THE GODS OF THE HILLS

PIETY AND SOCIETY
IN NINETEENTH-CENTURY VERMONT

T. D. Seymour Bassett

VERMONT HISTORICAL SOCIETY

Montpelier

Copyright © Vermont Historical Society, Inc.

Cover design by Janet North
Cover: Aristide Piccini's statue "Ethan Allen," Vermont State House; woodcut of the Angel Gabriel weathervane, Lyndon Universalist chapel.

Library of Congress Cataloging-in-Publication Data

BASSETT, T. D. Seymour (Thomas D. Seymour)
The gods of the hills: piety and society in nineteenth-century Vermont/T.D. Seymour Bassett
p. cm.
Includes bibliographical references and index.
ISBN 0-934720-43-6 (alk. paper)
1. Vermont--Religion--18th century. 2. Vermont--Church history--18th century. 3. Vermont--Religion--19th century. 4. Vermont--Church history--19th century. I. Title.

BL2527.V5 B37 2000
200'.9743'09033--dc21
00-033037

Printed in the United States of America

00 99 98 97 1 2 3 4 5

First Printing, May 2000

ISBN: 0-934720-43-6

Contents

Preface

The bias of this book is that the touch of the holy upon life is the most important fact in history and the most difficult to identify. Every single, solitary or associated Vermonter has practiced some kind of religion, from Day One as the ice receded, to the eleventh hour of the last day of the victory celebration in the war against Spain, and beyond. Human experience of the sacred in the place that became Vermont includes Indians learning the lore of their ancestors by their winter campfires. It includes the story of "St." Ann Story, who hid her fatherless children in an Otter Creek cave and thanked her God for survival. Neither primitive man nor pioneer woman nor most people after them could understand it well, yet they have known a little of the awe and the ecstacy, the doubt and the assurance, the stumbling and the striding of their dark lives. "For most of us, there is only the unattended moment, the moment in and out of time," T. S. Eliot wrote at the end of "The Dry Salvages." When the illumination comes, with glimmerings of meaning, people begin to join others of like minds to form churches.

Religion is concerned with the ways the sacred affects human behavior. It includes but is not limited to belief in the supernatural, for the boundaries between the natural and the supernatural are not clear. Was the Indian, believing in the spirits of animals, trees, and rocks, finding the holy in nature or assuming a world of disembodied ghosts of everything presented to the senses? The spirit of something is its essential character, not the separable half of a dualism.

I am a universalist interpreting Jesus' prayer that all may be one as praying that humans come to recognize that most importantly they *are* one. At the same time I am a particularist interpreting differences as a paradox. Each particular group is a chosen people, secure in the knowledge that its peculiarities are worthy, against the vast majority that do not share them. Like Mowgli in Kipling's *Jungle Book*, each species, proud to be what it is, can greet any other, "We be of one blood, thou and I."

Although religion does not change at state boundaries, the gods of the hills of Vermont have not been quite like the gods of the valleys, or of other hills. Like no other part of coastal English America, the

Vermonters' period of settlement was the revolutionary, not the colonial era. And in spite of the turbulence of that era, Vermont settlers were able to squat on New York land with impunity and with mere threats of violence, such as Ethan Allen's "the gods of the hills are not the gods of the valleys" (1 Kings 20:23, 28). In spite of revisionist proof that Indians *were* there, they were not there as an effective military force to contest the settlers' advances, as they had been effectively when combined with a few French soldiers. The comparative non-violence of Indian removal distinguished the "Old West" in Vermont from trans-Appalachian settlements. Although American religious pluralism was invented elsewhere, Vermont, after Virginia, was the second of nine states with some form of establishment to separate church and state. Throughout the nineteenth century, no central place in Vermont dominated the outback the way seaports and Tidewater ruled the eastern hinterland elsewhere, and the power of Vermont's seaports (Montreal, Boston, and New York) was mitigated by their competition.

The history of the Vermont process from intimations to institutions and their changes under the weight of accommodation to society and new inspiration, has scarcely been attempted beyond 1850. The exercise involves trying to look at the whole of the Vermont past from one perspective out of many. It means taking Vermonters' reports of communications from the Holy Spirit, the ultimate authority after all spirits have been tried, whether they be of God (1 John 4:1), and telling the story of how it changed their particular behavior.

Although I compiled more titles about religion for my *Vermont: A Bibliography of Its History* (1981) than for any other category except government and politics, most of the titles contained only materials for a history. Church manuals contain lists, documents, and a few paragraphs of "history." The annual reports of state organizations contain the bones of proceedings. Town histories with few exceptions have expanded the skeletal outlines with more names, dates, and places. Beyond these arid but necessary sources are the rare biographies of beloved pastors. These are especially rich when based on personal friendship and personal papers, like Joseph Torrey's "Remains" of President James Marsh of the University of Vermont, or Alfred H. Gilbert on Parsons Pratt of Dorset.

With the sources skewed as they are, I proportion my study to focus on changes in the major churches and on the new elements seeping in or bursting into the religious landscape. Both kinds of new life embody gropings toward fresh expressions of experience of a holy spirit. As the prophets and the priests feel their way through the murky ambience of their mixed-up world, their particular personalities and the characteristics of those they attract give new forms to the churches they develop. And behind the solid, glacially moving main bodies ("like a mighty turtle moves the church of God") is the larger mass of the more uncertain or oblivious, walking their ways without benefit of clergy or church.

In the almost infinite variety of religious experience among the thousands of Vermonters in these hills, sometimes a vignette of a leader, sometimes the story of a conflict, sometimes the description of a ritual will evoke the mood of a particular religious situation. I try, in a series of pictures, to illuminate a century very unlike the one I have lived through. By weaving the diverse threads of ethnic origin, hard-scrabble farming, meetings of Masons, Methodists, Democrats, or Patrons of Husbandry, I aim to produce a series of samplers that tell what Vermont was like in that bygone age. Sometimes, tiny points of colorful detail may produce a kind of historical pointillism which can be luminous, seen from the proper perspective.

The roots of the nineteenth century go deep. I cannot, however, adequately trace each feature to European origins. I have crammed into one chapter a few words on the presence of Indians and French (both defeated), their interaction with first settlers, a chaplains'-eye-view of the American Revolution, and some of the basic religious behaviors of pioneers with few preachers, meeting houses, or organized churches.

Until most recent times, a large proportion of the people continued unattached to any church. What bound them and the church members into one civil religion was love of their town, state, and country. The development of this patriotism I trace in the second chapter. The motto, "Freedom and Unity," merged loyalty to Vermont with loyalty to the nation. Gradually, over the century, Vermont developed a set of rituals, holy days, symbols, and saints, and a myth or story of its continued fight for liberty.

Until the War of 1812, Vermonters were concerned with external affairs, while at home, minority groups joined to end Congregational hegemony. Below these shifts in politics and power, voluntarism, leaving religious choices to the people, led to a pluralism of churches, each sure that it was the One True Church. In their competition for converts, the winning way was revivalist until the Millerite miscalculation. I sketch the profiles of the denominations as they appeared early in the century, and repeat the review to show changes after the Civil War with respect to their places of worship in the landscape, their liturgies, ministries, theologies, polities, and relations to government.

My host of helpers, who have tried to answer my endless questions, are more numerous than tongue can tell. My family have tolerated my preoccupations. University of Vermont Professor William E. Paden's Religion 100, "The Interpretation of Religion," helped me deal with my dilemma, that I found "secular" people religious. Professor

Paden has faithfully commented on successive revisions. The University of Vermont's Bailey/Howe Library staff has secured many interlibrary loans and provided invaluable reference aid. Susan Bartlett Weber has penetrated my confusions, insisted upon clarity, and helped me to say what I want to say. Samuel Allen, Elizabeth Bassett, David J. Blow, Howard J. Coffin, Forest K. Davis, William Goss, William A. Haviland, Jeanne Milling, Elizabeth Nordbeck, Marjory Power, Michael Sherman, Neil R. Stout, and Stanley Yarian have read parts at different stages and suggested improvements. Alan Berolzheimer, editor for the Vermont Historical Society, has helped shape the final result.

1

Religion in the Woods Before 1791[1]

Abenaki Religion

Before any other humans occupied the part of the northeastern woodland that became Vermont, the Western Abenaki and their forerunners told the first tales of their acquaintance with the sacred. A dense cloud hides the religion of these first Vermonters. Only scraps of evidence are left: oral tradition, a few artifacts, inferences from what is known of neighboring groups, and the few observations Europeans bothered to record.[2] Yet to start the story of religion in the area that is now Vermont with the arrival of people bringing European culture would assume that aboriginal people had no religion. Because the original Vermonters' religion flavored their whole life, we need to understand their life in order to understand their religion. Indians eventually clashed with white settlers, with a far different religion. How did these differences affect the conflict?

Human occupation of the northeast can be traced some eleven thousand years back, or about half the time since Asiatics came over the Bering isthmus, or by boat from the western Pacific, into the Americas. Changes in climate and therefore vegetation and its dependent animal life had consequences in culture. The Paleoindian (9,300-7,000 B.C.?) followed big game northward as glaciers melted and retreated. Then as species like the caribou and mastodon either died out or moved north with the tundra, the hunters or their successors of the Archaic period in Vermont (7,000-1,000 B.C.?) had to turn to smaller game, fish, and fowl, while the women gathered plants, roots, nuts, and berries.

The Abenaki were predators and gatherers with supplementary horticulture. They managed their game and therefore their population at a quarter of the land's carrying capacity, in time-honored, seasonal cycles. With near zero population growth, they had reserves for times of dearth. Over the centuries, the habitat of the hunted and the weapons of the hunters changed. Fishing likewise changed as Abenaki learned to make better nets, traps, and other equipment. So with nutting and berrying:

Those who knew passed on their knowledge of where to find game and edible plants. Indians began to modify the habitat by burning or otherwise selecting the species they wanted. They domesticated a few plants but more important, learned to cultivate corn, beans, and squash from Indians in the Middle West. They gardened on the alluvial flats near the mouths of major rivers on the Champlain shore, or on the terraces of the lower Connecticut, both with more than four-month growing seasons.

To acquire these resources, the Indians developed a stable, seasonal pattern of life, centered on water courses. They followed late winter moose hunting with sugaring and spring fishing at rapids and falls. As the earth warmed, the women planted plots of vegetables, with special ceremonial tobacco tended by the men. Through the summer they fished from dugouts on lakes and ponds. In the fall they left the villages in small bands for upland hunting. They tanned, dried, smoked, ground, baked, or piled animal and vegetable surpluses for use in times of scarcity, and when worse came to worst, they ate their dogs. In early winter the men checked their traps and assaulted beaver and muskrats in their lodges. In the dead of winter, they returned to their village to process what they had caught, wait out the cold, eat their earlier harvests, and repair their equipment until time for the next cycle. They prepared their "raquets" or snowshoes and toboggans for the late winter hunt in the deep snows. There was plenty of time to tell stories about their history and about the animals identified with their bands.

An Abenaki village consisted of a string of row houses for each band, between their gardens and the river banks. As the cycle of birth and death changed the size of households, spouses shifted between bands. During seasons of hunting and fishing away from the village, those who would be more hindrance than help (the aged, the infirm, and the children) stayed in the longhouses with a cadre of the able-bodied to tend and protect them.

Each band identified with a territory, typically defined as a system of trails related to watercourses. The main trail ran along the main stream to its farthest source; the secondary trail bisected the tributary, dividing the territory into quarters. As in other foraging societies, the Abenaki used only a quarter of the land's capacity to supply the group's necessities. This allowed the animals in the unhunted areas to multiply undisturbed so that four seasons later, the harvest would be abundant. In times of unusual dearth they could invade the unhunted "fallow" enough to survive. The band decided who could hunt its territory, but it could not sell land, in the European sense.

The European sense of property contrasted with the Indian sense of place. Here lay the crux of cultural difference: The Indians felt they belonged to the land; the Europeans felt the land belonged to them. From this difference, and from European land hunger that did not see what one did not want to see, sprang the mistaken European notion that there were "no" Indians in Vermont. Indians used most of the land only as a hunting ground---as if hunting were not a major way of using the land to earn a living. Not only moving seasonally, they even moved their villages when the refuse of occupation became too noisome. Yet compared to the mobility of contemporary Americans, their regular rotation suggested permanence.

They subsisted by a stable economy; they governed themselves for centuries without major changes in a decentralized, small-scale, egalitarian way. Because family clans were related they had mostly mutual, not conflicting interests, yet conflicts arose in large families under one roof. Abenaki conflict resolution started with persuasion combined with the deterrent of social disapproval. They found their leaders among those who had the personal ability to mediate into consensus.

They had no authority to use force; no Abenaki of either sex could tell another adult what to do. When John Williams, the Deerfield, Massachusetts, pastor captured in the raid of March 1704, sought to redeem his captive daughter Eunice through negotiators from Massachusetts Bay and New York, Governor Philippe de Rigaud, Marquis de Vaudreuil, cooperated but did not force her Indian captors to give her up. The Indians would have negotiated an exchange if she had been willing to return, but they let her make the decision.[3] In more serious and difficult cases the Abenaki struck a bargain by arbitration, and as a last resort, in the case of a murder, for example, the family or band of the victim notified the chief or council of the offender's band that they would seek revenge.

The usual family band ranged from fifteen to forty in one to three households, all related to each other. In the Mississquoi watershed all the family bands contributed their leaders to a council of elders with a peacetime chief (occasionally female) or a wartime chief (always male), who served, as it were, during good behavior, or for the duration of the war, or for life. Like the leaders of the family bands, these elders and chiefs earned the role by charisma and by wisdom as providers and negotiators. The leader's role most of the time was to preside at councils, to represent the band at gatherings with other bands and tribes, and to lead in ceremonies.

War was uncommon between the Western Abenaki and their Algonquian-speaking neighbors. With three quarters of their land held as a reserve, they rarely experienced a dearth that would drive them to seize others' goods. Besides, they believed it would be futile to hunt in the territory used by others because they could not control the spirits there. But the Mohawks, nearest of the Iroquois to the Abenaki, picked on the Abenaki to prove their superiority, control the fur trade, and replenish with tribute the deficits caused by their overuse of their resources.

Abenaki religion, like that of other early North Americans, linked their humanity to their relatives the animals and the rest of nature. In dangerous waters and dangerous woods, the Abenaki felt protected by shamans because these "ministers" best understood, interpreted, and made use of the spirits of each part of nature. So European priests understood the Christian tradition and "justified the ways of God to man," as Milton wrote. Shamans or medicine men (and sometimes women) cultivated special gifts for dealing with animal and other spirits.

Toward the end of the Archaic period, artifacts traded from the Caribbean and across eastern North America, found in special cemeteries, suggest that shamans led elaborate rituals concerned with the spirits of the dead. Then, for unknown reasons, the vast trade network was broken or the idea of what the dead needed in the afterlife changed. Thereafter, Indians paid little attention to burials, disposing of bodies without goods in former village storage pits and hearths.

In the prescientific world of the sixteenth century, on the eve of European penetration, both Europeans and Indians believed in the supernatural and that the body had a soul. The Abenaki believed that their "vital self" or spirit had qualities of blood-redness, symbolic of liveliness and emotion, transparent whiteness, and sky-blue-greenness, symbolic of the thinking and social aspects of life. This vital self depended on the body but could for short periods leave the body, usually in the form of an animal, and interact with others.

The Abenaki believed that every living thing could use its supernatural powers, but that shamans had greater powers over the spirit world than others. They could enhance this control by practice. Their clairvoyance could tell if an unauthorized hunter trespassed; they could divine where the game was; they healed by their control of spirits. Everyone sought animal helpers, but shamans were most skilled in using them. While in trance, a shaman could will his vital self into his helper's body and do his work, or without entering the helper's body, send the animal on errands. The shaman, speaking with spirits through his drum and his cedar flute, could call game, lure enemies, and attract women. The shaman took seriously his skill at sleight-of-hand and ventriloquism. To be a good magician proved his power, just as success in business proved the Puritan godly.

The Abenaki world was flat, focused on rivers running through woodlands full of animals who also had spirits. Indians ate but also respected their game. They threw the wild goose bones back in the water with a prayer that the breed might multiply. Before eating they said grace by putting the grease of the kill on the fire to thank Tabaldak, the "Owner." He was the most important spirit in their pantheon, the Creator who made everything except the topography (as in Psalm 24, "the earth is the Lord's and the fullness thereof").

Odzihozo, "He Makes Himself from Something," transformed the flat earth into the varied landscape. The story of Wo-ja-ho-se (another transliteration of Odzihozo) is the Western Abenaki form of the "Transformer" legend widespread across North America. Gordon Day, the pioneer anthropologist-ethnohistorian of the Western Abenaki, learned his story from their descendants, the St. Francis Indians in Quebec. Odzihozo transformed the earth into river channels and lake basins and piled dirt to make the hills and mountains. When he was finished, like Jehovah in Genesis, he surveyed his work and found it good. Last he made Lake Champlain and found it very good indeed. He liked it so much that he sat on an island off Shelburne Point and changed himself into stone so that he could sit there forever and enjoy the view. At least until World War II, Abenaki who boated past Odzihozo used to leave offerings of tobacco or corn. If they did not, they believed that the spirit of the rock would raise a storm and wreck their canoes. The Dutch fur traders, not knowing the Abenaki story, called it Rock Dunder, and the name stuck. The Abenaki explained how Odzihozo made Split Rock, near Essex, New York, and the falls of Otter Creek from Center Rutland to Vergennes, and reduced giant prehistoric animals to their present size.

After the creation stories, other tales accumulated. They told of Bedgwadzo, "Round Mountain," a shaman who tamed whirlwinds and thunders, and of semi-human, underwater beings, safe to talk about only when winter locked them under ice. One was a big lizard, another the Champlain sea serpent who might carry off young girls. The swamp spirit lured children in to drown. There were also the shy "Little People," who would do you no harm and made the button-like stones on the shore of Button Bay. There was the young woman who taught birds to sing. The Forest Wanderer was a cannibal giant. He, with the Thunderer, the Wind Bird, the Earth Grandmother, and Pmola (in eastern Abenaki lore, roosting atop Mount Katahdin), personified the frightening side of nature, which might be manipulated to one's advantage. Azeban, the raccoon, was chief character in the Abenaki version of the trickster stories told throughout North America. Clever and curious, or arrogant and foolish, his antics were meant to amuse as well as instruct.

The original Vermonters on the eve of European contact had more leisure, ate better, and lived a bit longer and more peacefully than most people then in Europe. Small wonder that some modern Vermonters, worried about the overuse of global resources, look back at the Indians, living in balance with their environment, with wistful admiration. The Abenaki were satisfied with their outlook on their world, which had not changed for a long time.

Indian-European Contacts

For more than two and a half centuries, Indians followed a collision course toward near extinction. The Abenaki, being ground to death between the millstones of imperial France and Britain, decided in each case which Europeans were least likely to hurt them and supported that side when they could not remain neutral.

The forces were unequal. Perhaps six thousand Indians occupied the valleys of Vermont. At the British conquest, the French *habitants*, settlers of New France stretched thinly along the waterways from Quebec to New Orleans, numbered about sixty thousand including a few officials, soldiers, priests, and *coureurs des bois*, the fur traders. Near the Atlantic coast a million land-hungry colonists represented a population pressure that shattered the Abenaki and defeated the French. During the hundred and fifty years after 1609, when Samuel de Champlain entered Lake Champlain, the Indians had less and less room to maneuver. They tended to side with the French, who had fewer settlers to disturb them, whose priests took the trouble to learn their language and live at their level. The Abenaki kept the native beliefs that "worked" for them, such as those relating to crops and hunting, but they found the relative immunity of the French to the diseases deadly to them a sign that Catholicism had some magical power. Hence they accepted conversion as far as they understood it.

From the French point of view, missions to Indians were both a goal and one of the ways to win North America. Almost the only Europeans on the Vermont land for most of a century, they provided priests and chapels for their soldiers at most outposts, and blocked the British until defeated in 1759. French captains marched their troops to Mass, while their priests served and suffered with soldiers and *habitants*. A Sulpician ministered to the scurvy-ridden garrison throughout the first winter of 1665-66 at Fort Ste. Anne on Isle La Motte. Sixty years later, Father Emmanuel Crespel, assigned to Fort St. Frederick (Crown Point, 1735-36), repeated the same old refrain, featuring the numbing winter cold, scurvy and malaria the worst among ever-present diseases, little game they knew how to catch and kill, and the social intangible, important for a lonely, educated man on the frontier, no one "with whom we could converse."[4]

The French occupation from Crespel's time was no longer just a network of paths connecting forts and trading posts. *Habitants* occupied the lake shore near Chimney Point and also at Alburg and near the mouths of rivers, stopping places on trade and raid routes. Transient priests began to record both French and indigenous baptisms and deaths near the forts. Beginning in the 1740s, the Abenaki village of Missisquoi, near Swanton, had a resident priest and chapel. Missisquoi, like the villages of Odanak (St. Francis) and Mohawk Kaknawake near La Prairie, across the St. Lawrence from Montreal, had a mixed population of Indian refugees, survivors of defeats in southern New England.[5]

It is hard to even outline the complicated nature of red-white attitudes about their colonial contacts. Historians have justified the European invasion or excoriated the invaders for the destruction of the first Americans. Faced with strange beings from out of their worlds, each side was wary. Each side borrowed what glittered as things that seemed to make their life better. As a result they were transformed, frontier whites partially Indianized and reds partially Europeanized. Both sides (and few could yet find a middle) were willing to die for the ways they held sacred, although the Indians, rather than die in a lost cause, retreated before superior power or hid where they could.

Ever since Champlain recorded how his Canadian Algonquian allies cruelly tortured their Iroquois prisoners, stereotypes built up in a series of horror stories. Did soldiers hear repetitions of Champlain's advice? "It would be better for them to die fighting, or kill themselves," he wrote, "than fall into the hands of their enemies."[6] Massacre matched massacre; whites avenged scalping alive by burning aborigines in their huts. Zadock Steele's *The Indian Captive* (1818) is notable in a long line of stereotyped stories of superstitious French bigots and bloodthirsty savages who tortured, hatcheted heads, and killed captives who could not keep up with their forced marches. Indeed, if you take prisoners live, expect pursuit, and the captives cannot keep up, do you leave them to die of hunger and cold, with a small chance of rescue, or do you wait and risk being overtaken by pursuers? Woods warfare, of course, was no Sunday school picnic; tree-to-tree and hand-to-hand combat aimed to force retreat, if not to maim or kill.

The roots of this hostility lay in opposite attitudes toward the land. Watching out for their land, as they viewed it from opposite sides, both peoples misunderstood each other. Yet many New England captives found that after the battle, one to one, their enemies were kind. Take, for example, the experience of pious Nehemiah How, caught while cutting wood outside the Great Meadow (Putney) stockade one October day in 1745. "I cried to God for help and ran and hollowed as I ran to alarm the fort," he wrote. He felt it was God's will that he be captured, but he found favor with God, for the captors "were generally kind to me while I was with 'em." One old warrior, "the best friend I had," took care of him, and another gave him a better pair of shoes. At Crown Point he conversed with those he had known in the Connecticut Valley. One, the husband of an earlier captive, inquired about the captive's relatives in the English settlements, and "showed a great deal of respect to me." "The French treated us [prisoners] very civilly." How was a prisoner eighteen months, serving as informal chaplain and recording forty-nine prisoner deaths at Quebec until another hand recorded his own.[7]

When Susanna Johnson arrived at Number Four, a fort at present Charlestown, New Hampshire, the first thing she saw was a war dance of "rummed-up Indians" from the nine or ten families living in huts near the fort. For a decade the Johnsons lived on that frontier, where "the Indians were numerous and associated in a friendly manner with the whites," a mixture "of savages and settlers, without established laws to govern them." Whites who compartmentalize their lives between "religion" and humane association would call this behavior secular. But the decade of peace and trade at Number Four demonstrated that Stone Age and Iron Age lifestyles under favorable conditions could coexist. The settlers knew, however, that if war with France broke out they would be hit first.

The blow came in August 1754: the Johnsons were captured and taken to Canada. On August 31, in a corner of Cavendish, as her husband was holding her on a horse, she was seized with labor pains. Her captors made her a lean-to near a brook and waited aloof while her husband and sister attended the delivery of Captive Johnson. These "savages" brought clothes for the baby, and a needle and pins to fasten them. They made porridge and johnny cake, and brought a cup to steep roots in for tea, and a wooden spoon to feed the baby with. They let Susanna rest for a whole day and made a stretcher for the prisoners to carry her on.[8]

Compare this special care with the apparently normal treatment of one of their own women in childbirth. On Sunday, May 3, 1730, near Springfield on the Black River, "an old pregnant squaw that traveled with us stopped alone and was delivered of a child, and by Monday noon overtook us with a living child on her back."[9]

The story of Jemima Sartwell shows how, in the midst of bloody warfare, border people mixed with their enemies. Indians killed Phipps, her first husband. Twelve years later, when they killed her second (Caleb, son of Nehemiah How), they carried her and her seven children to Odanak. The captives survived the eight-day march back to the canoes on Otter Creek, but her four-year-old son's captor put permanent dents in his head with his tomahawk handle. An Abenaki family adopted one of the small boys, who turned Indian. Jemima's two eldest daughters went to a convent. The nuns sent one to France where she married. The other was so satisfied with her life in French Canada that she flatly refused to return to New England—unusual disobedience in the days of strong parental authority—until her mother got an order from the French governor.[10]

The last Vermont captivity narratives of the colonial genre came out of the Royalton raid of October 1780. Young settler George Avery was husking corn "with other comerads" when "an old lady" went by "with solemn countenance agoing to meeting." He guessed it was Sunday because she "had on her Sabbath day mouth." The next day raiders burned the cabins in the clearings up and down the river and captured Avery. From a cabin his captors were going to burn he took a Bible and Isaac Watts' hymns, "consoling to use when prisoners. . . .We used to read them and meditate in our journey," he wrote.[11] George was religious, but he put getting food for survival above losing good daylight "agoing to meeting." From the "infidel" perspective many young woodsmen, like Yankee sailors, observed "no Sundays off soundings," and had no tithing men, no justices of the peace, who would keep them from traveling on Sunday and make them go to meeting. Independent Vermont courts and justice paid attention to property law, not often to religious delinquency.

Captivity tales demonstrate the individual piety of prisoners. Organized Protestantism first entered Vermont with the outbreak of Grey Lock's (or Lord Dummer's) War in 1723. The Province of Massachusetts built Fort Dummer (in present-day Brattleboro) the next year. At least three Congregational chaplains served at the fort, for the benefit of the garrison and "to instruct the Indians thereabout in the true Christian religion."[12] The other English outposts on the upper Connecticut seem to have had no chaplains. Chaplain Ebenezer Hinsdale preached to some of the Indians coming to the trading post to sell pelts, skins, and moose tallow. One of their women brought her baby for baptism but could not understand why the chaplain would not baptize the baby unless he could baptize the mother too. Hinsdale felt he had to explain, but could not explain across the chasm of vastly different cultural experiences, what baptism is. The French missionaries had no such scruples, but gave the standard answers and went ahead to save the Indian's soul.

Europeans could not explain Christianity to people willing to listen politely but satisfied with their superior nature lore and equally sophisticated ideologies. Whites, although often dependent for survival on native maize and healing herbs, valued most their European Iron Age technology, because that is what Indians were willing to trade for. They were not interested in the religion of the first Americans. Yankees, forgetting that they had taught terrorism by their example in the Pequot massacre of 1636 in eastern Connecticut, were sure that these were treacherous, dirty, inferior "Indian givers." Except for the need to watch out in wartime for raiders, traders, and skulkers coming out of the woods, settlers' attention was in the opposite direction, on the towns they had come from. Most whites, however, treated them as devil-worshippers whose heathen practices must be wiped out, preferably by wiping out the Indians. Even the Roman Catholic missionaries in New France, who tried the hardest and came the nearest to converting them, assumed that conversion meant the complete substitution of Christianity for shamanism.

A few colonial whites like Roger Williams, the Rhode Island leader, some Quakers, and such Spanish apologists as Bartolomé de las Casas, Dominican missionary in the West Indies, respected Indian humanity and their rights to be on the land. They recognized the possibility of learning from their way of life "and the spirit they live in," as the Quaker minister John Woolman wrote.[13]

Vermont frontiersmen saw and committed plenty of violence and bloodshed in the long years of warfare, first against the French and then in the Revolution. In peace time, however, as Dorothy Canfield Fisher was the first to assert, the woods were quiet in spite of white invasion, not like Kentucky's "dark and bloody ground." Vermont had no Indian wars except as adjuncts of imperial wars. One probable exception was that George Sheldon "on several occasions. . . murder[ed] certain Indians" who protested Sheldon's invasion of Abenaki territory and burned his barn. In military terms, this was a preemptive strike by a representative of such a preponderant power that the murders were sufficient deterrents.[14]

Memories of the French and Indian War and the folklore of Indian raids poisoned the minds of settlers with suspicion. They could not see the Indians' peaceful and positive side, which captives experienced when their captors were sober and in control. The Indians combined a habit of "creative procrastination," common to all weaker foes, with tactics to scare the enemy into yielding, and killed practically nobody. Colonials, notably Ethan Allen according to Michael Bellesiles, adopted this "terrorist" stance.[15] The Vermont frontier was quiet because the Indians were hopeless in the face of advancing settlers, the low population density (not as low as Mrs. Fisher imagined it) allowed Indians to fade into invisibility, and to some extent because of the religious self-restraint of individuals on each side.

Chaplains in the Champlain Theater, 1775-1777

Indians may have had some glimmer of hope in joining first Carleton's and then Burgoyne's advancing armies. Opposed by daily increasing swarms of New England militia, the Indians earned further settler hostility by choosing the side that failed to conquer the rebels. While the hot war swirled up and down the Champlain corridor during the first years of the American Revolution, chaplains accompanied New Englanders invading Canada on the old trails of the scouts and captives, or served at the forts and bivouacs in the Champlain Valley.

Young college graduates, often in their first southern New England parishes, caught the war fever and hastened into service, to pray with the dying, write letters to their families, and revive morale by raising the divine standard among the men. From the capture of Ticonderoga, unblessed by any chaplain, but taken "in the name of the great Jehovah" (if we can trust Ethan Allen's story), to the capture of Burgoyne's army at Saratoga, there were never enough chaplains. For those three years, 1775-1777, each chaplain had to serve more than a thousand troops in the Champlain theater. These pious youths were shocked at the breakdown of morals under the stress of military hardships: cowardice, desertions, profanity, drunkenness, camp followers, Sabbath-breaking, dumping the corpses of enlisted men into mass graves. Nevertheless, they steadfastly served for love of country and their fellow soldiers. Their duties and risks were severe, they had no military rank, and the pay--twenty dollars a month in 1776 and only thirty-three dollars the next year--was usually in arrears and in depreciated paper money.[16]

Congregationalist David Avery, one of the most famous of revolutionary chaplains, served in the Battle of Bunker Hill, helped build fortifications at Ticonderoga, and distinguished himself by exposure to German fire at the Battle of Bennington. A carpenter's apprentice called to the ministry, he had read theology and tutored at Eleazar Wheelock's Indian Charity School at Lebanon, Connecticut. After study at Yale he served two stints teaching the Oneida in central New York. When the news of Lexington reached his Gageborough (now Windsor) parish in the Berkshires, he told his people he was going to join the army, without the usual church council to clear his dismissal until two years later. He recruited a company who chose him captain, joined a regiment in Cambridge on April 29, 1775, and the next day preached a red-hot sermon to the entire army in the open air. "His fame is Great throughout the Camp," wrote Chaplain Ebenezer David after he had met "that good Soldier" Avery at Lake George. "A worthy man. . . . I long for an interview with him."[17]

Ebenezer David appreciated the few who responded to his own chaplaincy: "Notwithstanding their great distress found them in general as stupid as the beasts that pearish--yet. . . some. . . appeared not past fealing. One Evening a number I had almost said of Skellitons after prayer [came up for questions and exhortation]. . . . One say, 'Oh how I doe love to hear Minister talk.' This was a boy. I have ever found the Chaplains visits taken well by the sick."[18]

Congregationalist Ammi Ruhammah Robbins also admired rugged David Avery, who could breeze by the stinking hospital beds and eat afterwards like a logger. "I want a constitution of brass to tarry here," wrote Robbins. I am "utterly unable to go through the hospital." He had already survived the 1775-1776 invasion of Canada and the disastrous retreat.[19]

David Avery was the only chaplain in the Champlain theater who stayed in Vermont after the war quieted down in the north. In 1780, the Bennington town church, then the prime Congregational parish in Vermont, called David Avery to serve as its second minister. His call was not unanimous. The members of longer standing, who were Separates, were uneasy with his doctrine. Moved by the revivals in the Massachusetts towns they had come from, the Bennington Separates or New Lights believed that growing up in members' families was not enough; acceptance depended on evidence of a full religious conversion.[20] The church had been without a pastor for many months, and perhaps compromised for a war hero with Yale polish. Through his Yale connections he might parley Clio Hall, the Bennington academy established in 1780, into becoming the state college. They had secured John Witherspoon, President of the College of New Jersey at Princeton, as their patron, and hoped to attach Timothy Dwight to their cause.[21]

Avery's years of military service seem to have unfitted him for his postwar career. As a junior when Yale abolished "placing" (the ranking of students by their father's social status), effective in 1768, Avery rejoiced that "the finest coat and largest ruffles"[22] would no longer be marks of distinction, compared to scholarship and elocution. But as a pastor his imperious manner demanded the deference his congregation would be damned if they would give (and they *were* by Avery for not giving it). The church had neither expected nor agreed to yield all power to its pastor. When the congregation wearied of wrangling with him and dismissed him three years later, it waited another three years before calling his successor. The charge that Avery refused to manumit his personal slave has not been fully investigated.[23]

Cabin Religion, 1759-1791

Bennington, the first Vermont town with an organized church (1762), the first to settle a pastor (1763), and build a meetinghouse (1765), was the exception to the norm of the new settlements. Throughout those woods there were practically no outward signs of organized religion. "I have rode more than 100 miles and seen no meeting house!" wrote Nathan Perkins in the spring of 1789 from Governor Chittenden's farm in Williston.[24] This absence of architectural focus makes clear that the overwhelming majority of Yankee settlers were without benefit of clergy or meetinghouses. Only ten Congregational ministers were settled before the Revolution, and four had yoked parishes.[25]

Even before hostilities ended, the number of pastors had doubled: Twenty-one Congregational pastors settled over Vermont parishes by the end of 1780. Ezra Stiles must have been thinking of towns without Congregational churches when he told his diary in 1780 that Vermont had sixty churches without pastors.[26] In fact, only four organized churches (Halifax, Hartland, Royalton, and Windsor west parish) lacked settled Congregational ministers that year. The next most numerous Baptists organized only three churches before the Revolution, and twenty-three more by 1791, with the Anglicans, Presbyterians, and Quakers worshiping in a few more congregations. Even when Vermont joined the Union in 1791, almost three quarters of its towns had no church organizations of any denomination.

The pious in these awesome, dark forests had to get along with lay readers. "For a long time," wrote a historian of West Fairlee, "the inhabitants were few, and generally poor, unable to build a house of worship, or support a pastor. . . . Hon. Nathaniel Niles for many years held religious meetings in his own house, and in other private dwellings and barns, as would best accommodate those who were interested in assembling for worship."[27] This situation continued in West Fairlee until 1821, but it was the common experience of early Vermont settlers. A woman who came to Springfield as a child in 1772 recalled that her father was called "Bishop" because he read sermons in the house where people gathered for public worship.[28] Reuben Bigelow, who had spent some time at college, came to Peru in the 1790s. He "read the Bible. . . and sermons. . . whenever they had no preacher."[29]

Organized religion did not follow the English frontier as closely as it did the Spanish and French partly for reasons of financial and governmental policy. Many pioneers, from the Israelites to the Catholics, had moved with their religious institutions on their backs. Massachusetts had funded chaplains at Fort Dummer, but for a decade after Burgoyne's surrender, economic depression, disruption of trade patterns, uncertain land titles, Shays' rebellion, and new constitutions turned the attention of Congregational New England away from church-planting in the new settlements.

Shakers were the only missionaries to brave the northern woods in the early 1780s, partly because of persecution farther south. Mother Ann Lee, to her followers the embodiment of the Second Coming of Christ, won a "sizable number of adherents" at Guilford, Lyndon, and Pittsford, but they, like Mormon converts of the next generation, joined Shaker "families" in neighboring states.[30]

The main reason why most of the settlers were not immediately organized into churches was that they did not want the Standing Order. This was a system in Connecticut, Massachusetts, and New Hampshire that assumed a community where magistrates and ministry cooperated to maintain religious standards, with grudging allowances for Anglicans, Baptists, and Quakers. The system required that some form of religion must be supported. That usually meant the preponderant Congregationalist order. To destroy this unity of church and state destroyed religion for the advocates of this multiple establishment.

A majority of Vermont settlers, not liking the rules of the churches they escaped from and not wanting the religious restrictions built into the town governments they knew, were slow to work out the modifications they liked. First they wanted to own land as a basis for independence. Other matters could wait. They accepted a good deal of their religious tradition, and knew that they would choose their own churches eventually.

Nathan Perkins, on leave from his Connecticut parish in 1789, made a typically critical statement in the private diary of his Vermont missionary tour:

> About 1 quarter of the inhabitants & almost all the men of learning deists. . . . People pay little regard to the Sabbath; hunt & fish on that day frequently. Not more than 1/6 of the families attend family prayer. . . . About 1/2 would be glad to support public worship & the gospel ministry. The rest would choose to have no Sabbath—no ministers—no religion—no heaven—no hell—no morality.[31]

Such were Perkins' brief impressions based on visits to about two dozen households, traveling a hundred and fifty miles to the edge of west side settlement and back in forty-seven days.

The Vermont frontier was a safe place for travelers like him because the Indians had been cowed and the settlers were preoccupied with killing forest giants and letting sunlight into clearings, and not with killing their neighbors for the land or their wives. In their wilderness anarchy, they feared other settlers less than they feared poverty. Seth Hubbell's trials in Wolcott were repeated for some poor beginners in every town.[32] Nature, not humanity, committed most of the violence. Falling trees were more deadly than guns in the Vermont woods. In spite of the folklore about the frontier rifle, eighteenth-century smooth bores were in short supply and rifles very rare. Their range was short and their accuracy poor. George Sheldon probably murdered an Indian for burning his barn in Sheldon, and a decade before the Revolution one Neal reportedly murdered an Indian in Newbury during a drunken dispute. He received a prison sentence in Portsmouth.[33]

Even Jonathan Carpenter, prospecting for land after the main military action was over in the northern theater, had little to fear as he ranged over the four southern counties.[34] On the edges of Burgoyne's invading army, however, Tories and Patriots played for keeps. Isaac Clark murdered one "Protectioner," John Irish, "a Quaker in principle," who had stayed on his ninety acres in Tinmouth after Burgoyne's troops recaptured Ticonderoga. Irish got papers promising British protection and had come in from reaping his wheat when he was shot. His widow Rebecca's cabin was looted, but she stayed on with her three infants and harvested the hay, grain, and flax. In November she was told to leave because the farm had been confiscated and sold as Tory property.[35]

No one has discovered a case of a white killing a white in eighteenth-century Vermont in peacetime. The settlers were better at fraud than force: Smuggling, counterfeiting, and horse stealing flourished.

The frontier paradox of high alcohol consumption and little lethal violence is epitomized in Ethan Allen, whose toping and violent Old Testament invective were not followed by mayhem and murder. From the preacher to the pauper, people in this early period consumed more alcohol per capita than at any time after. Stills were numerous, with taverns every few miles along the road, and applejack figuratively in every cellar. In this context, we can assume much violence in the household, while not against strangers like the Rev. Perkins. How could Nathan Perkins open the curtain on the famine year of 1789 with the dictum, "Woods make people love one another & kind & obliging & good-natured"?[36] A few days later he noted as he passed through that infidel town of Burlington, "Col. Stephen Keyes whipped bruised & nearly killed a Dr. Stephens last month because he brought in a high bill for attending his father-in-law, Col. Sheldon."[37] Keyes kept a tavern on the Burlington waterfront and had a short fuse, perhaps from excessive use of his own liquor. Randolph Roth, who has combed the scarce sources, concludes that many spouses, especially if alcoholic or mentally disturbed, were violent but not lethally violent. Fear of penalties deterred some, but most, in the prevalent household subsistence economy, needed partners alive.[38]

Frontier people who did not "go to church," who drank heavily, and who went unpunished for that and fishing, frolicking, extramarital sex, and all the other misbehaviors that blue laws had been condemning and trying to curb for years, were "godless." Most woods people simply did not want the multiple establishment favoring the "standing order." Therefore, in missionary eyes the settlers were infidels.

Gradually a few people in some of the oldest towns such as Bennington and Brattleboro found common denominators in articles of faith and covenants that could be the rocks upon which they would found new churches. Until well past 1791, however, only a very small percentage of the population were church members.

Recent scholars have rejected the traditional view of the godless frontier and have found Vermont's religious diversity central to the understanding of successful resistance to New York's political and Congregationalism's religious authority. Donald A. Smith, using every available scrap of information about individual migrants who became Vermont settlers after several moves before the Revolution, found a solid majority opposed to reproducing the Congregational establishment of Connecticut and Massachusetts in Vermont. Their religious orientation, he claimed, was most important in their active and ultimately successful resistance to New York authority. He identified the variety of religious persuasions in the New Hampshire Grants and made a quantitative case that "pre-revolutionary Vermont was a microcosm of the principal forces dividing New England society."[39] And after the Revolution, the thousands who came pouring in with an even greater variety of religious attitudes, at least united in wanting to keep the contending forces in balance.[40]

Four kinds of dissenters from the dominant Congregationalists had settled in Vermont before the Revolution. Quakers from Dutchess County, New York, had met for worship in Danby since the late 1760s. Quakers also seeped into western Vermont from coastal New England.[41]

The Anglican Society for the Propagation of the Gospel in Foreign Parts supported missionaries who visited the small pockets of Episcopalians in Bennington County, from the late 1760s. Between times, these immigrants, mainly from Newtown and New Milford, Connecticut and Amenia, in Dutchess County, New York, got along with lay leadership. James Nichols, Yale 1771, ordained in England, was the first settled minister in Arlington for a year from 1786. Dismissed for intemperance, he served briefly in Sandgate and Manchester. The only other Episcopal clergy before 1791 were Reuben Garlick of Alburg and Bethuel Chittenden of Tinmouth, Governor Thomas Chittenden's brother, ordained deacons in 1787. Garlick doubled as a doctor and tripled as a teacher.[42]

In Ryegate the Scots American Company of Farmers bought a ten-thousand-acre block of land in 1773, and came to dominate the town although constituting only half the population. The company's agents had searched the eastern seaboard as far south as North Carolina for over four months. They chose Ryegate because of its good farm land, its cheap price of sixteen pence an acre, its water privileges, and because "we are within six miles of a good Presbyterian meeting. . . .[the Newbury Congregational church] very strict about keeping the Sabbath." In Barnet, the next town to the north, the United Company of Farmers for the Shires of Perth and Stirling was a smaller, later imitation of the Ryegate company. Both depended on visiting ministers from a distance: President John Witherspoon from the College of New Jersey at Princeton, Thomas Clark from Salem, New York, others from Londonderry, New Hampshire, or the nearby parson at Newbury. Barnet first installed David Goodwillie, an Associate Presbyterian, early in 1791, but Ryegate had to wait another eight years. Goodwillie preached sometimes in Ryegate too. It was "a poor man's country in which some grew rich," notably James Whitelaw of Ryegate and Alexander Harvey of Barnet, original agents and leading citizens.[43]

On both sides of Vermont Baptists were early pioneers. By 1790 they had established thirty-five churches, ordained twenty-eight elders (their name for minister), and licensed fifteen preachers for about sixteen hundred members.[44] John Peak, after building up the church in Windsor for over five years, had a long career as a pastor in New Hampshire and Massachusetts. The order of service at Windsor started with singing, then prayer, more singing, Bible reading, and concluding with "remarks on what was read or exhortation and prayer as the brethren felt freedom." Peak earned his living as a tailor, because in those days Baptists thought "it wicked for the people to give or the minister to receive any thing for preaching."[45] From Pownal to Rutland the "revolutionary stir" produced flocks of Baptists in Pownal, Shaftsbury, Wallingford, and Clarendon.[46] Shaftsbury Baptists, the largest flock, had no elder until 1780.

Considering the Methodists' leading place among the denominations by 1840, one tends to forget that they were few and within the Anglican communion until 1785, when the Baltimore convention consecrated Francis Asbury as an independent American bishop. Before that, a few Methodist Episcopalians, followers of Wesley, had found their way into the American backcountry. "Mother" Margaret Peckett, housekeeper for Methodist founder John Wesley, and her husband Giles, were part of this diaspora. They opened their Bradford log cabin in 1780 "for religious services for any Christians, ministers, or people, that love the Savior, irregardless [sic] of their denomination," serving their neighborhood much as many other pious leaders did in their towns. Yet only two Methodist itinerants reached Vermont before 1791: Samuel Wigton assigned to the Champlain Valley in 1788, and Jesse Lee in Windham County in 1790.[47]

Dutch Reformed churches dotted the Hudson Valley, but sent no colonies to Vermont. A group of Dutch farmers settled early under New York's Hoosac Patent in Pownal, but were driven off by the Green Mountain Boys. A few individuals with Dutch names (Van Buren, Vanderlip, Hendricks, Westinghousen) in the first two Vermont population censuses in western Bennington County, did not make a critical mass to form a church and support a dominie. They were less intense about their religion than many New Englanders, and as joint heirs of Calvin, could accommodate to the Congregational order. Scots-Irish Presbyterians from New Hampshire also joined with Congregationalists except in Barnet and Ryegate.

Because so many minority groups settled early in western Vermont, many thought of that area, the stage of the extralegal activities of the Green Mountain Boys, as radical in every respect. In 1914, John

M. Comstock pointed out that nearly all the Congregational churches organized before 1777 were in the Connecticut Valley.[48] Historians since have used "the Bennington mob," and the early imbalance in church formation, to show how soberly conservative the east side was. The differences, however, were more between hill towns and valley villages in the same counties on both sides of the Green Mountains. Settlers from southern New England entered the eastern side during the war, usually buying land with risky New Hampshire titles. Towns such as Brattleboro, Newbury, and Townshend hedged by paying charter fees to both New Hampshire and New York. Even those with New Hampshire titles had the comfort of distance and the mountain barrier between them and the Yorkers.

The gathering of Congregational churches in the western counties was subject to greater obstacles. It took a risk-taking investor to buy a shaky New Hampshire title to land right next to New York. Fear of raids rolled back settlement north of a Castleton-Pittsford line until 1780.

The Multiple Establishment Weakened

By 1780 the religious question was whether to have churches with preferential status as in Connecticut, Massachusetts, and New Hampshire, or a government with separation of church and state. The eventual solution favored a "reformed Christian republican policy," as Smith called it. The General Assembly had enacted the multiple establishment and the blue laws, but the towns decided whether and how strictly to enforce them. The multiple establishment required financial support of the "majority" church by all taxpayers except those certified as supporting a nearby dissenting church. Financial support meant a town-collected tax to build and maintain a town meetinghouse and pay a moral teacher of the whole population, who doubled as pastor of a church within the town.

Vermont immigrants brought a "dual heritage" of Old Light versus New Light, Arminian versus Calvinist. Old Lights were gradualist, rationalist, upholders of the traditional, organic community and the "halfway covenant." This assumed that children should have membership for most purposes as a birthright, because if they were brought up in Christian members' families they would turn out Christian. For them, "Christian liberty" was obedience to minister and magistrate. New Lights, products of revivalism, assumed that the first step toward salvation was the realization that one could do nothing by one's own efforts to escape one's thoroughly sinful situation. This they called "conviction of sin." Then came personal experience of God's grace, transformation by the Holy Spirit, and joining a church of saints gathered from the world and sanctified. New Lights discounted the trained ministry and wanted no cultural distance between elder and congregation. They wanted their clergy to earn some of their livelihood themselves, usually by farming, and receive the rest by subscription of parishioners. In some situations they accepted town taxes for religious purposes.

Arminians, named after a Dutch theologian, Arminius, rejected the Calvinist doctrine that God has predestined only a few for salvation. Deists, Episcopalians, some Baptists, and some Friends were various shades of Arminian. In the 1790s the Free Will Baptists, Universalists, and Methodists would strengthen the majority with this belief in Vermont.

Although the newcomers wanted to escape the old conflicts, they brought most of them along, and the situation "magnified the legacy of dissent," Donald Smith concludes.[49] Each year brought new settlers, shifting the balance between cliques, or adding new groups from different towns with different religious habits and customs. This made the achievement of community a will o' the wisp ever fading as towns aimed and moved toward it.

In the 1780s thirty-two more Congregational churches had been organized, nineteen on the west side, with a majority of some forty ministers settled in Vermont churches arriving in the eleven years from 1780 through 1790. In the same period traveling elders formed some thirty Baptist churches, half from Pownal to Brandon and half from Guilford to Woodstock. Examination of a good many records of churches organized in this period leads to the informal conclusion that few of any denomination had over twenty members each at the start. Even as late as 1805, the first religious society in Burlington organized with fourteen members.[50]

Those farthest from Puritanism were the many deists, among both the leadership and the woodsmen, feeling no need to organize into churches. Ethan Allen churned out 477 pages of verbose argument, entitled *Reason: The Only Oracle of Man* (1784), against superstition, miracles, and anything that violated natural law, and paid Anthony Haswell of Bennington to be his vanity printer. Like the rest of his generation, Ethan was saturated with the Bible. His quick response to his Yorker enemies threatening him with war attests to that: "The gods of the hills are not the gods of the valleys" (I Kings 20:23, 28).

"Ethan Allen's Bible" became notorious, judging by the horror-stricken reactions of the author's opponents. Perhaps a thousand copies of the original, abridgements, and facsimiles have circulated over the centuries. But the people who agreed with his beliefs in the rationalism of common sense, immortality, morality, and progress did not read it, any more than the patriots who agreed with Thomas Jefferson's Declaration of Independence had read the works of John Locke, upon which Jef-

ferson based so much of his philosophy. Perhaps they heard about it
when someone in a tavern bar threw out a phrase such as "God is in-
finitely good. . . [therefore] there cannot be an infinite evil in the universe,"[51] and those present spent the evening debating the proposition.
Like Robert Ingersoll a century later, Ethan Allen delighted in pointing
out "the mistakes of Moses" and in scoffing at superstition. There was
plenty of superstition among the settlers. Letters often state something
like this: "I had a presentiment he would die at the very time he died."
There was also a largely unexamined faith in Providence as ordaining all
things regardless of nature, which Ethan scoffed at.[52]

Christian Practice

All Christians in the Puritan tradition, and that included nearly all
Vermonters, had common practices governing baptism, joining a
church, worship, "Christian walking" (living a Christian life), and dying in the care of the community. Even the few Episcopalians, unless
they had been royal officers or had come directly from England, carried a
good deal of Puritanism with them when they left their Congregational
churches. Baptism was a ritual symbolizing the experience of initiation
into the "mystical body of Christ" (the Quakers called it "convince-
ment"). If you were a Catholic, Episcopalian, Presbyterian, or "Old
Light" Congregationalist like Samuel Williams of Rutland, you
baptized as soon as the infant could stand the sprinkling, and as soon as
a minister of your faith could be found. The ceremony aimed to pledge
the parents to bring up the child into a religious life, as godparents
pledged in other denominations, allowing a "confirmation" of the
baptismal promise after the member reached responsible age. The New
Lights, or Separate Congregationalists, and the Baptists, as well as the
new sects sprung from the Baptists or Separates, felt that joining
should be the conscious act of an adult. They delayed baptism until a
person could report a life-changing experience of grace. Quakers agreed
with those like the Baptists who believed that membership should be
by the joint decision of the reborn or converted individual and the
congregation. But baptism to them was an inward change, of the Spirit
and fire, and not by water.[53]

The regular practice in settled places of bringing a letter from one's
home church to the new abode was rare in Vermont, unless transfer certificates were so normal that they did not need mentioning. Aaron
Hutchinson's church consisted of those persons in Hartford, Pomfret,
and Woodstock "who brought their church membership with them." In
1796 John Conant took his letter from Ashburnham, Massachusetts, to
the Brandon Baptist church. Until 1801, Baptists, Universalists, and
Episcopalians had to present a letter from their minister to the town

clerk, vouching for their membership. In Rockingham, for example, one Baptist secured a letter from his former pastor in Dudley, Massachusetts.[54] But these were exceptional.

In such an important event as founding a church, settlers became members by subscribing to articles of faith and a covenant. A missionary such as Nathan Perkins helped them get started by drafting a theological statement and list of members' duties, or a deacon brought from his old church the articles and covenant. Articles of faith showed remarkable uniformity, but the implications of each article allowed for what outsiders have called endless bickering and insiders have thought of as earnest searching for the truth. The organization of a visible "church of the baptized brethren," as the Royalton Baptists called themselves, included sisters equally. The more churches emphasized the conversion experience, the less need they had for certificates. In some churches they were expected to relate their experience of Christian conversion. Sometimes they would be "propounded," after they had told the pastor they were ready to join; that is, they would be announced as a candidate, so that the existing members could have time to consider the applicant's "conversation and Christian walking."

Members' most important duties were "watch and ward" (helping each other live as if heaven was their destination), household worship, Bible study, and attending public worship. At its best, watch and ward meant caring for fellow members; at its worst, it meant malicious gossip and charging personal enemies with sinful conduct. Each member was responsible for admonishing a neighbor for profanity, frolicking, intemperance, and family violence. The injunction in Matthew 18:15-17 was to admonish privately, member to member; if the tension continues, repeat your complaint with witnesses; if that does not work, tell the church. The resulting church trials, the soap operas of those days, required confession by the guilty or excommunication of the intransigent. Expulsion of an irreconcilable member set a powerful example when the whole town participated in the activities of one church. In the woods, however, the privileges of membership were few, other churches could welcome the errant, and dissenters could usually vote down church taxes. Disowning, as the Quakers called excommunication, became the advertisement of a fact, not a means of discipline.

Church discipline called for maintaining the family altar (worship in the household before and after work) and regular Bible reading and study. Believers assumed that God's Word, revealed in Holy Scripture, is inerrant and subject to only one interpretation. The highest literacy in the world,[55] intense curiosity about the terms of salvation, and freedom to pore over the sacred texts resulted in marvelous diversity of belief, multiplying disagreements. One would expect devout and literate settlers would find religious outlets in diaries where churchgoing was impractical. Aside from the journals of revolutionary chaplains and the reports of Connecticut missionaries, hardly any private diaries have survived from the eighteenth century. Apparently the only men who committed diaries were those who committed war, that is, soldiers and chaplains who believed that for once in their lives they were doing something important that should be recorded for posterity. Jonathan Carpenter, who settled in Randolph after the Revolution, carried a pocket diary on his campaigns and scouts. Betweeen excursions he noted quality of land and even when his wife occasionally went to meeting.[56]

Most of the time people did not object to worshiping with Christians they disagreed with. They were willing to sign a church's articles of faith, and pass time arguing with an infidel deist or Quaker. Non-members attended services appointed by passing preachers or the town minister when convenient. If the minister preached in a nearby cabin or barn, if the streams were fordable or the drifts not too deep, if the work was in hand and nobody was sick, and if they felt like it, they came. For fellowship settlers had the choice of a tap room in a public house or going to meeting. How many attended is guesswork. Perhaps two hundred could have crammed themselves into Daniel Foot's 40-by-75-foot barn near the center of Middlebury.

Death punctuated the life sentence of a member with a ritualized, funereal period of mourning, yet each loss was counted the gain of the glory of eternal life, the promise of the resurrection of the saints at the end of the world. By "saints" they meant members, sinners forgiven by the saving grace of God. When life was shorter, death was a familiar visitor to frontier families. They knew the importance of sitting up with the dying and comforting the family. They deemed it significant to catch the last words of the dying because of the awesome act of meeting one's Creator. Funerals were not to eulogize first families so much as a minister's mission opportunity of rededication. Burial shifted from the spot where death occurred, in the earliest frontier, to family property, and in the early nineteenth century, to church or town lots. In 1790, Jonathan Arnold, major St. Johnsbury proprietor, deeded one of the earliest public cemeteries to trustees for the "South Parish," what became the principal village, for a burial ground, school, or other public use. Markers were either non-existent, or of wood or stone with nothing but initials and year of death.[57]

The Ministers

Few were called to minister, teach, or oversee the discipline of the church. Gospel order was a mixed government, under Christ the King, with officers ruling as an aristocracy but democratically elected and re-

moved by the members of the church. (Methodist, Episcopal, and
Catholic bishops had power to appoint and remove.) Ordination recognized a person's gifts in the ministry (the Quakers called it "recording").
Ordination sermons outlined the duties of these religious leaders. Each
congregation might have several recognized exhorters, evangelists,
teachers, and deacons, but only one pastor, unless he was infirm and
needed an assistant. It was more likely in the earliest days for one pastor to serve two or more towns.

A church "called" a minister to the parish after listening to candidates and negotiating a covenant or contract with him. If he accepted the
call, the church "settled" him for life by covenant between the pastor
and his parish. If he was the "first settled minister" in town, he was entitled to a lot, usually the worst land in town, which he might swap or
sell for fewer acres that he could farm and sell when he left town. The
parish felt defrauded by those who sold too soon after arrival. In
Sandgate, "Minister's Hill" was only three miles from "Swearing Hill."
Churches sometimes hurried the call to settle the first minister in town
because he would receive a bonus of land reserved for him by New
Hampshire or Vermont charters. In Sunderland when two Congregationalists were ordained on the same day, instead of dividing the bonus,
they asked the court to decide who was the first settled minister. The
judge decided in favor of the man who was ordained a few minutes earlier, according to one story.[58]

The tendency was strong to lease the minister's lot and use the income for schools. Shaftsbury Baptists declined this bonus for their
minister and the town assigned the income from leasing the minister's
lot to be used for schools. Some towns divided the rent from land reserved for church use in proportion to the number of members in each
denomination. In towns chartered by New Hampshire, the glebe land
was reserved for the Anglican Society for the Propagation of the Gospel
in Foreign Parts, but the General Assembly tried to divert its income
for schools. After a generation of litigation, the courts decided in favor
of the Episcopalians. Although the Quakers were the first majority in
Danby, they were not given the minister's right, and it went to the Baptists, organized in 1781.[59]

The covenant recorded the religious expectations and mundane
agreements in bushels of wheat, cords of firewood, annual increases, and
other stipulations. Like marriage, the bond was expected to last, and
occasionally it did. For example, Asa Burton tended his Thetford flock
from 1779 until his death in 1836, and David Goodwillie served the Associate Presbyterians in Barnet from 1790 to 1830. Among Presbyterians and Congregationalists the trained clergy still expected deference,
and where they achieved it, had long tenure and were often called "Father."[60]

All but three of the Congregational clergy settled in Vermont before 1791 were college graduates. Of these three, Jedediah Dewey of Bennington had experience as a pastor in Massachusetts and Lemuel Haynes read divinity with Daniel Farrand in Connecticut. Yale supplied sixteen, Harvard twelve, and Dartmouth ten graduates to Vermont Congregational churches before 1790. Yale and Dartmouth men were mainly in the Connecticut Valley. Gradually from the 1760s to 1791 fewer Harvard men and more from Yale, who took their theology from Joseph Bellamy, Samuel Hopkins, and Nathaniel Emmons, won posts in the new settlements. More liberal Harvard was failing to prepare preachers fit for frontier parishes. Daniel Clarke Sanders, Harvard 1788, who served over twenty years in Vergennes and Burlington (1794-1815), was glad to get back to the neighborhood of Harvard.[61]

Pastors were officers, not professionals. Members were "professors" who professed their faith. Charisma maintained revivalist leadership, and since this gift is unpredictable, the ministers had trouble maintaining unity until they evolved a discipline in the 1790s and after. But the prestige of clergy trended downward. The scarcity of candidates in wartime put the pious more upon their own resources during the long periods between "supplying" or temporary preachers, and gave them confidence from experience in ruling themselves. Even the settled pastors had drinking, sex, and business failings which damaged their image.

The realities of dissatisfaction with the minister, and the minister's disappointment at the congregation's failure to fulfill their part of the covenant, led to the breakdown of the ideal of lifetime commitment between parish and pastor. Some towns had superannuated ministers released from a prosperous church in a prosperous town. Under the guise of mission they lived out their days on a frontier that paid them little heed and fewer victuals. Other towns found recent college graduates who could not get a call to a parish in settled country. Although the fact that they persevered through college proved ambition, all but two or three Harvard or Yale men in Vermont parishes, who graduated when ranking was by social position (until 1768-1769), were near the bottom of their class socially. They plied their trade with brief appointments in towns that "hired preaching." Nathan Perkins ran into a Yale acquaintance who had tried for eighteen years to get a job as a settled preacher in ninety places and still depended on temporarily supplying one church after another.[62] Whether hired for short terms or called and settled, in either case, John E. Goodrich wrote in 1907, "there was an unusual proportion of unworthy men among the Vermont clergy" before 1791.[63] Goodrich judged in comparison to later clergy. Yet these pioneer preachers were the best available and they did the best they could and scraped a living any way they could.

In a good many towns, difficulties collecting church taxes led to voluntary subscription for part or all of the costs. Proposals to hire town preaching were often defeated because too many would not pay for it. When they did vote the church tax and looked for a preacher, they accepted whomever was available, of whatever religious persuasion, although they haggled long over the terms of his hire.

When Vermont negotiated admission to the United States in 1789-1791, the stream of its history dropped some of its load while other things continued their drift and the river picked up new cargo. Admission ended the independent republic with its failures in dealing with the British in Canada and with the United States. Admission confirmed victory over the Allen faction, over the British, hoping for a dependent buffer state, and over New York claims in Congress. The political tension between the southern-oriented Connecticut Valley and the northern-oriented Champlain Valley continued, with southwestern Vermont (from Rutland and Castleton to Bennington), oriented toward Albany, exercising its balance of power. Vermont still had a mainly subsistence economy but the commercial tail wagged the subsistence dog: Settlers aimed to barter their surpluses of skins, ashes, timber, cattle, and wheat, if not at the ports, then in the neighborhood.

As producers of goods had started to compete in the markets, so did wandering preachers, peddling their brand of the gospel to people free to choose. The multiple establishment continued, favoring the Congregational churches, but was less and less enforced. Although people still congregated in cabins, a few barnlike meetinghouses without belfry or tower, like the one in Rockingham built in 1787-1801, were raised on town taxes and/or the subscriptions of the zealous. Since "the revolutionary stir," a wave of revivals in the southwestern part of the state, the mobile population was more open to revivalist religion. Timothy Rogers, the Ferrisburg Quaker entrepreneur, found people along his way ready to discuss the fine points of theology and morals. The first "raving arminian methodist," as Nathan Perkins called him (probably Samuel Wigton), had appeared in Sunderland to compete for souls with the Calvinists.[64]

Wilderness required people to do it themselves and not depend on laws or ministers to dictate their religion. Even in tightly settled England, the Puritan ancestors of these "foresters," as Timothy Dwight called them, had taught that the Bible is literally the Word of God, and you can read all about God's good news in the good Book yourself. They wanted no bishop of an established church, no fixed dogmas devised by Congregationalists or Baptists on the model of the Presbyterians' Westminster Confession, to maintain social order, nor did most of them care to be served by second-rate itinerants. A century after the first settlers arrived, a nineteen-year-old school teacher in northeastern

Vermont, coming back from church, recorded in her diary, "I do not. . . believe all I ever heard any minister say on this point [hell], but. . . I have a mind of my own."[65]

Frontier scarcity taught them that if they *did* want to hire preaching, or to raise a meetinghouse, they should welcome the help of those who might differ on the fine points of doctrine. A generation later, when there were enough of various birds of a feather for several flocks, Yankee combativeness had more to fight about. While they enjoyed the conflict, they tolerated differences and the principle of voluntarism—all could go to their chosen churches or stay home.

Notes to Chapter 1

[1] I published much of this chapter in an earlier version as "Cabin Religion in Vermont, 1724-1791," *Vermont History* 62 (Spring 1994): 69-87.

[2] The following summary of Indian religion is based on Haviland and Power, *Original Vermonters*. They introduce the current state of knowledge from archeological and ethnohistorical sources, as detailed in the "Bibliographical Notes" and list of titles, 283-326. They guess at the Western Abenaki worldview (186-197) partly from the findings of Gordon M. Day, ethnohistorian, and by extrapolation from what is known of the ßEastern Abenaki, especially the Penobscot. See also other sections indexed under Ideology and Myths/Storytelling.

[3] See Demos, *Unredeemed Captive*, 77-81, 93, 112, 115-117, 168.

[4] See his *Travels in North America*, 40-46. François Dollier de Casson's account of his service on Isle La Motte, in his *Histoire de Montréal*, is translated and abridged in Bassett, *Outsiders Inside Vermont*, 8-12.

[5] Coolidge, "French Occupation of the Champlain Valley," remains the fullest treatment of this subject.

[6] Quoted and translated from his *Voyages* (1632) in Bassett, *Outsiders Inside Vermont*, 6-7.

[7] *Captivity of Nehemiah How*, 3-9. As with slaveholders who sometimes treated their slaves well from economic motives, Indian captors had the economic incentive of ransoming their prisoners of war.

[8] Johnson, *Captivity of Mrs. Johnson*, 8-9, 32-33.

[9] Diary of a Fort Dummer scout in Cabot, *Annals of Brattleboro*, 1:13 (spelling modernized).

[10] Gay, "The Captivity of Mrs. Jemima Howe," in Jeremy Belknap, *History of New Hampshire*, 3:177-190.

[11] Reminiscence of about 1846 in Lovejoy, *History of Royalton*, 151, 153. Avery's full story suggests no connection with Chaplain David Avery, Yale 1769, pastor at Bennington. George "got religion" later. The Royalton Congregational church, organized in 1777, had no house of worship until 1791.

[12] Cabot, *Annals of Brattleboro*, 10; summarizes the fort's history, 6-10, 12, 16-17. The sketched plan, 9, shows no chapel. The chaplains were Daniel Dwight, (ca. 1724-1727), at a salary of a 100 pounds a year, larger than that of his brother Timothy, who commanded the fort; Ebenezer Hinsdale (ca. 1731-1742); and Andrew Gardner, Sr. (1748).

[13] Woolman was on a two-hundred-mile trip into the wilderness of the Wyoming Valley to the Indian village of Wyalusing, "to spend some time with the Indians, that I might feel and understand their life. . . if haply I might receive some instruction from them, or they be. . . helped. . . by my following the leadings of truth among them." John Woolman, *Journal*, 129-130.

[14] Indian oral tradition gathered by John Moody of Sharon confirms what H. R. Whitney recorded as lacking authentication, in Hemenway, *Gazetteer*, 2:370, 371, 376 (quotation). Fisher, *The Vermont Tradition*, 17-31, while wrong about racial antagonism and wrong about the number of Abenaki, rightly emphasized "how empty the country was" (22) from the white perspective.   Randolph A. Roth expresses the opposite view in *The Democratic Dilemma*, 15: "The [Connecticut] valley remained a violent place for many years" after 1764.   Cf. Earle Newton, *The Vermont Story*, 35.

[15] Bellesiles, *Revolutionary Outlaws*, 98, 186-187.

[16] Krueger summarized the chaplaincy in "Troop Life at the Champlain Valley Forts."   See also Headley, *Clergy of the Revolution*, 89-106 (on Samuel Spring, who served at Mount Independence), and 128 (on Thomas Allen of Pittsfield, who accompanied the Berkshire militia to the Battle of Bennington).

[17] Black and Roelker, *A Rhode Island Chaplain*, 27; Chase, *Dartmouth College*, 1:308-309; sketches of Avery in Headley, *Chaplains of the Revolution*, 287-299; Dexter, *Graduates of Yale College*; and in Sprague, *American Pulpit*, 1:697n.   The story that he was converted by George Whitefield is apparently apocryphal, with the kernel of truth that he was an evangelical or New Light.

[18] Letter from Mount Independence to Nicholas Brown, Providence, R. I., 31 August 1776, in Black and Roelker, eds., *A Rhode Island Chaplain*, 27. David, Brown '72, an ordained Seventh Day Baptist minister, had been principal of Providence Latin School before the Revolution. He died in service.

[19] Robbins, *Journal*, especially 25-26, 30, 33, 36-37.

[20] See David Avery, *Papers*, xxxi and passim. The lack of unity was over interpreting "Hopkinsianism," the theology developed by Samuel Hopkins between the Great Awakening of 1734-1749 and the publication of his *System of Doctrines* in 1793. See Conforti, *Samuel Hopkins and the New Divinity*.

[21] David Avery to David MacClure, August 16, 1780, Spargo Autographs, Box 1, folder 9, typed copy, in Special Collections, Bailey/Howe Library, University of Vermont.

[22] Quoted in Kelley, *Yale: A History*, 78.

[23] See David Avery, *Narrative*; Michael Bellesiles, *Revolutionary Outlaws*, 234-237. Was the "Revd Mr. Avery of Stamford, on mission to Vermont," who was "deeply mortified at ye Superior defference showed to" Nathan Perkins at the meeting of the ministerial association in Poultney, June 1789, the former Bennington pastor? (Nathan Perkins, *Narrative*, 55).

[24] Nathan Perkins, *Narrative*, 27. Jeremiah Day, "Missionary Tour, 1788," appears to be the only report of a minister's trip before Perkins. In 1780, the General Association of Connecticut released David Sherman Rowland of Windsor and Joseph Strong of Granby to visit the new settlements, but their church records show no evidence that they went, as Earle W. Newton, *Vermont Story*, 106, asserts.

Jennings, *Memorials of a Century*, opp. 24, shows a drawing entitled "First Meeting House Erected in Vermont."

[25] They were Jedediah Dewey (Bennington, 1763-1778), Peter Powers (Newbury and Haverhill, N.H., 1765-1782), Jesse Goodsell (Westminster, 1767-1769), Joseph Bullen (Westminster, 1774-1785), James Wellman (Windsor and Cornish, N.H., 1768-1774), Abner Reeve (Brattleboro and Guilford, 1770-1774, Brattleboro, 1774-1792), Samuel Whiting, (Rockingham, 1772-1809, and Chester, 1773-1778), Clement Sumner (Thetford, 1773-1778), Benajah Roots (Rutland, West Parish, 1773-1787), and Hezekiah Taylor (Newfane, 1774-1811). See Comstock, *Congregational Churches*, 35, 41, 52, 71, 94, 95, 110, 127, 142, 144, 149.

[26] Stiles, *Literary Diary*, 2:404.

[27] Alvah Bean in A. M. Hemenway, *Gazetteer*, 2:915, 1170.

[28] Hubbard and Dartt, *Springfield*, 72.

[29] Hemenway, *Gazetteer*, 1:208-209.

[30] Marini, *Radical Sects*, 94, 133; Bail, "Zadock Wright."

[31] Nathan Perkins, *Narrative*, 32. The most quoted passage in Perkins' often-quoted *Narrative*, used first by Stilwell in "Migration from Vermont," 76, and Ludlum in *Social Ferment in Vermont*, 19-28, to support their conclusions of frontier infidelity and west side radicalism.

[32] Hubbell, *Narrative*.

[33] *Vermont Historical Gazetteer*, 2:376, the Sheldon murder(s) substantiated by Abenaki oral tradition as told to John Moody of Sharon. Wells, *Newbury*, 44, cites two murders, also evidenced by oral tradition. This supports Randolph Roth's conclusion that "the [Connecticut] valley remained a violent place for many years " after 1764. Cf. Newton, *Vermont Story*, 35. Fisher, *Vermont Tradition*, 17-31, while wrong in denying racial antagonism, especially in the Missisquoi Valley, is right that Vermont had no Indian wars except as adjuncts of imperial wars, and that it is hard to imagine "how empty the country was" from the white perspective. (p.22)

[34] Carpenter, *Journal*.

[35] For the state of the Rutland County frontier during Burgoyne's invasion see my *Outsiders Inside Vermont*, 32-34, and Williams, *Danby*, 171-176. See also [Jehiel Johns], Huntington, to G. W. Benedict, Burlington, May 19, 1840, in Stevens Family Papers, 9-18, UVM, reminiscing about the Revolution. Attribution by J. Kevin Graffagnino.

[36] Nathan Perkins, *Narrative*, 27.

[37] Nathan Perkins, *Narrative*, 32. No connection between the Sheldons of Sheldon and Keyes' father-in-law has been established. See the references to Keyes in Hemenway, *Gazetteer*, *Index*, and the Chittenden County Historical Society *Bulletin* 17 (January-February 1982):3 on his character.

[38] Professor Roth has sent me a prepublication copy of his forthcoming chapter, "Spousal Murder in Northern New England, 1776-1865," in *Over The Threshold: Intimate Violence in Early America,* ed. Christine Daniels and Michael V. Kennedy (New York: Routledge, 1999), 65-93.

[39] Smith, "Green Mountain Insurgency," summarizes and revises the conclusions of his dissertation, "Legacy of Dissent" (quotation, 870). See also brief reference to the eighteenth-century revivalists in Donal Ward, "Religious Enthusiasm."

[40] See Randolph A. Roth's summary of Smith and his treatment of the religious forces to 1800 in *The Democratic Dilemma*, 26-39. Michael A. Bellesiles, *Revolutionary Outlaws*, 217-222 and passim, with his focus on Ethan Allen as a charismatic leader, thinks of the religious situation after the Revolution as secular because the sects cancelled each other out, and no one group could control religious observances. In a comparable study, Sweet, *Church and Community*, concluded that the inflexibility of Congregationalism prevented it from meeting the challenge of the New Hampshire frontier. The growth of dissenting groups broke down the unity of the town as both a government and a Congregational church.

[41] Hoag, *Journal*, 52, states Huldah Hoag's recording as a minister and suggests her husband Joseph's. Williams, *Danby*, 97-99, includes a list of thirty-two early Quaker settlers, with more biographical detail in the alphabetical "Family Sketches," 101-288.

[42] Brush, *St. James Episcopal Church*, 13-20; Manchester, Vt., *Zion Episcopal Church*, 1-5; Dexter, *Graduates of Yale College*, 3:425-427 (Nichols); Hemenway, *Gazetteer*, 2:496 (Garlick), 1:881 (Chittenden). Reports of Episcopal missionaries in Vermont to their English headquarters have not been used by historians of Vermont.

[43] Bailyn on Ryegate in *Voyagers to the West*, 604-637, quotations on pp. 619, 637; "Ecclesiastical History" of Barnet by Thomas Goodwillie, son of the first settled minister, in *Vermont Historical Gazetteer*, 1:284-302.

[44] Benedict, *Baptist Denomination*, 486; Peak, *Memoir*, 53.

[45] Peak, *Memoir*, 44, 63.

[46] Marini, *Radical Sects*, 40-48, discusses the wave of revivalism that sent New Light groups through northern New England and Nova Scotia. They won over many, probably a majority, who were dissatisfied with orthodox Congregationalism.

[47] McKeen, *Bradford*, quoted in Schwartz and Schwartz, *Flame of Fire*, 44; see also 67, 118; Mudge, *New England Conference*, 33. Wigton, and not the Quaker Timothy Rogers, as stated in my "Cabin Religion in Vermont," 83, must have been the "raving arminian methodist" in Sunderland Nathan

Perkins referred to in his *Narrative*, 20.

48 Comstock, *Congregational Churches* (1914), 8; (1942), 9.

49 Smith, "Legacy of Dissent," 868-872.

50 Burlington, Vt. First Congregational Church, *Hundredth Anniversary*, [9].

51 Allen, *Reason*, 118.

52 See Bellesiles, *Revolutionary Outlaws*, 217-244, and my columns in the *Burlington Free Press*, "Ira Allen and the Headless Woman." The journal of Timothy Rogers, Ferrisburg and later Yonge Street, Ontario, a Quaker, cites in his disputes with deists several cases where "the spirit" told some one of imminent death (typescript and original in the archives of Canadian Yearly Meeting of Friends, Pickering College, Newmarket, Ontario).
    Ethan Allen was not the only "frontier philosopher" devoting hours of old age to a theological dissertation. Former Congressman Nathaniel Niles a generation later left over two hundred pages of musings, now in the Vermont Historical Society, MSS 23, #92. See also Williams, *Philosophical Lectures*.

53 See "Baptism," in Dean Freiday, ed., *Barclay's Apology in Modern English*, 301-326.

54 Dana, *Woodstock*, 424; John Conant (1773-1856), "Extracts From an Autobiographical Sketch," 7, (n.d., typescript in Brandon Public Library); L. S. and W. D. Hayes, *Old Rockingham Meeting House*, 32.

55 Gilmore, *Reading Becomes a Necessity*, establishes high literacy in southern Windsor County as indicative of similar levels in the surrounding region and assesses the significance of Bible reading in the cultural complex.

56 See Carpenter, *Journal*.

57 Fairbanks, *St. Johnsbury*, 104-105; Sloane, *Last Gret Necessity*, 13-28, especially 4-5, Table 1.1, "Characteristics of American Cemeteries."

58 John M. Comstock, *Congregational Churches*, 126. This is folklore telling a truth about eagerness to win the minister's lot but inaccurate for 1790, when steeples and their clocks were non-existent, watches were scarce, and time was told by the sun.

59 See Chapter 3, p. 73, on the Episcopal recovery of glebe lands; Williams, *Danby*, 92-93 on Baptist Hezekiah Eastman as first settled minister of Danby.

60 Examples: "Father [Chester] Wright" of Montpelier, (Thompson, *Montpelier*, 130); "Father [Simeon] Parmelee" (Gilman, *Bibliography of Vermont*, 192); Father Joseph A. Sherburne, Methodist (C. D. and O. D. Schwartz, *Flame of Fire*, 208); "Father [Asa] Lyon, as he is generally denominated," *Vermont Chronicle*. 16 (27 January 1841), 13, col. 1.

61 Bassett in *University of Vermont*, 14.

62 Nathan Perkins, *Narrative*, 33.

63 Goodrich, "Immigration to Vermont, 74.

64 Nathan Perkins, *Narrative*, 20.

65 Melissa S. Dolloff's Journal at UVM, entry of August 15, 1858.

2

Vermont's Nineteenth-Century Civil Religion[1]

Between the American Revolution and the Spanish American War, the separate states of the United States of America were drawn closer together by the powerful forces of nationalism, a worldwide movement. Coming together at first as a coalition to win independence from the British Empire, the many different colonies only gradually, after much strife and mutual experience as states, came to realize that they belonged to each other.

Vermont brought its own brand of patriotism to the Union: its fifteen years of independence and its share in the Revolution. The unifying force in the independent state of Vermont had been opposition to outward foes, first New York, then the British, Indians, and Tories. Opposition to the Confederation was mainly because of its refusal to let Vermont join. Until 1796, the British occupied their fort at Block House Point, on a prong of North Hero commanding the trade on the direct route between the Isle la Mott Passage and the Carrying Place, a portage to the east shore of the island. Britain was indeed an enemy to be wary of, as well as a trading partner to profit from. Exposed to this British threat, and divided by factions with opposing political, economic, and religious interests, Vermont sat on a fence. Where did its interests lie? With the American Confederation? With British North America? Or as some would-be filibusters dreamed, in a greater Vermont carved out of Lower Canada and upper New York? When Vermonters got off the fence and decided to join the feeble, infant, federal union, only their patriotism, proven in the Revolution, could overcome the conflicting loyalties threatening to tear them apart.

When the end of the war and the admission of Vermont to the Union resolved old tensions over land titles and New York jurisdiction, British North America, touching Vermont's Canadian border, was the only enemy against which Vermonters could unite. Congregationalism, beleaguered by competing churches, had been retreating for years and

now could no longer impose unity. Vermont, which had held out for its
acceptance as one of the United States, needed to merge loyalty to its
past with loyalty to the nation. Vermonters needed to claim a share in
the victorious Revolution, to bind all their people together.

I have come to realize that this patriotism, this budding nationalism, eventually had all the elements of what historians have recently come to call a "civil religion." Vermont's declaration of independence at Westminster, January 15, 1777, outlined its creed and
promised mutual support "by all the ties that are held sacred among
men."[2] The rituals, scriptures, symbols, and saints of its patriotism
developed gradually over the next century and a quarter.

The Vermont Creed

Vermont's creed was clear from the start. Freedom and unity,
Vermont's motto in Ira Allen's design for the first state seal, and all the
words related to the doctrine it symbolizes, were often repeated abstrac-
tions. "Unanimity, the great Strength and Security of a free and independent People, is necessary for the Existence of a sovereign State," declared the preamble to the Act of June 21, 1782, against armed subver-
sion.[3] Vermonters valued their freedoms: liberty to acquire property and
use it with minimal outside interference; liberty to move without a by-
your-leave; liberty to meet, speak, and publish without restriction;
freedom to vote and hold office; freedom to worship without an established church.

Like most creeds, the declaration stated goals, some of which, like
equality, tolerance, and balance, were implicit, and mere gleams on the
horizon. Revivals and reforms in the first third of the nineteenth century
were new outlooks differing from those of the freethinking founders,
but the evangelical groups all identified their ideas of the kingdom of
God with the fortunes of the American republic.[4]

The Westminster convention, in its haste to draft a declaration or
creed, tried to state the ideal of human equality and the equality of
churches without choosing its language carefully. By combining language concerning the legal bondage of apprentices and convicts with a
prohibition of slavery, it left a loophole for minors to be held as slaves.
Cases continue to turn up of settlers bringing slaves to Vermont from
states still sanctioning slavery. They freed them, sometimes as late as
the 1830s and 1840s, when someone called their attention to Vermont's
intended prohibition, or courts forced them to give their slaves up.[5]

Aside from those civil rights embedded in the first ten amendments
to the federal Constitution, and derived from long colonial common law
tradition, the part underlying Vermont's attitude toward religion was
Article 3 of its 1777 declaration. No one can be forced to attend or

support worship or pay for preaching, it read, but all *denominations* "ought to observe the Sabbath . . . and keep up some sort of religious worship." Again, this was hasty and careless draftsmanship. The intention was to require *everyone* to go to some church on Sunday. But, literally, only a handful of the population belonged to a "sect or denomination"; the rest were therefore exempt. The General Assembly proceeded to enact blue laws and the multiple establishment as if everybody had to attend worship and toe the mark.

In most of the world that Vermonters came from—Great Britain, Quebec, and much of New England—the state gave advantages to what it considered to be the one true church. For Vermonters the principle of religious freedom rested on a broader assumption not yet fully articulated. Referring to Protestantism, and soon to Christianity instead of to one of its branches, they implied that there was not one true church but a communion of saints in many churches, each with special insights into the truth. And in 1777, they would have had to include members of the vast unaffiliated majority with *their* special insights.

Vermont in its first fifty years had a remarkably homogeneous population, compared to its later diversity. Compared to their places of origin, however—eastern New York, Northern Ireland, Scotland, and towns in southern New England "burnt over" by revivalism— Vermont's new settlements were remarkably heterogenous. As Vermont lacked a single established church, only the revolutionary creed could unite those thousands of early arrivals and the two hundred thousand people with varying traditions added in the first half century. They feted the Revolution in spite of the fact that escape from military service in the war for independence had been one of the motives driving young men out of settled New England into the relatively safe Connecticut Valley.

Toleration had to mean more than accepting the principle that other people's creeds made no difference or that heresy must be allowed but restricted. Samuel Williams wrote in 1794, "It is not barely *toleration*, but *equality* which the people aim at."[6] Those who favored this kind of toleration wanted a level playing field, where people who believed passionately could evangelize and those who did not care could be left to mind their own business. Williams' attitude was somewhere between recognition that others he did not agree with had rights, and an openness and willingness to learn from those who are different. Vermont was an immigrant society; it was not colonized like New France, but settled by individuals or families. But admission to the United States, a nation-state organized by the dominant English, cancelled the regime of the immigrant society.[7]

On this playing field political parties developed in Vermont out of a colonial background that had not needed them. It is hard to see how the English-speaking world shifted in the eighteenth century from factional to party politics. The early modern "faction" was a group that earned destruction because it plotted treason. The party, by contrast, came to be assumed loyal to the state whether in or out of power. Both factions and parties had interests and formed coalitions, but only the party loved its country more than its coalition or interests. The distinction is hard to make because party rhetoric then, as it does even today, labelled opponents as evil factions and subversives.

Colonial interests had been woven together in a combination of loyalties and frictions. A weak loyalty to the empire and stronger loyalties to one's colony and town created crown-colony and town-colony tensions. At home, habitual deference to the magistrates, the clergy, and the other wealthy, well-born, or well-educated men kept the community in balance. People running affairs through their business and family connections in the wider world had not needed parties as long as most people were quiet, isolated, and only superficially involved beyond their neighborhoods.

The Revolution allowed self-made men like Ira Allen and Matthew Lyon to develop followings, calling to their active support people who had hitherto taken no part against the traditional leaders. Allen's was a faction subordinating the republic's interest to his, while Lyon's was a party, accepting defeat at the polls until it won a seat for him in Congress and the presidency for Jefferson in 1800.

Patriotic loyalty overcame the evils of faction in this new situation, following the dictum of Jefferson's first inaugural, "We are all Republicans, we are all Federalists." Knowing that pure liberty is chaotic anarchy, Vermonters, like other Americans, believed in order created by coming to agreement. For them, unity did not mean absence of conflict. They loved verbal fights in court, church meeting, town meeting, and around the tavern or home fireplace. Ideally, unity meant that all the people could speak up according to rules of order and try to persuade the whole; that everybody should be represented in the General Assembly. In its first constitution, everybody meant white, male, Protestant adults who paid their taxes.[8] The creed allowed for growth to include more and more of the population eligible to take part. These liberties had limits, of course. No individual or group could be allowed to harm the life, liberty, or property of others or disturb their worship.

From the Revolution on, Vermonters recited their creed by developing rituals that embodied ideas and events from the new nation's revolutionary tradition and their own special part in it.

The first votive fires lighted on the altar of freedom were in the fireplaces of veterans' cabins, where their children and grandchildren heard about hardships at the seige of Quebec and the deadly trek back to the Champlain Valley, the battles on their borders, and doing one's bit as a ranger or private elsewhere. Baptist Elder Ezra Butler's Waterbury neighbors testified to his stories, probably not about himself, as he was never in battle, but about what others did, about why the Revolution was worth the sacrifice.[9] For those who had *not* done their bit, the patriotic pose was more important than for veterans. Repetition of Vermont's folk history, the exploits at Ticonderoga, Hubbardton, and Bennington, with all their metaphors and omissions, resonated in the people's memory and gave value and meaning to their later experience.

Patriotic scripture appeared in the reading of the American Declaration of Independence at various rituals, as recitations of creedal statements in common school texts, or in print after being proclaimed from pulpits. The publication of two Vermont histories by Samuel Williams and Ira Allen in the 1790s satisfied the personal needs of their authors and the considerable Anglo-American curiosity about this "Switzerland of America." More important, it crystallized the Vermont story that people like Butler had been telling each other.[10]

The Fourth of July and Other Civic Holidays

Just as at first in the new settlements the devout gathered privately to pray, sing psalms, and read the Bible, so citizens gathered at family altars and tavern celebrations to remember the birth of freedom and veterans who won it. By the time newspapers were reporting public gatherings to celebrate the Fourth of July, people felt that they had always marked the day. While Vermont was independent, celebration signaled the state's willingness to join the Confederation. After admission, people assembled to proclaim unity and to offer each other "mutual congratulation, uninfluenced by party," according to the program at Vergennes in 1796.[11]

Yet partisans promoted the celebrations, each claiming a monopoly of patriotism. Matthew Lyon and the Democratic Societies celebrated for Jefferson's party in western Vermont, and the Federalists countered on the other side of the state. In Vergennes people assembled at Captain Hollister's inn at noon, and ate "a plentiful Republican dinner" at three, followed by sixteen toasts. Then a deputation visited "the ladies assembled at a bowry on the bank of Otter creek to commemorate the day over a cup of hyson [tea]"; festivities ended with the mingling of ladies and gentlemen in song and dance until six. After so many toasts, one can imagine that many continued to celebrate far into the night.

The Rutland County Democratic Society that year heard an oration by Elias Buel of Fair Haven, where Lyon lived, while its Chittenden County counterpart heard veteran Udney Hay of Underhill. After Hay's speech the faithful gathered at Gideon King's tavern in Burlington for dinner at three, with fifteen toasts.[12]

The fully developed Fourth was dawn-to-dark excitement, no matter how good the haying weather was. Boys and young men saluted the sunrise with cannon firing and bell ringing. Parades, with militia first, and dignitaries, veterans, students at every level, and townspeople, kept in time by drummers and stirred by tunes on whatever musical instruments the town or its hinterland afforded, led to the meetinghouse, court house, or grove. Outdoor ceremonies featured militia inspections, banners and bunting, huzzas, volleys of musketry, and cannonades by the "black artillery," foreshadowing modern motorcycle gangs. "Dressed in long, black, swallowtail coats...with brass buttons...tall, bell-shaped leather caps, mounted by...black plumes," they dragged their cannon into position.[13] Indoors a Protestant type of "service" enveloped the oration with invocation and dismissal, hymns led by the choir, often with original words by locals, and a public reading of the Declaration of Independence. The morning and afternoon sessions were separated by feasting in local taverns.[14]

In 1811, at opposite corners of the state, Guilford and Fairfax celebrated the Fourth for their counties. Guilford, until recently the most populous Vermont town, followed the customary pattern, with a special feature, common to later decades, involving youth. After opening odes and prayers by the local pastor, "twenty-one youths of about ten years of age, of both sexes, emblematically arrayed" to represent the states and territories, proceeded up the meetinghouse aisle, "bearing the Declaration of Independence." Their spokesperson presented "the book" to his father, Royall Tyler, chief justice of the Vermont Supreme Court, who thereupon read it with his usual "elegant enunciation," and then gave the chief oration. Presumably, the crowd of "nearly 1,000" and the musicians had gathered from afar, so that it is reasonable to assume an oldtimer's memory that the din of fifty drums at a Brattleboro muster, ten of them bass drums, was duplicated in Guilford.[15]

Instead of a personage like Royall Tyler, the alternative for orator was an aspiring young man. At Fairfax, twenty-year-old Jacob Collamer, one year out of college, addressed a large Independence Day audience, his first step up the ladder that would lead him to the United States Senate. Pretense of nonpartisanship was gone. Like other orators since two parties contested federal elections, he called the Fourth our civil "sabbath," and claimed the altar of freedom for the Republicans, with "the cloud of war . . . on our political horizon."[16]

A typical oration, like those in other states, shouted the battle cry of freedom. Speakers in the meetinghouse or outdoors had to shout to be heard. They praised Vermont's contributions to the fight for freedom against the tyrannical British and declared that God had guided the patriots at every turn and had brought peace and prosperity to state and nation. Hard times were only a dip on the rising road of progress if people would be faithful to their God and work in the spirit of the Revolution. The program mixed patriotic music and the repetition of Vermont's tribal history with quotation of "scriptures" featuring the Declaration of Independence and the Protestant Bible. The exodus from British Egypt and the Conquest of Canaan (the New Hampshire Grants) from New York shared center stage with battles won.

In tandem with the national holiday (holy day), Vermont's Election Day, a state holiday since 1778, celebrated government's balance between freedom and unity. This celebration, when the General Assembly convened in October, had counterparts in the other New England states where the tradition of the partnership of church and state died hard. Vermont gave up appointing election day sermons in 1834, a year after the last state disestablishment, in Massachusetts. Civil religion continued to feature the inauguration of a new governmment without the counterproductive appointment of one divine as chaplain, to the displeasure of those disappointed.

States are "honorable and happy," declared Samuel Shuttlesworth, the Windsor Congregational minister, in 1791, "in proportion to their conformity to the essential laws of religion."[17] The General Assembly launched its annual session with an "order of worship" duplicated in Fourth of July celebrations, to consecrate the people's loyalty to the state and, from 1791, to the nation. When the legislature met at the Windsor courthouse on Thursday, October 13, 1791, "the day was ushered in by the beating of drums." About ten o'clock, Captain Hawley's cavalry met Governor Chittenden's party a few miles from town and paraded them to the green, where the local militia companies maneuvered in "beautiful uniforms." The canvassing committee thereupon declared Chittenden reelected and fifteen cannon boomed. Shuttlesworth, appointed at the previous session, then delivered the Election Day sermon "with his usual energy and pathos." After a banquet, with a long series of nonpartisan toasts, festivities closed with an elegant ball including guests from neighboring states. In 1792, the state reimbursed Governor Thomas Chittenden for his nine-pound contribution toward the expenses, probably for gunpowder. Militia officers were expected to provide the liquor.[18]

That booms, bangs and marching were important to the ritual of Election Day is suggested by the fate of the resolution introduced by Daniel Farrand of Newbury in 1796: "Military parade on days of election is inconsistent with the true dignity and principles of a republican form of government." Therefore there should be no military parade on Election Day and the legislature should pay none of the expenses. The House politely heard his resolution and promptly tabled it. Festivities and fireworks continued to flourish.[19]

Appointment to deliver an election sermon, although originally an honor awarded to a distinguished Congregational minister, came to follow the principle of rotation in office. Only Shuttlesworth and Asa Burton of Thetford preached more than one election sermon. Baptist Caleb Blood was the first non-Congregationalist, at Rutland in 1792. The General Assembly elected the Reverend Samuel Williams, Congregational pastor in East Rutland, chaplain of the session, presumably because Blood came up from Shaftsbury for Election Day only and could not open each day's session with prayer. To show the world what a *real* election sermon should have been, Williams dusted off his 1774 sermon on love of country for a rerun at his own Congregational church ten days after Blood's performance. Williams' eloquence showed that he had been to and taught at Harvard; Blood's was revivalist chanting rather than logical rhetoric.[20] From 1778 to 1816, only four Baptists and one Presbyterian were chosen chaplain, to deliver the sermon of the year. All the rest were Congregationalists. From 1817 until the practice was discontinued after 1834, however, the ministers of eight denominations took turns, and only four of them were Congregationalists.[21]

Other civic holidays carried over from New England colonial times were the movable feasts of Fast Day and June militia training in the spring, academic commencement in the summer, and Thanksgiving in late fall. Although holidays focused on some aspect of public or private life, all had a patriotic ambience. Counting one's sins and blessings were acts of worship by a population that still accepted God as dispensing rewards and punishments on earth. The special holidays for schools and militia publicly acknowledged the part of the creed that recognized learning and public security as sacred goals. As in Election Day ritual, forms inherited from the Puritans prevailed.

Although newspapers enjoyed no holidays but their staffs suffered double duty when they put out extras for holidays and special events, they considered their function of keeping the public informed a sacred duty. At the head of its editorial column, from its start in 1837 into 1855, the *St. Johnsbury Caledonian* quoted the American jurist, Joseph Story, "Pledged to Religion, Liberty and Law."[22]

The governor first proclaimed Fast Day to recognize "the frowns of Divine Providence" in the 1777 British invasion. God-sent disasters like the frost-filled summer of 1816 also called for special penitential proclamations. As defined in Governor Isaac Tichenor's 1805 proclamation, Vermonters, "from a sense of religious duty," annually devoted "a day at the commencement of the labors of the season" to pray for "Divine protection and blessing."[23]

They often chose a spring day, sometimes coinciding with Good Friday but essentially a civil celebration, after provisions and fodder had been used up over the winter. Although some governors suggested public worship, meetinghouses were even less occupied than at Thanksgiving. Nor has any evidence surfaced that anyone actually fasted. Governors' proclamations acknowledged dependence on the Creator and that public safety and prosperity depended on conformity to divine law. Except for the call to mourn the death of presidents, Fast Day was practically dead after 1870.

In the 1850s, four spring rituals competed to be Vermont's salute to the start of the growing season: the official state Fast Day; the traditional English May Day; the Christian sequence of Lent, Holy Week, Easter, and Pentecost; and a new movement for Arbor Day.

A ritual recognizing the Vermont farmers' cold weather hardships now reflected a shift of attention to the village. One element was the exuberance of prehistoric spring renewal, expressed by children hanging May baskets of arbutus on neighbors' doors.[24] Another, observed by Catholics, Episcopalians, and Lutherans, was Christian joy that Christ was risen. Unlike Thanksgiving or even Christmas, however, for those of Puritan background, Easter was not a climax celebration.[25]

The messiness of the farmstead was compounded as dwellings crowded together in villages, crying for beautification and yard cleaning at home or in the graveyard. Village improvement societies focused on the burial ground, by midcentury increasingly owned and operated by proprietary associations. Two dozen incorporated in the eight years before the Civil War, and after the war the trend continued. It meant distancing death from the living: letting professionals care for the dying, letting undertakers care for the corpse, and letting cemetery associations maintain graves. Either the new religious attitude was less concerned with the afterlife, or people, less sure, feared death more and wanted to put it out of their minds.[26] The family was still the focus, most of the plots being for sale or rent to families. Although all classes could use the cemetery, it reflected class structure based on wealth, and high Victorian individualism.

Beautifying the burial ground was still a community project, the towns contributing funds. On May 1, 1860, some two hundred people of Dorset met at the burial ground and planted maples, elms, and evergreens around the edge of the yard and righted stones, paying meet adoration to those who came to town before them. "At noon about 100 men sat down to a well set table in Mr. Baldwin's yard. . . .The second table was filled mostly with ladies."[27]

While towns were tidying, their dyed-in-the-wool localism and nostalgia for the early days found another expression in the spate of town histories in the half century after the Civil War.

With plowing and planting done but hay not ready for mowing, militia musters provided pauses in the rural year. The importance of June training, however, declined after 1840, partly because Independence

Day satisfied the same needs, partly because the temperance movement decried its alcoholic ambience, and perhaps because people did not see an enemy to prepare against. When their country gave them an enemy by declaring war on Mexico, Vermonters produced only one company of volunteers. Freedom and unity could not be served, they felt, in an imperialist war that extended slave territory. Drill revived, however, as hostility toward the slaveholding South increased in the mid-1850s.[28]

A cardinal principle of the Protestants' patriotic creed was that people must be educated, not only to read the Bible and understand their faith, but also to be good citizens. Every central place with an academy or college held an exhibition at the end of the scholars' final terms. They heard an eminent visitor exhort the young to uphold science (meaning the wide realm of learning), their church, and their nation. They heard the scholars declaim and honor the village for supporting "the higher branches," and the "land of the free" for its wide-open opportunities. Trustees gathered for business and, more frequently toward midcentury, alumni attended and contributed to a building fund. The seniors, besides declamations and student drama, had their final literary and religious society meetings with separate speakers from the learned occupations (lawyers, clergy, and editors), banquets, and excursions.

Commemoration of the battles of Lexington, Concord, and Bunker Hill glorified annually the role of Massachusetts in the Revolution. One wonders why Vermonters did not celebrate May 10 to commemorate the capture of Fort Ticonderoga when Bennington began its annual celebration of Bennington Battle Day the year after the August 16, 1777, battle. With the filiopietistic logic of "for want of a nail the shoe was lost," orators pointed out that the setback to Burgoyne's German dragoons on their side trip to seize munitions broke the spirit of the invaders in 1777 and led to American victory and independence. At least Vermonters could and did say over and over again, "We did our duty for our country."

For the first ten years Battle Day "was the busiest day in the year" in Bennington. Youths would find an old barn to burn, and volunteer firemen paraded in full uniform. In 1784, local thespians put on a play.[29] The heroes featured in Bennington Battle orations were John Stark, Seth Warner, and Samuel Herrick, commander of a company of rangers at the battle. It was always a local celebration, although in 1795 they observed the day at Manchester and in 1801 at Shaftsbury. Taking its cue from the antebellum movement to build the Washington Monument, the Bennington Battle Monument Association was incorporated in 1853, with statewide incorporators for fundraising purposes. By contrast, the Hubbardton Battle Monument Association, incorporated in 1856, never struck fire, although it had a site in the state rather than across the line in New York, where Seth Warner fought the Germans.

Both Washington and Bennington got boosts of public funding during the centennial enthusiasm of 1876. As a result of the wide publicity for the dedication of the Bennington Battle monument in 1891, the legislature named August 16 a state holiday in 1894. The monument is on the hill in Old Bennington, not at the battle site.[30]

In December, Vermont almost universally celebrated Thanksgiving but ignored Christmas. Governors usually proclaimed the first Thursday in the month and called for public worship, but families observed mainly by gathering and feasting. The event celebrated home and family, for which the patriots had fought ever since the Pilgrims landed. Where the Fast Day outlook was dark, Thanksgiving's was bright, in spite of the Vermont weather. To complete the seasonal round of ritual holidays, Vermonters used New Year's Day as a time to exchange gifts, pay social calls, and make resolutions. Lorenzo Dow recorded in 1799, "I . . . renewed my covenant to be more faithful to God and man."[31]

Partisanship and Patriotism, 1791-1831

Vermont in the early republic, especially from admission in 1791 through the War of 1812, preserved the paradox of bitter partisanship in church and state under a canopy of patriotism. Among the increasing output of published sermons and orations, songs and stories, the rhymes of Royall Tyler and Anthony Haswell combined loyalty and ardent disagreement about how to express it. They represented the two sides of the state and both Washingtonian and Jeffersonian orientations. The conflicts between the reigning Federalists and Democratic Societies that supported Matthew Lyon for Congress in the late 1790s continued between Washington Benevolent Societies and reigning Republicans, over the same principles, but with a new focus on the War of 1812.[32]

Above the local heroes towered General Washington, the Father of his Country. The eulogies that poured out after his death were mainly from Federalists and Congregational ministers but included such Jeffersonians as Anthony Haswell. They made plain that the retired president was the revolutionary word made flesh for all sorts and conditions of men. Endowed by God with almost superhuman virtues of solid judgment, acute discernment, perseverance in adversity, and prudence, he checked treason and held a neutral course in a war-stricken world. St. George slew the British dragon and kept the country united as plain President Washington.

His birthday, February 22, which Leonard Worcester claimed was annually observed before his death, came to be his saint's day. However, at the request of Bennington Masons, Anthony Haswell first mourned his death (December 14, 1799) on St. John the Baptist Day,

December 27, and the Reverend Heman Ball spoke in Rutland on New Year's Day, 1800. In the two and a half years before the battles at Plattsburgh silenced most Federalist guns, Vermont's Federalist Washington Benevolent Societies published twenty-one speeches on Washington-oriented holidays, invoking the patron military saint in opposition to the War of 1812. But after the war, Washington was a hero above party.[33]

Vermont's patriotism came near shipwreck in the cold and hot war conditions under Presidents Jefferson and Madison. The embargo and the War of 1812 inhibited Champlain Valley trade, travel, and social intercourse with Canada. Governor Martin Chittenden came near nullification when he refused to order Vermont troops to assist General Macomb, across Lake Champlain. He weaseled out of his Federalist hostility by encouraging volunteers, who streamed toward Lake Champlain and Plattsburgh. Yet sounds of secessionism came not from the Champlain Valley, where smuggling and trade with the enemy were subverting administration policy, but from the lower Connecticut Valley. Windham County Federalists sent a delegate to the Hartford Convention in 1815 and Secretary of State Josiah Dunham of Windsor attended as an observer, but the Republican General Assembly of 1815 repudiated the Hartford resolutions. After such bitter, unity-breaking partisanship the Federalists could do no more than crawl into their holes or join the Republicans, who won large and steady majorities after the war.

During the war, flags decorated martial maneuvers around recruiting stations, the Vergennes shipyard, the Burlington barracks, and on Lake Champlain vessels. Although the state established its militia flag in 1803, such symbols had little civilian use until the Whig and Democratic politicians of the era of Henry Clay and Andrew Jackson, when flagpoles were erected on village greens. Then Independence Day ceremonies officially opened and closed with the raising and lowering of the flag of the United States. The 1836 legislature authorized a state flag of thirteen stripes, alternately red and white, and one large white star on a blue field bearing the state coat of arms, but it does not seem to have had much use. Instead, Vermont troops in the wars from 1837 on carried a flag with the state coat of arms on a blue field. Not until the Civil War did this flag become a necessary symbol of Union. It was made official in 1923, to distinguish it more clearly from the Stars and Stripes.[34]

Unity, fractured by party battles of 1800-1815, needed rebuilding. President James Monroe, crossing the state in late July 1817, did his best to mend fences. He courted such Federalists as Josiah Dunham and emphasized the value of national defense by stopping at sites of recent military activity.[35] Still more effective, the return of the Marquis de

Lafayette in 1825 on a two-day trip via Windsor, Woodstock, Montpelier, and Burlington, drew large crowds.

Half a century after he first came, Lafayette's return reminded patriots inclined to say "we did it ourselves" of their country's broader Revolution.[36] In welcoming General Lafayette, Vermonters repeated the well-established Independence Day ritual of cheers, bell ringing, gunfire, wordfire, toasts, and illuminations rehearsed during President Monroe's visit. Celebrations were held in each town, and one innkeeper charged the federal government, which picked up the tab, $68.75 for 273 meals and $36 for "27 Gales [*sic*] Brandy, gin & spirits for solgers."[37] As far as one could see through the haze of patriotic enthusiasm and spirituous drink, the general public rejoiced to show the general how widespread were "the blessings of republican liberty" Vermont had inherited from the Revolution he had helped win. The Montpelier Congregational ladies entertained him, and one of them pronounced the welcome. Only one other woman on his ten-month tour had that honor.

Governor Cornelius P. Van Ness, the choice of three quarters of the voters in three elections, hosted Lafayette's Burlington visit. The general embraced veterans, laid the cornerstone for the University of Vermont's new building, and boarded the "sleeper," the steamboat *Phoenix*, for Whitehall.

While Lafayette's hosts had honored his republican leadership, they had toasted the Green Mountain Boys, because they were of two minds about equality. Guided through their first half century by the revolutionary declaration that "all men are created equal," they had the usual democratic dilemma of reconciling the uncommon individual with the common people. Americans canonized Washington, but Congress decided in 1789 to call him "President" and not "His Highness." Vermonters lauded President Monroe and General Lafayette, but were fond, in funeral eulogies, of praising an ordinary man as "nature's nobleman," a phrase widely used in Vermont by 1840. Titles of nobility could not be granted by the United States, according to the new Constitution, nor accepted when offered by foreign powers without the consent of Congress.

The revolutionary creed of equality, and the Christian creed of human equality in the sight of God, minimized distinctions, yet Vermonters used deferential titles to honor state officials, and militia and masonic officers. Vermont's House Rule 5, adopted in 1791, stated that "no other title than Mr. be required to address the members of the House." Rule 12, however, required that "whenever his Excellency the Governor, or any member of the Council" entered the House chamber, "all business shall cease" except their business.[38] But because representatives were chosen by the freemen, the legislators were always "honorable" and the titles of the governor and council exalted the people

through their servants. Extolling the merits of their leaders because of
their office, not their party, class, or social background, provided another bond between the people, the state, and the nation.

As in the case of legislative titles, the popularity of freemasonry
illustrated the paradox of belief in the simple equality of brother
Masons and the hunger of plain Yankees for ritual, costume, and mystery veiling inequalities of rank. Masonry, "a church outside the
church," provided another support connecting local, state, and national
affairs across the boundaries of party and church, at least in the eyes of
its organizers. All members had to believe in the Supreme Ruler of the
Universe, and, although each lodge served as a mutual benefit society of
brothers (no women were admitted), their larger goals were enlighten-
ment, education, morality, and upholding the members' religious obligations. They explicitly denied any conflict between their solemn Masonic duties and their domestic, civil, and religious responsibilities.
From five lodges operating in Vermont in 1794, the movement grew to
over seventy by 1826. Leaders of both parties joined; ministers of several denominations served as Masonic chaplains.[39]

Suspicion of secrecy and fear of conspiratorial power led to the
organization of a fanatical party against the Masons, driven by revivalistic emotions, fear of oligarchy, and economic uncertainties. This
rival religious party wiped out the Masons in less than a decade. John
H. Woodward, Westford pastor, concluded that "the anti-Masonic revolution. . . soured and alienated some minds, . . . dismissed some ministers, and. . . nearly wrecked some churches."[40] Had the Masons been
recognized as the religious society they were, the religious liberty section of the Vermont constitution ought to have protected them against
the antimasonic attacks of the 1830s.

By the 1830s the civic religion of Vermont had developed a
panoply of holy days, scriptures, rituals, and beliefs. It had suffered
schism in which each party believed it alone was patriotic, while others
invoked a plague on both their houses. Governors' messages for half a
century had outlined the dominant creed: minimal government; maxi-
mum freedom; frugality; thanks to God for benefits and confession of
sins that brought disasters. Governors were the most prominent ministers of this civic religion, but denominational clergy saw in their dual
membership no conflict between the civic and the sectarian societies.
All public servants down to common school teachers with their patriotic texts were also its ministers. Nature's noblemen did not run for office; the people called them as ministers to serve the commonwealth,
not just their party. This attitude faintly echoed that of the eighteenth-
century Congregational churches' Standing Order, with the minister
both pastor called to shepherd a church within the town and appointed
the whole town's moral teacher. Each civic festival had community

scale, although the centers attracted visitors from surrounding towns and speakers from farther away. The celebration took place on sacred ground, the town common or in the town meetinghouse. Each had a different emphasis, but used similar rituals.

Until the 1850s, Vermont's patriotism lacked two elements of its religion: a state capitol and a state hero to symbolize republican democracy and to epitomize what Vermont stood for. Ammi B. Young designed such a capitol in 1833-37, but Vermonters did not choose Ethan Allen until later.

The Second State House: Temple of Republican Democracy

In the thirty years after 1777 the legislature was peripatetic, meeting in thirteen towns, without a single place to call capital. Meeting permanently in Montpelier from 1808, the General Assembly occupied space satisfactory as a gathering place but very inadequate as a symbol. It was a simple wooden-frame meetinghouse like many others throughout New England, with a belfry surmounting a hipped roof and unusual porches on the second and third floors above the main entrance, affording covered walkways to the hall of the House and the Council chamber.[41]

Between 1808 and 1834, thirty-three newly organized towns sent representatives for the first time, to crowd the House chamber. From 1826 to 1836 pressure for a second chamber built up until a Senate of thirty members replaced the twelve-member Governor's Council. The cry for more space overcame parsimony. The presence of Ammi B. Young, an ambitious and talented architect with a plan, and the rising prosperity in the 1830s, brought the second state house into being.[42]

Vermonters have tended to name all their buildings houses, whatever their use, and so the term "capitol," reminiscent of the Roman temple of Jupiter, has never been popular in Vermont. Although the state used its "House" for its business only three to six weeks a year, it had the same practical requirements of use as most other "houses," especially meetinghouses, likewise used a small part of the time.

The Vermont creed, or complex of ideals to be symbolized, had changed in half a century. The scales between freedom and unity had shifted away from wild freedom as the turbulent frontier had given way to settled farming and trading villages. Instead of militia on the *qui vive* against the British Lion in the revolutionary spirit, June training was a farce and soon abandoned. The Democrats could whip up little practical support for the Canadian rebellion. Governors' proclamations were paeans of peace. The "ultraism" of antimasonry and the perceived excesses of other reformers and revivalists had lost majority support and

Second Vermont State House, 1837-1857. Daguerrotype ca. 1850. (Courtesy of the Vermont Historical Society.)

the Whig Party came into a long decade of dominance. The Whigs used the style of reformer-revivalists but promoted a new judicial syndrome: justice, order, thrift, openness to change only in the light of new evidence, and solid conservatism. Only independence continued as a cardinal principle in the Vermonters' creed. Architect Young expressed these conservative principles in his design.

Young and his building committee sited the capitol on the axis of travel up and down the Winooski valley. Necessarily in the valley trough, it could not be a beacon like the Old Mill's tin-covered dome at the University of Vermont, built a decade earlier on the crest of a hill, reflecting light to travelers miles away. Perhaps ex-congressman and ex-governor Samuel C. Crafts of Young's building committee was responsible for some of the refinements, such as extending the vista to maximize the approach by blasting into the hill. Congressman Crafts had experience on the Public Buildings Committee for the reconstruction of the U.S. Capitol after the British burned it in 1814.

From Berlin Hill to State Street the approach showed a subtly proportioned pile with the facade of a Greek temple merged with a Roman dome. A state gazetteer described it as simple, neat, pure, appropriate (i.e., functional), built for the ages.[43] Young had the base of the wooden dome painted gray to blend with the granite walls, while the copper sheathing of the dome and roofs oxidized in a few years to blend with the green pasture above.[44] The sergeant-at-arms contracted the hay-cutting inside the yard enclosed by an iron fence. The 325-foot approach, broken by a series of steps, allowed the visitor-worshiper to gaze on the shrine's Doric entrance and feel that gods and heroes dwelt within.

Entering ceremonially through the imposing portico or for business from either end, people found an interior design symbolizing the importance of each element of state government. The basic form of a Greek cross suggested the marriage of classical and Christian culture. This was the people's center, apparently never locked, where all could walk at any time into the people's meetinghouse.

Symbols and icons inside were almost as scarce as images in a synagogue. Portraits, not flags, hung in the chambers. George Gassner's copy of Gilbert Stuart's portrait of George Washington, behind the speaker's desk, was the first thing people thought of saving in the 1857 fire that destroyed the second capitol. This, with copies of the Declaration of Independence and of Washington's farewell address hanging in the state library, called to mind the glorious American Revolution in the tradition of the liberties fought for by the ancient Greek democracy, as contemporaries viewed it. The Greek revolution of the 1820s gave fresh meaning to the Greek revival when Jonathan P. Miller of Montpelier joined a foreign legion to fight for Greek independence from the Turks, and returned with a young Greek protegé. No one provided a portrait of Lafayette, who had aroused patriotic fervor in 1825.

The only portraits of Vermonters were a bust of Elijah Paine, judge of the First U.S. District Court, 1801-42, and an elegant full-length oil of Charles K. Williams, Vermont Supreme Court, 1829-1846, both in the Senate chamber by 1847.[45] By the 1840s, public poverty did not prevent ex-governor Charles Paine from giving to the state the bust of his father, nor the Rutland County Bar Association from presenting the portrait of retiring judge C. K. Williams.

The two jurists were appropriate symbols because in the popular mind both were free from partisan politics and epitomized probity and justice. They represented both sides of the state and both had links to early Vermont. Samuel Williams, the judge's father, an immigrant of the 1780s, was pastor, publisher, and first historian of Vermont. Paine's was the typical success story of a man with advantages who made good on the Vermont frontier. He speculated in Vermont lands in the 1780s, built a turnpike, invested in a broadcloth mill, and held major offices for fifteen years, climaxed by a term in the U.S. Senate, from which he was appointed to the U.S. District Court.

Ethan Allen, State Hero

The last element needed to complete Vermont's civil religion was the canonization of its saint, Ethan Allen. It will surprise those acquainted with Ethan Allen's heroic image that he had no icon anywhere until October 10, 1861, when the General Assembly dedicated Larkin G. Mead's statue in the portico of the third state house.[46] Nor had the state honored his greatest exploit by celebrating May 10 to commemorate the day Allen captured Fort Ticonderoga.

Why had they waited so long? No other early Vermont leader, either, had the honor of recognition with a public image. Was it Bible-based, Puritan hostility to icons or Yankee parsimony? Did people feel that nature's noblemen needed no glorification? The images of judges, senators, congressmen, and governors were not exposed to public view, although many of their families had portraits on their own walls.

All those long years of the early republic, the deist George Washington could be a hero, bathed in the glory of final victory; Ethan Allen, author of that infidel book, *Reason: The Only Oracle of Man* (1784) could not. The Green Mountain Boys chose not to elect Ethan to

"Ethan Allen," by Aristide Piccini (1941), after the original by Larkin G. Mead (1861). Portico of the Third Vermont State House. (Courtesy of the Vermont Historical Society.)

be their leader because they doubted his ability. He chose himself, however, to lead the company that took Ticonderoga and then led a quixotic invasion of Canada with a handful of men. When he tried to take Montreal, not, like Ticonderoga, a tumbledown fortress inadequately guarded, His Majesty's troops surrounded his men and took him prisoner, ending his military career.

Although Ira Allen tried to make his brother a hero, the deistical Allen could not win wide approval until revivalistic fires burned out after the 1830s. Then he could be remembered only as a romantic frontier character who struck a bold blow for freedom in capturing strategic Ticonderoga and then suffered under British captivity.

The 1779 charter of the Two Heroes (later divided into the towns of South Hero, Grand Isle, and North Hero) listed Ethan Allen and Samuel Herrick as the first of 365 grantees. Who were the two heroes if not the first two named? Exchanged after two years as a prisoner of war, Ethan spent the month of May, 1779, visiting General Washington at Valley Forge and lobbying Congress in Philadelphia. He came home with a brevet colonelcy in the Continental Army and back pay for the entire period of his captivity.

Finally reaching Bennington on the night of May 31, "he caused three cannon to be fired," arousing the town, and "brought out rum" to celebrate with his old friends. The next day, Samuel Herrick ordered a fourteen-gun salute, one for each state in the Union and one for Vermont. Allen spent the summer in further self-glorification, telling the story of his life as a prisoner of war, in the genre of the Indian captivity narratives. Before the year was out, he and other Green Mountain Boys had bought the two largest islands in Lake Champlain for ten thousand pounds.[47]

No contemporary evidence has surfaced to identify Ethan Allen as one of the Heroes. Ira Allen as surveyor general and state treasurer in charge of land grants could have stated officially that the Two Heroes were the first two grantees named. The Allens had enemies who would not like the idea. No one would have objected to Herrick. He had a sterling reputation as leader of a regiment of rangers with a large role in winning the battle of Bennington. But the Two Heroes cannot be identified. People believed for over a century, with no justification, that the Two Heroes were Ethan and Ira Allen. If one speculates that Ira Allen painted his brother golden, the dye was not fast. After his death it washed off.[48]

When Ethan died (February 12, 1789), Ira tried once more to make his eldest brother a hero. He delayed the funeral several days, saying that Ethan wanted to be "buried under arms" and therefore his former comrades had to be called from about the country. Witnesses recalled a large crowd, "considering the newness of the country," parading from Ira

Allen's house across the Winooski River on the ice and up the hill, with a cannon fired "every minute by the watch." Veterans laid their drawn swords across the coffin until it was opened for a final farewell and then closed and lowered with a six-platoon salute of musketry. Since by Ethan's request no clergyman was present,[49] Major William Goodrich, the marshal, then made a few remarks on how much General Allen had done for his country and suffered for it. Then all returned at quick step across the snow and ice to Ira's house, where they tapped a barrel of rum. Ira saw to it that the only two newspapers in the state, the *Windsor Vermont Journal* and the *Bennington Vermont Gazette*, had full accounts. The funeral ritual conformed to family practice near the frontier, with burial on family property, either with no marker or a simple wooden one. No one bothered to record the obsequies when Governor Chittenden died eight years later.[50]

Late in 1801, Levi Allen died insolvent in the Burlington jailyard and nobody in his family would claim his body and thereby assume his debts. It was therefore up to the town to bury him. But Green Mount Cemetery, Burlington's burial ground, was outside the jailyard and the authorities reasoned that he could not leave its limits even in death, so they gave him a pauper's burial in the field which became Elmwood Cemetery.[51]

Samuel Williams could have painted Ethan a hero, but devoted less than three pages to Allen in his *History of Vermont*, published only five years after Allen's death. He "placed himself at the head of the opposition" to New York, wrote Williams, and in May 1775, with "enterprising spirit . . . put himself at the head of the troops" he raised in a few days and bravely took Ticonderoga. He "placed himself," "put himself at the head"; he was not chosen. Williams closes him out as commander of the militia enforcing Vermont law against the Guilford Yorkers and in charge of the initial Haldimand negotiations.[52]

Williams wrote with restraint. The more common Federalist attitude, shared in a less lampooning tone by Ezra Stiles and Timothy Dwight, presidents of Yale, the Rev. Nathan Perkins, and many other orthodox divines,[53] found voice in the anonymous rhyme of about 1790 beginning "Allen's escaped from British jails. / His tushes broke by biting nails," and ending "One hand is clenched, to batter noses / While t'other scrawls 'gainst Paul and Moses."[54]

Favorable comments from outsiders accumulated over the half century after Ethan Allen's death. At the banquet for Lafayette in Gould's Hotel, Burlington, June 29, 1825, after twenty-two toasts to all the great from Washington to Simon Bolívar and the South American revolutionaries, Lafayette proposed "Ethan Allen and the Green Mountain Boys." The master of ceremonies rejoined with the "Patriotism of the Early Settlers," as if to say, "It was the rank and file,

not that infidel blow-hard." School histories by Nathan Hoskins and
Zadock Thompson expanded, repeated, and sometimes even plagiarized
Williams. The six printings or editions between 1779 and 1814 of
Ethan Allen's captivity narrative, none printed in Vermont, may have
accounted for upwards of a thousand copies that served to keep his name
alive. But the Vermont story, as Vermonters believed it, was about the
fight with New York, maintaining independence, and admission to the
Union on terms that recognized New Hampshire titles. The heroes were
the Green Mountain Boys, settlers, and frontiersmen, and only inciden-
tally their leaders, Ethan occasionally among them.[55]

Vermonters began to show more interest in Ethan as hero from
1834, when Hugh Moore published his *Memoir* in Plattsburgh.
Daniel Pierce Thompson's *The Green Mountain Boys* (1839) testified
to the new interest. But Thompson, although inscribing his story to
Ethan's nephew Heman, ex-minister to Chile, featured Seth Warner as
his hero. By calling Warner Warrington he suggested that Warner, a
hero of the battle of Bennington, was the Washington of Vermont.
Thompson treated the taking of Ticonderoga as a minor theme of only
thirty pages. Zadock Thompson's *History of Vermont* (1842), because
of its wide distribution, fanned the flame at Ethan Allen's altar. Ethan's
Narrative had its first Vermont imprint in Burlington in 1838,
followed by three more Burlington printings by 1852. Henry W.
Dupuy's *Ethan Allen and the Green Mountain Boys of '76* (1853)
enjoyed three more printings before the Civil War.[56]

Not long before he died in 1841, Jabez Penniman provided a marble
slab on a low granite foundation in Burlington's Green Mount
Cemetery to mark Ethan Allen's grave. It seems unlikely that Penniman's wife, Ethan's widow, could have remembered after more than
forty years where her former husband was buried. The inscription on
the slab ended denying Allen was an infidel: "His spirit tried the mercies
of his God, in whom alone he believed and strongly trusted." Penniman, after eight years as collector of customs in Swanton, farmed and
processed limestone near the high bridge over the Winooski gorge in
Colchester. The Pennimans must have started the story that when
Ethan's dying daughter asked him whether to believe her mother's faith
or his freethinking, he replied, "Believe like your mother."[57] Benson J.
Lossing, visiting in July 1850, sketched the tablet and noted, "A wil-
low drooped over the tombs of the patriot dead, and rose-bushes clustered around the storm-worn monument."[58] Although Lossing thought
he saw Ira Allen's grave, Ira died and was buried in Philadelphia. Jabez
Penniman probably created "the Allen enclosure" of 1850 when he ordered the memorial tablet, and his wife had to guess, after half a century, where Ethan was buried. Although she had long wanted a re-

spectable tombstone, Penniman's lime kilns had probably not provided a surplus until the prosperity of the 1830s, when travelers were beginning to ask where Ethan Allen's grave was.

What people thought of Ethan had become so favorable by 1850 that a local artist dreamed of carving Ethan's statue. At the 1850 session of the General Assembly, B. H. Kinney, a cameo-cutter from Rutland, exhibited his plaster casts of Ethan Allen, Governor C. K. Williams, and an Indian girl, hoping the legislature would commission the Ethan Allen in heroic marble. The legislature pleaded poor until 1855, when it authorized two thousand dollars for a statue over his grave. The movement supporting this commemoration evoked the effusions of college students like Constans Liberty Goodell of the University of Vermont Class of 1855, who wrote "Ethan Allen," a paean praising nature's nobleman, the "hero of Ti."[59] Ethan's was becoming a name to use: Two years later the Ethan Allen Engine Company Number 4 organized in Burlington.[60]

The state appropriation also sparked a search for the original marker. Workmen digging for the foundations of the new monument authorized by the 1855 legislature found bones near the old tablet "within the Allen enclosure." The *Burlington Free Press* concluded (9 June 1858) they must be Ethan's. "No more of the dust of the Patriot was disturbed than was necessary," because this had become holy ground. The taboo against removing remains had developed since family burial grounds had been plowed up after the family had departed. If Ethan had hero-worshippers all the years after his death, as Washington had, they would have beaten a path to his well-marked tomb.

Failure to raise matching funds prevented completion of Burlington's monument until 1873, with another sculptor's Ethan atop a Tuscan column. Larkin Mead had submitted a design and model for the Burlington job, but these became the ultimate choice for the portico of the third capitol. John Spargo, president of the Bennington Battle Monument and Historical Association, noted in 1937 that "since the middle of the last century" Vermonters had been looking in vain for a likeness of Ethan. Not enough people cared before 1850.[61]

By midcentury, as people called for public images of founding fathers, they first chose neither those aristocrats nor the self-made men of the first partisan period, but judges. Cooper's *Leatherstocking Tales* had romanticized the northeastern woodland frontier and his imitator, Daniel Pierce Thompson, had given it a Vermont flavor. But Ethan's full re-habilitation had to wait until the erosion of memory left little but the martyred captive and the hero of Ticonderoga. By then, the fires of religious revival had died down and multiple reforms had drained off into the antislavery crusade. Then Ethan's blow for freedom could be linked with freedom for slaves and his heterodox book, *Reason: The*

Only Oracle of Man, so long called "infidel," could be forgotten.

Ethan Allen was "oftenest on the lips of" Vermonters as their choice to be honored with a statue in National Statuary Hall, which Congress established in 1865. The joint resolution commissioned each state's senators to choose two of its deceased citizens, "illustrious for their historical renown or for distinguished civic or military services."[62] Ethan Allen represented Vermont's founding generation.

For their second choice, the commissioners claimed they looked for an antislavery crusader among the many Vermonters who had worked to end the evil. Passing over six-term Congressman William Slade (1786-1859), active supporter of the abolitionist petition campaign in the federal House, Charles K. Williams, first Liberty Party candidate for governor and ultimately elected as a Whig, and Erastus Fairbanks (1792-1864), first Civil War governor who had worked for gradual, compensated, emancipation, they chose Jacob Collamer (1791-1865), a conservative Republican opposed only to slavery in the territories.

Collamer had spent seventy years of his life in Vermont and thirty-two in public service on the bench, at the bar, in the state legislature, in the U.S. House, and briefly as postmaster general in President Zachary Taylor's cabinet, and had just died after ten Republican years in the U.S. Senate. Justin Morrill and the men he canvassed urged his solid combination of learning, jurisprudence, statesmanship, and eloquence. The qualities of Judge Collamer were the qualities of Judge Elijah Paine and Judge Charles K. Williams, the only images of state leaders in the second state capitol. Collamer represented the Republican Party, heir of Paine's Federalist and Williams' Whig parties, and for the next century, the Republican Party represented Vermont. But Collamer's career did not have the stuff folk heroes are made of. The speeches at the presentation of his statue in 1881 were his last hurrahs. Today, few know that Collamer's statue stands in the Hall with Ethan Allen's, and if they knew his name, they would not know why he was chosen.[63]

Civil Religion Revised

Right after the Civil War, civil religion cast a comfortable garment over differences and victory blurred the lines that divided Vermonters. There was more need than ever for a canopy that covered everyone, for the differences were greater than ever. The coming of new kinds of foreigners was an obvious source of difference. The multiplication of associations to meet particular interests needed common points of reference, too. Most of the new groups had Christian motivation, but the Christianity that worked its way into their statements of purpose was not far from the preamble of the federal Constitution, fundamental to the American Way.

Having suffered the agonizing experiences of the war, all survivors had to incorporate a sense of those experiences into their patriotism. They never focused on any one local war hero but they were unanimous in raising Abraham Lincoln to sainthood beside, if not above, George Washington. Funereal gatherings in April, 1865, immediately focused on the martyred president. Speakers recalled Lincoln's great unifying speeches assuring Vermonters that their dead had not died in vain.[64]

For a generation, people looked back on the Civil War with bittersweet feelings.[65] Hope for national renewal drove away sorrow over war losses. To their tradition of freedom and unity formed in their country's first two wars against Britain, Vermonters easily added their part in ending slavery and preserving the Union. They told that story in celebration of a new national holiday, proclaimed in General John A. Logan's order to observe May 30, 1868 as "Commemoration Day." Occurring at the start of the summer political season, Decoration Day, its common name until World War I, enabled Republican politicians to claim credit for the defeat of the Rebels and imply that the Democrats had not given their last full measure of devotion. Neither Fast Day, long indifferently observed in Vermont and last proclaimed by Governor George W. Hendee in 1870, nor Easter, nor Arbor Day, nor May Day could compete with the annual requiem of Memorial Day.

Even during the war, families had visited their cemetery plots or had transferred soldiers' remains from battle graves. In 1868, small groups of Vermont veterans and their friends quietly observed Decoration Day. Observance rituals developed from the traditional Fourth of July celebration, but in a minor mode. This simplicity struck the right note with veterans who had known and respected Johnny Reb and borne the sufferings of war.

At St. Johnsbury in 1868, a procession offered flowers and evergreens at the new soldiers' monument. Rain interfered at Woodstock in 1869, but on the following Sunday a silent company deposited a miniature flag, with wreath and staff, at each warrior's grave. Burlington emphasized the contributions of anonymous volunteers in speeches honoring the unknown soldier in 1870. At Bristol in 1872 they spent the day improving the burial ground. The crowds grew each year; business stopped; the floral arrangements became more elaborate, and bands, choirs, public officials, fraternal orders, fire companies, schoolchildren, veterans of earlier wars—especially the two new Civil War organizations, the Loyal Legion (commissioned officers) and the Grand Army of the Republic—and citizens afoot and in carriages joined the parade. But the bands played softly in the cemetery, barriers between Yankee, French, and Irish lowered for the moment, and the orators dwelt less on glory than on rededication. More and more celebrants found Lincoln's

Gettysburg Address worth quoting.

Governor John W. Stewart preached reconciliation at Burlington in 1872. Preferring quiet meditation to speeches and pomp, he called for remembrance of the devoted dead and for facing the trials and duties of peace. "Smother every remaining. . . spark of animosity between the sections," he concluded. "We cannot afford to perpetuate the hatreds of the war. We should feel today that we can shake hands across the graves with our Southern brethren."[66] Gen. W. W. Grout of Barton, not yet elected to Congress, echoed the same sentiments in 1878. Half a century later, schoolchildren recited Francis Miles Finch's "The Blue and the Gray": "We banish our anger forever / As we laurel the graves of our dead."

In spite of the exhortations of governors, in the dozen years after the conflict, the hatreds of the war fired the Radical Republican program to make the Southern rebels pay and to give former slaves power over their former oppressors. When Jefferson Davis ventured across the Canadian border at Derby in 1867, an indignant woman threw a stone at him, a crowd taunted and booed, and he was refused a visit to a famous herd of cattle. As Vermont carpetbaggers wrote home that the Ku Klux Klan and other Southerners were resisting the Radicals' program and rallying to deny them the fruits of victory, Vermonters hardened too.

The patriotism of those who took part in the victory of the Union in the Civil War was part of the religion of all church people and the centerpiece in the religion of those who were not adherents to any particular religious organization. Some were like the original settlers, not connected with any association, except perhaps the family, through which they could express their sense of the sacred.

The Grand Army of the Republic, open to Union veterans honorably discharged, established a Vermont department in 1868, which promoted Memorial Day. But the G.A.R. did not grow because veterans put re-establishing themselves in civilian life over nostalgia. Toward 1880, however, veterans began to win political offices, thanks to Redfield Proctor's and Wheelock G. Veazey's Reunion of Vermont Officers, and the annual encampments attracted larger numbers. G.A.R. peak membership of 5,445 at the time of the Burlington encampment, February, 1891, represented a sixth of all those who had served in Vermont units, a very high percentage of veterans still alive, well, and in the Vermont department. Another sign of the growth of the G.A.R. was the founding of the Women's Relief Corps, consisting of wives of veterans, and devoted to patriotic education and the distribution of flags to weekday schools and Sunday schools.

Other patriotic societies aimed to garner the unearned increment of the members' ancestors who fought in earlier wars. The Sons of the American Revolution organized in Vermont in 1890, the Daughters of the American Revolution in 1892. The Society of Colonial Wars followed in 1894, and the Society of Colonial Dames in 1897.[67]

For Vermonters, the Civil War had achieved "one nation, indivisible, with liberty and justice for" the ex-slave too. They trusted the Union, "under God." They were confident that the democracy they practiced, which had become the common name for patriotism, had proved its validity and could meet new challenges. Unfinished business between Protestants and Catholics required no revision of the mode of operation: majority rule, minority rights, and by peaceful acceptance of election results, gradual accommodation to gradually changing conditions.

For another half century or more they would need no restatement of the American Way. In Vermont the essentials of its patriotic faith had crystallized. "The mystic chords of memory, stretching from every battle field and patriot grave, to every living heart and hearthstone," as Lincoln appealed to them in his first inaugural, bonded them beyond all difference.

Notes to Chapter 2

[1] This chapter appears with minor changes in *Vermont History* (Winter/Spring 1999) with the same title.

[2] Vermont, *Records of Governor and Council*, 1:51, with supporting documents and commentary, 48-54.

[3] *Laws of Vermont, 1781-1784*, ed. Williams, *State Papers of Vermont*, 13:98. The annual printing of a session's enactments, variously entitled, will be cited as *Vermont Laws*, with date.

[4] See Goen, *Broken Churches, Broken Nation*, 41.

[5] For example, see True, "Slavery in Burlington?"

[6] Williams, *History of Vermont*, 336; 2 ed. (1809), 2:382. The second edition, "corrected and much enlarged," reprinted the 1794 chapter on religion with two inserts dated 1806. According to Walzer's classifications in his *On Toleration*, Williams' attitude was one of openness and willingness to learn in a diverse society ruled by a nation-state in which the toleration offered by one dominant group, the Protestant anglophones, was being widened by diverse immigration.

[7] Walzer *On Toleration* has analyzed a continuum of five attitudes toward toleration and discusses how these attitudes play out in five regimes of toleration.

[8] The restriction of militia to white males in the Act of March 10, 1797, continued in the Act of November 1, 1837, was not thought of in the original act of February 1779 establishing the militia. See *Vermont State Papers*, 307; *Vermont Laws to 1824*, 431; *Vermont Laws* (1837), 19. Voters in *town* meetings, according to R. S. (1840), 86, were limited to those "whose list shall have been taken in any town the year preceding his voting," or those "exempt from taxation" because aged sixty and over.

[9] See Butler's typical pension file, R. 1555 under the Act of June 7, 1832. In it, ex-Governor Butler, 68, recorded his service as a private in Lt. Col. Henry Dearborn's Third New Hampshire Regiment, in the Veterans' Records of the National Archives and Records Administration. He marched in the spring of 1780 from his Claremont, New Hampshire, farm via Springfield, Massachusetts and Danbury, Connecticut, to West Point. His unit went as far south as Hackensack, New Jersey, before returning in the fall, crossing the Hudson to the Highlands, and building log huts for winter quarters in

November 1780. During his six-month enlistment, they served as sentinels in a foot of snow at the top of the mountain, with forays to Long Island Sound for forage, and then returned home "over the frozen ground."

[10] Williams, *History of Vermont*; Allen, *History of Vermont* and the succession of state histories after them.

[11] *Rutland Herald*, 8 Aug. 1796, 2:3. All the quotations in this paragraph relating to the Vergennes celebration refer to this report.

[12] Fair Haven *Farmer's Library*, 8 Aug. 1796, according to McCorison, *Vermont Imprints*, #382; *Burlington Mercury*, 17 June, 3:4, 1 July, 4:4, 8 July, 1796, 3:2-3.

[13] Recollection of a Brattleboro company at June training (*Vermont Historical Gazetteer*, 5:50).

[14] See Spargo's "composite description" of the Bennington ritual in his *Anthony Haswell*, 142-143. See also Curti, *American Thought*, especially "The Nurture of Loyalty," 123-143.

[15] See the account in the *Windsor Vermont Republican*, quoted in Crockett, *Guilford Congregational Church*, 14, and the recollection of a Brattleboro muster, ca.1815-1823, in *Vermont Historical Gazetteer*, 5:51. In 1811 there were twenty-three states and territories.

[16] Collamer, *Oration*, 5, 14.

[17] Shuttlesworth, *Discourse*, 6.

[18] *Records of the Governor and Council*, 4:3; *State Papers of Vermont*, v.3, pt.4:266 (appointment of Shuttleworth, January 24, 1791) and pt.5:ix, 215 (reimbursement of Chittenden "in hard money," November 8, 1792, for election day expenses). Fifteen seems like a remarkable collection of artillery, no doubt for this special celebration in honor of Vermont's admission to the Union.

[19] *State Papers of Vermont*, 3(7):227. Previous references to Election Day show that officers had advanced money for the purchase of gunpowder to perform "the common exercises and manoeuvers of the day," (October 8, 1795, 6) likewise in 1796, 210, and were reimbursed.

[20] Blood, *Sermon*; Williams, *Love of Country*, first delivered as a Thanksgiving Day address in Salem when he was the pastor at Bradford,

Massachusetts. He used Psalm 137:5-6 for his text in 1774 and Psalm 122:7-8 in 1792, but extensive passages are the same. Even when he professed loyalty to the British Empire--we live, he wrote, in "the great community, . . . believe in her religion," favor "her laws and government, share her fortunes"—(1774, pp. 7-9), he smoothly transferred the sense to the federal government of 1792.

[21] See list by P[liny] H. W[hite] in *Historical Magazine*, n.s. 3173 (March 1868), or in Gilman, *Bibliography of Vermont*, neither with denominational identification.

[22] Noted in E. T. Fairbanks, *St. Johnsbury*, 219.

[23] Tichenor broadside *Proclamation*, recommending "to ministers and people of every religious denomination . . . to assemble on Wednesday," April 24.

[24] See the *Burlington Free Press*, 4 May 1848, 2:1, on the poetry of May Day. Governor Levi Fuller's 1893 proclamation named May 18 as Arbor Day, "following a now well established custom" (*Burlington Free Press*, 2 May 1893, 4:1).

[25] Easter is not indexed in M. A. McCorison's *Vermont Imprints*, or M. D. Gilman's *Bibliography of Vermont*, nor the eight volumes of *Bibliographies* of the Committee for a New England Bibliography.

[26] See Sloane, *Last Great Necessity*, 98.

[27] Gilbert, *Parsons Stuart Pratt*, 4-5.

[28] See Bassett, *The Growing Edge*, 47, 129-130; Blackwell and Holway, "Waitsfield Militia Petition of 1836," 5.

[29] Drysdale, *Bennington's Book*, 84-85; the *Bennington Vermont Gazette* (15, 23, 30 Aug. 1784), advertised a proposal to print the "tragedy."

[30] Jacob, *Poetical Essay. . . .* The introduction to the reprinted edition in Vermont Historical Society *Collections* outlines the elements of the ritual. See also Noah Smith's speech to the same assembly, 1:255-261. McCorison, *Vermont Imprints,* nos. 359, 529, 603, 629, 853, 1010, 1089, 1174, 1757, 2173, and 2192, and 147A (1788) in "Additions and Corrections," (1985), show steady celebration from 1795 to 1820. Note also Anthony Haswell's joining the patriotism of Independence Day and Bennington Battle Day in no. 2269-2270, *Songs for the 4th of July and the*

16th of August. For the incorporation of the Bennington Battle Monument Association, see *Vermont Laws* (1853), 135-136; the charter of the Hubbardton Battle Monument Association, *Vermont Laws* (1856), 191-192; and the establishment of the state holiday, *Vermont Laws* (1894), 112.

31 Dow, *Journal*, 57.

32 Tyler, "Ode Composed for the Fourth of July, [1796]," "The Fourth of July [1799] Poems," *Verse*, 46-48, 96-109. John Spargo, "Anthony the Ballader," *Anthony Haswell*, 137-170, with all the poems Spargo could find, set to the popular tunes of the day and sung on the Fourth of July (189-208), and Bennington Battle Day, August 16 (209-229). There is a short section, 221-229, commemorating American victories in the War of 1812.

33 Tyler, "Oration on the Death of George Washington," in his *Prose*. 269-280; Worcester, *Oration*. See McCorison, *Vermont Imprints*, index entries for Washington Benevolent Society and Washington's farewell address.

34 Nye, *Vermont's State House*, 11.

35 Crockett, *Vermont*, 3:142-147.

36 Ibid., 3:201-208. The account of Lafayette's visit in Burlington by Auguste Levasseur, one of the general's party, is in Bassett, *Outsiders Inside Vermont*, 59-61.

37 Canfield, *Lafayette in Vermont*, 25-26.

38 *State Papers of Vermont*, 3(5):12. An interesting note needs to be written on the evolution of the meaning of "Esquire," from its medieval meaning of shield-bearer preparing for knighthood, to the British landed gentry with local power, to identification in early Vermont with justices of the peace and therefore a notch above Mr., to an honorific.

39 Coates, *Masonry*; Brown, *Christianity and Freemasonry*, preached to the Masons in Danville, and *Utility of Moral and Religious Societies*, Brown's Putney sermon.

40 In *Vermont Historical Gazetteer*, 1:895. Deborah Clifford called my attention to Woodward's opinion. David Ludlum, after sketching the growth of Masonry in Vermont from 1781 to 1826, concluded, "the socio-religious sentiment aroused by the blessed spirit" of militant antimasonry then turned to a new enemy, the slaveholder." (*Social Ferment in Vermont*, 89-94, 133.)

[41] Robbins, "Montpelier Becomes the Capital," in his *Vermont State House*, 14-17 (illus. on 17).

[42] I have examined the inventories of the sergeants-at-arms during the life of the State House, 1836-1856, to create a portrait of the building, in "Vermont's Second State House."

[43] Thompson, "Vermont State House," *History of Vermont* (1842), 2:130-132, based on consultation with the architect, with woodcut. Young designed the engraving of the Vermont State House in Hayward's *Gazetteer*, opposite 187.

[44] I have found no evidence that, like the dome of the third state house, the dome was painted red. See Robbins, *Vermont State House*, 54.

[45] Henry Kirke Brown's bust of Judge Paine is now in the Supreme Court building; Benjamin Franklin Mason's Williams is in the governor's ceremonial office. See Nye, *Vermont's State House*, 60 (Williams), 80 (Paine), 82 (Washington).

[46] Nye, *Vermont's State House*, 14; "J. Q. D." in *Rutland Herald* (October 12, 1861), 2:3.

[47] Unfriendly report of Ethan's arrival in Bennington, by the son of Seth Warner, who commanded the Vermont regiment at the battle of Bennington, quoted in Thompson, *Independent Vermont*, 349. The legislature granted the charter of the Two Heroes October 27, 1779, on a petition four days earlier (*Vermont State Papers*, 2:192-195).

[48] Swift,*Vermont Place Names*, 262; Stratton, *History of South Hero Island*, 6.

[49] Or did Ira ascribe the prohibition to Ethan because no minister would come, not even Governor Chittenden's brother Bethuel? There were then at least fifty ministers in Vermont.

[50] Reminiscences of Hawley Witters, Ethan's chore boy, Huldah Lawrence, who witnessed the funeral at age six, and Henry Collins, a Burlington lad of twenty-five at the time, in the *Burlington Daily Free Press*, 5 June (Witters) and 19 June 1858. See the account in the *Vermont Gazette*, 23 February 1789, and Table 1.1, "Characteristics of American Cemeteries" from the seventeenth century to the present, in Sloane, *Last Great Necessity,* 4-5, also 14-15, 17, 24-25.

[51] Cockerham, "Levi Allen," 253 and n47.

[52] Williams, *History of Vermont* (1794), 219, 223, 226, 244, 248, 249.

[53] Timothy Dwight, *Travels* (1969), 2:283, Thompson, *Independent Vermont*, 157-158.

[54] Barnes, *Ebenezer Allen* (1852), appendix, 15, quoted in *North Country Life* 13 (Spring 1959). Peladeau did not index by first line in Tyler, *Verse*. Francis Parkman, on a tour of French and Indian War sites in 1842, reported an old storyteller near Lake George who told "one about Ethan Allen . . . scarcely to be put in writing." See Parkman, *Journal* (1947), 1:50.

[55] Griswold, "Ethan Allen," in *New-Yorker* (July 10, 1840), 275, originally printed in the *Southern Literary Messenger*. Seventy-eight lines of rhymed iambic tetrameter claim that Ethan's fame will outlast the Green Mountains. See also Hoskins, *History of Vermont*; Thompson, *History of Vermont* (1833); Gilman, *Bibliography of Vermont*, 5-7; Graffagnino, "The Vermont `Story'"; and McWilliams, "Faces of Ethan Allen."

[56] Moore, *Ethan Allen*; Thompson, *Green Mountain Boys*; Allen, *Narrative of Captivity*; De Puy, *Ethan Allen and the Green Mountain Boys*. See also Sparks, *Ethan Allen*, and Melville, *Ethan Allen*.

[57] A. M. Hemenway told the story in rhyme in her *Vermont Historical Gazetteer*, 1:568.

[58] This first tourist guide to an Ethan Allen monument, as David J. Blow of the University of Vermont Archives described it, appeared in Lossing, *Field-Book of the Revolution*, 1:161, with drawing.

[59] In Hemenway, *Poets and Poetry of Vermont*, 132-137.

[60] Ethan Allen Engine Company, *Exercises*, 17.

[61] Kinney in Montpelier: *Bradford Green Mountain Gem* 8 (Nov. 1858): 274; Zadock Thompson's March 1852 lecture on Ethan's life, occasioned by Kinney's exhibiting in Burlington, is in the *Vermont Historical Gazetteer*, 1:560:2. A. M. Hemenway's poem about Ethan's daughter is ibid., 1:569. Spargo's comment is in the Battle Monument Association *Report* (1937), 4.

[62] Morrill and Edmunds, *Report on Statuary Hall*, 5. See also Senator Morrill's canvas of leading Republicans, in the Morrill Papers, Manuscripts

Division, Library of Congress, for the year before this report.

[63] [Collamer]. *Presentation of Statue, 1881.* The state paid Larkin G. Mead $6,500 for Allen's statue and Hiram Powers $8,000 for Collamer's. See Windsor *Vermont Chronicle* (17 Nov. 1866), 3:1.

[64] For a sample of the spontaneous outpouring of Vermonters' grief, see H. A. P. Torrey, "In Memoriam—Abraham Lincoln." The development of this hero worship over the next two generations was marked by a movement exalting Lincoln's Gettysburg address, started by the publication of Andrews, *Perfect Tribute. Laws of Vermont* (1939), No. 1. (April 6, 1939), 2, added Lincoln's Birthday to Vermont's ten other legal holidays.

[65] Bassett, *The Growing Edge,* 155-219, provides economic and social background and detail for some of my conclusions about the postwar period to 1880.

[66] *Burlington Weekly Free Press,* 7 June 1872. The whole state press annually gave the holiday full coverage.

[67] Stone, "Military and Patriotic Societies," in *Vermont of Today,* 2: 599-619.

3

The Open Race Between the Denominations, 1791-1840

Looking back to 1790, when he settled in Vermont, Quaker minister Joseph Hoag wrote in his journal, "In a new country. . . filling up with people of every [religious] society, or nearly so. . . the priests not being anxious to crowd in until some more favourable prospect of pecuniary advantage could be obtained, the people were thus left destitute of preachers, so there was a great openness."[1]

Joseph Hoag was unfair to the clergy; in spite of some imperfect saints, as a group they were also-rans in avarice. He assumed correctly, however, that *nearly all* the settlers had *original* connections with some religious society. There was something in their background that preachers who braved the wilderness could appeal to.

In any new country, open to all, competitors for the attention and energies of newcomers include preachers, homesteaders, speculators, and fugitives from civilization. Preachers in the Northeast reached few at any one time, but few could grow up without having been aware of or exposed to at least one nearby revival.[2] Ever since the Puritans arrived there had been times and places of refreshment, when the tides of the spirit flowed full, and times of dryness.

Believers are sure that revivals are the work of God, while the historian sees the phenomena of prophets and preachers proclaiming God's work and sinners in situations "accepting Christ." Those who caught converts knew where the fish were biting, because of "conversion readiness." The potential converts had to be dissatisfied with their situations, whether lacking any religious connection or claimed by a group that no longer met their needs, however cloudily understood.

In religion nothing fails like success. New members, convinced emotionally, and perhaps understanding a few main points of doctrine, still wander among the seasoned members, wondering how this new faith they have embraced applies to their daily lives. As the pool of potential converts is drained, sponsors turn their attention to defining for the neophytes the centers and boundaries of their church. At first the new cadres march enthusiastically to the same drummer. They develop useful habits of attendance and support of church activities. Then some begin to find the boundaries to be barriers against some of the behaviors they brought from outside or developed as beginners. Before long, reformers call members to come out from the evils they see inside the fences. Age after age swings from rules to rule-breaking enthusiasm and back again.

So with the heirs of the Puritans. In spite of several times of rich harvest from Jonathan Edwards to George Whitefield and down through the eighteenth century, the New England churches were suffering from habitual rather than freshly spirited religion. Max Weber, in dealing with the sociology of religion, called this a development from charisma to routinization. The bulk of the population in the northern settlements had escaped from the churches, but they were an open market to be won by religious enterprise.[3] To win that market, the preachers would have to brave the hardships of travel, and speak to willing listeners. Church authorities would have to accept barely qualified preachers.

The ministers of the first knots of Vermont settlement before the Revolution—Congregational, Baptist, Episcopalian, Presbyterian, and Quaker—insofar as they adhered to the Calvinist tradition, and most of them did, all faced a population that, by and large, did not believe it. Each faced their own particular obstacles to capitalizing on the "openness." These groups failed to monopolize the field or win the unchurched either because their methods did not work or the obstacles were too great.

Congregational Handicaps

Beyond the Calvinist handicap, the main obstacle for Congregationalists was their attitude toward leadership. They wanted their ministers to have more than college training, and they wanted them to settle, not itinerate. Consequently, they could not provide enough ministers. After the exploratory journeys of Jeremiah Day and Nathan Perkins in 1788 and 1789, Connecticut's General Association from 1793 and its Missionary Association, organized in 1798, sent at least forty missionaries before 1815 to the Connecticut and Champlain valleys. The missionaries arranged with their churches for leaves of absence, sometimes lasting several months, to preach the gospel, establish churches, and then report the need for young college graduates to tend the new flocks.[4]

Too few men of any sort who supported the Congregational Standing Order were willing to accept calls to the new settlements.

There were better jobs closer to home. Even Berkshire County, Massachusetts, was closer than Addison County, Vermont. Daniel Clarke Sanders, Harvard 1788, candidated and taught school for six years before he accepted a call in Vermont, and that was to Vergennes, whose leaders expected their town to be the leading city if not the capital of the state. Harvard graduates like Sanders and Samuel Whiting of Rockingham were less missionary-minded than Yale alumni, and those with a sense of mission had many opportunities, if not in Massachusetts, then in southern New Hampshire and the near parts of the District of Maine. In this period, Yankee traders and whalers were discovering profits in the Pacific, the African slave coast, and the Mediterranean, while the impulse for foreign missions, which founded Andover Theological Seminary, began to send Vermonters to the Sandwich Islands, Liberia, the Ottoman Empire, India, and Burma. Samuel Austin of Worcester, writing for the Massachusetts Missionary Society in 1801, explained that they had only enough funds to send two or three missionaries into Maine and one to join two others along the Genesee River.[5] This tacitly acknowledged Vermont as a Connecticut sphere of influence.

Another handicap was Congregational reluctance to adopt what turned out to be the successful Methodist tactic of circuit riders who could serve several feeble groups. Congregational tradition was to settle one minister with one congregation and help out away from home as way opened. Also, they remembered itinerants during the eighteenth-century revivals stirring up trouble when they invaded parishes without or even with the permission of the pastor. In Vermont, however, there were no parishes to invade. The only step toward the circuit system they would take was to yoke parishes, and only four early pastors served congregations in more than one town: Abner Reeve, in Brattleboro and Guilford; Grant Powers in Haverhill, New Hampshire, and Newbury; Aaron Hutchinson in Hartford, Pomfret, and Woodstock; and Samuel Whiting in Rockingham and Chester. Another form of minor itinerancy was the exchange of pulpits, or holding services in schoolhouses in different districts. The Congregational principle, however, was for one congregation to call, maintain, and dismiss its pastor, and receive his full attention. Temporary, properly authorized missionaries to the lost sheep of the Connecticut house of Israel, yes. While in the field they would feed whatever lambs were there when no other shepherd was around. But appointment just to itinerate was going too far. Vermont society was too turbulent for churches to maintain their vitality only by the nurture of members and members' children in one place, without moving from place to place to win and cultivate members.

Timothy Dwight, on his several visits to both sides of the state, never recorded in his published *Travels* that he preached a sermon or appointed a meeting for religious instruction on his way. He was careful to stop for the Sabbath and attended Congregational worship, if any was available. As "Pope Dwight," the most influential minister in Connecticut and president of Yale College, he gave valuable advice to the founders of Middlebury College, to the consociations, and to the ministers, especially the Yale alumni, whom he visited. In at least one case, at pastor-less Middlebury, he probably led worship. Arriving on Friday, 28 September 1798, Dwight baptized the son of Seth Storrs the following Sunday, and consulted with the town leaders that evening. In 1813, Dwight delivered the opening sermon at the Windsor, Vermont, convention that founded Kimball Union Academy of Meriden, New Hampshire, "to assist in the education of poor and pious young men for the gospel ministry." It could be argued that a man in his late forties and fifties, with a heavy load of ruling, teaching, preaching, and politics, needed a real vacation.[6] But itinerant Methodist Bishop Asbury took no vacations.

Other Colonial Churches

Throughout the colonies the Baptists had grown not so much by immigration from Britain as from Congregational castoffs during revival stirs; their whole posture was revivalist. Except for starting and staying more in the hills, owning less property, earning less income, and having less schooling, on average, the Baptists' story repeats the Congregationalists'. In Vermont they grew by migration from southern New England and, like the Congregationalists, soon lost their anti-Calvinists. The potential members of the Free Will Baptists were basically the dissatisfied or nominal Baptists and Congregationalists who could not stomach predestination.

Episcopalians had long had a few devoted leaders with large hopes in small places such as Tinmouth, Arlington, Manchester, and Shelburne. Theirs was a middle way as in England, less swayed by the movements for revival and reform. Quiet or openly Tory in the eighteenth century, they had accommodated toward contemporary Protestantism in its minimal ritualism partly because they could not afford the things to show forth the beauty of holiness in the liturgy. Held firm by their Book of Common Prayer, they bowed toward the evangelical outlook, but accepted no "new measures" coming from the revivalism of western New York.

One wonders whether a dozen clergy in a score of parishes with a total membership of 1,169 needed to be made into the Diocese of Vermont in 1832. The reason came from pressures outside the state. Except for sharing Alexander Viets Griswold since 1810 as bishop of the Eastern Diocese (consisting of the four New England states except Connecticut), Episcopalians in each state had always held their own conventions and sent their own delegates to the General Convention.

Also, an endowment of lands reserved for the Church of England in every Vermont town chartered by New Hampshire encouraged the Episcopalians. The Vermont legislature, while recognizing New Hampshire land grants, had asserted its right to use the income from these lease lands (also New Hampshire grants) to support all the religious teachers in each town in proportion to their resident taxpayer members, and for common schools. Pursuit of this endowment preoccupied churchmen's attention and consumed their energies for decades. After a generation of litigation the U.S. Supreme Court ruled in 1823, as it had in the Dartmouth College case, that the state could not violate the previous grants because they amounted to contracts. The church victory continued hostility against it rather than increasing its influence, but it gave the Episcopal bishop a fund to pay part of his salary from the small rents of these glebe lands. The rest he earned as rector of St. Paul's in Burlington.[7]

John Henry Hopkins, elected bishop in 1832 by a seven to six vote of the clergy, the laity confirming,[8] was a native of Ireland, a man with the restless energy of a convert, a popular speaker and prolific pamphleteer.

Like Bishop John Henry Hobart of New York before him, Hopkins was convinced that the Church of England, American version, had a unique role as the preserver of the true Christian tradition in liturgy, polity, and theology. It should not trail along in the wake of the evangelical churches in the Puritan tradition, as rector William S. Perkins was doing.[9] So strong was the low church influence in Hopkins' diocese that he felt it necessary to declare that the Roman church's use of the cross was a poor reason not to use this "edifying and wholesome" symbol. Among all his drawings of church interiors, however, only one had a cross, and that a very small one.[10]

Hopkins' considerable gifts and varied background prepared him to be useful in his poor diocesan home and throughout the Anglican world. Of Presbyterian upbringing, Hopkins ran a book business in Philadelphia as a young immigrant, then operated an iron forge and furnace in western Pennsylvania, and became a lawyer. Though his own denomination was dominant in the Pittsburgh region, he chose on principle to ally himself with a struggling little group of Episcopalians. With the zeal of a convert he studied for the priesthood, was ordained in 1824 at Trinity Church, Pittsburgh, and participated enthusiastically in the conventions of his diocese. By the late 1820s he had found friends among the High Church party, who encouraged his ambition to rise in the hierarchy. He became assistant rector of Trinity Church, Boston, on hand when the new diocese of Massachusetts needed a bishop. He did not win that election, and again he chose the hard task with a small group, to build the Diocese of Vermont. In his thirty-six-year episcopate, the number of priests, communicants, and houses of worship doubled.[11]

This growth, however, occurred more because of what the Episcopal church stood for than through the persuasiveness of its bishop. Hopkins was not strong as facilitator or conciliator. He saw clearly what was right and stuck to that, alone or with a multitude.

Hopkins was not part of the Oxford Movement in America, although he sympathized with much that the movement stood for. He was not of the High Church party; he was usually a party of one. He did his own studying and published his own conclusions, usually at variance with the popular views of the day. He opposed the antimasonic movement (some of his best friends were Masons), the antislavery movement, and the prohibition movement, while believing in the roots of their causes: Christian benevolence, Christian emancipation of slaves and care for them, and temperance. He believed the church should stay out of politics. He believed in education but not educational reform. His lifelong ambition was to establish a theological seminary to supply diocesan clergy and a school to train the laity for service. When he laid his first proposal before the diocese, it replied, "We can't afford it." He went ahead anyway and was soon bankrupt. His successor as bishop, William Henry Augustus Bissell, who taught in his first school, found him an autocrat.

This headstrong and talented man's exuberant energies, interests, and goals, so often at odds with those of his people, led him away from full-time pastoral care of his diocese into a variety of creative activities. He published a book on Gothic architecture (1836) and tried to persuade vestries to build according to his plans. He was more puritan than catholic on images "utterly out of place" in a house of worship; "a species of idolatry," he called them. Acceptable were Bible subjects or images with "a place in the Church's calendar."[12] He fostered music in the home by publishing *Twelve Canzonets* (1839). Desperate for money, he and his children created and colored lithographs of Vermont flowers and landscapes. He poured forth a steady stream of polemical publications and participated vigorously in the deliberations of the American House of Bishops. Like so many versatile Vermonters, his contributions were to the world.

Some converts from the village elite, repelled by the bare, sermon-focused Congregational service, the hard-line covenants, and revivalism, appreciated the rich sixteenth-century prose of the Book of Common Prayer, based on the medieval missal, the paraphernalia of the service, and the relaxed theology. This yearning for more ritual sent many to Masonry and a few to the Shakers. Among the converts to Hopkins' church were Timothy Follett, Burlington merchant, and Senator Dudley

Chase of Randolph and his family. After a quarter century with the Springfield Congregational church, pastor Robinson Smiley turned Episcopalian, apparently disgusted with the new measures of the revivalists. One family feud, aired at length in 1834 while the Windsor Congregational church was without a guiding pastor, led to the resignation of William Tileston, the church treasurer. He wrote, in requesting dismissal to the Episcopal church, "Matters of discipline are much better handled in the Episcopal church."[13] I have not found a record of what attracted Zadock Thompson, Burlington naturalist-historian. After teaching in his own private schools and editing short-lived magazines, he was ordained deacon and taught in Hopkins' school. These recruits came before 1840. Others like Governor Charles K. Williams, son of a Congregational minister, were attracted by what the English Oxford Movement stood for: veneration for the ancient Christian tradition, personal piety reinforced by traditional church liturgy.

The Episcopalians were like the Catholics in their emphasis on ritual, episcopal authority, non-Calvinist theology, and a penchant for the Democrats. Examples of leading Episcopalian Democrats are Supreme Court judge Isaac F. Redfield, editors Charles G. Eastman of the *Montpelier Vermont Patriot* and Hiram Atkins, his successor on the *Montpelier Argus and Patriot*, and lawyers Charles Linsley of Rutland and Edward J. Phelps of Burlington. Apart from these leaders, the rank and file were more often than not Federalists and Whigs. Both denominations grew with the growth of villages after Bishop Hopkins arrived.

The Quakers of Vermont, one of its five original denominations before the Revolution, still numbered over a thousand in 1828. They grew by in-migration and birthrate, and declined by becoming "worldly" or marrying non-Quakers and being disowned (excommunicated), by schisms in 1828 and 1845, and by death and departure. Joseph Hoag, the leading Quaker evangelist of this generation in Vermont, had escaped from restraining elders in Dutchess County, New York. They said he was not a good farmer and he had better learn to harvest a crop before he went afield to harvest souls. But in the woods along small side streams of Little Otter Creek and Lewis Creek and from Starksboro to Ferrisburg, where many Friends settled, he found he could do both, with full cooperation from his wife Huldah, also an approved minister, and his many children. His role was like that of the missionaries sent from Connecticut before 1815 to change nominal adherents into live, practicing Christians. Because of Hoag's establishing work, and the questing religion and substantial property of a few other early arrivals like Thomas Robinson and Timothy Rogers of Ferrisburg and Clark Stevens of Montpelier, remnants of Friends survived in eastern Addison County, Danby, and one or two other towns.[14]

Preoccupied with scratching a living under adverse conditions, Friends lacked a critical mass[15] in many towns where they settled. A minority of the minority of affiliated Christians, late-colonial Friends had been numerous, widespread, and well-known to be both prickly and reliable, from Georgia to Maine. With the Anglicans they shared patriot hostility because of their ambivalent loyalties during the American Revolution. They became fossilized, maintaining a protective shell of custom by rigorous excommunications, while stiffly upholding their peace and antislavery testimonies.

What happened to these disowned Quakers? Untended by enough traveling ministers and weighed down by worldly worries, they joined, like many other settlers, the group of whatever itinerant came along. The Quaker Harknesses of Ferrisburg, for example, moving within the limits of Peru, New York, Monthly Meeting, became Methodists of Harkness, New York. The exhortations of Methodists Lorenzo Dow, and Fanny Newell in southern New England,[16] also show Quaker contact. Many of those Quaker farmers who followed the flow of settlement into the interior joined any handy Baptist or Congregational group, but more often the new denominations: Free Will Baptists, Universalists, Methodists, and the Christian Connection. These newcomers adopted some of the Quakers' terminology, their asceticism, their "puritanical" detachment from the "world" in matters like dancing and tavern-haunting. Another way of putting it: Residual Quakerism reinforced the same Puritan elements in other descendants of seventeenth-century dissenters.

As Quaker Henry Miles of Monkton wrote, if the seed sown by Joseph Hoag "has germinated and sprung up in plants very unlike the sower,—if these plants have, under the training of Methodism or Congregationalism, or any other religious influence, blossomed in brighter colors, or borne fruit of more spicy flavor than the Quaker tree, the sectarian may repine, while the true Christian will rejoice at witnessing another evidence that Divine Truth cannot be confined within the narrow limits of a sect." Miles concluded by quoting William Penn: "The humble, meek, merciful, just, pious and devout souls are everywhere of one religion; and when death has taken off the mask they will know one another though the divers liveries they wear here makes them strangers."[17]

How the Methodists Grew

None of the itinerants venturing into the northern woods were as callow, eccentric, and minimally qualified by downcountry standards as Lorenzo Dow. A native of Coventry, Connecticut (1777-1834), Dow was one of the earliest Methodist travelers. At eighteen he answered what he believed to be God's call to preach. For almost a year he preached on his own in southern New England. Later his Methodist presiding elder sent him home four times as unqualified, but his stubborn persistence in spite of opposition, the hallmark of his whole career, was rewarded with a temporary license for the Cambridge, New York, circuit in 1798. Good results led him and his older companion to expand their mission into northwestern Vermont. Dow visited from house to house, "and where there was freedom," exhorted and prayed, even "in the middle of the day." He wore ordinary traveler's dress, not clerical garb, held meetings every day of the week, rebuked his opponents severely, and argued from Scripture. His favorite device was to catch his hearers in "covenants." He got some in every audience to stand up and promise before God and the congregation to read the Bible and pray frequently for a period of several weeks.[18]

Tobias Spicer, a preacher and presiding elder in the Hudson-Champlain Valley, 1809-49, recalled that Dow was the first Methodist in Middlebury. With three or four companions Dow began singing on the bank of Otter Creek and attracted "scores" who thought someone was drowning. Lorenzo prayed and was invited to preach that evening. He came back and planted a Methodist cell. In Brandon he made a covenant with a militia major and his niece, which led to the formation of a Methodist society in that town. Spicer called him eccentric, but a "holy, zealous and useful preacher."[19] Neither storm nor sleet nor gloom of night kept Dow and other ceaseless travelers from their appointed rounds. A common saying to describe bad weather declared, "Nobody's out but crows and Methodist preachers." They started Methodist "classes" or "societies" in many places. These freely circulating beggars for God sowed and various churches reaped.

When Francis Asbury visited Vermont, six times from 1803 to 1811, he preached every day wherever he was. He faced a situation where it would be impossible to find support for a young man in one place with few converts and nearly all of them poor. He set an example of "living off the land" as invading armies do. The hand-outs of sympathetic, hospitable backwoodsmen helped the preachers on their way, and sometimes some of them joined the Methodists.[20] Until Asbury died in 1816, few Methodist preachers married after they committed themselves to circuit riding. If they were married before they were licensed, preachers left their wives behind and visited them occasionally.

Ebenezer Washburn was two years married when he hit the road. He left his wife in Petersburg, New York, and came home to her every few months. Joseph Sawyer converted him in the Berkshires in 1798, made him leader of a class of three couples four days later, and gave him a hymnbook and a discipline to go with his Bible. Reinforced by a covenant with Lorenzo Dow, Washburn attended every prayer meeting and class he could get to, with some thoughts of preaching. He was soon handed a license to exhort, and at his second quarterly meeting, a license to preach. Assigned to Vermont circuits, 1801-02, he argued with Calvinists, Universalists, and Episcopalians, and aimed at the convertible.[21]

One needed the strength of conviction to endure the harrassment to be expected regardless of protection from the respectable. A man in St. Albans threatened to thrash Lorenzo Dow, but Dow eluded him in the dark. The tribulations of St. Paul were felt over and over by many a circuit rider. "I have had stones and snowballs cast at me in volleys," wrote Ebenezer Washburn, "great dogs sent after me to frighten my horse. . . . But I never was harmed by any of them." Some saluted him with "Glory, hosanna, amen, hallelujah." Others, greeting him with oaths and profanity, scattered and fled when "I turned my horse to ride toward them." There were subtler forms of discrimination. Sometimes shareholders in a meetinghouse did not let the upstart Methodists use it. The Hartford Congregational church expelled a member for letting a Methodist preacher into his house.[22]

The fishing analogy works as far as hooking converts goes, but you only dress and eat fish, while converts need to be nurtured. The Methodists were right that it was better to have a young man be there more often for newly formed "classes," as they called their beginners' groups, than to have a more experienced, more Bible-learned, and better trained man come less frequently. Their strategy was simple. People needed to participate several times a week, to tell what God had done for them, to sing His praises full voice, to petition for His help, to take courage from the intentions of the others in the group. The group needed to be small, so that everybody had a turn, and to divide as it grew. It helped to have at least one substantial citizen offer his house for class meetings, by his status in the community to attract the curious and to protect the group from harrassment by rowdies.

As a consequence of such fortitude, persistence, and coverage, the Methodists were so successful that their rapid rise reshaped Vermont's religious constellation in this period. Represented by isolated individuals like "Mother" Margaret Peckett of Bradford and the itinerant Samuel Wigton before 1791, they were abreast of the Congregationalists and ahead of the Baptists by 1840. They outraced the Universalists and Free Will Baptists, among the new groups who also ran, and rivaled the Baptists as the most vehement.[23]

Free Will Baptists, Universalists, Christians

One large, liberal wedge of the religious pie included the Free Baptists, Universalists, Christians, some "free" or "union" churches, some of the Congregationalists who eventually became Unitarians, and some of the Quakers, who divided into two branches in 1828. While all except the Quakers accepted the primary authority of the Bible, they wanted to test it themselves. That is, their final authority was individual interpretation of the Bible. Since reasoning varies with the reasoner, these latitudinarians put little emphasis on written creeds and left the expression of beliefs to individual conscience. And each, starting at different places and times, and objecting to different particulars cherished by their parent group, could not unite in one large, liberal church. They liked being small and slightly different.

A group of Baptists in Strafford formed for worship in 1792, but had trouble agreeing on articles of faith. Each side called for outside help, and those believing in universal atonement called Elder Benjamin Randall, the first Baptist who had pulled away in New Durham, New Hampshire, in 1780. After a sermon joust of champions, Randall drew off the majority. From Strafford their revivalists fanned out among the poor farmers in the hills of Orange County and beyond in the backwoods of northeastern Vermont. Until 1801, new religious groups had a hard time gaining recognition as legitimate dissenters. In 1800, Free Baptist Joseph Boody, Jr., found five Baptists in Hardwick, excommunicated as freewillers, who had property distrained to pay the ministerial tax to support town preaching.[24] The next year the General Assembly exempted anyone from church taxes merely by their asserting that they disagreed with "the majority" view. Hardwick was among sixteen Vermont towns with Free Baptist churches organized between 1798 (Corinth) and 1805. Four more organized before the War of 1812, a score more from 1817-29, and thirty-four more in the 1830s. Less than a fifth of these churches were in the southern four counties.[25]

Woods people welcomed unconventional exhorters. In northwestern Vermont, Free Will Baptists supported the missionary efforts of Charles Bowles (1761-1843), three-quarter African American. Bowles' maternal grandfather was Daniel Morgan, Revolutionary officer, and his father was African American. Farmed out to foster parents, he served the entire War for Independence, two years as the servant of an officer and the rest as a private. He farmed in New Hampshire, joined the Baptists, then the Free Baptists, went to sea as ship's cook, and began preaching about 1808. He came to Huntington, Vermont, in 1816, bought a farm, started a church, and was ordained. From this base he traveled for eighteen years in Orange County, the Winooski and Missisquoi valleys, Grand Isle, Clinton County, New York, and the Eastern Townships of Quebec, and organized Huntington and Enosburg quarterly meetings. Once, on "a preaching tour," he went all day with no food. He prayed and let his horse choose where he would ask for shelter. A Methodist had appointed a meeting where he stopped, but the preacher was late, so

Bowles filled in and felt that God confirmed his call.

He often encountered racists. In Hinesburg they threatened to put him on a sawhorse and throw him into the pond if he held his meeting. When the liquored-up men in their face-blackened disguise had heard him preach on Luke 3:7-9 ("How can you escape the wrath to come?"), he announced their scheme at the end, challenging them to let their leader face him, for though he would make no resistance, he would preach again on the way, "and we will have music, glory be to God!" This display of courage paralyzed them; many were converted in the next few weeks.[26] Because the Free Will Baptists were backwoods New Englanders, at home or in upstate New York and the upper Middle West, they were relatively isolated from the South. Their isolation made it easier to unite in public testimony against slavery as early as 1835.[27]

John Colby of Sutton, meteoric evangelist in eastern Vermont, upstate New York, Ohio, and Rhode Island, 1809-17, won Clarissa Danforth for Christ about 1809. Danforth's father built up a business around his Weathersfield Bow tavern, with an ashery and a wharf above Ashley's ferry to Claremont. Born about 1792, Clarissa escaped home by conversion, and went on tour all over northeastern Vermont and eventually in rural New England, especially Rhode Island, as an attractive young preacher. She was in fact, but not in formal ordination, the first non-Quaker woman preacher in Vermont. This shows how hill people were free from the convention requiring white, male preachers. But in matters of church governance, pastoring, and eldering, again with the Quaker exception and the later circulation of Spiritualist mediums, Vermont women were excluded in every denomination until after the Civil War.[28]

It seems likely that a Quaker leaven influenced the Free Baptists, as expressed in their terms (e.g., monthly, quarterly, and yearly meetings) and their emphasis on plain dress and plain speech (common, however, to all the churches of the Puritan heritage), their acceptance of female and African-American ministers, their early antislavery stance, and their serious avoidance of any kind of "frolic." John Colby's parents were born in the Quaker centers of Amesbury, Massachusetts, and Weare, New Hampshire, and moved to Sandwich, where he was born, where there was another Quaker meeting. Places where successful revivals were held include towns with Quaker settlements such as Smithfield, Rhode Island; Parsonsfield and other inland Maine centers; Dover and Unity, New Hampshire; Strafford, Huntington, Richmond, Charlotte, Grand Isle, Vermont; and Peru, New York. The Free Will Baptists used other female exhorters besides Clarissa Danforth: Martha Spaulding, Nancy Towle, and Salome Lincoln Mowry.

One reason why a single congregational, liberal denomination did not develop in Vermont was the propensity of one leader or another to emphasize this or that tenet as central. Free Baptists, while objecting to their parent church's Calvinist creed, still insisted on adult immersion. The Universalists had "certain leading points" upon which they united, especially that the God of love would save all in the end.[29]

The Universalists were the noisiest opponents of the contemporary versions of Calvinism. In a debate of champions held in Lemuel Haynes' West Rutland Congregational church in 1805, Hosea Ballou summarized his *Treatise on Atonement*, the Universalist campaign document he issued later that year. Haynes replied with *Universal Salvation*, expressing the evangelical orthodoxy he had preached for a quarter century, thus crystallizing the Calvinist and anti-Calvinist sides in the Jeffersonian period.[30] This and similar contests enabled sharp-eyed missionaries to identify those ready to form Universalist societies in every second or third town east of the mountains, more thinly in western Vermont. Certificates exempting dissenters from supporting the usually Congregationalist establishment before 1807 were most often for the two kinds of Baptists or for the Universalists. These same groups, with the new Methodists, provided the troops bringing this establishment to an end. Universalists were the first to compile a *denominational* hymnbook (not a psalm book with a supplement of hymns).[31] Universalists were the last to have one of their ministers chosen to preach an election sermon, in 1824.[32] They were the chief scoffers at revivalist hoopla: Universalist Rev. Russell Streeter led the 1835 attack on Jedediah Burchard in Woodstock.

A tinge of racism coloring Hosea Ballou's harangue against the African-American Lemuel Haynes suggests that the bulk of Universalists, least revivalist, were also less vehemently antislavery. Thus their members favored the mainly Protestant Democratic Party after their original opposition to the Federalist multiple establishment, and their antimasonic excitement of the 1830s.[33]

Most Universalists felt that "it doesn't make any difference" whether we sprinkle or dunk our new born-again members. They were by habit congregational and depended on their press,[34] for lack of enough itinerants, to draw their congregations together. Not having the Methodists' network of classes and districts, they depended on short stands of their too few able preachers, trying to serve several nearby groups. Not having enough well-to-do members to complete the subscription of pittances from many working men, although they had over a hundred congregations in 1844, only two-thirds of them had meetinghouses and less than half had preachers attached. Not caring about the fine points of theology, they could not attract seekers whose main need was detailed certainty. Universalists, like others sure that all Christians should be one, could not figure out how to extend ecumenism beyond some benevolent enterprises. Yet a few thousand adherents expressed a point of view much more widespread than their numbers indicated.

Some made Christian unity their one distinctive, just as their forebears in the colonies had called themselves "the Church of Christ at" Dartmouth College or wherever they lived. Refusing to accept any more particular label than Christian, they became a new denomination with thirty or forty churches in the state, fluctuating according to the availability of leadership. Their two Vermont founders, Abner Jones of Lyndon and Elias Smith of South Woodstock, had been Baptists, then Free Will Baptists, and they drew mainly from those groups in Vermont. The Free Baptists and the Christians were close in origin, belief, and behavior and considered union. Although in the first quarter of the nineteenth century they "shared revivals, accepted each other's ministers and attended each other's meetings," they could not merge because they were at different stages of development, from the charisma and chaos of "gospel liberty" to the routinization of a rational church polity.[35]

They felt that the only things they had to agree upon were the authority of the Bible and the congregational order. They practiced open communion like the Free Baptists and aimed to live "a godly, righteous, and sober life," as the Episcopal Book of Common Prayer put it. Outsiders called them Christ-ian, perhaps to distinguish them from generic Christians, all of whom nodded acceptance of Christ's injunction that his followers be one.

They did not merge with the nationwide Disciples of Christ, also called Campbellites, themselves a union of some Presbyterians and Baptists on the same basis of Bible Christianity. Elder Worden P. Reynolds, who made his living as a carpenter and cabinetmaker, organized the Manchester "Disciples," a Baptist secession, in 1829, which lasted a generation. After they sold their building to the town for a school and were cleaning out the attic, they found some baptismal garments, "heavy black woolens weighted with wire."[36] In 1831, Reynolds started a "Church of the Disciples" at Pawlet that lasted forty years. They had a spurt of life after they built a meetinghouse in West Pawlet in 1847 and Alexander Campbell, founder of the Disciples of Christ, preached there once. As Rising and Nelson's slate business expanded, the Baptists and the Welsh Methodists provided the religious services. A "Church of Disciples," organized in West Rupert in 1837, lasted through the century.[37]

Like so many Baptists, the Christians were avid antimasons because they believed that secret societies were neither democratic nor Christian. Quakers, and Congregationalists like Chester Wright, agreed with the antimasons but eschewed politics. Although from 1836 through 1881 Christian ministers and lay representatives met annually to consult and confer, these associations lacked the power either to maintain order or promote growth. Otherwise they could have corralled more of those with this majority view and rivaled the Methodists. They merged with the Congregational churches in 1931.[38]

Roman Catholics

Anti-Romanism, sometimes called nativism, shifted in the 1830s from a fear of a faraway threat to hostility against Roman Catholics in Vermont. At the other end of the religious spectrum from the descendants of the Puritans, Roman Catholics appeared as the most important new element on the religious scene in the second quarter of the century. Stereotyped as devils incarnate, owing allegiance to the papist Anti-Christ, the Whore of Babylon, they were unknown to early Vermonters, except those who hired transient French Canadians, or the few who traded in Lower Canada, visited Atlantic ports, or sailed abroad.

The 1777 and 1786 constitutions of Vermont required a "religious test" of assemblymen. In addition to the oath to behave as a "guardian of the people," each member before taking his seat swore or affirmed that he believed in one God, a divinely inspired Bible, and professed the Protestant religion.[39] According to folklore Ethan Allen refused to take this oath and was disqualified. He found swallowing the whole of Scripture too much but he scaled that hurdle as representative of Arlington.[40] If Ethan could make it, the bar was obviously an anti-Catholic gesture against bogeymen not in Vermont, whom most Vermonters had no personal experience with.[41]

"Catholic," meaning universal, was in common usage among Vermont Protestants. Episcopalians reciting the Apostles' Creed believed in "the Holy Catholic Church." Timothy Dwight wrote in 1798 that many new settlements were "divided in their religious opinions," but he praised the Manchester people for their "catholicism" in agreeing to hire qualified preachers of different denominations. The Universalists at Woodstock were called the "Independent Catholick Society" (1794), in Reading (1796) the "Reformed Catholic Society," and at Hartland Four Corners (1802) the "Catholic Benevolent Society." The Burlington Congregational Church announced a series of "Lectures to Young Persons" by five Congregationalists, the Episcopal bishop, and a Presbyterian from Plattsburgh, on Sunday evenings in 1833. It assured the public that they would be "catholic," and not in a "party and sectarian spirit."[42]

Before the Champlain Canal and other improved inland waterways eased travel, and before Catholic Emancipation (1829) climaxed a long series of British acts restoring Irish Catholic civil rights, many Irish crossed the Atlantic on returning lumber boats. Quebecois joined them to earn their keep as choppers and farm laborers in the Champlain Valley. First dependent on rare visits from Richelieu Valley and Massachusetts priests, they served themselves with the occasional "dry mass," reciting the prayers they remembered, and reading from books of devotion. When John De Cheverus became the first bishop of Boston in 1810, he had the care of these distant, scattered Catholics. A hundred or so, mainly French Canadian, clustered near Burlington in 1815. Exploitation of iron and copperas ores early attracted Irishmen to lonely mountain mines in Bennington, Chittenden, Tyson in Plymouth, and Shrewsbury, and to the little furnaces and forges of Forestdale in Brandon, Vergennes, and Pittsford. Because Catholics were few, few Protestants worried about them.

The returning prosperity of the 1820s attracted more, with strongest seepage still in the Champlain Valley. After a decade of relatively quiet recovery from the angers and anxieties of the second war with Britain and its aftermath, partisanship and political rancor revived, along with religious enthusiasm. Governor C. P. Van Ness ran unsuccessfully for the U.S. Senate in 1826, perhaps rounding up Irish votes and triggering a bit of nativism. This first tear in Vermont's garment of good feeling led immediately after his defeat to his joining the Democratic Party. Because different towns treated aliens differently, in 1827 the Council of Censors proposed and the subsequent constitutional convention adopted the first amendment to the Vermont constitution, defining these privileges to include naturalized immigrants.[43]

The statewide total of Vermont Catholics, conservatively estimated, grew to more than a thousand by 1830 and at least three thousand by 1840. Protestants had viewed Catholics from afar as foreign "Papist" enemies of true religion. Now they saw them as misguided prisoners of the priesthood who should be converted. Because Protestants succeeded in "freeing" only a few, Catholics became a growing threat and nativism a growing fear.

Nativism was only one of the reform movements that characterized the second quarter of the nineteenth century. This and the temperance, antislavery, and antimasonic reforms, all born aiming to persuade and not compel, began to grow strident. Temperance people stayed calm longer, until they came to associate the social evils of poverty, intemperance, and crime with the Catholic immigrant. Two main reform movements—anti-alcohol and antislavery—provide the background of this growth.

Vermont's steady opposition to slavery began with the 1777 constitutional requirement than all adults be free. A handful of slaveholders in the early years did not immediately manumit, but whenever Vermonters thought of it, they were antislavery. Their first institutional expression was the Vermont Colonization Society, founded in 1819. Tacitly racist, it proposed to remove the evil of slavery by ridding the country of blacks, and focused on Liberia. Vermont politicians felt discomfort with the Missouri Compromise of 1820, extending the possibility of slavery to western public land. In 1828-29, William Lloyd Garrison fired the first editorial shots in his Bennington *Journal of the Times* for action more positive and immediate: the gradual emancipation of slavery in the District of Columbia.[44] To the Catholic workingmen, feeling oppressed themselves, antislavery reform had a low priority.

Antimasonry, the hottest political issue for a decade (1827-1836), was in one sense a crusade against "a church outside the church." It vented democratic feelings of little people against the village power structure, united in a clique operating secretly across denominational lines. Masonry satisfied some Protestants' hunger for magic as a means of getting one's way in an adverse world. It satisfied the ascetic Protestants' hunger for trappings when they would not accept the Anglican or Roman versions. To the heirs of the Puritans, Masons were a kind of Catholic, full of secret, medieval hocus-pocus.[45]

Benedict J. Fenwick, who succeeded Cheverus as bishop of Boston in 1823, toured Vermont in 1826 and realized that time had come to establish a Vermont mission. Four years later, Jeremiah O'Callaghan presented himself as the man for the job. His eccentric, medieval passion against charging interest had blocked his finding a parish in Europe. (After all, Deuteronomy 23:19 commands, "You shall not lend upon interest to your brother"—but you may to a foreigner.) Even in America in 1823-24 he had looked in vain from New York to Baltimore to Quebec, being refused chiefly because he would not give extreme unction to a usurer. Bishop Fenwick, in sending him to Burlington, may have felt that this oddball priest was better than none, and, besides, Vermont Catholics were too poor to have money to lend at interest.

Fenwick's successor, Bishop John Bernard Fitzpatrick, noting O'Callaghan's death in Holyoke on February 23, 1861, described him as "a man of fair natural talent, slender education, limited knowledge and indomitable spirit as well as great presumption," who devoted all his resources to the welfare of his church, and had "no chance to enforce his queer notions on. . . usury" because all the Catholics in Vermont were poor.[46] At fifty when he arrived in Vermont, O'Callaghan had the basics of what the Irish immigrant needed: credentials to administer the sacraments, willingness to cover the ground, and sympathy for the poor and outcast, as he had been an outcast himself. He spoke Gaelic, but in spite of a brief sojourn in France, never learned enough of its language to understand the French or sympathize with French Canadians.[47]

O'Callaghan in residence and on the move presented a new test of tolerance, beyond putting up with "Crazy Dow," "ranting" Methodists, and the unshaven, unwashed visionaries of various sects wandering through the villages. The new priest's main functions, besides confirming the solidarity of the Irish in the faith, were to reclaim lost sheep, to confront anti-Catholics with anti-Protestantism, and to deal with the emulsion of Irish and French. His circuit was larger than any Methodist's except Asbury's and he covered it with persistent travel. It was larger than Bishop Hopkins' diocese, for O'Callaghan crossed Lake Champlain and the Connecticut River and reached below Vermont's southern border.[48]

Only a few lambs were lost, to Baptist and Adventist revivalists in northwestern Vermont, or an occasional servant in well-to-do village families. The membership list of the First Calvinistic Congregational Church in Burlington includes the names of a few French and Irish who joined during John K. Converse's pastorate, 1833-45, but they had left the church before the Civil War. Perhaps they had left town, or were uncomfortable with the old Yankees, or the old Yankees were uncomfortable with their working clothes, habits, and speech.[49]

Roman Catholics were by the 1830s no longer other people far away, but under foot. Nathaniel Hawthorne found the Irish unavoidably noticeable on the Burlington waterfront in 1835. "Nothing struck me more, in Burlington, than the great number of Irish emigrants," he wrote. "They swarm in huts and mean dwellings near the lake, lounge about the wharves, and elbow the native citizens entirely out of competition in their own line. Every species of mere bodily labor is the prerogative of these Irish. . . . The men exhibit a lazy strength and careless merriment, as if they had fed well hitherto, and meant to feed better hereafter; the women strode about, uncovered in the open air, with far plumper waists and brawnier limbs, as well as bolder faces, than our shy and slender females; and their progeny, which was innumerable, had the reddest and the roundest cheeks of any children in America." [50]

Hawthorne's description of the Irish Jim Crow was fairly typical of Yankee first impressions. The sources and consequences of this prejudice are complicated. There is always aloofness between the settled and the newcomer, but the peasant Irish had a peculiar impact. They left poverty and oppression in the Old Country, had a hard trip across the ocean, and arrived with their prejudices against English-speaking Protestants intact.

Yet they expected things would be different in the United States. Jeremiah O'Callaghan told his countryman that "all tribes of nations" live "in union and friendship" in the United States. Here, he boasted, is "peace without interruption," protected by militia ready "to die for the common welfare. There are no cattle houghed, no White Boys sounding the horn, nor haggards in flames: because. . . people [are not] goaded into rebellion by Orangemen or tithe-proctor."[51]

He soon found a usurer in each Whig manager of a local institution and played the broken record of his obsession against banks and usury until his dying day. Long experience in Ireland, and O'Callaghan's incessant hammering on Protestant "false teachers," both in print and by word of mouth, framed an Irish mindset and created an "Irish brigade" not only in Burlington, but wherever else clumps of Irishmen settled.

Protestant hostility matched the Catholics'. In 1835, fifty-six men, including several Scots Presbyterians from Barnet, petitioned the General Assembly to prohibit the erection of monasteries and nunneries, asserting that they enslave the mind, restrict liberties, and favor despotism. George Perkins Marsh of the Governor's Council, chairman of the select committee to which the petition was referred, reported out a bill favoring the prohibition. It lingered into the next session and died.[52]

When the priest-pamphleteer had attacked the local Protestant clergy, the *Burlington Free Press* retorted, on October 13, 1837, that it was "perfectly right for an itinerant foreign priest to take upon himself the whole subject of politics—to preach it in the church, proclaim it at the corners of the streets, and publish his opinions to the world! Such are the monstrosities of the times." But "this reverend Paddy," the Whig editor continued:

> according to his own showing, has thrice been spewed from the church and his native country as a shatter-brained disorganizer. That such an individual should find our religion, our laws, our institutions, and the whole frame-work of society wrong, is certainly not wonderful; and that he should content himself with simply denouncing our business men as cut-throats, our clergy as impostors, and our statesmen and legislators, as bribed and venal orators, indicates a degree of modest charity [equalled only by the Democratic *Burlington Sentinel's* giving him space.]

The burning of St. Mary's, Burlington, the night of May 8, 1838, was widely assumed to be the act of an anti-Catholic terrorist, although no one was ever charged. The correspondent of the *Boston Pilot* claimed that a Canadian heard a storekeeper harangue a dozen college boys drinking in an upper Pearl Street tavern the night of the fire. Was this a perverted form of spring fever, inspired by the animosity of their Protestant elders? St. Mary's was under repair; a careless smoker could well have knocked live ashes out of his pipe to smolder in the shavings.[53]

We will never know who did it. We do know that the fire occurred not only in the context of religious and class tensions but also in the tensions between increasing numbers of Gaelic and francophone newcomers, all Catholic, able to support additional priests. For the Irish, Father John B. Daly served the four southern counties of Vermont from Castleton, 1837-1850, while the bilingual Fr. William Ivers came briefly to St. Albans, 1841-1842, with a mission to the concentration of Catholics in northwestern Vermont. Fr. Amable F. G. Petithomme, a French missionary to Maine Indians diverted to Burlington by Bishop Benedict J. Fenwick, converted a schoolhouse not far from St. Mary's, May 1834-October 1835.

It did not matter who burned the first Burlington Church of St. Mary's in 1838, or that Protestant "lords of the manor" gave land for a church and cemetery in several towns or let Father O'Callaghan use their buildings for Mass; or even that the priest was the most effective strike-breaker.[54] In spite of the usually sincere tolerance of alien ways by Yankee Protestants, the burden of poverty and adjustment fell on the Irish immigrants and they blamed the Whig bosses. They were all Democrats.[55]

The fewer Quebecois were not Democrats, for reasons unclear, perhaps because of their hostility to the Irish as well as the Yankees. French Catholics in Quebec were in the habit of managing the material aspects of their parish life and talking back to their priests. They had francophone missionaries in Burlington from 1835, and would have francophone priests in Burlington's St. Joseph's, established in 1850, the first ethnic parish in New England. Unlike the Irish, they could walk home to their relatives north of the border if things got too bad. They were more literate and more concerned for parochial schools. Most important, their language, which they used much more than the Irish used Gaelic, insulated them from both Irish and Yankee. A few were at least temporarily converted by revivalistic Protestants, but their basic reaction, if poverty did not require them to live among anglophones, was to form non-political enclaves. Few Franco-Americans voted Whig and none favored any reform except temperance.

Burchardism

Many Catholics, Episcopalians, and conservative Congregationalists objected with Bishop Hopkins to the emotionalism of revivalists and reformers, in different proportions and for varying reasons. Neither these pastors nor any others objected to the awakening of religious "sentiment." Annual parish reports of evangelical churches to their state conventions focused on the statistics of those "hopefully converted," the "serious" beyond mere occasional church attendance and support, the youths drawn from dissipation to prayer. They wrote of seasons when enthusiasm infused cold reason with earnest desire for

God's free grace and undying love. Maybe they were backsliders whose wives kept praying for their redemption. All were as familiar with revivalism as modern youth is with TV.

Revivalists won souls because they persuaded the lost to seek God's kingdom and righteousness first (Matt. 6:33), trusting that their needs would be met. In the turbulence of rapidly changing America, holding onto their parents' faith in the tried and true was not good enough in the face of expanding unknowns. For some, impending or actual loss of status, decline in business prospects, or removal of family supports drove them to their knees. For others, the attraction of a new minister, or the new rhetoric, or a new location, brought them into the church.

An element of anxiety about salvation entered the psyche of most applicants for church membership, along with the mundane pressures of pleasing one's family and friends, personal help through church connections, a crush on the pastor or singing master, and enjoyment of the liturgy. Calling to the "anxious seat," the front bench where exposed sinners could be prayed into conversion, was only a "new measure" of the late 1820s. Persuasion by parents, leaders, or other role models was only secondary. They were anxious when they had time to think about it, if they were unemployed, but with some of the most intense revivals coming during times of "full" employment, there was time to be anxious during as well as after dawn-to-dark work.

It is hard for us to conceive of how "leisurely" work was. With so much of it manual, short periods of rest were essential to get through each day. Those interstices of rest allowed for the brooding uneasiness which could lead to insanity, innovation, or conversion. Perhaps whether anxious people became Methodists or Mormons depended on the random encounter with stimuli, from preachers, exhorters, or neighbors.

The increased harvest of Protestant converts during flush times of the early 1830s might suggest that people could afford the luxury of daily and nightly religious meetings when they were prosperous. The theorists who equate heightened religious interest with trouble in the marketplace could argue that prosperity at best is selective, but anxiety in the face of rapid and little understood change is universal. What of the grain farmer who watched declining yields in the best of times? The wool grower who saw the erratic price fall as he went to sell, or suffered losses from a blizzard or sheep-killing dogs? A graph of Vermont Baptist membership, based on annual reports to the state convention, shows a peak in 1843, not matched until the end of the 1870s. Both peaks came at the ends of long economic depressions. Perhaps the difference between temporary conversions and membership shaken down after the contrived enthusiasm waned explains the large gains in flush

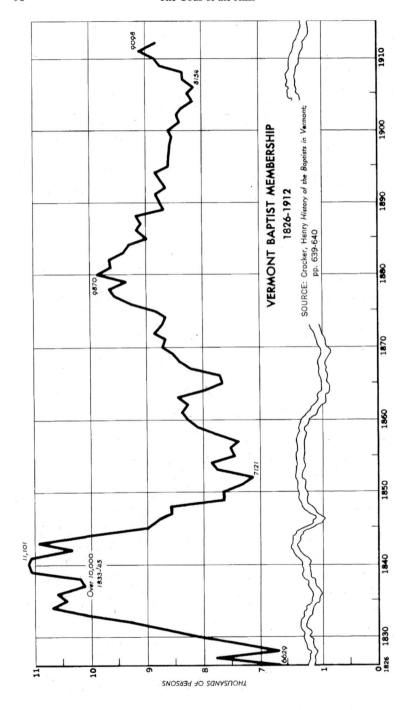

VERMONT BAPTIST MEMBERSHIP
1826-1912

SOURCE: Crocker, Henry History of the Baptists in Vermont;
pp. 639-640

THOUSANDS OF PERSONS

times and the peaks at the end of hard times.[56]

The waves of revival throughout the first half century of the republic had many features in common. While revivals converted the teenage children of the pillars of society, they also reached down into the poorer classes and confirmed their worth. Political parties were likewise acknowledging their worth by giving more poor farmers and artisans the vote and encouraging them to use it. Revivals were noisy, because the poor, when they felt free, let off steam. They gave those hitherto slighted working people front-row seats, anxious seats, where in churches supported by pew rents the substantial members paid for the front rows, just as in modern theaters and concert halls. It emphasized salvation, redemption, sanctification, and not denominational distinctives. When the converts believed themselves saved, they believed themselves obligated to "try to live a Christian life," and that led to reforms, as David Ludlum recounted them in *Social Ferment in Vermont*.

The Congregationalists were not winning their share of the converts. It seems they had lost the common touch. Reuben Smith, pastor of Burlington's Calvinistic Congregational Church, 1826-31, with solid Middlebury College and Princeton Presbyterian training, followed a common pattern in winning forty-four new members during his first six months but few thereafter. His successor, young John Kendall Converse, proposed soon after his arrival to stage a protracted meeting. The congregation balked.

They did not object to a serious, awakened concern for religion, but the "new measures," among which the protracted meeting was a central feature, emphasized what human effort could do to insure salvation. Presbyterian Charles Grandison Finney had successfully applied these methods in Rochester, New York, and out from there in the late 1820s. Faith and practice should be God-centered, said the objectors, not person-centered. Whip up short-lived emotions with sensational, impromptu preaching, altar calls, anxious seats or mourners' benches, and constant pressure to follow the flock into the fold, and the emotionally worn will tire, leaving the "converts" ready to relapse.

The success of their competitors gradually persuaded Congregationalists like Converse in Burlington and Daniel O. Morton in Springfield to adopt more lively revivalist techniques. Morton wrote that most of the time it "seemed like one continuous Sabbath" with the large house of worship filled daily.[57] As so often the case, the means affected the ends and the doctrines. The "new measures" called all sinners not only to recognize their parlous state, but also to *do something* for their salvation. This belied the Calvinists' deterministic doctrine of predestination and moved people's practical beliefs toward the Arminian side of the spectrum. "New measures" had been gradually coming. This also shifted the emphasis from quiet prayer that God would convert, to a belief that revivalists were influential, more than merely instruments, in conversion.

Into this environment of renewed discontent and social division, one set of Congregational leaders, seeing their group outdistanced, capitulated to the new revivalist mode and in 1834 invited Jedediah Burchard, an upstate New York preacher, to visit their churches. His reputation as a seasoned evangelist was second only to Finney's. That Burchard and Finney were Presbyterian made no difference in revivals, for the two denominations were close in how they understood the gospel and how they should preach and teach it. The stream of revivalism had been gathering to flood proportions with no outside help, except from God, the preachers said. Competition had fueled the revivals and competition was not going away, as more and more minority groups collected members enough to build houses of worship and pay parsons. And now in the 1830s even the Papists were raising their alien voices, coming into view.

Burchard began auspiciously, welcomed by President Joshua Bates of Middlebury College and the local Congregational pastor in the fall of 1834. Moderate revivalist Daniel O. Morton of Springfield found no fault, nor did Windsor and Dartmouth College Congregationalists, although Burchard took a beating in liberal Woodstock and the Dartmouth students were divided. Burchard's fifteen-month tour in 1834-36 through the Champlain and Connecticut valleys was a short-lived movement akin to antimasonry in that the revivalist aimed at the souls of ordinary people and attacked respectable hypocrites.

On sparse evidence, historians looking for the sensational have painted Burchard as a circus rider (he was a circuit rider), a barnstorming actor, a coarse, vulgar, sensation-seeking charlatan. They granted that his colloquial speech was effective in persuading all kinds to commit themselves to Christ, but they charged that his conversions were temporary and lacked the proper preparation and grounding. They could not find fault with his theology, which was orthodox, although he oversimplified as spellbinders do. He was well grounded in Scripture, and his Episcopalian wife helped him by organizing the youth, among whom he made numerous converts.

Knowing that controversy gets attention, he ridiculed the pompous, referred disrespectfully to local personalities, even attacked his host church, "cold as Greenland" before he came. A slave "under conviction" after only two days, he said, was as good as his master, who took years to be converted. His plain language suited people with little education. He used "ain't," with a ready wit told vivid short stories in plain language, and welcomed all, rich and poor, to open communion and front-row anxious seats. People paid good money for front pews in most churches. He assumed you don't reason with the sinner, you excite his emotions: the fear of hell and the love of Jesus. As a fisher of men and women he would hook the drowning sinner and pull that poor fish out of the flood of perdition. Any bait or lure would do.[58]

By the end of May he was in Montpelier, where he converted the forty-year-old lawyer and Middlebury College graduate Daniel Pierce Thompson, his wife, sister-in-law, and maid. Describing the experience to his cousin, Thompson said the "new measures" were nothing more than an

> immediate application of the promises & commands of
> the gospel. . . . I saw with alarm that there was rank
> rebellion in my breast to the very God that had been
> sustaining me all my life, and this led me to call in
> earnest for forgiveness & mercy. . . . Mr. Burchard is
> truly an extraordinary man! With power of eloquence
> capable of throwing a whole audience into tears at will,
> he yet chooses to address the understanding & first
> convince the mind. With a thorough knowledge of. . . .
> all that is now going on [in] the world, every department
> of science & literature, united with indefatigable labor,
> he catches all classes, and particularly the most intellec-
> tual.[59]

Burchard concluded his Vermont campaign with stands in Burlington before Christmas 1835, Williston and Hinesburg running on into January 1836. As Thomas A. Merrill, the Middlebury pastor, had introduced him to Vermont with favorable publicity, the Rev. John K. Converse was equally favorable.

Elam Comings, a twenty-three-year-old University of Vermont sophomore, wrote his family a full account after two weeks' regular attendance at Burchard's meeting, while he "kept along one recitation per day most of the time." He concluded that Burchard's battle was the Lord's and the new measures were

> the same as were used in 1831. . . .There is but very little
> excitement. Yesterday I took a tremendous trimming
> from Dr. Marsh for being an enthusiast. . . . carried away
> with Burchard. . . . On the whole I *like him*. He is a very
> active man & in the heat of his zeal he says some things
> which he had better not say, but I think he means well. .
> . . [He] puts more confidence in prayer of any person I
> ever saw. Dr. M. calls him a fanatic on this account.
> Among the converted are. . . men of all ages & ranks.
> The old & the young, the rich & poor, the learned & the
> illiterate.[60]

Comings finished out the year in Burlington and then transferred to Oberlin College where Charles G. Finney, principal exponent of the new measures, had just come to establish a theological department.

The University of Vermont faculty, led by President James Marsh, campaigned quietly against Burchard, charging that his flamboyant ways did not prepare converts for membership thoroughly. They mounted a deliberate and successful campaign to turn the regional associations and the *Vermont Chronicle*, the state Congregational organ, against Burchard, or at least to neutralize the *Vermont Chronicle* and persuade congregations to rescind their invitations to him.[61]

Since Burchard was the talk of every village, printer Chauncey Goodrich sought to publish a best seller by assigning two college students to report Burchard's sermons. Shorthand stenography had become accurate enough to catch a speaker's words as they flowed, and shorthand was used to record what Burchard said on his tour. The strain of a year's protracted meetings must have worn Burchard thin; opponents were able to make him look like an enemy of civil rights when he used dubious means, buying a reporter's notes, not answering Goodrich's offer to let Burchard correct the copy before it was published, and trying to keep the reporters out of his meetings. Of course he was right that the cold type of an unsympathetic report can distort a dramatic message delivered in a vibrant voice speaking to a sympathetic audience. His enemies effectively disturbed his meetings while staying within the law.

George Perkins Marsh conceded, in a letter to his father in Woodstock, that Burchard captured attention for religion, but his "manner is highly objectionable," because it produced shallow, temporary conversions.[62] Indeed, most of some hundred who joined Burlington's Congregational Church during the protracted meeting of December 1835 had been crossed off the list before the Rev. Converse left the pastorate in 1844. Did the converts slide back into their sins "the morning after" their intoxicating excitement? Burchard warned them of the danger. He told them to practice what they professed after the thrills wore gone and they had to earn their living and do their family and civic duties. He told them that to grow in grace they needed a different kind of preaching, for "a man is best instructed by his own pastor."[63] They may have dropped off because they did not feel welcomed, because they did not dress right, or because they did not speak the language of the counting room or the classroom.

Several pro-Burchard clergy lost their jobs: in Royalton and Woodstock, right away; in Burlington and Middlebury within a few years. Some, like the venerable Jedediah Bushnell, who had served Cornwall Congregationalists since 1803, were dismissed for objecting to Burchard's coming to his church. President Bates of Middlebury resigned too. Sherman Kellogg came from Rochester, Vermont, as pastor of the newly organized Montpelier Free Church, free of pew rent and full of the Oberlin theology, Finneyite fervency, and antislavery reform. Elam J. Comings served, 1844-47, and the church died the next year.

John Kellogg, Benson lawyer, town clerk, and Democratic candidate for the U.S. Senate, transferred to the Methodists in 1838 because the ruling Congregational clique could not see how he could be a Democrat and a Congregationalist, and because he opposed Burchard.[64] Burchard concluded, as he left Vermont after the excitement of his Chittenden County finale and prepared to work the New York shore of Lake Champlain, "I've had a hard time of it here."

The Vermont Congregational Conference never issued a statement siding for or against Burchard. No Congregationalist after Burchard tried to evangelize the unchurched majority of village artisans and laboring classes until Edward Hungerford in 1867.[65] It was becoming harder to convert the unchurched poor to Protestantism as Roman Catholics filled the low-paid jobs and had priests to serve them. The Burlington Congregationalists established a church in Winooski late in 1836, but while it served some of the mill village's Protestant minority it failed to attract the Catholic operatives, who crossed the river to the French or Irish churches in Burlington. Latter-day Episcopalians, Unitarians, and Congregationalists had a higher proportion of substantial farmers and business and professional people, usually Whigs, than other Protestants.[66] Congregationalists transferred their revivalistic zeal to elect William Henry Harrison president and swamp the state Democrats in 1840. They also transferred a good deal of patronage from Middlebury College to Burlington College.

Religious   Statistics

After a half century of competition for members, using specialists in revivals, the number of adherents to Protestant churches had grown more than tenfold while the population had increased less than three and a half times. Catholics had increased from near zero to several thousand.

When Vermont entered the Union in 1791 there were nearly a hundred organized churches: some sixty Congregational, half as many Baptist, two or three Episcopal, two Quaker monthly meetings with several worship groups in different towns, and one Presbyterian church in Ryegate. Half a century later, nine new denominations had entered the field: Methodists (who began sending circuit riders to Vermont in 1788), Free Will Baptists, Christians, Universalists, Unitarians, Reformed or Covenanter Presbyterians, Reformed or Protestant Methodists, Roman Catholics, and Latter Day Saints (Mormons).

By 1840, the Methodists, because they were organized by circuits, probably covered more towns[67] than the ninety Congregational churches. Three years later each had clergy in 140 towns.[68] Some seventy-five Free Will Baptist groups had separated in this period over theology and style, but about 120 small Calvinist Baptist churches continued.[69] The list also included, depending on how defined, forty-six Universalist,[70] twenty-two Episcopalian, eleven locally organized Quaker congregations, several in the "Christian Connection" or "Disciples," over half a dozen Roman Catholic flocks, four Unitarian churches, and occasional missionaries for Mormons and Shakers. With this distribution of churches, public worship occurred frequently in most towns, although not every Sunday.[71]

Notes to Chapter 3

[1] Hoag, *Journal*, 68-69.

[2] Cross, *Burned-Over District*, 7-8.

[3] Finke and Stark, "The Upstart Sects Win America, 1776-1850," in *Churching of America*, 54-108, treat the population as a market and explain why the Methodists and Baptists won, the Congregationalists and Episcopalians lost, and the Presbyterians kept pace with population growth but won a smaller share of the market.

[4] Their reports are in the Connecticut Missionary Society Papers in the office of the Connecticut Conference, U.C.C., Congregational House, Hartford, Conn., and have been microfilmed. The General Association apparently recommended that Joseph Strong of Granby and David S. Rowland of Windsor, Connecticut, visit the new settlements in 1780 but I have found no evidence that they toured.

[5] Austin to Hon. J. Treadwell, Chairman, Missionary Society of Connecticut, c/o Abel Flint, Hartford, 13 April 1801, in Connecticut Missionary Society Papers, Congregational House, Hartford, Conn.

[6] Dwight, *Travels*, 2:287-288 (visit to Middlebury); Lawrence, *New Hampshire Churches*, 464-465 (Kimball Union address). Robert V. Cushman, Middlebury Congregational church historian, found the Storrs baptism recorded in the church archives. Dwight may have assumed that his readership would not be interested in the weekly work of a reverend professor on vacation, and omitted references to Sunday preaching, as he did the Middlebury baptism. The Timothy Dwight Papers in the Yale University Archives may contain evidence of his preaching in Vermont.

[7] On the Episcopal fight to recover their glebe, see Bogart, *Vermont Lease Lands*. Vermont (Diocese, Episcopal), *Documentary History*, 232-235, summarizes the background of the U.S. Supreme Court decision.

[8] Vermont Episcopal *Documentary History*, 401.

[9] See c. 4, p. 32, on Bishop Hopkins' removal of Perkins, rector of St. James, Arlington.

[10] Hopkins, *Gothic Architecture*, 36, plate 4B. He also shows, as models for grave monuments, two free-standing crosses where, in medieval times, travelers could stop on the highway and pray or hear preaching friars, 45,

plate 13. To fit Hopkins into his architectural background, see Stanton, *Gothic Revival.*

11 Bailey, *Episcopal Church in Vermont*, 16.

12 Hopkins, *Gothic Architecture*, 14-15.

13 Skinner, *South Church, Windsor*, 36-37.

14 Joseph Hoag, *Journal*, 52-69; MS journal of William Dean at UVM; Hughes and Bradley, "Quaker Meetings in Vermont"; Bassett, "Migration of Friends to the Upper Hudson and Champlain Valleys"; Zielinski, *Farnham Meeting.*

15 A critical mass has enough parts or members to produce a chain reaction, as in dominoes close enough to knock the next one down, or sticks of wood, once on fire, raising nearby pieces to the kindling point, or in a religious community, where two or three are gathered and set afire by the Holy Spirit, they kindle the novices, probationers, or seekers into the fire of faith and action.

16 See Dow*Journal*, especially of his Irish trip in 1798, and Newell, *Memoirs.*

17 In *Vermont Historical Gazetteer*, 1:739-740.

18 Lorenzo Dow, *Journal*, 33-37 (1796), 46-47, 50-57, 64-69 (1797-99), 154 (1802), 238 (1805).

19 Spicer, *Autobiography*, 227-231. Compare the equally friendly description of Dow when he visited Lynn, Massachusetts, in Young, *Autobiography*, 95-97.

20 Asbury, *Journal and Letters*, 2:59, 394-396 with map of places he visited, 437, 508-509, 538-539, 606-607, 676. Asbury did not reach north of a line from Burlington to St. Johnsbury except for Westfield, probably a mistake for Westfield, Massachusetts.

21 Washburn's narrative is in the New York *Christian Advocate and Journal*, 16 (20 July 1842): 193:1, 16 (3 Aug. 1842): 201:1, 16 (10 Aug. 1842): 205:1-2, 17 (12 Oct. 1842): 33:1-2, 17 (26 Oct. 1842): 41:1-2, quoted in C. D. and O. D. Schwartz, *A Flame of Fire*, 78, 92-93.

22 Williams, "Christian Church, Woodstock," 5.

23 I find my conclusions about why Methodists surged ahead confirmed in the "design of victory" by Goss, *Statistical History of American Methodism*, quoted in Finke and Stark, *The Churching of America*, 104-108.

24 Stewart, *Free Will Baptists*, 170. See Chapter 4, 27. It is clear that the collector of the church tax picked on the excommunicated Baptists. It is not clear whether the Congregationalists or the Calvinistic Baptists were exempt or taxed, as the minister was Baptist Amos Tuttle who was later called to preach for the Congregationalists!

25 This summary is based on Buzzell, *Benjamin Randal*; Stewart, *History of the Freewill Baptists*; Colby, *Life and Travels*; Baxter, *Freewill Baptists*; Henderson and Phillips, *Vermont Yearly Meeting of Free Will Baptists*; Records of Tunbridge Monthly Meeting, 1825-1876, in Vermont Historical Society; Williams, *Rhode Island Freewill Baptist Pulpit*, 9-22 on John Colby; *Free Baptist Cyclopaedia*, 663-673; *New Hampshire Yearly Meeting of Free Baptists*.

26 Lewis, *Charles Bowles*, 5-25. Bowles' pension file S44640 is in the Veterans Records of the National Archives. Stewart, *History of the Free Will Baptists*, 307-310, has the most detailed account of the Hinesburg episode.

27 Burgess and Ward, eds., *Free Baptist Cyclopaedia*, 20.

28 On Clarissa Danforth: *Life of John Colby*, 2:45-46; Henderson and Phillips, *Vermont Yearly Meeting of Free Will Baptists*, 16; Stewart, *History of the Free Will Baptists*, 306-308, 310, 377, 386; Burgess and Ward, eds., *Free Baptist Cyclopedia*, 148-149, 666, 668. For other female Free Baptist preachers, see Towle, *Experience in Europe and America*, and Davis, *Memoir of Salome Lincoln*. Davis did not argue for female *pastors*. The minutes of the Stanstead Freewill Baptist Quarterly Meeting (MS. in the Special Collections of the Bailey/Howe Library of the University of Vermont) record Martha Spaulding's organizing a circuit of eight churches in the Stanstead district, in the Eastern Townships of Canada.

29 Samuel C. Loveland expresses the Universalist version of these liberal views in Zadock Thompson, *History of Vermont* (1842), 2:192-193.

30 See Saillant, "The Hopkintonian and the Universalist."

31 Hosea Ballou, Abner Kneeland, and Edward Turner, *Hymns, Composed by*

Different Authors (1808), contained only American hymns, all by the editors. Cited in Hughes, *American Hymns*, 276.

[32] See Gribbin, "Vermont's Universalist Controversy of 1824."

[33] D. M. Ludlum, *Social Ferment in Vermont*, 134-198, does not mention the Universalists in his treatment of the antislavery movement. See Table 7.12, "Religious Status of Political Activists, 1835-1850," in R. A. Roth, *The Democratic Dilemma*, 259, showing 62.5% of all church members and only 27.3% of Universalists were on Whig Party committees.

[34] See Chapter 4, p. 127 for the *Christian Repository and Universalist Watchman* and its predecessors from 1820.

[35] Fulop of Columbia Theological Seminary, Decatur, Georgia, "Gospel Liberty," used Weber's theory of church development from charisma to routinization to explain why Free Baptists and Christians did not merge. See also Williams, "Christian Church, Woodstock."

[36] Bigelow and Otis, *Manchester*, 55.

[37] Hollister, *Pawlet*, 148-149; last listed in *Walton's Register* for 1871. The three "Disciples" church buildings appear separately from the list of eleven Christian buildings in Schedule VI of the 1870 MS. Census.

[38] See Abner Jones, *Autobiography;* Abner Dumont Jones, *Memoir of Abner Jones*; Smith, *Life of Elias Smith*; Morrill (author of a general history of the denomination), "The Christians."

[39] This declaration, in Chapter II, Section IX of the 1777 constitution (*State Papers of Vermont*, 12:13), and Chapter II, Section XII of the 1786 constitution (ib. 14:132), was omitted from the 1793 constitution (ibid., 15:169). In eighteenth-century usage, professors were church members, then only a small minority of Vermonters, but the intent of the clause was to exclude non-Protestants.

[40] In the October session, 1778 (*State Papers of Vermont*, 3(1):33-34, 39). Allen refused to take the religious oath, was made a non-voting member, and served on committees, according to Bellesiles, *Revolutionary Outlaws*, 191.

[41] I wrote a more detailed account of Roman Catholics in Vermont to 1843 in a series of columns in the *Burlington Free Press*, 2, 9, 16, 23, 30 Apr., 7, 14, 21, 28 May, 4, 11, 18 June, 23, 30 July, 6, 13 Aug. 1978.

[42] Timothy Dwight, *Travels*, 2:285. For the Universalist societies, see Henry S. Dana, *History of Woodstock*, 398; MacDonald, *Rebellion in the Mountains*, 109; Child, *Gazetteer of Windsor County*, 150; for the "catholic" lecture series, *Vermont Chronicle* (15 Feb. 1833).

[43] Sanford and Gillies, *Records of the Council of Censors*, 318-319; Lund, "Vermont Nativism," assumes that fear of foreign influence caused the adoption of Amendment I. I did not find any such evidence in preparing "The Rise of Cornelius Peter Van Ness."

[44] Bassett, "A Letter by William Lloyd Garrison."

[45] Ludlum, "Antimasonry," *Social Ferment in Vermont*, 86-133; Walter John Coates, *Masonry, a Church Outside the Church* . See Chapter 2, 13.

[46] Fitzpatrick's diary, 4:275, for February 23, 1861, copied by David J. Blow, along with other correspondence with the bishops of Boston, from the original in the archives of the Archdiocese of Boston.

[47] O'Callaghan, *Usury* (1828), contains a "Narrative. . . of the Sufferings of the Author," mixed with argumentation, 2-34; O'Callaghan had a fourth edition printed in Burlington in 1834, and piled more pages into the fifth edition, revised and enlarged (New York, 1856; 551pp.), as the final monument to his defiance of modernity.

[48] Smith, *Diocese of Ogdensburg*, 184: "Father O'Callaghan. . . seems to have discovered and visited every Catholic family on either shore of Lake Champlain." See also 196, 320. Until Father John B. Daly arrived in 1837, O'Callaghan ranged as far south as Pittsfield, Mass.

[49] The *Membership Record* of the First Calvinistic Congregational Church, Burlington, includes eleven German, African-American, Indian, Irish, and French members, 1825-1848: #386, 462, 580, 602, 632-633, 844-847, 855. Most continued in membership less than eight years, according to the investigation of David J. Blow.

[50] See the excerpt from Hawthorne's sketch of Burlington in Bassett, *Outsiders Inside Vermont*, 63-64, from *The New England Magazine* (November 1835), and Bassett. "Irish Migration."

[51] O'Callaghan, *Usury* (New York, 1824), 116.

[52] State Archives, Petitions, filed 12 October 1835. D. Gregory Sanford,

Office of the Secretary of State, to author, December 30, 1983.

[53] O'Callaghan wrote his bishop that when a Canadian testified that he was told about the nativist plot the investigating committee stopped work. But he noted also that Protestants were liberal in subscribing for the new building.

[54] The newspaper account of the strike on the Vermont Central near Jonesville in July 1846 does not name the priest, but O'Callaghan was the nearest of the three English-speaking priests in Vermont. See Bassett, "Vermont Railroads," 134.

[55] Lucey, "Diocese of Burlington," 132, concludes, "The anti-Catholic feeling never was organized in Vermont as elsewhere."

[56] See Fig. 1.

[57] Morton, *Revival in Springfield*, 5-6.

[58] Eastman, *Sermons by Jedediah Burchard*; Streeter, *Jedediah Burchard in Woodstock*; Duffy and Muller, "An Aesculapius of the Soul"; Potash, "Burchard and the Revival of 1835." Potash found that Burchard's Addison County converts were mainly substantial citizens and the children of members, the same kind as in other revivals.

[59] Daniel Pierce Thompson to Josiah Pierce, Gorham, Maine, 17 June 1835, in Vermont Historical Society, MS-127 #53, called to my attention by Weston Cate.

[60] Elam J. Comings, Burlington, December 23, 1835, to his father, Capt. A[ndrew] Comings, East Berkshire, in the Comings Papers, Oberlin College Archives.

[61] A collection of eighty-two letters to the Rev. Edward W. Hooker of Bennington, in the Congregational Library, Boston, shows how energetically President James Marsh campaigned against Burchard. See, for example, Marsh in Rutland to Hooker, January 27, 1836, from this collection; also H. H. Cooke and G. B. Eastman to Prof. Benjamin Hale, March 24, 1836, in the Dartmouth College Archives, MS 836224.1; Ebenezer C. Tracy, editor of the *Windsor Vermont Chronicle*, to Marsh, October 18, 1835, and Marsh to President Nathan Lord of Dartmouth College, December 1835, both in Duffy, *Correspondence of James Marsh*, 173-175, 177-191. Rutland pastor William Mitchell indirectly attacked Burchard and defended the sufficiency of regular ministry in "The Utility of

Modern Evangelists." A balanced summary by John E. Goodrich appears in Burlington, Vt. First Congregational Church, *Hundredth Anniversary*, 23-25, 28-29.

[62] George Perkins Marsh, Burlington, to Charles Marsh, Woodstock, 29 Dec. 1835, in the Dartmouth College archives.

[63] C. G. Eastman, *Sermons by Jedediah Burchard*, 68.

[64] See Kellogg, *Withdrawal from the Congregational Church in Benson*. A magnifying glass on the town's history for the previous quarter century would disclose a complex of personal tensions involving temperance, politics, and theology.

[65] For Hungerford's efforts, see Chapter 6, pp. 194-95.

[66] Barron, *Those Who Stayed Behind*, 20, found Congregationalist farmers "only marginally better off" in Chelsea, according to the 1820 census and Chelsea's 1837 grand list. R. A. Roth, another sociometrist, found "few socioeconomic differences among" various rural Protestants. Perhaps the village tail wagged the rural dog: Without much difference in the country, village Whigs called the tune. Or the poor Methodist, Free Baptist, Universalist, when he got religion, became ascetic, temperate, hardworking, and elevated his farm until it was "only marginally" below the Congregationalist's.

[67] Assignments made by the Troy Conference in early June 1842 are listed in the *New York Christian Advocate and Journal*, 16 (13 July 1842): 191, with Vermont circuits in three districts: Poultney (six circuits in New York, ten in Vermont), Burlington (twenty-two in Vermont), and Plattsburgh (sixteen in New York, two in Vermont—Alburg and Grand Isle). East of the Green Mountains there had been 603 Vermont members of the New England Conference in 1799 but hardly a tenth as many two years before (James Mudge, *New England Conference*, 50, 65). Briefly (1800-04) in the New York Conference, the Vermont District was returned to the New England Conference, 1804-24. When the Troy Conference was established in 1832 to include western Vermont, the Vermont and New Hampshire Conference went somewhat unhappily by itself. "The Great Debate" for the next century, after much pulling and hauling, was settled in 1940 by putting all of Vermont in the Troy Conference (C. D. and O. D. Schwartz, *A Flame of Fire*, 145-175).

[68] "Clergymen in Vermont," in *Vermont Almanac for 1844*, 82-88. Its errors were mainly of omission, e.g. in Burlington, Richmond, and Shelburne, and of location. Two years later it listed Methodist ministers in

only 119 towns.

[69] "Roll of Baptist and Free Baptist Churches Alphabetically Arranged," in Henry Crocker, *Baptists in Vermont* (Bellows Falls: Vermont Baptist State Convention, 1912), 628-631.

[70] MacDonald, *Rebellion in the Mountains*, 58-121.

[71] Roth, *The Democratic Dilemma*, 187, concluded that by the end of "the great revival" of 1827-1843, 43% of the population in the Connecticut Valley were church members. I do not find evidence for his further assertion that "the vast majority [of these members] attended church regularly." There are practically no records of church attendance except almanac diaries, not yet exploited. A variety of reasons, such as travel away from meeting, weather affecting travel to meeting, illness (of members, their animals, or the preacher}, or dissatisfaction with the minister kept well over half of the membership absent when there was a service.

4

Structures, 1791-1840

Under the canopy of love of one's home town, state, and nation and of revival-fanned enthusiasm for salvation, common features emerge on the religious landscape of the early national period. Meetinghouses became churches with towers or steeples, their interiors shifting pulpits to the end of an oblong instead of opposite middle doors. Sermons, under revivalist influence, lost some of their studied, written formality. Choirs and congregational singing improved. A trail of family training and schooling, vocation and settling, brought pastors for shorter terms to their flocks. They believed, and taught their people to believe the Bible as the clearly revealed Word of God and chief guide for life. Government at every level aimed to support them in establishing a Christian republic. They were evangelical in wanting to persuade outsiders to their views and behaviors. It is possible to find general characteristics because membership and distinctives rested lightly upon the newly saved and there was much shifting of allegiances. This chapter provides some details to support these generalizations.

Meetinghouses and Parsonages

In 1791, pious settlers had gathered to hear itinerants in large barns, log houses, or in the open air, but in only a handful of places to hear settled ministers in meetinghouses.[1] By 1840, some 175 towns had a house of worship, "sacralizing the landscape," modern historians of religion point out. The four hundred meetinghouses, the largest human structures added to nature except for a few village mills, were distributed according to how many denominations had a foothold in some corner of the town. Perhaps forty-five towns had only one house of worship and most of these were "union" meetinghouses, occupied by two or more denominations, in proportion to contributions toward its construction or to number of taxpaying adherents.

Here was another case of an ecumenical spirit that recognized competing churches as Christian, but joined them for the convenience of having a public building over whose use they could fight (radicals excluded "per order selectmen") rather than not having any at all. They first fought over where the center would be, because the meetinghouse had been and would continue to be for a while the prime symbol of unity in the town. As several church buildings appeared in the same settlement they symbolized the pluralism that replaced community. Settlements developing before members decided where to locate the meetinghouse contested issues of access and probable growth. Donors of church lots had strong influence on decisions. Once the townspeople had located the meetinghouse, they fought over shares in its use.[2] Often the union building was erected by a private religious society organized under the Act of 1798 to sustain public worship, whose articles spelled out how the occupation of the house should be apportioned.

The first meetinghouses were scarcely to be distinguished from the large barns they superseded. The great Rockingham meetinghouse, started in 1787 and completed in 1801, the only surviving Vermont Congregational example, stands lonely on a rise off Route 103, forsaken by its bygone congregation.[3] People entered by a door on the broad side, opposite a high pulpit with its sounding board, a structure over the pulpit to direct the preacher's voice toward the congregation. Since the prime purpose of worship for the heirs of the Puritans was instruction in the Bible, the central location of the pulpit provided optimum eye contact and hearing. The dropleaf table in front of the pulpit could be opened up for communion but was otherwise out of the way because communion was infrequently celebrated among churches in the Puritan tradition. The congregation sat in box pews had benches on three sides. On hinges, they were pulled up for more standing room during the pastor's prayer, and came down with bangs as people prepared to sit. Light came from small-paned windows, shuttered against storms. Tallow candles, later whale oil lamps, lighted the rare evening meetings. Heat came from bodies, rum, footwarmers fueled with coals from home, or as in Middlebury from stoves in the vestibule. Toward the 1820s, they added more stoves with stovepipes leaking the hot air on its journey to the roof. A gallery over the entrance or on three sides held the choir opposite the pulpit, flanked by children, servants, persons without property, African Americans, Indians. If membership grew, they added porches for stairs to the galleries, to save space for more pews, and as covered vestibules to entries.

Near 1800, builders gradually shifted toward the medieval plan whose focus is on the altar, where the mystery of the Word made flesh is realized or memorialized. The worshiper entered the gable end and could walk up the nave to the chancel, containing the altar rail and the steps up to the central communion table, the holy of holies. Few went farther toward the medieval than to orient the interior lengthwise. Those who sat near the door would not have heard as well as before the change, except that even if they took away the sounding board, the gabled ceiling compensated. To accent the welcome of the entrance, the congregation added a tower with belfry, spire, and vane.

Lavius Fillmore's designs in Old Bennington (1803-1805) and Middlebury (1806-1809) are unique adaptations of an English tradition stemming from Christopher Wren via the plans published by Asher Benjamin and worked out in the new meetinghouses of lower New England from the 1790s. Lesser villages and lesser denominations, without the moneyed members, cut the decoration and imitated as much of their rivals' buildings as they could manage. The Woodstock Methodists in 1836 instructed their builder to copy the details of the Universalist chapel. Except for the cross over its four-square belfry, you could not tell whether St. Mary's in Burlington (1841) was a Catholic or Protestant Greek revival building.[4]

Bishop John Henry Hopkins, in writing an *Essay on Gothic Architecture* to help Episcopal building committees deal with common house carpenters, straddled the issue of focus. Two plates, including the plan and elevation of the chancel drawn for St. Paul's church, Burlington, show a central communion table with pulpit behind it; two show a central communion table with desk for Scripture reading on one side and the pulpit on the other. Hopkins did not make room in the chancel for the choir, hitherto in the gallery. In fact, he never mentioned sacred music in the essay, which assumed that the Gothic tradition enhanced worship. His interpretation of the Middle Ages assumed that all Christians were equal in God's sight, and shared standing room or free pews.[5]

A few designers in this period chose for unknown reasons a reverse church plan with two entrances on either side of the pulpit, as in the East Montpelier Center Methodist church, built in 1822-1823. Perhaps they hoped to discourage tardiness, because latecomers had to walk toward the facing assembly.

Belfries and their bells heralded the coming of commerce. Businessmen in commercial villages wanted to know when to meet at the tavern to talk business or take the stage or steamboat. Those who had accumulated surplus wealth in the villages subscribed for the purchase of bells to be hung in meetinghouse belfries. Ropes hanging down to the vestibules enabled strong young men to call people to worship, to town meeting, to funerals and ordinations, to ring curfews. Unitarian businessmen in the aspiring commercial port of Burlington built an edifice in 1816 with both a belfry, Revere bell, and a $750 clock. The Norwich Congregational Church, erected in 1817, had a town clock and a Revere bell. Former governor Isaac Tichenor bought a bell for Old Bennington's Congregational Church, first formally rung at the ordina-

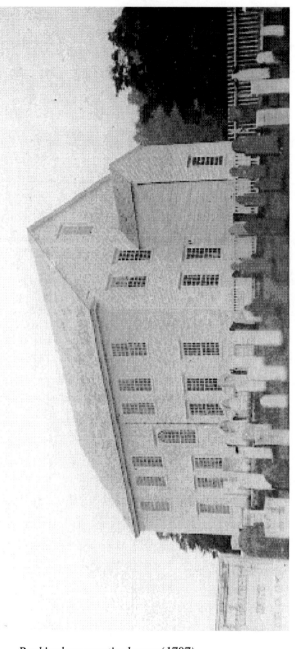

Rockingham meetinghouse (1787).

*Old Bennington facade by Lavius Fillmore (1803-05). Fillmore's
steeple survived two centuries of storms.*

tion of Absalom Peters on July 5, 1820. Middlebury, the most populous west-side town in 1820, added its bell in 1821.[6] For funerals the practice was to ring as many times as the years of the deceased. Before the days of undertakers, some towns kept a town hearse garaged in a hearse house near the meetinghouse, or in one of the sheds.[7]

Communities with no bells marked time with horns. The stage driver blew his horn as he approached the village; the sexton's horn announced the hour of worship; college boys warned with their tin horns that they were out looking for mischief.

Rectories or parsonages were not an assumed perquisite of preachers. Most first settled ministers, who received free land, had to build their own cabins on their lot or sell it and build near the meetinghouse. When Bishop John Henry Hopkins came to Burlington in 1832 only one of the thirteen Episcopalian clergy had a rectory. Whether the minister found his own lodging or accepted whatever leaky shack or tenant house the church made available, and whether it was well supplied with wood for the fireplace or stove, were matters of local bargaining. How many ministers sought dismissal because their wives could not stand the stove?

Public Worship

As the number of ministers, members, and meetinghouses increased, the character of the observances at their places of worship changed. For the many towns still without settled ministers or itinerants to lead worship, "reading meetings were stately held."[8] Isolated Catholic laity read a "dry mass" from prayer books brought to Vermont from abroad. The Sabbath still ran from Saturday sunset to Sunday sunset. For pious Christians, this ruled out Saturday night dances. Sunday was filled with two or three public services plus travel by wagon, horse, or foot to and from church. When Sabbath schools spread in the 1820s they preceded or followed worship or shared the noon hour between services with those eating their light lunches. The Sunday evening service was not regular, but occurred when a new minister was trying to whip up enthusiasm or during other revivals. In liturgy few sources document the changes in music, in the length, shape, and content of pastoral prayers, the form and content of sermons.

Since the churches of Puritan lineage (all but the Romans and Anglicans) no longer depended on prayer book or missal, each minister developed his own habits and repetitions. Baptist and Congregational worshipers continued the colonial custom of rising to honor God during the pastor's address to the Throne (his prayer), but singing seated. This practice was not reversed in Bennington until 1849.[9] Kneeling was another way to humble oneself before divine authority and rest the body by changing position during the long services. Perhaps the practice declined because it was too Roman or Anglican, or the floors were too cold and cushions too expensive.

Church Music

In colonial times New England worshipers used to sing the psalms as Isaac Watts shaped them. A strong male voice would line them out for the congregation, that is, he would sing one line for the people to repeat after him, because many could not read or remember the words and tune. As psalm books became available, as the congregations learned to read them, and as teachers encouraged singing, lining out gradually disappeared. In Vermont the conservative Presbyterians of Barnet Center did not give up the old practice until about 1845.[10]

Music came a close second to the pastor's voice as the most important element in public worship. While congregations sat for singing, the choir carried the burden of the hymns. For normal worship something between a mixed quartet and an octet sang, with more voices and an occasional stringed or wind instrument on special occasions.

Historians of sacred music report a general decline in quality of performance and creativity of composition throughout New England in the late eighteenth century. Perhaps near the new settlements the social benefits of singing together made up for lack of skills. The rise of singing schools and the publication of hymn tunes showed a renewed interest from 1791 to the War of 1812. Gradually singing masters trained a choir to sing from hymnals ornamenting the psalms or other Biblical passages, sometimes of the masters' own composition. Singing masters like Justin Morgan of Randolph even wrote anthems for their more proficient choristers. Many of these teachers, like Justin Morgan, Jr., were tenors, who would carry the tune. When choirs came to lead the singing the congregation would rise, turn their backs to the pulpit, and "face the music" (the choir in the gallery at the rear). Nearly all of this liturgical change occurred in Congregational churches.[11]

The white spirituals of the hills, presumably developing unrecorded among the Baptists and other rural groups, were absorbed into the later nineteenth century hymnals without documentation, or merged with the poetry and tunes of Charles and John Wesley, Methodist founder and his brother, brought to America in Methodist hymnbooks. Perhaps the missionaries of the Society for the Propagation of the Gospel in Foreign Parts led the chanting for isolated Episcopalians in Arlington and Alburg. Apparently no hymnbooks survive from this period. Bishop John Henry Hopkins composed and published *Sacred Songs* in 1839, one of which was "Home, Sweet Home," (not to be confused with Stephen Foster's song of the same title), but Hopkins' songs were sheet music for use in the home.[12]

The Quakers of this generation, of course, did not sing at worship. Their liturgy consisted of gathering in silence, with hats and bonnets on, seeking to hear the voice of the divine spirit, and taking off their hats while one of their number, of either sex, knelt in prayer or rose to deliver a message in that spirit. Their recorded ministers developed a sing-song chant when they spoke in meeting. Their benediction was a friendly handshake to signify that their worship together was over until midweek morning, for those near enough the meetinghouse to break off work and pray together.

Camp Meetings

While most people worshiped indoors most of the time, in warm weather, by special appointment, camp meetings were drawing crowds out to the pasture or grove. You could get away from troubles at home; you could hear several ministers for the price of one; you would meet co-religionists from other places; you might even get religion and change your life. And camp meetings were more respectable than tavern-haunting. By 1840, the Methodists in particular had made a virtue and an institution out of the original necessity of not having anywhere else to gather sinners except the outdoors. "Come to the church in the wild woods" in those days meant "Come to a place where the woods give shade, next to a pasture for the horses, where the owner will let you cut firewood and poles for your tent."

The plan of the camp meeting site came to include both individual and "society tents" big enough to hold the delegation from one church. Here, those familiar with each other would open and close the day with prayer. Tents formed a crescent around the "holy ground" or assembly area. The plank seats, if the terrain allowed, faced away from the sun and toward the preachers' stand, raised several feet above the ground. A slanting roof protected the preachers from the sun and also helped project their shouts over the hundreds in the crowd.

If the meeting lasted over two weekends, attenders brought a lot of food. The local arrangements committee regulated the local merchants' provision stalls, cook shops, or refreshment stands, and enlisted those who knew the local rowdies and how to defuse them before they exploded into dangerous damage.[13] The picnic and circus qualities of camp meetings attracted people who wanted to hear good oratory, see friends, and make acquaintances, including, hopefully, those of the opposite sex.

Legal protection, proof of popularity, came in an 1827 law regulating behavior near camp meetings. It prohibited liquor sales, shows, games, horse races, and gambling within two miles of a camp meeting while it was in progress and the sale of *any* "victuals, drink or merchandize within half a mile"—established merchants and innkeepers excepted. Methodist Orange Scott, presiding elder in Springfield, Massachusetts, published a camp meeting hymnbook that had at least five editions between 1831 and 1836. The editor of the Methodist *Christian Advocate and Journal* wrote in 1842 that "these gatherings and protracted meetings in the woods" made a more vivid impression than meetings held in the available meetinghouse space. In his forty years' experience there was no reason to fear "disorders," claimed by non-revivalistic groups from Catholics to Universalists. However, Eli Ballou, Montpelier Universalist editor, opposed "such demoralizing meetings" with their "nocturnal scenes of evil," but admitted that they won converts.[14]

In spite of these variations in outdoor or indoor worship, the common elements were more important than the differences. The Bible was central, whether in exegesis, exhortation, song, or prayer. People sang what they were familiar with, from whichever tradition the hymn came from. They had common wants, which they and their ministers prayed for. They all rejoiced in what God had done for them, in death's release from pain, the return of the native, the escape from famine, flood, and fire, and the help of neighbors when catastrophe did strike.

Even when the Catholic missal and the Episcopal Book of Common Prayer prescribed the order of worship, poverty limited the decoration of the service.[15] The Episcopalians tended to be low-church and Bible-oriented rather than high-church and medieval-oriented. Benjamin B. Smith, Episcopal rector of St. Stephen's, Middlebury, and editor of the *Episcopal Register*, wrote a long series in that organ defending prayer meetings and revivals as common to all orthodox Christians.[16] Friends studied the Bible less and less directly, but learned it secondhand from their earlier writers. Except for the Anglican manual for all sorts of worship, and later Presbyterian and Methodist forms, the lack of any means to imagine Protestant public worship, presumably the central activity of the pious, frustrates the historian of religion before the day of printed orders of service.

Clergy

Protestants continued to consider their preacher essential to the prosperity of their church. They hired him for his sermon. Before the War of 1812, Congregational and Presbyterian ministers wrote out their sermons and read them to the congregation. The form was architectural: biblical text; proposition derived from the text, and a series of proofs, frequently citing the Word of God, i.e., the Bible, from "firstly" to "finally," substantiating the proposition. As the eighteenth-century Age of

Reason left its mark on ministers' minds, they used rational proofs or referred to God as revealed in nature. When called to supply neighboring churches they might pull out an old stand-by and note on the copy when and where it was used again. Perhaps only the nipping cold in the barnlike meetinghouse kept the congregation awake. While it was not a legitimate cause for dismissal, the aging parson's old-fashioned sermon, "strictly Calvinistic. . . methodical. . . slow and deliberate, almost to a fault,"[17] set a restless congregation to looking for a younger, livelier man. "It is said of Rev. Mr. Blood, that in preaching he was very dull for the first two hours, but eloquent and powerful for the third hour."[18] Thomas Rowley of Shoreham poked at the parsons with the quatrain: "By our pastor perplext / How shall we determine? / "Watch and pray," says the text; / "Go to sleep," says the sermon.[19]

With increasing competition from itinerants or exhorters who held their audiences' attention better with extempore rhetoric, the orthodox began to abandon their formal writings and get along with notes.[20] Their long, impromptu prayers prepared them to reduce reliance on the written word.

"For whatever doctrine might be," wrote Daniel Pierce Thompson of early Montpelier, "it was preaching, and that seemed to have sufficed with a people too seldom served to be very particular."[21] It sufficed, provided that it did not cost his congregation much. Baptists and Methodists and their spin-offs survived on very small freewill offerings. Quakers depended on hospitality when they traveled in the ministry and were not paid to preach at home. One Ira Allen (not Ethan's brother) thought paying the preacher "pernicious," the root of all religious tyranny.[22]

Because estimates of attendance were so few and the few so inaccurate, we cannot tell whether sermons reached more ears than the talk in the tavern taproom, teaching in common schools, or whether newspapers, available in the same taprooms, reached more eyes. Religious observance, however, whether appointed by itinerants or in the regular worship of churches, continued to be a major educator of the population, outside the home.

People have assumed that the prestige of preachers declined from colonial times. Evidence cited is in the career choices of college and academy students and other youths: increasingly for business, law, newspaper work, teaching instead of the traditional divinity. But these choices were consequences of the rewards and punishments of preaching. Did the congregation flock to hear him, call him "Father," pay him deference, and contribute from their stores at donation parties, keep him until he died—in a word, love him? Or did they pay him little attention and less salary? If he kept calling his people to lay up their treasures in heaven, was he satisfied to have his own treasure there? Or did his people recognize that his labor was worth his hire?

Yes, deference to the office of pastor did decline, but for their services of consolation and counsel, for instruction and marking the rites of passage at birth, marriage, and death, people valued their ministers as helpful equals. Opportunities expanded with the growth in churches and academies, the widening missionary fields at home and abroad, the staffing of benevolent agencies promoting the Bible, Sunday schools, seamen's rests and temperance, and distributing tracts for all these good things.

The paradox of lowered esteem for ministers and needing more of them characterized the second quarter of the nineteenth century. A visiting English Baptist reported, "Such is the want of ministers, that every one of good character and talent, from any shore, is eagerly sought and immediately employed." He was referring to David A. Jones, who came from England in the summer of 1835 with twelve years' experience, and received a call from the Danville Congregational church "within a fortnight of his arrival." James Buckham, a Scot who had preached fourteen years in England, was able in 1834 to win a Congregational pastorate in equally substantial Chelsea on the recommendation of President John Wheeler of the University of Vermont, after only a few months in the United States. Unitarians in the villages of Burlington, Brattleboro, and Montpelier were exceptional. They never seemed to have trouble hiring a Harvard man.[23]

To address the perennial minister shortage and not lower the standards of a trained ministry, the Northwestern Education Society, founded soon after the War of 1812, provided tuition scholarships and maintenance for Congregational theological students. These grants had no requirements that the scholar return to the region that sent him.

Beliefs

Aside from worship we have other windows through which we can see people's thoughts and attitudes. The founding missionary or pastor spelled out for each new church the confession or articles of faith, copying a good deal from the manual he had brought from his home church, in his head or pack, and the men and women who became the first members signed them. Most articles were boiled down and simplified versions of the Standing Order of the colonial Saybrook (Connecticut, 1708) or Cambridge (Massachusetts, 1648) "platforms" upon which the Puritans "stood." They varied according to where and with whom the local minister had read theology.

Few articles were as simple as those of the Plainfield Congregational Church, organized November 13, 1799, with six members. Six months later the church voted that because "some members are dissatis-

fied with the articles of faith. . . [they] have liberty to select such articles as they are satisfied with, which shall be considered the church articles of faith," but the others can believe "them as they are now."[24]
Nicholas Snethen, Methodist rider on the Barre circuit, soon detached
half the congregation and formed a class. Not only were the Plainfield
Congregationalists soft on the articles; they put up with a pastor,
Jonathan Kinney, for more than a decade, who was licensed but never
ordained because he did not believe in infant baptism. In 1805 the modest presiding elder of the Methodist Vermont District expressed similar
latitude: "We oblige no private members to believe in every point as we
do, in order to become a member of our community." He went on to
say that if probationers show evidence "of their acceptance of God,"
Methodists accept them as Christians even if they are Calvinistic.
Their preachers, of course, had to agree to the "leading doctrines" of the
Methodists.[25]

The almost complete absence of transfer certificates for the founding
members of a congregation may merely show that the church clerk had
no desk with pigeon holes and discarded them after their purpose was
accomplished, to introduce a church member in a new place. On the
other hand, not to depend on them may well have been a matter of principle rather than lack of archival discipline. Like their predecessors on
the *Mayflower*, they were starting a church of Christ anew. As the
Vermont Chronicle put it, Congregational churches were organized "as
they would have done in a heathen land, or had there existed no visible
church on earth."[26] Their qualifications were not that they had belonged
to a down-country church, as many of them had, but that they subscribed to the articles of faith of the new church and the by-laws of the
new society, the latter dealing with procedures and resources.

Churches differed in their processes for accepting as members those
who had been attending worship. How much reliance would the church
put on a candidate's "relation," a statement of religious experience by
the person propounded, that is, proposed for membership? This statement might be written, declared in private to the minister and deacons,
or pronounced before the congregation. Did the church accept a
"half-way covenant," that is, could the adult children of members participate in some church decisions without evidence of their hopeful conversion? No conversion could be more than "hopeful" because God only
knows whether one is saved.

Diaries and letters, especially at times of conversion, illness, and
death in the family, help us understand each individual's unique complex
of beliefs and how those expressions related to their behavior. Sylvia
Drake, Weybridge seamstress, enjoyed her feelings of guilt and confided
to her diary from 1821 through 1823 her pride in her self-abasement, re-
iterating how sinful she was, barely worthy of salvation. "Rude I am,

in speech and manners," she wrote, yet actually she was literate, capable of rhyme, and at ease in the society of the respectable Congregational church members with entree to Middlebury College functions. She was comfortable to be always busy sewing and housekeeping, or doctoring her mild dyspepsia. Her fondness for her partner, the older seamstress Charity Bryant, instead of for God alone, she probably thought of as a sin; likewise her "neglect" of her mother and siblings. And like all those who turned "serious," she was proud of having given up the "vain and foolish perversities" of youth.[27]

Most Christians Vaguely Trinitarian

Nearly everyone still believed abstractly, but perhaps less intensely and not very specifically, in the apostles' creed. It centered on God the Creator, Jesus Christ the divine incarnation, and the Holy Spirit, the Counselor Jesus spoke of at the Last Supper (John 14, especially verses 12, 16-17, 26). If people paid attention to what the "holy catholic church," "the communion of saints," or "the resurrection of the body" meant, it would be worth pausing to analyze their various interpretations. Some earnest souls spent much time searching their Bibles, arguing the fine points, and concluding an infinite variety of meanings. It is enough here to look at what people did pay attention to and act on, and how they treated those who disagreed with them.

One result of the acceptance of whatever preachers were available and the similarity of conversion experiences was the pilgrimage of seekers through several denominational connections. Many Vermonters like Orestes Brownson, who became a leading Roman Catholic editor, Mormon Joseph Smith's family, and William Miller, Adventist founder, passed through a series of religious connections with slightly different accents before finding their spiritual homes. Less well-known was Jason F. Walker (1819-1880), principal of Troy Conference Academy, Poultney. Assigned to Pawlet, he left Methodism and organized an "Independent Religious Congregation" there, went West and became a Unitarian minister, then was reordained an Episcopalian.[28] Leaders like these represented hundreds of followers who also migrated from church to church and became generic Bible-based, revival-converted Protestants. Their experience, their exposure to different preachers, their intermarriage and daily life with Christians labeled differently, disposed more and more to agree with Henry Miles that "Divine Truth cannot be confined within the narrow limits of a sect."[29] A good many Protestants still assumed, however, that members of their sect would be saved and the rest damned. Damning Catholics to hell, and vice versa, lasted a good deal longer.

God the Creator; Atheists; God of Nature and History

Their disbelief in hell excluded atheists from testifying in court. An atheist cannot be trusted as a witness in court, declared the editor of the *Vermont Chronicle* in 1833, because he does not fear eternal damnation if he lies. The penalty for blasphemers, who "shall publicly deny the being and existence of God, or the Supreme Being, or shall contumeliously reproach his providence and government," was up to two hundred dollars, close to a year's earnings, but not to my knowledge prosecuted.[30] Roswell M. Field of Newfane introduced in the 1835 General Assembly a resolution permitting the testimony of atheists, which the House defeated. In 1845, Eli Ballou, editor of the *Montpelier Universalist Watchman*, supported the bill repealing the "antiquated superstition." If an atheist witness perjures himself he may testify, but if he is honest, he is declared unreliable, wrote Ballou. "We regard it as wrong for Christians to take an oath," he concluded, reflecting the testimony of his Quaker parents. The repeal bill passed the House but lost in the Senate. Finally in 1851 the legislature spoke: "No person shall be deemed incompetent as a witness in any court. . . on account of his opinions on matters of religious belief."[31] This repeal opened the door to those who were unwilling to declare their belief in a supreme being. Nevertheless, the same two-hundred-dollar fine hitherto in effect for publicly denying the existence of the supreme being remained a dead letter until the 1981 revision of the statutes.[32]

Most of the time people behaved like deists, as if God had merely created the world, which thereafter operated by natural laws. Yet most people believed that God could intervene in human affairs and even in nature. When bad things happened, they felt and wrote that God was punishing them for their disobedience. Abraham Lincoln a generation later could still appeal in his second inaugural to Vermonters' and other Americans' long-held belief in divine punishment for sin. The Civil War was somehow the fruit of God's wrath because the whole country had allowed slavery. In the realm of nature, if heavy snow caved in a roof, people searched their souls to discover what evils they had done to deserve this punishment. "Acts of God," the more violent aspects of nature such as floods, hurricanes, tornados, and forest fires, were not understood by the embryonic and mainly amateur natural scientists. Science consisted of observation, description, and pigeon-holing (the technical term is taxonomy). The philosophical framework was Newtonian mechanism, and although Newton was a devout Christian, his scientific assumptions were not based on Christian theology.

Jesus Christ, Savior

For a majority of Christians, Jesus was the second person in the Trinity, the incarnate Christ, the Word of John's Greek gospel made flesh, who redeemed humanity by his sacrifice on the cross, for sinful humans could not save themselves. Pious Roman Catholics, emphasizing their belief that Jesus was born of the Virgin Mary, had long prayed for Our Lady's intercession in every trouble, before Pope Pius IX declared her immaculate conception a dogma in 1854. To Protestants, this was a form of idolatry, Mariolatry.

Since for the heirs of Calvin, there was no certainty of election, one had better do good works as Jesus had commanded. Christians could only watch and pray, and one mysterious day they would wake up to glory and know they had been saved. People expected to give hospitality to strangers and receive it, although fare might be poor and beds infested. They sat up all night with the dying, helplessly and lovingly, assuring them of their place in heaven and in their hearts. They went to church, took communion if members, or if not members, when invited in open-communion churches. They brought produce for the preacher when they could and remembered to, gave orders to wife and family, fed the hungry. And having fed the least of the brethren, etc. (Matt. 25:35-45), Christ, interceding with the Father, would reward them openly and in heaven. Still, works were not a ransom necessary for salvation, and Calvinistic uncertainties did not satisfy some, who sought blessed assurance with the "Arminian"[33] Methodists and other dissenters from doctrines of predestination.

The Calvinist view fitted the European situation, where in this world many were called but few were chosen, better than it did the open society of the English New World. With the windfalls of forest, fish, and game, it was hard for the settler to conceive of reverse Russian roulette, where all but one chamber was loaded against you. Common sense said that every one could win; all would have prizes.

As the eighteenth century wore on, the mood of confidence and comfort replaced anxiety for work and daily bread. Survival in this world and the next became, instead of a long-odds lottery, a come-all-ye chorus. Justification by faith and election, reflecting those few who did well in this world, faded in the minds of many, and an "Antinomian" view widely replaced it. Essentially that meant that legalism, the law of Moses, the law as Paul wrote of it in his New Testament epistles, law as a set of rigidities binding humanity, gave way in the free atmosphere of the New World to free grace, undeserved. Members trying to live a Christian life would fail, confess, and be forgiven. Yet saved-by-grace was a belief putting renewed emphasis on behavior, especially in giving up liquor and frolics. What came to be called "puritanical" was really

the behavior of Christians saved in revivals. Strangely, the view of the
Savior as stern judge, consigning to outer darkness or glory, softnened
into a soft Christ of love as portrayed by Murillo, while reformers were
stiffening into judges and prohibitionists.

The Holy Spirit

Behavior could be guided by the law, what it says you should do to
be saved, or by the Holy Spirit, what it inspires you to do. The third
person of the orthodox Trinity had always been important since Pentecost demonstrated what Jesus taught. The heirs of the Puritans put
much emphasis on the Holy Spirit in their revivals, but they had different ways of discerning God's spirit from other spirits.[34] The clergy of
every denomination were ordained when an authorized body confirmed
that God's Holy Spirit had called them to proclaim the Gospel. Pious
members as well as preachers prayed to know what God wanted them to
do in their daily work. They consulted dreams and visions; some opened
their Bibles at random to learn what Word to obey.[35]

In the nineteenth century a growing number believed in some form
of second blessing or sanctification by the Holy Spirit. The tradition of
John Wesley's brand of perfectionism was available to the fast-growing
Methodists. They won thousands by preaching the glory of the blessed
assurance of salvation and sanctification through Christ's atoning sacrifice, based on conviction of sin. John Humphrey Noyes, a former
Congregationalist, issued "perfectionist" publications from Putney for a
decade after 1838.[36] Quakers had always asserted that anyone, properly
prepared and attuned, could minister by the aid of the Holy Spirit and
could know, tell, and do the will of God at a particular moment. They
qualified their "infallibility" as the other heirs of the Puritans did, by requiring group corroboration and steady diligence and watchfulness.
Even then, they recognized the possibility of falling away.[37]

Joseph Hoag, Quaker minister, had a vision which he recalled near
his death in 1846 as coming to him while working in a Monkton field
in 1803. The Holy Spirit warned him that unless Americans abandoned
slavery and the evil ways of Europe and returned to faith in God, they
would suffer many schisms. It won attention during the Civil War because it seemed to predict that war. But his fear was not unique; many
during the sectional conflict threatened that the course of their political
enemies was leading straight to sectional violence. Hoag, an habitual
Old Testament reader, wrote in the mode of the eighteenth-century
jeremiad (the people have erred and strayed and incurred God's wrath).[38]
The vision was probably an insight about the nature of schism, possibly triggered by the excommunication of the Hudson, New York, liberal Quaker Hannah Barnard in 1802 (foreshadowing the Quaker separa-

tion of 1827), and recalled during the painful schism of New England Friends in 1845. It is more remarkable as a vision of the centralization following the Civil War, sustained by the triumphant Republican Party.

Several short-lived groups surfaced in this period, following a charismatic leader and receiving direct inspiration from God and the angels and spirits. Several young women, chiefly near the Maine-New Hampshire border, went into trances during Free Baptist revivals and, coming to their senses, caused great excitement about their claim to have spoken with angels. These precursors of the spiritualists converted many in the decade after 1809.[39]

Some people believed in angels and others in devils. John S. Pettibone recounts a story told him by an eyewitness, probably from the 1790s, that a "demon vampire" was sucking the blood of Captain and Deacon Isaac Burton's second wife Hulda. They exhumed "the liver, heart, and lungs, what remained of them," of his first wife, three years dead, and burned them at the blacksmith's forge before a crowd of hundreds, in the belief that this exorcism would cure Hulda's consumption.[40]

Similar in their reliance on inspiration were the communitarian-vegetarian Dorrilites across Vermont's southern border in Leyden, Massachusetts, in the 1790s,[41] and the followers of Isaac Bullard of Ascot, near Sherbrooke, Lower Canada. Seemingly driven out by the hardships of settlement in the Eastern Townships of Quebec and the cold summer of 1816, these "Puritans" followed Bullard southward, surfacing in Hartford, Woodstock, and Sherburne, eventually floating down the Ohio River and breaking up at New Madrid, Missouri. What little property they had, they had in common. Spectators fixed on their filth, common to tramps and the homeless.[42]

The Church of Jesus Christ of Latter Day Saints, based on the visions of native Vermonter Joseph Smith at Palmyra, New York, drew its Vermont converts westward like the earlier communitarians, but unlike them organized into a durable church. Almost immediately after the publication of the Book of Mormon in 1830, the Mormons sent missionaries back to Vermont. Jared Carter, whose brother John led a Free Will Baptist church in Benson, was converted in western New York, came back to his brother's church in October 1831, and converted it en masse to Mormonism. Orson Pratt held a Mormon conference at Benson in August 1832, sent missionaries through Vermont, and gathered a slim harvest. The considerable literature on Mormon origins explains why Joseph Smith could attract poor, marginalized people hoping for magic to liberate them into the state of Adam before he fell, with dashes of quasi-Masonic ritual and Bible communitarianism. The Methodist itinerant Tobias Spicer attended a Mormon meeting in order to "try all spirits, whether they be of God" (1 John 4:1). He called their claims to heal the sick and raise the dead ridiculous, but admitted, "they made some converts, from among a certain class." Orson Pratt healed an elderly Methodist woman, but only temporarily. The Mormons closed the Benson church, and led the converts to Kirtland, Ohio, where Mormons were swarming. Heber Chase Kimball of Sheldon, ordained one of the Mormons' twelve apostles in 1835, converted elsewhere and came back as a missionary to New England the next year.[43]

Evidence about changes in Mormon attitudes toward African-Americans may be buried in the Benson story. Charles Bowles, black Free Will Baptist revivalist, spoke at the dedication of their stone chapel. The census shows ten or more blacks in Benson in this period. If any of them were Free Baptists and went west with the Mormons, their experiences in Missouri and Illinois may have been pertinent to the development of Mormon racism.[44]

The family of Oliver Cowdrey, native of Wells, moved to Palmyra, New York, like Joseph Smith's family. Oliver, involved with Smith's money-digging, became his disciple and scribe recording of the Book of Mormon. Cowdrey's father harbored a counterfeiter, a fugitive from Orange County justice named Winchell, a. k. a. Wingate, who began using the witch hazel or "St. John's rod" to locate buried treasure. Many believed he used the rod as a cover-up for another counterfeiting scheme. He connected with the Woods in Middletown, whose patriarch, Nathaniel, had been excluded from the Congregational church and was preaching to his large family the supernatural judgments of God in the form of earthquakes destroying "the gentiles." The connection with the Mormons is circumstantial, but it shows the backwoods context of belief in spirits which would lead to treasure, health, finding lost valuables and children, and foreknowledge. What still needs study is why the conditions that produced Joseph Smith did not produce many followers in Vermont. Were there too many alternate paths from the same backwoods base?[45]

One cannot begin to catalog all the people drawn hither and yon by will-o'-the-wisps. The Hardwick "New Lights," however, deserve attention as the most noticeable of lower-class, counter-culture groups that would multiply in the twentieth century as Holiness churches. They grew out of two score years of feeble pluralism on a poverty-laden frontier. Amos Tuttle (1761-1833), Litchfield, Connecticut, Baptist, first settled minister, 1795-1799, town clerk, 1799-1801, and town minister invited by the Congregationalists, 1803-1806, left Hardwick when called by Fairfax Baptists.

Pioneer Hardwick took on the flavor of the maverick Methodist Lorenzo Dow from a remarkable series of connections between the Dows and Bridgmans of Coventry, Connecticut. Capt. John C. Bridgman made the first settlement in South Hardwick (near the present village) in 1797, according to his son. He married Lorenzo Dow's eldest sister Ethelinda while her sister Orrilana married a Fisk of Hardwick. Lorenzo visited two of his sisters in the fall of 1802. On his 1799 visit to northern Vermont and the Eastern Townships along the Canadian border, he called "the people in this part of the world. . . the offscourinq of the earth," debtors or criminals, out to make money.[46]

Hardwick had the usual disagreement over where to locate the meetinghouse. Samuel French, who married Lorenzo Dow's younger sister Tabitha, went ahead on his own in 1820 and built the south meetinghouse near his South Hardwick settlement. He would not sell the building to the Congregationalists, who built on a hill nearer the Center. He wrote "Liberty of Conscience" on the front of his meetinghouse and let all comers use it, including the Methodists and Free Will Baptists who had each won a few followers in town. When the Congregationalists divided (their second church lasting from 1825 to 1843, with pastors a third of the time), this great diversity left the people open to any new winds of doctrine.

The only surviving record of a witness to the excitement of 1837 is the hostile Rev. Chester Wright. This sixty-year-old Middlebury College graduate opposed Masonry, so Montpelier Masons in his church dismissed him in spite of his twenty-two-year service. In 1836, after more than five years without a charge, he began preaching in Hardwick.

Wright declared that since the winter of 1837 the devil had been at work in the south meetinghouse. "Tumultuous noises" silenced some ministers invited to preach there, and elsewhere they broke up services with heckling. A group of a dozen or more, who had not shaved for months, started their meetings sitting in silence. Then someone would scream a Bible text; more silence, and then more Bible, a few words at a time, vituperating regular ministers and vilifying the hypocrisy of regular churches. For over a year "the droll meeting" attracted crowds to "the Hardwick Theater" as the south meetinghouse came to be called, where they could see "jumping, swinging the arms, rolling on the floor, . . barking [like] dogs, foxes, cuckoos, &c."

One woman baptized her son as Jesus Christ, saying she was the Virgin Mary. For many years this group had believed that the gospel dispensation nullified the fourth commandment to keep the Sabbath and turned it into a holiday. John Humphrey Noyes's *New Haven Perfectionist* circulated among them, an indication that they were open to his as well as other forms of holiness doctrine. They claimed "extraordinary sanctity" "by the spirit of Christ," which enabled them to foretell the future. Some from the Second Congregational Church and other churches attended, approved, and occasionally exhorted, Wright claimed.

He called this witchcraft, or worse, insanity. When he preached his denunciation, they tried to interrupt him, but he had a magistrate ready who arrested one man for disturbing worship. Whereas these proto-Pentecostals put the authority of the Holy Spirit over Scripture, Wright along with most mainstream Protestants believed the opposite. Joseph Torrey, a successor of Wright in the Hardwick pulpit, 1860-1875, repeated Wright's story, adding, to further discredit the movement, that one leader hanged himself after the excitement died down. These charismatics disappeared from the record, either because of dispersal in the hard times of 1838-43, or because Wright persuaded the "pious" among them not to countenance such ranting.[47]

The Hardwick experience was a theme with variations. Thomas Davidson, an adventist revivalist who, like the Shakers, preached that Christ would return as a woman, stirred northwestern Vermont for a year, 1829-1830. Vigilantes, accusing him of instigating murder and suicide, escorted him forcefully into Canada.[48] John Truair (1780-1845), a charismatic Congregational revivalist and planter of churches in Lamoille and Franklin counties, 1809-1813, returned twenty years later after being excommunicated by both New York Presbyterians and Massachusetts Congregationalists. His teaching seemed to fit the Christian Connection in calling all Christians to belong to one Union church, "free to all" whose faith was based on the Bible. But he combined ecumenism with perfectionism and more millennial enthusiasm than the founders of the Christian Connection a generation earlier could stomach.[49] In church after church throughout Vermont, tenure was precarious for ministers not in line with the new revivalism, such as Chester Wright, Thomas Davidson, and John Truair.[50]

Church Polity

Charismatics, who obey the Holy Spirit as they experience it, cannot conform to the rigidities of church government, least of all to a superstructure beyond the local congregation. In early Vermont, however, all denominations were congregational. To adapt an old Spanish-American saying, God was in the sky and the bishop was far away; therefore locals kept control, even in churches with bishops, whether Roman, Anglican, or Methodist.

A Roman Catholic example of local independence is the eccentric missionary priest, Jeremiah O'Callaghan, appointed by Bishop Benedict J. Fenwick of Boston in 1830. Fenwick told him to build St. Mary's on the hill in Burlington, to serve the Catholics at Winooski Falls as well as the downtown Irish, and although he protested, he built it as directed. But within a month after it burned in 1838, O'Callaghan started rebuilding where he had always wanted to, in the village center, competitively across the street from the Episcopalians. O'Callaghan sent his bishop a detailed report June 6, enclosing the deed for the downtown lot, with the comment that "some Episcopals and Calvinists . . . would rather" the Catholics were "*out of sight* in the suburbs." Although almost the entire hierarchy had abandoned the medieval view that taking interest is sinful, O'Callaghan consistently refused the sacraments to usurers.[51]

The Episcopal bishop of the Eastern Diocese (all of New England except Connecticut) let the small, isolated parishes on the Vermont frontier run themselves. From 1832, when they elected John Henry Hopkins to preside over the new diocese of Vermont, they continued to follow their own directions while Bishop Hopkins followed his. Hopkins wanted a theological seminary but his parishes did not support him enough to maintain it. He was not entirely powerless, however. While usually letting his clergy and vestries run their own parishes, he was able soon after he arrived to get rid of evangelical rector William S. Perkins of St. James, Arlington, for violating the canons. Perkins had delivered the election sermon at the opening of the 1831 legislature and led one of the oldest and strongest parishes in the diocese.

The only episcopal church whose bishop had substantial power was the Methodist Episcopal. Constitutionally, the bishop's power had been delegated by the General Conference, a quadrennial gathering of all the ordained circuit riders.[52] The bishop appointed the presiding elders of districts and delegated to them the supervision of the circuit preachers and stewards, who, with other circuit preachers, left much to be done by local leaders. Asbury's conference assignments to circuits, his successful insistence that his circuit riders have neither cabin nor wife, as Jesus commanded when he commissioned the twelve apostles (Matt. 10:10, Mark 6:8, Luke 9:3), testify to his power. He wrote from Peru, New York, to a lieutenant, "An arm of just and decisive authority in our General Conference and the same in the superintendency will be necessary. Other denominations have it not, they are local, they are all bishops."[53]

He did not always have his way. Elijah Hedding, who was converted in Starksboro and first served on Vermont circuits, married in 1810, stopped traveling, and was stationed in Boston. Married clergy and stations, that is, pastorates in towns instead of circuits, multiplied after Asbury's death in 1816. Succeeding bishops on the west side of the state, in the New York Conference to 1832 and thereafter the Troy Conference, operated out of the Albany area, and delegated much authority to the presiding elders of the Vermont districts. The same was true of the east side, originally in the New England Conference, 1800-1830, then the New Hampshire Conference to 1844. Some Methodists who thought that their bishops had too much power broke away to start Reformed or Protestant Methodist churches, which had a few congregations in Vermont.[54]

The elements of a representative or federal system were in place and available for congregational bodies to use. Although all denominations in the Puritan tradition were congregational in gospel order, all had ways through regional gatherings to overcome their isolation, adjust differences, compare notes, help settle church quarrels that locals could not handle, and ordain those recommended for the ministry by single congregations. The crucial question was how much power these associations or quarterly meetings had.

Abner Reeve of West Brattleboro led in organizing the Windham Association of Congregational ministers in 1776, and other Congregationalist associations of roughly county size followed from 1788. These groups provided a sort of in-service training for young ministers and consultation on the problems of their parishes. At ordinations, the ceremony when a young man was accepted in his first parish, installations of ordained ministers in new parishes, or dismissals, the host church convened councils to advise them. Reasons for dismissal, on the minister's part, were that the church was not supporting him as well as it had agreed to, or he had a better job offer elsewhere, that is, he was called to a wider sphere of usefulness.

When the University of Vermont invited John Wheeler of Windsor's South Church to be its president in 1824 he did not want to go and accepted the advice of council to stay in Windsor. But after he had been there twelve years and the university called again, the council could find no reason to divorce Wheeler from the Windsor church, but recommended his leaving for greater service at the university. The church argued that fights would break out when he left, and they did. More and more as the century advanced, ministers were becoming professionals climbing a ladder of better pay, prestige, and power, instead of officers of a church, like Asa Burton of Thetford, who stayed with his church in spite of conflicts and alienation of parishioners.

After the Congregationalists, other denominations developed regional gatherings. The regular Baptists had associations from 1780 but fiercely guarded their local autonomy. The Universalists followed with a Northern Association, covering all of Vermont, in 1804, later subdivided. Methodists with circuits and districts and Free Will Baptists and Quakers with quarterly meetings, wielding considerable power, were like the Congregationalists in having regular regional meetings, chiefly of ministers. While the Methodist districts did have power over the circuits, the others, in the congregational stream, although they heard appeals, usually confirmed the decisions of the local churches and were labelled advisory.

On the next level, the few Episcopalians met in annual state convention from 1790, and chose their own delegates to their national General Convention. The Congregational churches created their annual state convention in 1795. Only ministers attended, two representing each association, until 1822, when laymen were allowed. In 1823, when the Baptists drafted a constitution for a state convention, influential leaders like Aaron Leland of Chester opposed this trend away from local control, but accepted the state body. The first General Conference of Free Will Baptists at Tunbridge in the fall of 1827, with delegates mainly from northern New England, accepted the Vermont Yearly Meeting organized the previous February.[55] Universalists followed in 1833 and the Christian Connection in 1836.

Statewide organizations wanted a statewide publication to speak to their members, just as they kept trying to establish statewide academies to train their members and ministers. The General Convention of Congregational Ministers launched the *Adviser; or, Vermont Evangelical Magazine*, a monthly that was more magazine than newspaper, in January, 1809, and sustained it for seven years. After the postwar depression, Walter Chapin of Woodstock published the *Evangelical Monitor* fortnightly for two years, 1821-1823. The General Convention tried again in 1826 and kept the weekly *Vermont Chronicle* going until 1898, mainly in Windsor from 1828. Its survival, like that of the rest of the Vermont religious press, originally depended on editors whose salaries came from their congregations and on subscriptions from the core groups in each church. After the Civil War, when Lyman J. McIndoe bought it, it depended primarily on being a department of his general weekly.

A series of vigorous pastors willing to work double overtime started and sustained a Universalist periodical with various titles in Woodstock, 1820-1834. As the Montpelier *Christian Repository and Universalist Watchman* (1834-1870), under the editorship of Eli Ballou from 1840, it maintained a circulation of over two thousand.[56]

Episcopalian growth sustained the monthly *Episcopal Register* in Middlebury for four years from 1826. The Episcopalians were the first denomination in Vermont to give up their state journal and depend on a national organ. The Christian Connection depended on out-of-state papers except for a few months of 1827 when Abner Jones helped Elder Jasper Hazen publish the *Gospel Banner* in Woodstock. The Roman Catholics circulated the Boston *Pilot*; the Adventists, Joshua V. Himes' Boston *Signs of the Times*, and others.

The Methodists, with the weight of the Troy Conference south of Vermont looking toward Albany, and the little Vermont Conference looking toward Boston, found their national metropolitan press serving their needs adequately until after the Vermont Conference separated from New Hampshire in 1844. The *Montpelier Christian Messenger*, started in 1846, spoke for the Vermont Conference, east of the Green Mountains.

The Vermont State Baptist Convention started the *Brandon Vermont Telegraph* in 1828, bought by twenty-eight-year-old Orson S. Murray in 1834 and continued for ten years under his increasingly radical editorship. In the early 1840s when the Baptists excommunicated him and withdrew their patronage from the *Telegraph*, they tried to publish their own short-lived *Vermont Baptist Journal*. They did not try again until 1879, when the Rev. J. K. Richardson of Rutland started the *Vermont Baptist.*

The rise of Orson Murray illuminates many Vermont religious developments in the period of revival and reform: upward mobility via the ministry; the fluidity between Baptists and Free Baptists, indeed among most active Protestants, without reference to theology in revival situations; the close connection between revival and reform. Many reformers were able to compromise and moderate their goals. Others like Murray went on to connect one cause with another until they felt the absolute necessity of fundamental change in the whole of society.

Murray was born in Orwell in 1806, the eldest of eleven children of poor, pious Connecticut immigrants, converts from Congregationalism to the Free Will Baptists. Orson worked on the farm, but showed a bent for letters and soon was teaching district school. Baptized, backslid, and reconverted, he felt a call to the ministry and although already saddled with a wife and children, worked his way through Shoreham and Castleton academies by 1832.

Many Christians, once revived, soon saw that the world needed reformation. Murray became a teetotaler, he said, when he saw an agent for the Vermont Temperance Society, a Congregational minister, tipsy with wine at a wedding. Next came opposition to the secrecy and aristocracy of Masonry, followed by conversion to "Abolition Now" after reading Garrison's *Thoughts on African Colonization* (1832) and his weekly *Liberator*. As agent for Garrison's New England Anti-Slavery Society in 1833 he was banned in Bennington and endured corn-throwing Middlebury College students, but organized twenty local societies. On his 1833 tour he converted Jonathan P. Miller, Berlin representative in the General Assembly, to whom he fed resolutions against the slave trade and slavery in the District of Columbia. Murray was in on the organization of the American Anti-Slavery Society in Philadelphia, December 1833, and played a leading role in forming the Vermont Anti-Slavery Society the next year.

How he was able as a Free Will Baptist (or had his second conversion of 1829 brought him back to the larger body?) to take over the editorship of the *Vermont Telegraph* by 1835 is unclear. In his wide travels he must have met an angel who would give him the few hundred dollars he needed to buy control of the paper. As in the case of Lyman J. McIndoe's acquiring the *Vermont Chronicle* after the Civil War,[57] the denomination could not control its organ unless it owned the paper and chose its editor.

For more than seven years, while the rest of the denominational press in Vermont printed religious opinion and reported revivals, missions, Bible and tract distribution, Sunday school activities, and ministerial changes, Murray paid increasing attention, not only to the old reforms for education, temperance, and antislavery, but also to nonresistance, women's rights, health reform, and, finally, the need to achieve these in a believing community. The turning point in his losing touch with his constituency was around 1838, when William Lloyd Garrison organized the New England Non-Resistance Society. The effects of the Crash of 1837 seemed to show that solid institutions like banks, turnpikes, and canals, even the British government of Canada, were not impregnable. What kept his courage up, in spite of protests and withdrawals of support, was the apparent acceptance of antislavery action by statewide Baptists. This too failed on the rock of "no fellowship with slaveholders," for the American Baptist Convention, with its large southern membership, could not countenance it. In 1842 the regular Baptists gave up on Murray and found ministers to edit their *Vermont Observer*, which lasted until 1846. Murray did not further splinter the Baptists with an antislavery denomination, as Orange Scott did the Methodists. Instead, as the wheels of repudiation and excommunication turned slowly through 1841-1842, Murray grew more insistent on universal reform. Late in 1843 he brought his family to New York and started the *Regenerator* in line with the communitarian principles recently announced by a small group in Ohio. He lived until his death in 1885 a doctrinaire communitarian.[58]

The statewide denominational press influenced its churches by dispensing information. Another element of control over local congregations was the home missionary. Vermont Congregationalists fielded a few itinerants from 1818, and as their domestic missionary associations developed, they exerted some power through their grants to keep itinerants in the field and build houses of worship. They never could distribute enough aid, however, to influence the weak churches they assisted. Unlike the Congregationalists, the Baptists did not have a state missionary society, except for a few evangelists sent by the missionary societies in Massachusetts and Maine in the decade after 1807, and local societies in some churches. Their feeling was that the local church is its own missionary society.

Church and State

What divided Vermonters more than their theologies, rituals, or ideas of church government was their attitudes toward the revivals that undulated through the half century. The first apostates from any of the original five groups (Congregational, Baptist, Quaker, Episcopalian, and Presbyterian) were those who could not stomach their Calvinist elements, especially election and predestination: Free Will Baptists, Christians, Methodists, and Universalists.

Old and new dissenters combined in a swelling chorus of opposition to the multiple establishment of 1783 that favored the Congregationalists. The law required exemption from the church tax only by certificate, signed by a "Minister of the Gospel, Deacon, or Elder, or the Moderator in the Church or Congregation to which he, she or they pretend to belong," vouching "the Party to be of their Persuasion," and recorded by the town clerk.[59] The opposition was substantial. In Rockingham, in the eighteen years until the law was watered down in 1801, the town clerk recorded the certificates of fifty-five Universalists, fifty-three Baptists, and fifteen Episcopalians.[60]

This was only a minor hindrance to the Congregationalists' ability to pay their minister or build and maintain a meetinghouse. They felt far greater pressure from a majority that repeatedly voted down proposals to hire preaching or build. In that sense one can say that the multiple establishment law of 1783 was a dead letter in many towns by the 1790s.

By 1801 the Congregationalists had reached their fall-back position: A new law allowed anyone to opt out of church taxes by merely stating, "I do not agree in religious opinion with a majority of the inhabitants of this town." This was not good enough for the Baptists and their fellow dissenters. Many might forget to file or fail to follow the strict specifications for filing and be liable. The law still falsely assumed that the first church to organize represented the majority opinion in town. Why should the burden of proof be on the dissenter? They entered politics as Republicans committed to repeal the whole establishment and succeeded in 1807. Strong Congregational towns, with a minister and a meetinghouse, such as Thetford and Rockingham, kept collecting the church tax for a few years more. In Rockingham, the 136 who certified disagreement included those through 1809.

Once in politics, the anti-Congregationalists continued as Jeffersonians and Jacksonians until their antislavery and/or nativist sentiments drew them off in the 1840s. During the 1806-1807 campaign to repeal the law favoring the Congregationalists, some Baptists near Chester objected to Elder Aaron Leland's descending to worldly contests. Nevertheless, he and Ezra Butler of Waterbury continued to lead Baptist cohorts in state government until the late 1820s. Butler served a term in Congress (1813-1815) and as governor (1826-28); Leland served as lieutenant governor (1822-27). Vermonters also elected clergymen to Congress who opposed the Democrats: Congregationalist Asa Lyon of Grand Isle in the Federalist sweep of 1814, Congregationalist Reverend Professor James Meacham of Middlebury, from 1848 to his death in 1856, and antislavery Whig Baptist Alvah Sabin of Georgia, elected in 1852 and 1854. Die-hard Whigs put John Wheeler, retired Reverend President of the University of Vermont, on their ballot for governor in 1856, in spite of his declining the honor. After Meacham and Sabin, no ministers were elected to federal office until the Progressive wave of 1912.[61]

Church and state, according to most Vermonters in the nineteenth century and well into the twentieth, should be separated only to prevent Catholics from hampering the free exercise of Protestant religion. They saw in European history Roman Catholic, Lutheran, Calvinist, and Anglican establishments choking liberty. The American Revolution broke the Anglican establishment and the First Amendment prevented Congress, but not the states, from establishing religion or interfering with the free exercise thereof. Thomas Jefferson's Virginia statute for religious freedom (1785) led a national trend away from any kind of establishment. Jeffersonians in Vermont made it the first of the Congregational states in New England to implement this shift.

While the Protestant denominations wanted fair competition, they regularly availed themselves of the advantages to be gained through state and local government. Tax exemption of church property had become established in the colonies when churches performed welfare functions. No church was about to give that up. As already mentioned, religious societies used town houses and schoolhouses, and observed religious holidays proclaimed by governors. The original corporation of the University of Vermont deliberately included representatives of the state's four main denominations. Turnpikes exempted from tolls those going to and from public worship. From 1797 until 1819, ministers settled or hired for a year or more enjoyed a thousand-dollar exemption of their grand list.[62]

Election sermons to 1833 proclaimed the necessary conjunction of the state and religion to uphold morality and justice. Perhaps preaching election sermons at the opening of the legislature stopped because the joint houses chose too many Jacksonian Methodists, Baptists, and Universalists as legislative chaplains and election-day preachers and not because Vermonters had given up the principle of a Protestant republic. Baptists, Methodists, and Congregationalists contended for the small office of legislative chaplain in 1861. It took three ballots to elect Baptist Leland Howard of Rutland over Montpelier's Congregationalist William

H. Lord. Congressman William Slade proclaimed in 1839, opposing a motion to dispense with the congressional chaplaincy, that the New Testament was "the great charter of popular freedom---the basis of genuine and safe democracy."[63]

In the half century after Vermont joined the Union, Christians of every description changed the ways they worshiped, in public and at home. They changed also their ways of thinking about God, of dealing with differences, of spreading the Word and competing with other religious societies in the race for converts. Changes in the churches affected society and as society changed it influenced the churches. But the changes of the first half century were small compared to the reorientation of religion in the next sixty years.

Notes to Chapter 4

1 *A Map of the State of Vermont As It Was About A. D. 1791* (Montpelier: Vermont Department of Highways, 1941), reproduced in Earle Newton, *The Vermont Story*, 93, shows a dozen meetinghouses on the west side as far north as Cornwall and half a dozen on the east side. For an unusually detailed account of the trials of the Royalton Congregational Society and the town in building its 1791 meetinghouse (not on the above map), see Lovejoy, *History of Royalton*, 236-241. Jennings, *Memorials of a Century*, opp. 24, shows a lithograph by A. Meisel, Boston, of the first Bennington meetinghouse, 1765, with porch on the side instead of the gable end as in Rockingham.

2 "The Town Meeting: A Comi-Tragic Poem," unsigned, in the handwriting of Samuel C. Crafts, n.d. [about 1804-07], MS. in the Crafts Papers at UVM, sides with the Baptists of Craftsbury in their failed attempt to win equal use of the town meetinghouse.

3 See Desmond, "A Forgotten Colonial Church" and L. S. and W. D. Hayes, *Old Rockingham Meeting House*. The Walter Harvey meetinghouse built by the Covenanter Presbyterians of West Barnet in 1831, illustrated in the *Burlington Free Press*, October 18, 1970, continued the bare, eighteenth-century style.

4 Freeman, *Congregational Church of Middlebury*, 29-37, discusses the tradition, the builder, and the building. MS-28 in the Vermont Historical Society contains specifications for the 1836 Methodist chapel in Woodstock. Sketches of the similar Woodstock Christian and Universalist chapels and St. Mary's, Burlington, appear in Zadock Thompson. *History of Vermont* (1842), 190, 192, 201.

5 Hopkins, J. H., *Gothic Architecture*, 17-18, 34, 38; plates 3, 4, 6, 7.

6 Meetinghouse records of the First Congregational Church (Unitarian), Burlington; *"Know Your Town": The 1940 Survey of Norwich. Vermont* (Norwich: Norwich Woman's Club, 1942), 52; Isaac Jennings, *The Old Meetinghouse in Bennington*, 61-62 and note; S. A. Freeman, *Middlebury Congregational Church*, 34.

7 For example, see *Official History of Guilford*, 178.

8 Lawrence, *New Hampshire Churches*, 683, concerning the Church of Christ in Colebrook and Vicinity, organized in 1802, with attenders from both sides of the Connecticut River.

9 Isaac Jennings, *The Old Meeting House in Bennington*, 55. See also the untitled reminiscences of David Hanchett (born 1820), a Suffield, Connecticut, Baptist, written ca. 1890 (refers to "the great snow storm" of March 1888), in the possession of his descendant, Janet Chater of Shelburne, Vermont. Pages unnumbered.

10 Wells, *Barnet*, 134. For general background see Hughes and Smith, *American Hymns*.

11 For aid in imagining a typical church service of this period I am indebted to Betty Bandel, who directed the performance of church music as it had been performed since 1785, on 20 May 1969, at the United Church, Hinesburg, at a meeting of the Chittenden County Historical Society. See her *Justin Morgan*. Miss Bandel and James Chapman, director of the University of Vermont Choral Union, have produced recordings of a selection of the church music of this period.

12 [Hopkins, J. H.], *Sacred Songs*, advertisement dated 20 Dec. 1839 (and paid to run for several issues) in *Burlington Free Press* (10 Jan. 1840), 4:1; M. D. Gilman, *Bibliography of Vermont*, 127, lists a London & New York imprint, 1839.

13 Francis Asbury, *Journal and Letters*, ed. J. Manning Potter et al. (Nashville: Abingdon Press, 1958), 2:471, described a camp meeting June 6-11, 1805, at Stillwater, New York, with preachers from Canada, Vermont, and elsewhere in the Northeast, with "little intermission, night and day, of labour and praises." Roger Finke and Rodney Stark, *The Churching of America*, 92-108, explain the effectiveness of the early-nineteenth-century camp meeting.

14 Vermont Laws (1827), 31, sec. 2 added to an 1819 law penalizing disturbance of worship; R. S. (1840), 395 (Title xxi, c.82, sec.7); *New York Christian Advocate and Journal*, 17 (31 Aug. 1842): 10; *Boston U. S. Catholic Intelligencer*, (1 Oct. 1831): 1, called them "licentious"; Scott, *Camp Meeting Hymn Book*; *Universalist Watchman & Christian Repository*, 17 (11 Oct. 1845): 97.

15 New American editions of the Book of Common Prayer, 1789, 1800, 1828, removed royal and other obsolete references. Ambrose Atwater of Burlington ordered the 1810 printing of William Vicars' *Companion to the Altar* on the importance of preparing to receive Holy Communion.

16 "Prayer Meetings," *Episcopal Register*, 2 (July 1827): 97-99, (Aug.

1827): 113-116, (Sept. 1827): 129-132, (Nov. 1827): 161-163, 3 (March 1828): 37-41, (Apr. 1828): 53-56, (May 1828): 77-80, (Nov. 1828): 176-179, (Dec. 1828); 192-195; "Revivals," 2 (May 1827): 74-75, (June 1827): 92, (July 1827): 105-106.

[17] Pliny H. White on Walter A. Chapin of Craftsbury, in *Vermont Historical Gazetteer*, 3:168:2; Erastus P. Williams' diary for Sunday, April 16, 1837, quoted in Nash, *Royalton, Vermont*, 21: "I went to meeting. Old Mr. [Azel] Washburn [1764-1841] preached. He was rather tedious but was the fault in him or me?"

[18] Perrin B. Fisk (1837-1913), in *Vermont Historical Gazetteer*, 4:783, about Baptist Elder Friend Blood in Waitsfield about 1838.

[19] Biddle and Escholz, *Literature of Vermont*, 44. Mary Grace Canfield, *Valley of the Kedron*, 207, cites a contemporary as recalling how "Uncle Joseph Sterling, after a long sermon, asked the preacher to shorten his prayer as the people were freezing."

[20] Some continued to write their sermons, perhaps most often, beginners like twenty-eight-year-old Alexander Huntington Clapp, who graduated from Andover Theological Seminary in 1845. Mellen Chamberlain, Brattleboro East Village schoolmaster, recorded in his diary for 25 Oct. 1846 (Chamberlain Papers, Boston Public Library), "Went to church to hear Mr. Clap on the duties of people to their pastors. Well written and delivered." T. S. in the *Vermont Chronicle* (2 June 1866), 1:4-6, blamed ministers' writing out their sermons so that they could get a better parish, as one of the reasons for the decline of the evangelical denominations.

[21] Thompson, *History of Montpelier*, 92.

[22] Ira Allen, *Hiring Preaching*.

[23] Cox, *Baptists in America*, 177; Bassett, "James Buckham," 4. The dozen settled Vermont Unitarian ministers, 1810-1865, graduated from Harvard College and/or Harvard Divinity School.

[24] Dr. Dudley B. Smith in *Vermont Historical Gazetteer*, 4:726. Many churches were like the Waitsfield Congregational church, whose eleven founding members organized June 27, 1796 without any articles of faith, voting to "take the Bible for our rule." See Jones, *Waitsfield*, 99.

[25] Sabin, *Gospel Discipline*, 67.

[26]*Vermont Chronicle*, June 11, 1845, 92:1-2. None of the organizers of Burlington's Congregational church in 1805 or of its orthodox branch in 1810 had letters from their churches in Connecticut (J. E. Goodrich in *Burlington First Congregational Church Centennial*, 18).

[27] Murray and Rodney, "Sylvia Drake," especially 126-129. In Emerson, *Religious Experiences*, the text is supersaturated with piety and preoccupation with death, like the diary of the tubercular daughter in Mark Twain's chapter on the feud in *Huckleberry Finn*.

[28] Marcus D. Gilman, *Bibliography of Vermont*, 319; UVM *General Catalogue*, 72.

[29] See above, chapter 3, page 8.

[30] *The Revised Statutes of the State of Vermont, Passed November 19, 1839, to which are added Several Public Acts now in Force, and to which are prefixed the Constitutions of the United States and of the State of Vermont* (Burlington: Chauncey Goodrich, 1840), chap. 99, sec. 11, p. 444, against blasphemy (hereafter referred to as R.S.), continued in *The Compiled Statutes* (1851) (hereafter, C. S.).

[31] *Vermont Laws* (1851), 8-9; *Vermont Chronicle*, 8 March 1833, 4:1; *Centennial Proceedings, Newfane*, 47; *Universalist Watchman and Christian Repository*, 2 August 1845, 11; 15 November 1845, 14:3; Ballou, *Genealogy of the Ballous*, 994-997 (Eli Ballou, #3253).

[32] *Vermont Statutes* (1947), 8493; omitted in *Vermont Statutes Annotated* (1981).

[33] Named after the Dutch theologian, Arminius (1560-1609), who rejected extreme predestinarian Calvinism and left room for universal salvation. Not to be confused with Antinomianism, a theological view that the Christian by faith and grace is freed from all legalism.

[34] See Nuttall, *Holy Spirit in Puritan Experience*.

[35] Henry Crocker, *Baptists in Vermont*, 58-59, reported a woman's dream that her father told her to go to Wheelock and tell Barnabas Perkins to preach at the Danville courthouse on the gospel of John, 21:22. He came at her request, preached on that text, and converted three young women.

[36] J. H. Noyes, *Religious Experience*, 158-160 and passim; *Way of*

Holiness; G. W. Noyes, *Putney   Community.*   See also Walter, "Perfectionists in Westminster."

[37] Barclay, *Barclay's   Apology*, 155-170, Propositions VIII-IX, "Perfection," and "Perseverance in the Faith and the Possibility of Falling From Grace." Editor Freiday claims, "Barclay's doctrine of perfection and its correlative, perseverance, were adopted by a major part of English-speaking Protestantism—partly through Methodism," xxv.

[38] Hoag's vision is most accessible in *Vermont Historical Gazetteer*, 1:740.

[39] Isaac D. Stewart, *The History of the Free Will Baptists*, 275-276.

[40] Pettibone, "Manchester," 158.

[41] See David M. Ludlum, *Social Ferment in Vermont*, 239-240.

[42] Ludlum, *Social Ferment in Vermont*, 243-244; Zadock Thompson, *History of Vermont* (1842), 2:203-204.   Thompson was in the neighborhood of Woodstock when the Bullardites were there. Also disturbed by the bad weather of 1816 and intense Bible study was Origen Packard of Wilmington, whose "Packardite" followers believed "that all Christians should be united." Since this seemed to be starting still another sect, they broke up but carried their "spiritual" interpretation of the Bible back to their former denominations.   Sketch by his daughter in A. M. Hemenway, *Vermont Historical Gazetteer*, 5(pt.3): 20.

[43] See Barnouw, "Mormon Converts"; Tobias Spicer, *Autobiography*, 111-113. For background see especially "I was born in Sharon," in Brooke, *Mormon Cosmology*, 129-146, and two summary paragraphs in Bratt, "Reorientation of American Protestantism," 71-72.

[44] See Elise Guyette, "Black Lives," for which she prepared a database of Vermont blacks. A plausible hypothesis puts the blacks of Benson in the Free Baptist church with no "Negro pews." In Benson's 1803 Congregational meetinghouse, financed by a pew auction, "the two rear pews were reserved for blacks." See Aiken, "Benson in Epitome," 150.

[45] Hill summarized "the Wood scrape" in *Yankee   Kingdom*, 214-215. Barnes Frisbie elaborated the story in *Vermont Historical Gazetteer*, 3:810-189.

[46] See Lewis Joseph Bridgman's story in the *Vermont Historical Gazetteer*,

4:363, and Dow's *Journal* (1848), 65, 154.

[47] Chester Wright, *The Devil in Hardwick*, iii-14.   Various pastors
summarize Hardwick church history in *Vermont Historical Gazetteer*, 1:326-
329.   See also Joseph Torrey (1832-1917), "New Lights," ibid., 1:329-330,
followed by a sketch of Amos Tuttle by his son David, 1:330-331.   Daniel
Pierce Thompson recounts the life of Chester Wright in his *History of
Montpelier*, 201-203.

[48] Henry Crocker, *Baptists in Vermont*, 416-419; Elsie Wells, *Bakersfield*,
103; retold in J. J. Duffy and H. N. Muller, III, *An Anxious Democracy*, 34-
35.

[49] Truair's orientation and tone of voice show in his *Alarm Trumpet*, a
Federalist diatribe against the "bloodstained annals of Atheism and
Democracy," and *Christian Holiness*.   Truair's story is told by J. J. Duffy
and H. N. Muller, III, *An Anxious Democracy*, 32; Wagner, "Truair's Vermont
Ministry," and Edwin Wheelock in *Vermont Historical Gazetteer*, 2:620.

[50] Congregational ministers dismissed: Amariah Chandler, Waitsfield,
February 3, 1830; Alexander Lovell, Vergennes, November 10, 1835;
Simeon Parmelee, Westford, August 8, 1837; John K. Converse October 7,
1844 (but a revolt had been quelled earlier).   Reasons for dismissal are
neither well recorded nor simple, but in each of these cases one important
element was a split in the congregation over the new forms of revivalism.

[51] "Several persons are withheld from the sacraments," complained William
H. Hoyt to Bishop Fenwick on May 22, 1847, and extreme unction denied
the recent convert, Archibald W. Hyde, because they were usurers.   David J.
Blow copied both letters from the archdiocesan archives.   For the story of
the fire see Chapter 3, 19.

[52] To maintain the connection between American and British Methodism,
John Wesley appointed Thomas Coke and Francis Asbury co-superin-
tendents, but Asbury, instead of accepting Wesley's appointment, insisted
on consecration by the Baltimore Conference in 1784, virtually asserting
the independence of American Methodism.   Although Coke held his title for
twenty years, he spent little time in America.   For Asbury's strategy for
winning converts on the frontier, see Chapter 3, pp. 77-78.

[53] Francis Asbury to Solomon Sias, 30 June 1811, in *Journal and Letters*,
3:451-452.   Writing from Lynn, Massachusetts, to Stith Mead, presiding
elder of the Richmond, Virginia, District on 15 July 1805, Asbury lauded
Elijah Sabin's *Gospel Discipline* as "excellent and [as] well calculated for
the meridian of Virginia as Vermont," ibid., 3: 321-322.   See also Emory

Stevens Bucke, gen. ed., *The History of American Methodism* (Nashville: Abingdon Press, 1964), 1:469, and C. D. and O. D. Schwartz, *A Flame of Fire*, 135-136, on Asbury's strong preference for unmarried clergy.

54 I have found some evidence of Reformed or Protestant Methodist churches in Pawlet, Readsboro, Shelburne, Somerset, Springfield, and Sudbury, totaling over two hundred members. See *The Reformer's Discipline* (Readsboro, organized in 1814); Elijah Bailey, *Thoughts on Government*; Sprague, *Annals of the American Pulpit*, 7:249 (Nicholas Snethen); "Reformed Methodist Church," in Rupp, *Denominations in the United States*, 399-403.

55 Freewill Baptist Connection. *Minutes of the General Conference*, vi-vii.

56 M. D. Gilman, *Bibliography of Vermont*, 214; Henry S. Dana, *History of Woodstock*, 250-252; *Vermont Historical Gazetteer*, 4:409-410; newspaper circulation statistics in the U. S. MS. Census, Schedule VI, 1850-1870 (copies in the Vermont State Library and the National Archives and Records Administration).

57 See Chapter 6, p. 213, on McIndoe and the *Chronicle*.

58 Hamm, *God's Government Begun*, xvi, 1, 18-29, and other indexed references, has collected the most information about Murray, "the leading light of ultraism in Vermont" (Ludlum, *Social Ferment in Vermont*, 57).

59 Act of October 17, 1783, Section II, in *State Papers of Vermont*, 13:196.

60 L. S. and W. D. Hayes, *Old Rockingham Meeting House*, 31-32. The sample certificate by a Baptist minister in Dudley, Massachusetts, suggests a source for the history of migration to Vermont.

61 The eight clerical town representatives through the Civil War, as listed in Comstock, *Principal Civil Officers of Vermont*, are remarkably few, with three quarters of the terms before 1815: Ezra Butler, Waterbury (1794-97, 1799-1804, 1807); Asa Lyon, South Hero (1799-1802, 1804-06, 1808), Grand Isle (1810-14); Aaron Leland, Chester (1801-07, 1809-10, 1813); Reformed Presbyterian David Goodwillie, Barnet (1805); Alvah Sabin, Georgia (1826, 1835, 1838, 1847-49, 1861-62); Alexander L. Twilight, Brownington (1836, when he was an academy principal, not preaching regularly); John H. Woodward, Westford (1856); and Orville G. Wheeler, South Hero (1863-64). An occasional minister, like Edward P. Wild, Congregational, Craftsbury, one term, 1872, showed that there was no taboo on preachers in politics.

State senators from 1836 were consistently lawyers or businessmen. Clerical exceptions: Rev. Orville G. Wheeler, Congregational, South Hero, elected from Grand Isle County, 1860-61; and John Gregory, Northfield stock breeder, ordained Universalist in 1833 but only occasionally preached after 1850, elected from Washington County, 1856-1857.

62 William Slade, comp., *Laws of Vermont* (Windsor: Simeon Ide for the State, 1825), 388, 395.

63 *Speech of Mr. Slade of Vermont on . . . Appointing Chaplains to Congress. . . .Dec. 27, 1839*, (n.p., n.d.), 6-7.

5

Catholic Growth; Protestant Reorientation, 1840-1865

Vermont's early-nineteenth-century revivalists shaped religion until the 1840s. Although the technique became habitual in the camp meetings and urban revivals down through Billy Sunday and Billy Graham, they did not have the power to deal with the new problems of the depressions of 1837-1843 and after, industrial consolidation, and the growth of cities. In the unexpected trauma of the Civil War experience, comrades and chaplains tried to meet human needs regardless of religious persuasion. Pious soldiers, buffeted but unbowed, mostly kept the forms of their faith, but revivals were scarce among Vermont troops. The bare practice of familiar rites in the army was difficult under war conditions and Catholic soldiers, without Vermont chaplains, had little access to their priests.

Revivalists in Vermont continued to recruit many converts to carry the gospel across the world, and in the state they worked against liquor and slavery, but focused on new, political means. Moral suasion had changed personal and social habits, but some reformers were not satisfied. These exhorted their audiences, regardless of denomination, to lobby and vote for reform laws. Abolitionists organized the Liberty Party to end slavery and teetotalers organized the Temperance Party to pass and enforce the Vermont prohibition law of 1852.

About 1838 the moderates split from the ultras. The Congregationalists led by the Christian transcendentalist James Marsh had defeated Burchard. The Baptists would soon defeat Orson S. Murray, and after losing heavily to the Millerites, consolidate their forces.[1] Murray and other communitarians retreated from society in despair at the vision of the industrial ogre looming on the horizon.[2] The revivalist Millerite hope for a second coming died with the failure of Miller's prophecy, but an Adventist church rose again on the creedal rock of perpetual readiness for the millennium. The Methodists continued to use the old methods, but by the 1850s in Vermont (earlier elsewhere) they were domesticated and had stopped growing.[3] A holiness segment did not join the trend toward respectability and bureaucratic management of the large mass converted earlier in the century.

Methodists, Millerites, and Baptists plied the same old revivalist ploys on scattered, priestless Catholics, and had remarkably little success, while the Catholics forged to the lead in numbers among organized Christians.

Those born into their faith and those born again presented the paradox of crying a catholic message and gathering separate denominations. Actually, while building schools and other institutions strengthening their own churches, the Protestant denominations were getting along with each other better because they were becoming more like each other as many of them participated together in benevolent associations. In Vermont they agreed about slavery, but would not force the split that Methodist Orange Scott and Baptist Orson Murray demanded, until their national bodies were ready in the mid-1840s. They agreed about nativism and sometimes other reforms and benevolences, while trying to preserve their own peculiar institutions against the erosion of out-migration, competition, and indifference. They worried about their loss of members, especially in the hills. Ministers of many faiths mourned the desecration of the Sabbath, the indifference that shrank the practice of family prayer.

Political attention shifted from revivalism to hullaballoo and Tyler too, the Whigs' name-calling campaign of 1840 to elect General "Tippecanoe" Harrison and blame the Democrats for the depression. In Vermont, a growing minority in each Protestant denomination called on its state body to pass antislavery resolutions. Quakers kept out of party politics but often petitioned the state legislature and Congress whenever antislavery issues arose. Too few in Vermont after their second, 1845 schism, Quakers lost some influential members such as Rowland T. Robinson of Ferrisburg, who resigned from the Society of Friends, disappointed that it was too timid to support immediate emancipation. A few scattered Covenanter Presbyterians from Braintree to Barnet were as activist for abolition as the Quakers. While abolitionists clamored to "end slavery now," northern moderates reached the intransigent Republican position of refusing to allow slavery in the territories.

The last shouts of the Vermont revivalists founded two new denominations, the Wesleyan (antislavery) Methodists and the Adventists, the ultras of the ultras, expecting the end of the world.

Wesleyan Methodism

Abolitionists in the Methodist church created a new denomination when they, like some seventeenth-century Puritans, ultimately came to advocate "reformation without tarrying for any." Methodists had earlier divided over the powers of the episcopacy, with the Protestant or Reformed Methodists wanting the bishops to have less power.

Orange Scott (1800-1847) tried for a decade to convert the majority to abolitionism, to its great annoyance. Since national Methodism had almost equal proslavery and antislavery wings which did not split until 1844, Scott had either to be patient a few more years or separate from northern Methodists who would not yet abandon their Southern brethren. He chose to separate.

Scott was born in Brookfield, Vermont, the eldest in the large family of a rootless farm laborer. His father, requiring his labor until he was twenty-one, allowed him to accumulate only thirteen months of common schooling as a minor, but he was constantly educating himself. Converted at a Barre camp meeting in 1820, ordained in 1825, he rose rapidly to be a popular presiding elder by 1830.

According to editor Abel Stevens of the Boston Methodist organ *Zion's Herald*, Scott sold more Methodist literature than anyone else in the East. His "noble trumpet" voice, Stevens claimed, while not directed by the mental discipline that higher education could have provided, appealed to those classes who admired a coarse but aggressive fighter. Stevens called him second only to Wilbur Fisk as a Methodist preacher, and unexcelled at camp meetings and quarterly meetings. His career prospects ended when he converted to abolitionism in 1833.

Scott fought a losing battle in the columns of *Zion's Herald* and in the General Conference to convert his church to an antislavery platform. As presiding elder of the Providence, Rhode Island, district, he led a movement to win the General Conference of 1836 for abolition, and lost—both the vote and his presiding eldership. Cleared of Bishop Elijah Hedding's charge that he used "coarse and disrespectful language," but still unruly, he accepted election as pastor of St. Paul's Methodist church of Lowell, Massachusetts, without the approval of his bishop. As agent of the American Antislavery Society he increased his pressure on the Methodist majority. Failing again to convince the General Conference of 1840, and with consumption threatening his life, he retired with his family to Newbury, Vermont.

There his children could attend Newbury Seminary, and he could try to recover his health with outdoor physical labor. Meanwhile he prepared antislavery polemics for the periodical press and Sunday school books at the nearby press in Wells River. As soon as he effected his transfer to the New Hampshire Conference, which included eastern Vermont until 1844, the seminary used his talents to raise money and recruit students. By the end of 1842 he had lost patience with his temporizing northern colleagues and withdrew with two other antislavery leaders from their Methodist Episcopal Church. From January 1843 the seceders published the *True Wesleyan* to prepare the way for the Utica convention of May 31 which launched the new Wesleyan Methodist denomination. At least six Vermont Wesleyan congregations had a house of worship by 1870.[4]

Miller and Adventism

Baptist William Miller of Poultney, Vermont, and next-door Low Hampton, New York, figured out from his intensive reading of the Bible and especially from the Old Testament book of Daniel, that Christ would come again in 1843 or 1844. After years of pondering, he published a series of articles in the *Brandon Telegraph* in 1832 and began to preach this fearful good news. His success was pedestrian until 1839, when he met and convinced Joshua V. Himes in Boston. Himes's promotional skills exploded a minor hill-town movement into northeastern wildfire. Himes grew up a Rhode Island Episcopalian, became a Garrisonian abolitionist, and was the successful pastor of a large church of the Christian Connection when he met Miller.[5]

Miller was not the first to emphasize the injunction to "work the works of him who sent me, while it is day" (John 9:4) and the parable of the foolish virgins who were not prepared for the midnight cry that

Golden Gabriel was not an adventist weathervane but above the Lyndon Universalist chapel roof by 1850 (see Shores, Lyndon: Gem of the Green, *170; used by permission of the Lyndonville Historical Society).*

the Bridegroom was coming (Matt. 25:1-13). This outlook was part of a common Christian tradition. Perhaps the significance of the Millerite "delusion" that Christ was indeed coming soon, was that many no longer believed in the possibility and mocked those who did. They caricatured the Millerites as disposing of all they had and climbing hills and housetops in white "ascension robes" with muslin wings to be closer to Jesus when he descended from the clouds, as predicted by William Miller for that cold October 22, 1844.

There is little firsthand evidence to support the "ascension robes" story. An East Braintree teenager wrote to her beau seeking his fortune in Missouri, "Millerism is pretty much down. . . . it has done a great deal of injury. . . . Some. . . did not harvest their grain until very late if they have at all, they were so sure the world would come to an end this fall. . . . Therefore their families are. . . destitute."[6]

Some sold their property because the movement needed the money to finance its feverish press, telling the prophecy to more and more people. True, persons preoccupied with their immortal souls are likely to neglect their mortal business. Spending time at revivals, except for the value of contacts with prospects, whether you are a Millerite or a Methodist, will lower the profit margin in the short run.

Like many other beliefs in prophecies, wrong in particulars but right in essentials, Adventism contained the wise advice that the disciples of Christ are to live *as if* he will come tomorrow. One believer replied to an inquirer who asked, "What shall I do if it [the Second Coming] does not come. . . I shall be. . . stronger in the belief of my Lord's speedy coming," as I am stronger now than I was a year ago.[7] Around this principle the Adventists continued to grow and divide.

The visions, itinerant ministry, and writings of Ellen Gould Harmon White, originally a Portland, Maine, Methodist, contributed mightily to the movement. White persuaded a majority to become *Seventh Day* Adventists because, after their "great disappointment," they agreed to obey the fourth commandment (Exodus, 20:8-11) and rest on the seventh day of the week, not the first. She blamed the Catholic Church for causing the shift from Saturday to Sunday. Her visit with her husband, James Springer White, to the hills of Johnson, Vermont, led to the organization of a Seventh Day Adventist church there in 1862. Joshua Himes went with a minority to form the Advent Christian Church in 1861, over the issue of the soul's immortality, and eventually came full circle back to his Episcopalian roots. Some two dozen small Adventist churches, scattered all over the state, in hill-towns and among hill town migrants to villages, had organized before the end of the century.[8]

From Persuasion to Prohibition

In the half century that followed the failure of William Miller's prediction that the world would actually come to an end, the world of excited revival and fervent reformism—what John Higham has called "boundlessness"[9]— did indeed come to an end. Whatever religious zeal, whipped up by the revivals, that had not burned out seemed sucked into the vortex of antislavery emotions, especially in the rural districts.

The intensity of revivalist and Adventist excitement left people emotionally drained and their churches hurting, if not from revivalism, from out-migration. In the villages the Protestants gained numbers and lost no power, but their priests had had their fill of their prophets. Both Orson Murray, calling for comprehensive community, and Jedediah Burchard, calling backsliders high and low to be saved and lead a Christian life, had lost their audiences. The Reverend Professor James Marsh and his phalanx had neutralized Burchard; Baptists like Cornelius A. Thomas of Brandon stood for a different kind of religion than Murray's. The new piety stressed support of community enterprise, benevolence, and respectability. From one point of view, this means hypocrisy. From the dominant Whig point of view, supported by most weighty Democrats, it meant approval of economic and social projects for the benefit of the community.[10]

While Protestants' desires for technological and economic change grew stronger, the will to resist religious change crept into their churches, and affected the unchurched Vermonter too. The reforms that survived aimed to change other people elsewhere, or the poor, Catholic dram drinker. Educational reformers sought new ways to get back to basics for the benefit of business. They all tended to be negative. They had prohibited Masonry in the 1830s, and while the Masons quietly returned to work after 1845, now the mood was to prohibit liquor, to prohibit slavery, and to get after those who violate the prohibitions. To cleave to the old was the mood of the new generation.

The Methodist metamorphosis from the rough and rugged, minimally trained, young itinerants of their growth period was complete by the middle of the century. Even by 1840 at least half the clergy were "located" at "stations," that is, they were responsible for Methodists in one place rather than a circuit. By 1840 seventy-five Methodist churches had houses of worship of their own and perhaps a score more shared union meetinghouses. In 1845 the Vermont Conference required presiding elders to oversee the furnishing and maintenance of parsonages, although more than half failed to meet the requirements. The 1857 minutes of the Troy Conference had a new column listing the value of parsonages for each charge, and more than half (98 out of 194) had parsonages. With a necessary concern for real estate came a calming of zeal.[11]

The work of William G. T. Shedd, a disciple of James Marsh, was characteristic of the Congregational stance. He completed what Marsh started, editing Coleridge's works soon after he finished seven years on the University of Vermont faculty and started a lifetime of seminary teaching. In his 1858 address to the Congregational Library Association he declared, "The only power that can unify" us "is. . . a self-chosen denominational creed." This was neither the come-all-ye spirit that invited Jedediah Burchard to revive Protestantism in Vermont, nor the stern, old-fashioned, hell-and-damnation spirit that looked backwards to the harsh side of Calvin. Shedd was urging his generation, like his mentor before him, to think about God so that theology could inform an even-keeled behavior. This spirit called Congregationalists in 1878-1879 to be ruled by recent statements of faith.[12] But the effect of emphasizing enlightened dogma was nevertheless to build a fortress. Loss of zeal and loss of a quarter of their membership while the Episcopalians and Catholics kept growing, tempted the evangelicals to hold tight to what remained.[13]

The Roman Catholic Diocese of Burlington

The main reason for Protestant defensiveness was the arrival of thousands of Roman Catholics, more from Ireland than from Canada, to work, not only in the fields and woods, but also on the railroads and in the mills using or making the new machines. Natives were ambivalent about these newcomers because they appreciated their cheap and lusty labor, yet were baffled by their behavior and fearful of their religion.

The rise of the Roman Catholic Diocese of Burlington to become a major force is the most important theme in the religious history of Vermont during the half century after 1840. Only one veteran priest and a few short-term missionaries tended Vermont Catholics in 1840, off in a distant corner of the Diocese of Boston. When Louis De Goesbriand retired in 1892, after four decades as first bishop of Burlington, his statewide diocese had fifty-two priests. The two church buildings of 1842, in Burlington and Middlebury, had multiplied to seventy-two.[14]

The Irish flood of the late 1840s had overwhelmed Burlington priest Jeremiah O'Callaghan and his cohorts. Beginning at an age when most men of his period expected to give up control, O'Callaghan had traveled far and wide, served St. Mary's parish in two Burlington buildings, bought and started a parochial school, and held the fort for twenty-three years. But his eccentricities and combativeness irritated Protestants predisposed toward nativism. O'Callaghan did not moderate his attack over the years. "We had lately a fortunate escape from a vile faction of idlers who made a desperate attempt to get our village incorporated," he proudly reported to the *Boston Pilot* in 1853, "for the exaction of heavy loads of fresh taxes. But they were defeated by the honest portion of the natives, and our Irish Brigade."[15] It was time to bring order into the immigrant chaos and improve public relations, the Catholic hierarchy thought.

In 1853 it established the Diocese of Burlington, and chose Louis De Goesbriand to run it. The new bishop, born in Brittany in 1816, served his American apprenticeship in Louisville, Kentucky, and Cleveland, Ohio. He spent his first year in Vermont surveying the diocese, found temporary help in two French priests and five Oblates of Mary Immaculate, and then recruited a new team of young Irish and French clergy in Europe the following winter. Bishop De Goesbriand's poor flock, he wrote a Breton bishop on December 18, 1853, was "famished for the Word of God and the Sacraments." In 1849 there had been three resident priests and three transients. De Goesbriand assembled nine priests and a deacon for his first diocesan synod late in 1855, at the peak of the nativist Know Nothing Party's influence, and by the outbreak of the Civil War there were fourteen settled priests, mostly under thirty-five years old. The older clergy against whom antipathy had built up were swept out. Their young replacements could reach the lost sheep and strengthen their resistance. The majority were francophone (seven Bretons) and most of the Irish had studied in Paris. The first synod established sacramental standards and registers, the use of a common English edition of the catechism, annual inventories, and the bishop's control of buildings and the movements of priests beyond their parishes. O'Callaghan would have been unhappy that parish money now had to be deposited with usurious bankers.

When they had enough priests they needed their own buildings, to free themselves from dependence on non-Catholics. A vigorous building program expanded diocesan property in the decade from eight church structures in five counties with a capacity of forty-six hundred, worth $43,000, to twenty-seven in ten counties, capacity ten thousand, value $110,000.[16] Even then the total capacity was only half big enough to shelter the nominal Catholics in Vermont. Nine tenths of the churches built and the priests resident were in large towns and industrial centers, where they had gotten along in rented paint shops, schoolhouses, railroad shanties, private homes, or abandoned Protestant churches. Rev. John B. Daly had used "the old `Ball Alley' on Main Street" in Rutland. The Rev. Zephyrin Druon, who came from France a few months after De Goesbriand, bought or constructed chapels and churches in ten towns, often acquiring prominent sites, as in Montpelier next to the statehouse.

The bishop hoped to climax these gains with a cathedral, but on his return in the spring of 1861 from a second trip to France he postponed building on account of the Civil War. Better times allowed a start on St. Patrick's Chapel in May 1862, a cornerstone ceremony in September 1863, and a dedication December 8, 1867 as the Cathedral of the Immaculate Conception. The doctrine that the Virgin Mary was conceived and born without original sin (1854), had long been a prominent element in popular piety.

De Goesbriand early faced the problem of getting French and Irish to live peaceably in one religious family. Quebecois had had French-speaking priests in Burlington off and on since 1835. In 1841, the second French priest, Francois Ancé, used a chapel near the orginal building that had burned in 1838 rather than share the new St. Mary's downtown. He had trouble getting along with people and after a stormy twenty months in Burlington, his Boston bishop removed him.[17] An early hint of Protestant bias for the French over the Irish is the extensive airing of pro-Ancé arguments in the *Burlington Free Press*. Its editor had been steadily critical of O'Callaghan, but praised the French priest for forgiving the parishioners who attacked and robbed him, and generally defended his side of the conflict. This can be called divide-and-rule policy or accepted as the genuine preference of these Protestant outsiders.

In 1850 Bishop John Bernard Fitzpatrick, Bishop Fenwick's successor, had approved the establishment of St. Joseph's, the first ethnic parish in New england, in the care of Fr. Joseph Quévillon, the first settled French Canadian priest in Vermont. French Canadians conducted

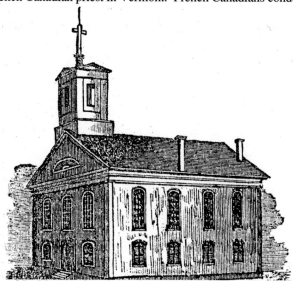

Woodcut of St. Mary's church, Burlington, 1832. (From Thompson's History of Vermont, Natural, Civil, and Statistical, *Gazetteer, p. 201.)*

Cathedral of the Immaculate Conception interior, 1863-67. (Used by permission of the Diocese of Burlington.)

their own church business through *marguilliers*, members of a prudential committee called a *fabrique*. Bishop De Goesbriand aimed to centralize the care of property. For a man not yet forty to be telling elders
of the *fabrique* what to do produced tension. The Canadians erred, wrote
the bishop in his diary, when they bought an old store in Lowell for a
church. Another group decided to have a building in Enosburg, "perhaps
because I said I thought a chapel had better be nearer East Berkshire."
He found the Canadians "very poor *in every respect*."[18]

When he dealt with the Irish O'Hears and Hannas of Highgate, he
began to change his mind about the French. Catholics had settled in
Highgate since 1824. They had bought a lot in 1849, and finished the
Church of St. Louis by 1856. Fr. MacGowan of St. Albans had financed the pews by subscription, but did the parishioners have any
property right in them? Their new French priest explained that church
buildings and contents belonged by canon law to the bishop of a diocese. Of the twenty-six pewholders, all but the O'Hears and Hannas and
two others turned them over to De Goesbriand in December 1854, in return for three dollars each, but threats of excommunication could not
budge the four. So the bishop ordered their four pews taken out of the
church with crowbar and force.

His enemies called the sheriff, who jailed him for trespass, but
parishioner John Menard (referred to as John Minor in the court record)
put up his farm to bail him out. Illness postponed the trial to April
1859, when the bishop, defended by Benjamin H. Smalley, a St. Albans Catholic convert, before Congregationalist judge Asa O. Aldis,
was found guilty and fined $10.83 damages and costs. Roman Catholic
law, said the judge, "has no force in determining what the rights of
these parties are" unless by agreement. The Vermont Supreme Court
heard the bishop's appeal in January 1861 and affirmed the verdict. It
granted that the bishop had title to both land and building, but was only
"trustee" for pewholders, who had sole right of possession and use for
public worship. The bishop then used his ultimate weapon: He immediately interdicted the Church of St. Louis. No services were held in it
until Nicholas Hanna and Thomas O'Hear, the only recalcitrant pewholders left in town, capitulated in July 1865. The damage from the
bitter fight left a deep wound; the parish did not recover enough to support a resident father until 1886.[19]

Roman Catholics were unhappy with the Protestant-dominated
common schools, where Protestant teachers could read from the Protestant Bible daily, Protestant ministers influenced school boards, and
Protestant kids ridiculed and abused Catholic children. Therefore they
gave high priority to developing a parochial school system as fast as
limited resources allowed. Before the Civil War, only in the major villages with substantial Catholic populations could Catholics afford

parochial schools: in Burlington (1854), Rutland, including West Rutland (1855), St. Albans, including Swanton (1857), and Highgate (1858). The St. Albans and Highgate schools soon failed. Laity staffed the schools except in Burlington, where thirteen Sisters of Providence from Montreal also cared for fifty-one orphans, as reported in the 1860 census. For a poor membership, support of parish schools was a heavy burden. Although local taxes had long paid some of the costs of common schools, parents had to pay a substantial part until the 1864 law made schools entirely tax-supported. Henceforth, Catholics paid taxes for public schools and tuition for parochial schools, a double burden.[20]

Protestant Reactions

Vermonters who came earlier, committed to freedom for people to be different, did not like heterogeneity when it happened, whether those who pushed in were Baptists coming in 1775-1815, Methodists in 1800-1840, or the Catholics who came in threatening numbers after 1840.[21] Bishop De Goesbriand was marshaling a squad of priests and a team of nuns to protect and teach his flock. They were not a Protestant bad dream that would go away. Although they held to their official welcome, the natives were alarmed at the consequences of the latest invasion and wondered whether the naturalization laws should be stiffened. James Marsh's brother Leonard was sure that if Congress had such naturalization requirements "as would have excluded the putrid masses of foreign ignorance and vice from the polls," the United States would have escaped the "disgrace and dangers of the present time."[22]

One Congregational reaction was to celebrate the landing of the Pilgrims in December 1620 as Forefathers' Day. Initiated in 1842 by Philip Battell, a Middlebury College and Yale-trained, well-to-do lawyer who inherited Connecticut money, the annual event gathered Middlebury's elite to dine and hear an address extolling the Puritan virtues.[23]

Protestants were happy to use the immigrants as cheap labor—not only in the new industries, but always as farm laborers, barbers, hostlers, stage drivers, teamsters, boatmen, and woodsmen. They hoped that these people could learn the principles of democracy as the natives thought they practiced them in church, society, and state. Mill and quarry owners gave land for churches or contributed to building funds mainly so that their Catholic operatives would feel at home and stay on the job. Archibald W. Hyde, collector of customs during Democratic administrations from 1830 to 1845, sympathized with the French Canadians especially, and allowed them to use a building or build on his land near the streets named after him, Archibald and Hyde, in Burlington.

The history of Protestant-Catholic joint activities has not been written, partly because so much of history is oriented toward conflict as well as because joint activities were limited. Curiosity brought Protestants to the consecration of St. Mary's, Burlington, in 1832, and continued to attract outsiders, in spite of family taboos, to Mass. More often than not, selectmen permitted the use of the town house for Mass. Bishop John Stephen Michaud remembered his mother's mentioning that Cornelius P. Van Ness' Spanish wife attended Mass in the Burlington courthouse after St. Mary's burned.[24] Protestants felt responsible for bringing French children under their care or in their employ to Sunday schools, or bringing Sunday schools to them.[25] They tried to give them Bibles, to take them to church if they lived in the family, include them in family prayers, reprove their intemperance, and help them help themselves. In return they hoped that the grateful aliens would accept the right (Protestant) way.

On the other hand, many masters, poor or mean, treated dependents poorly and meanly, whether native or immigrant, and in between most Yankees and foreigners went their separate ways and helped their own. There was no widespread conspiracy to down the foreigner, nor were many imbued with the ideal of mutual aid among all citizens regardless of differences. Evidence is scarce of discrimination in stores, or in places to watch parades or civic ceremonies, or at the ballot box, either because there was little, or because the wounded did not dare squeal.

More than twenty years of nativism lay behind the eruption of a pimple of a party called the American or Know Nothing Party of 1855-1856. By the mid-1850s, the temperature of politics was feverish. The Kansas-Nebraska Act of early 1854 shocked Vermonters into assembling a new coalition of reform groups for containing slavery and for their pet causes.[26] During the summer of the anti-Nebraska movement, a strident anti-Catholic itinerant calling himself "Angel Gabriel" harangued on Sundays in the streets of Burlington and came near causing a riot.[27] Gabriel's trumpet heralded an anti-foreign conspiracy. The Know Nothings, who aped the secrecy and rituals of fraternal orders, surprised the major parties with their success in electing local candidates in 1855. They controlled the 1855 Council of Censors, which quixotically proposed to reapportion the state house of representatives according to population, perhaps so that the large towns could control their foreigners better. Reapportionment came in the 1960s.

The case of English-born Charles H. Joyce makes it clear that nativists had no objections to foreign Protestants. A Northfield Know Nothing leader in 1855, he became a Republican state's attorney only two years after naturalization.[28] The Whig leadership was so completely in agreement with the Americans' blaming Catholic immigrants for the ills of society that the Whig element of the Republican coalition had no trouble absorbing the Americans and paying them off with the governorship of radical Ryland Fletcher in 1856-1858.

Perhaps it was more than a coincidence that during the two terms of Baptist Governor Ryland Fletcher, Know Nothing leader turned Republican, someone revived the election sermon. This feature of political ceremony, asserting that religion is essential to upholding the state, had been discontinued after 1834. The three "preachers of the year," 1856-1858, were elders with long tenure in strong churches: Willard Child of Castleton, Silas McKeen of Bradford, and Cornelius A. Thomas of Brandon. Governor Hiland Hall, Fletcher's successor, apparently did not see the need of the sermon, although legislative chaplains continued. In 1861, Baptists, Methodists, and Congregationalists took three ballots to choose Rutland's Baptist Leland Howard legislative chaplain over Montpelier's Congregationalist William H. Lord.[29]

Protestants proselyted more than Catholics and won more Catholics as temporary adherents. Nobody has counted the long-term adherence on either side but probably neither side harvested many. Comfortable Congregationalists had trouble accepting lower-class converts as equals, especially during the excitement of 1835 stirred up by Burchard. A Franklin Methodist reported the conversion of one Pelletier, a Canadian immigrant, who testified at a Berkshire camp meeting to "the gracious change. . . in his heart and mind." He concluded that there were a lot more like Pelletier "in the frontier towns of this county."[30] The Baptists had more immediate success near the border than the Methodists. They maintained a mission and school at Grand Ligne, south of St. Jean, Lower Canada, which trained evangelists, some of whom worked among the wooded hills of Franklin, Berkshire, Richford, Enosburg, and Montgomery. French-speaking congregations with French-speaking leaders lasted through the 1850s, dying out because of out-migration, trouble with ministers, and reconversion to Catholicism by visiting priests.[31]

A trickle of well-to-do, upper-class Vermonters converted to Catholicism: William H. Hoyt of St. Albans, the Barlows and Smalleys of Fairfield; George Allen, son of Heman of Milton; in Burlington, Archibald W. Hyde as he approached his deathbed in 1847, the Tuckers and Demings, related to Hoyt's wife, and Abby M. Hemenway.

Hoyt's was the most important defection/accession because of his highly educated gifts, his connections, his wealth, and his position in the Episcopal church. He was a New Hampshire Yankee of old stock, son of a Sandwich storekeeper, Jeffersonian legislator and later Liberty Party and Free Soil candidate for governor, in retirement president of the Carroll County Bank. The son had prepared for the Congregational ministry at Dartmouth and Andover Theological Seminary, but found its tradition, theology, and polity wanting.[32] He dropped out of Andover and took Episcopal orders after training at General Theological Seminary in New York. He lived briefly with Bishop John Henry Hopkins and helped with his school in Burlington, then filled in at St. Stephen's in Middlebury. On August 21, 1838, he married Ann Deming and brought his bride to the vacant St. Albans parish. Ann had recently inherited over $58,000, almost a third of the estate of her father, Eleazer Hubbell Deming, an early Burlington trader. In the decade following the 1836 departure of the previous rector, George Allen, communicants of the St. Albans Union Church nearly doubled, while the growing village gained less than thirty per cent.

Relations between Hopkins and Hoyt were uneasy. Both men were converts to the Anglican way and both highly appreciated church history and valued the traditional liturgy. Perhaps Hoyt acted according to his Congregational tradition more than he realized in resisting his imperious Irish immigrant bishop. When most Episcopal priests in Vermont parishes tended to act independently of their bishop, Hoyt's Congregational background reinforced his independence. He could hardly help looking down on the self-taught upstart instead of giving Hopkins the deference due his station.

Hoyt was in touch with the Oxford Movement and preferred the clarity of its leader, John Henry Newman, who turned Catholic in 1845, to the *via media* of the Anglican Church, inevitably ambivalent because it was a middle way. After seven years as rector of Union Church (Episcopal) in St. Albans and a very deliberate debate with himself as well as with his bishop, Hoyt wrote Bishop Hopkins on July 24, 1846, resigning his care of the parish, went to Montreal, and was received into the Roman Catholic Church.[33] Hoyt took a few parishioners with him into the Roman Catholic church. From a peak of 111 communicants in 1845 the Union Church dropped to 101 in 1850 but recovered and grew. The town expanded with the railroad. He had the Vermont versatility, which served him well as a St. Albans lawyer after his conversion, for a decade as editor of the Democratic *Burlington Sentinel*, and finally, after his wife's death, as Roman Catholic priest.

The Episcopal Diocese of Vermont

The loss of a talented priest to the Catholics caused no earthquake among the Episcopalians. They continued to grow on villagers' hunger for more ritual and less stern dogma. Convinced members can always claim that their churches grow because more and more people see the truth of their way, but questions still arise: why these particular converts at this particular time? A twenty-five percent Episcopal gain in the 1840s, contributing to a doubling in the diocese during Hopkins' episcopate, 1832-68, cannot be ascribed to the harmonious energy of bishop, clergy, and laity before the Civil War, for there was disagreement on the major issues.

The Episcopal church received notable accessions of distinguished Congregationalists, such as Whig Charles K. Williams, judge, governor, and son of an early Rutland pastor, and the Democrat Isaac F. Redfield, judge of the Vermont Supreme Court. The drain continued: William J. Harris, Yale 1856, bought an Episcopal prayer book his junior year but had Congregational ordination in 1862 and served two parishes before he went to Boston and was confirmed Episcopalian. Such devout Christians wanted less emphasis on what they considered harsh, negative theology, less "ultraist" reform, and more emphasis on benevolence, with due deference to household and village traditions. The attraction for some was what the English Oxford Movement stood for: veneration for the ancient Christian tradition, and personal piety reinforced by traditional church liturgy. By seniority Hopkins became presiding bishop in 1863. Having long refused to take sides on the slavery issue, he helped hold his denomination above the fray and together when antislavery and Civil War divided other denominations. Protestants uncomfortable with the radical Republicans found Hopkins's stance attractive.

Education of Clergy and Members

Most Episcopalians in the Diocese of Vermont were cool to Bishop Hopkins' lifelong desire for a theological seminary. They had failed to sustain Bishop Hopkins' school in the 1830s, but the undaunted bishop tried again before he had even paid off its $13,000 debt. For five years after 1854 he begged throughout his diocese and in eastern cities, raising about $30,000 in paid-in pledges, with some $5,000 more out of his own $1,200 salary and outside earnings. He added his fees from lecturing widely, his salary when he substituted for Bishop Alonzo Potter of Philadelphia, and what the University of the South (Sewanee) paid him for surveying its campus and lands. In 1860 he dedicated the Gothic building of the Vermont Episcopal Institute at Rock Point, Burlington, whose architecture he had inspired if not designed, and straightway started another drive for a girls' school. The Institute's theological students, however, never supplied Vermont's needs for clergy, who prepared most often at General Theological Seminary in New York City, or in Cambridge, Massachusetts, or Alexandria, Virginia.[34]

With the fading of revival zeal fewer young men in the Puritan tradition felt called to the ministry. Out-migration bled congregations, funds were short for paying what ministers could be found, and congregations called for ministers with more training. By the 1840s, Congregationalists no longer hired ministers who had merely read divinity with an older man after graduation from college. From its establishment in 1808, Andover Theological Seminary's three-year course trained the largest number of them for Vermont pulpits, while Yale, Princeton, Hartford, and Bangor, with shades of doctrinal difference and varying spheres of influence, supplied the rest.

The Baptists, Universalists, Methodists, and Christians had once been satisfied with preachers who got along with little education and less money and farmed to earn their meagre livelihood. By mid-century even they had come to feel that would-be preachers should attend academies. For Friends, a yearly meeting boarding school was available from 1796 in Dutchess County, New York, and even earlier in New York City, but few if any Vermont Quaker ministers had academic education. At the academies someone, usually the principal if he was a minister, would give special attention to those potential ministers whom their churches had encouraged with funds. In all these minority groups, including the Catholics, the pastors often had to travel to more than one town to tend their flocks and had short tenures. So their in-service training had to be on the run or at ministers' conferences and association meetings.

Only the Baptists at Fairfax and the Methodists at Newbury had theological departments with their academies. The Methodists' Newbury Seminary (1834-1868) received New Hampshire Conference approval in 1841 to start a theological program, headed by Rev. W. M. Willett, a scholar of Hebrew. They raised enough to endow one theological professorship, hire another instructor, and publish the quarterly *Newbury Biblical Magazine* (1843-1846). New England Methodists promoting theological studies transferred their hopes to Concord, New Hampshire, and finally settled on a School of Theology at Boston University.[35] Vermont Baptists, with supply of clergy chiefly in mind, persuaded the New Hampton (New Hampshire) Institution, despairing of support from its state Baptist convention, to transfer to Fairfax, Vermont, in 1852. Vermont Baptists struggled until after the Civil War, but had no better luck than their New Hampshire brethren. Roman Catholic clergy in this period most conveniently attended La Grande Seminaire in Montreal, available to anglophone as well as francophone because the instruction was in Latin.

The age-old feeling that churches need schools to indoctrinate, that is, teach what they believe, at first combined the dual purpose of raising up ministers and teaching the faithful. To eke out a skinny and uncertain income, many a Congregational minister and his wife (less often, clergy of other faiths) kept school for parishioners' children and any others they could lure to the parsonage. If successful and the town or the town leadership would help, the school rose to the level of academy, which with more success might last beyond the tenure of the founders, although not often with clerical heads. Affluent church members would find money to help promising boys to attend academies under denominational control.

In the 1830s the Baptists founded and controlled several academies, and added New Hampton in 1852, while the Methodists had four by 1847, and the Universalists started three between 1848 and 1863. Free Will Baptists began talking about an academy in the 1850s, but did not open one until after the Civil War.[36] Lack of enough patronage and financial support for all these schools forced Protestants to aim at transmitting the faith through one statewide or conference-wide school. Except for the Episcopalians, who had none to begin with, their efforts were realized in the decade of prosperity that began during the Civil War.

The Troy Conference Academy, West Poultney, chartered in 1834, opened in 1835, and two years later moved into its own $40,000 building. It survived competition from half a dozen other Methodist schools in the New York part of the Conference, notably Fort Edward, New York, Institute, headed for half a century from 1854 by Joseph E. King, successful principal of Newbury Seminary (1847-53). Unable to pay off its construction debt, the Conference leased the Poultney school to a Methodist minister in 1855. He sold it in 1863 to a former principal and a professor. With a dearth of available males, they turned it into a girls' school called "Ripley Female College."[37]

As in secondary schools, so in colleges, the weight of attention and activity turned on providing moral, nonsectarian programs. President Benjamin Labaree stabilized Middlebury College by downplaying the evangelical and Congregational hallmarks of its first thirty-five years, raising money, and attracting a young faculty, strong in science. Middlebury managed the appointment of its professor of geology, Charles Baker Adams, as first state geologist, and saw the benefits of releasing the Rev. James Meacham, professor of rhetoric and English literature, to serve in Congress, 1849-56. Adams was capable of reconciling geology and Genesis. Meacham was capable of reconciling the peace movement, which he supported, with the warlike tradition of the Green Mountain Boys.[38]

Norwich University had a hard time keeping afloat under the shadow of Dartmouth College, and more than once in its early years the trustees thought of escaping to a less competitive site. After its first escape to Middletown, Connecticut, Norwich University was chartered in 1834 under Universalist patronage. The Universalist influence had obviously waned when Norwich chose as its president in 1847 the Rev. James Davie Butler, Congregationalist. In 1851, when the Universalists sought a college under denominational control, not Norwich but

Brattleboro was among the proposed sites. President Edward Bourns, an ordained Episcopal priest (1850-1869 with minor gaps), followed Butler. Bourns conducted services in Hanover Sunday afternoons, and at St. Mary's, Northfield, until succeeded by President Roger S. Howard, previously Episcopal rector at Woodstock. Under Bourns the university had Episcopal "support."[39]

The University of Vermont continued under President John Wheeler (1833-49), next to Joseph Fairbanks of St. Johnsbury and Thomas A. Merrill of Middlebury, probably the most influential Vermont Congregationalist. During Wheeler's tenure and that of Worthington Smith (1849-56), over a fifth of the graduates went into the ministry.[40] After that the percentage shrank steadily to less than seven percent toward the end of the century. In the nineteenth century, the last ministers co-opted to serve on the board of trustees were installed in 1865; the legislature elected two in 1887. Wheeler's successors, also Congregational ministers, followed his conservative orientation through the Civil War.[41]

The school reformers, responding to the needs of business and industry, claimed that the common schools were not giving a good education to the people to fit them for the modern world of exchange; therefore the state should tell them what to do. And in the more populous places, during the half century after William Miller said the sky was falling, graded elementary and public high schools began to eclipse the church-related schools and academies.

The growing minority favored nonsectarian if not anticlerical education in private academies, too. Chelsea citizens chartered an Orange County Independent Grammar School in 1833, perhaps emphasizing its freedom from the strong Congregational influence at Randolph's Orange County Grammar School. People's Academy of Morrisville, chartered in 1847, provided that "there is not to be taught any particular religious creed or sectarianism." Yet all students had to attend Sunday worship unless with parental excuse, and the Rev. Septimius Robinson, pastor of the local Congregational Church, 1835-60, was long chair of the trustees.[42]

Changes in the 1850s

Meanwhile statewide Protestantism, stark as truth, was in the villages a growing, physical presence reorienting its objectives, while in the hills it was halted or in defensive retreat. People, especially men, cared less about their churches, but they were enthusiastic about the business outlook. They worshiped the miraculous new inventions: the steam locomotive transforming transportation, the electric telegraph speeding communication, steam stone channelers chiseling jobs away from many Irishmen, scales and machine tools ushering in the age of accuracy and interchangeable parts for the miracle machines. The clergy, like the press, supported the business that made villages and village churches strong.

The Brandon Congregational and Baptist churches illustrate the co-operation of village churches bound together in support of a village's main industry. Both organized in 1785 and sharing the "minister's right," the two churches maintained friendly relations partly through family connections and partly through mutual interest in the iron industries developed by Baptist deacon John Conant from 1820. The first long-term Congregational minister, Ebenezer Hebard (May 1799-September 1821), and Elder Cornelius A. Thomas's tenure, 1836-1875, at the stronger Baptist church, steadied the relationship.

An unusual record of preachers, texts, and attendance at the Congregational church, 1855-1856, suggests how the Baptists' lesser partner kept its balance in the period of rapid economic change and growth after the railroad reached Brandon. Surprisingly, the church was better served by a variety of visiting ministers passing through town, from the Middlebury and Burlington colleges, or missionary agents, than had they accepted less capable men wanting to settle there. Elder Thomas preached for them or they visited his church eight times in less than two years and they maintained two and sometimes three Sunday services, with attendance ranging from 150 to 200. Only strong village churches continued to support the double dip of morning and afternoon worship.[43]

The Universalists stopped growing in the 1840s, and had less success than the Baptists in the centers. After having large shares in the union meetinghouses of the early years, and a strong missionary push against the revivalism of the 1830s, they lost steam. The fading of the fear of hell among the heirs of Calvin cut into the Universalists' potential market, with many in other churches adopting their distinctive belief in salvation for all. James Buckham, Congregational pastor in Chelsea, 1834-1841, after he had buried three of his babies, said in a sermon that he believed all infants (not just *elect* infants) would be saved. His old-guard enemies called a council, but although it did not condemn him, he left rather than try to lead a divided church.[44] In many places like East Randolph, because of the Universalists' minister shortage, congregations long suffered without a settled pastor or even infrequent calls from a missionary. In Windsor and probably Burlington, Universalists were always part of the Unitarian congregations. John Gregory of Northfield, one of their ablest evangelists for reason and reform, tried in 1830 and again in 1845 to plant a church in Burlington, but each time the plant withered. In Barre, where Universalists had organized in the southern part of town in 1796, they were

able to move into the center in 1852, and hold on as the granite industry transformed Barre into a city.[45]

Free Will Baptists and the Christian Connection, born in the country, had an even harder time invading the villages, but continued to hold
on where they had started, from the softening of Calvinism.[46]

Protestants built more churches and added members in the growing
villages, 1848-64. Internal migration, evangelism, prosperity, and
Catholic competition stimulated this growth. The Congregationalists
paid the best ministerial salaries in the state and sustained costly building programs in St. Albans, Burlington, Brandon, Rutland, Bellows
Falls, and Woodstock after 1851. The other denominations, especially
the Methodists, showing signs of rising status, followed suit. They
became in 1846 the fifth denomination in Vermont to establish a
statewide organ, the *Montpelier Christian Messenger*. The Vermont
Conference could afford it, perhaps, because the Rev. Elijah Scott was
willing to devote his life to editing the organ. A few hundred Welsh,
mainly Methodist, who struggled and built in the slate region, were the
only substantial group of Protestant immigrants to Vermont in this period.[47]

Booster optimism caused the Congregational churches in St.
Johnsbury and Burlingon, and the Burlington Methodists, to feel so
confident they would grow that they released a colony in the same village. Earlier, in at least twenty-five towns with more than one nucleus,
two or more Congregational churches served the separate centers and a
few other congregationally organized groups added a second church to
make access easier. In Burlington the Roman Catholics had a reason in
1850 to give French Canadians a priest who could speak their language.
St. Mary's and St. Joseph's were a long mile apart, and served two connected villages, Winooski Falls and Burlington.

In October 1851, the Congregational church on St. Johnsbury
"Plain," near the Fairbanks scale factory, organized the South Church
with a colony of seventy-five of its members. Was it "the difficulty in
securing seats for all worshipers," or a disagreement between members,
or a guess that the village would grow enough to support two Congregational churches, or a pre-emptive strike to keep the Methodists off
Main Street? The only recorded motive was the need for more space.
They dedicated their new building, a third of a mile down the same
street, the following January.[48]

In 1855, the Burlington Methodists organized a second church three
blocks from the first, and in 1860, the College Street Church split off
and built three blocks away from its parent.[49] While the same expan-
sionist hopes seem to have inspired all these pairs, circumstances suggest that both faith and practice differed enough between the Burlington
Methodist and Congregational twins to make separation more comfort-

able for both. And if the prospect of growth had not been good, factions could not have afforded the dangerous luxury of two churches of one mind but with inadequate resources. We can always assume, while the record is silent, that clashing personalities affected the outcomes.

"The mightiest revival that Burlington ever saw" established a second Methodist church in 1854-1855, that lasted a dozen years. As a result of three weeks of protracted meetings, so "many were converted and many believers were sanctified" that the little Methodist meetinghouse on White Street and its lecture rooms could not hold them all. Protracted meetings were revivals every evening led by imported evangelists, plus daytime prayer meetings for women who gave their housework a lick and a promise. Sanctification or perfectionism, in Wesley's original doctrine, meant in the exhorters' simple words that beyond the experience of God's grace converting the soul of the sinner, a "second blessing" through the spirit of Christ could infuse in believers the ability to overcome sin. Troy Conference leaders wanted to corral this enthusiasm by building larger, but agreed to the local urgency to swarm off.

Twenty-seven members and forty-nine probationers transferred to a new site on Pine Street, nearer the new shops but still with a respectable address—quite a load of green wood for a few families to season. The new membership included "a class which had never been reached before," given to "violent gesture and passionate and loud vociferation." They probably had lower economic status, less education, briefer residence, and needed a church for social solace.[50]

Rivaling the parent church, the Pine Street Methodists' building was a little bigger, had modern improvements of gas light, hot-air furnaces, and an above-ground lecture and Sunday school assembly hall. It was a "free" church; that is, attenders gave free will offerings instead of members paying pew rent as in the First Methodist Church. A hostile witness claimed, however, that the new church hypocrites made a local African-American barber and his wife sit in a Negro pew. Their Sunday school became the largest in Burlington. Optimistic boosterism ran afoul of hard times after 1857. By 1860, both churches were in trouble. The First Methodists, without the balance of artisan-oriented enthusiasm, had veered in a liberal direction. Genteel eloquence, tolerance, and freedom of expression seemed more important to them than the rigors of orthodoxy and Pine Street's hallelujahs of sanctification.

After the war, Bishop Matthew Simpson came, conciliated, and won agreement to build a noble new house of worship for both congregations. After a fair trial, Conference leaders had re-established middle-of-the-road Methodism and headed off for another generation the tendency of their holiness wing to break away.

Two different kinds of revivals in the late 1850s showed the split

between the anti-church extremists and the church-oriented village revivals. The "businessmen's revival" of 1858 gave birth to young men's
new Christian activities. Unlike the holiness flare-up creating Burlington's Pine Street Methodist church, the religious revival of 1858,
started among New York City businessmen, was sedate and orderly.
Accessions to Vermont Protestant churches in the 1850s were either
children of members, people moving to the villages, or the harvest of
this revival. With frequent and protracted prayer meetings, this Yankee
labor-saving device of praying by steam, as one newspaper quipped,
used the age-old call to repentance and salvation. Like the earlier revivals, it minimized denominational differences and avoided theology
and politics. It differed from earlier revivals in several respects: It was a
reaction against the excesses of reformers; it comforted those uprooted
from their rural homes; it fed on the depression of the late 1850s; and
its less boisterous style appealed to young village businessmen, the
"yuppies" of the day. In a sense it was an outlet for the unrecognized
fear of the rising tide of anger and intransigeance leading to the Civil
War. This antislavery discomfort was a current swelled by repeated
tributary incidents over a long generation.

Newspapers of both parties welcomed this respite from partisanship. Instead of working in harmony to build Christ's kingdom, wrote
John Cain in his Democratic *Rutland Courier* of November 28, 1857,
"the churches have been. . . divided and paralyzed by side issues. . . .
The human mind. . . can entertain but one absorbing question at a
time." "Business-Men's Prayer Meetings" gathered daily at the Congregational "chapel" on West Street, Rutland, in the spring of 1858, and
like all the other services, they were non-denominational. Adventists led
by Elder Miles Grant of Boston capitalized on the ferment, as did the
"evangelicals."

The revival's institutional products were Young Men's Christian
Associations, which budded in 1855-59 in several villages, lay dormant
during the Civil War, and blossomed after. The purpose of the twenty-
one St. Johnsbury young men who organized a sort of Christian
lyceum in late October, 1855, was to do "ourselves and others good."
The purpose of the Rutland YMCA in 1858 was "to promote evangelical religion among all classes. . . of this town, and especially among
its young men; feeling the great value of concentrated efforts."[51] The
Rutland group behaved like a fraternal organization and the lyceum it
had been before the revival. When Daniel Russeguie died of lockjaw the
Rutland Courier (12 November 1858) mentioned that he belonged to
the "Y" and would have a large funeral. The young men also heard
ministers lecture on such subjects as the mythology of the ancient
druids. But when the Rutland Young Men's Association in 1855 could
not agree to invite the Rev. Antoinette L. Brown to lecture to them,

they referred the question to the ladies, who voted "No."[52] Similar organizations appeared in West Rutland, Brandon, and Norwich (with a "Young Ladies' Christian Association"), constant in prayer, acting as missionaries and tract distributors to districts bereft of access to pastors, and generally taking themselves very seriously.[53]

With the moderate reformers captured by the Republican coalition, the Rutland Free Convention of 1858, billed as a gathering of all kinds of reformers, was also underneath, the spiritualists' first step toward becoming a denomination. Spiritualists were a new phenomenon with itinerant mediums whose messages from the spirit world were mainly anti-establishment. Off on the left edge of the scene during the depression after 1857, the gathering was hosted by spiritualists and attended by "no-government" abolitionists, feminists, and other radicals.

A Garrisonian abolitionist convention preceded the Rutland meeting January 26-27, 1858, in Bradford. The same kind of radical signed its call: Governor Ryland Fletcher, Rev. Nathan R. Johnson of the Covenanter Presbyterian church in Topsham, and Monkton Quaker Henry Miles. Commended by Daniel Pierce Thompson's *Green Mountain Freeman*, it presented African-American speakers from the Boston area.

The only detailed sources documenting this Rutland Free Convention are a report of proceedings by participants, an account in the spiritualist organ, *Banner of Light*,[54] and adverse comments in the newspapers. By 1858 the Republican Party had absorbed moderate reformers, leaving extremists wanting company and publicity.

The organizing committee, including the two Rutland spiritualists and the Boston publisher of the proceedings, chose a format of discussing resolutions without voting on them. It amounted to a vote if attenders signed the many petitions for various causes. Dr. H. S. Brown of Clarendon told the *Rutland Herald* that more supported woman suffrage than any other cause. A list of those who signed the petition to call the convention shows a sprinkling of "friends of human progress" from Burlington to Bennington: Harvey Howes of West Haven, who cast the only vote in the 1870 constitutional convention for woman suffrage; four Universalist ministers; Joshua Young, Burlington Unitarian; Jon R. Forest, the Winooski critic of the Pine Street Methodists; B. J. Heineberg of Colchester and eight other doctors; Rowland T. Robinson, Ferrisburg ex-Quaker; Achsah Sprague and several other spiritualists. Jason F. Walker, ex-Methodist then of Glens Falls, delivered the keynote address.

The local Republican *Herald* roasted them in its annual New Year's doggerel: "The Holy Word is freely set aside / As being too severe on Human Pride. / 'Free Love' talks long, the Marriage Rite ignores! / Convenient Creed for Session held outdoors. / 'Spirits' appeared — I'll call them Diabolic, / A better term perhaps is *Alcoholic*. / The former sort, if present, were self-willed, / And if the latter, they were well distilled. / . . . / And said Convention didn't stop to say / How much it hastened the Millennial Day."[55]

At a time when every other wanderer had a plan for national salvation in his pocket, spiritualists, who both believed in and experienced communication with the spirits of the dead, had a more modest goal: personal comfort. Bret Carroll, the latest analyst of this new movement, quotes with approval Sydney Ahlstrom's characterization of the spiritualists as sharing the principles of "harmonial religion" common to mid-nineteenth-century liberal Americans. They assumed that "spiritual composure, physical health, and even economic well-being...flow from a person's rapport with the cosmos." Carroll analyzes the relationships of spiritualism with the other religious and reform movements of 1820-1860, and concludes that, like the Mormons, Adventists, and Shakers, Spiritualists criticized the creeds, clergy, and polities of their competitors to improve rather than destroy their principles. Commonly dismissed as a transient fad, arising out of the socioeconomic malaise of the period and attracting sensational attention in séances, it became "a fully elaborated religion" with "mutually hostile Christian and rationalistic wings."[56] Its tensions between liberty and order coincided with Vermonters' balance between freedom and unity. Its semi-private circles provided the same reinforcement of believers that the Methodist classes provided. Its itinerant mediums were its ministry, mediating between divine angels and humans needing a scientific grounding. Its communitarian tendency appealed to Vermonters' localism, as Orson Murray did.

The fame of the Fox sisters of Rochester, New York, who claimed in 1848 to be mediums for messages from the dead, spread with telegraphic speed, especially in communities away from the telegraph and railroad lines. Charles Morris Cobb's diary as a fifteen-year-old in Woodstock testified to the excitement in his town in the winter of 1851. Miranda Briggs Randall, wife of Nathaniel and probably the first medical-college-trained woman doctor in Vermont, was a member of the Mt. Tom Spiritual Circle. She wrote a pamphlet containing a long letter from George Washington recorded by Austin E. Simmons, local medium, giving advice on current issues. He no longer favored neutrality in foreign affairs, but with Daniel Webster, would help the oppressed everywhere. The Hungarian republican, Lajos Kossuth, was then in the United States promoting his aborted revolution against Austria. Washington (in life a slaveholder) wanted no slavery in the territories and urged California Forty-niners to turn from gold-seeking to agriculture. Letters from the Sherman family in Fairfield, 1852, witness to the same excitement during the dull days of winter.[57]

Vermont's most significant spiritualist missionary was Achsah W. Sprague of Plymouth (1827-1862), a child prodigy, local school teacher at twelve, crippled with arthritis. Lying useless in a darkened room for two years, doctors ministering in vain, she began to get better, like Mary Baker Eddy, when she found her vocation. Her sister reported spirits promising her a useful career as a trance speaker. Starting in 1854, her health improved as her fame spread and she widened her field. She reached Iowa and Missouri before her disease and the war ended her activity. She is one of many examples of women's advancement in this period as healers, counselors, and unordained clergy. She used her popularity to advocate antislavery, temperance, women's rights, and prison reform. She was in demand for funerals and planted many seeds of spiritualist churches.[58] Beginning with the Rochester rappers, there was always an element of vaudeville in the evangelistic performances of mediums. Some went to see them as they would the performances of dancing bears and magicians. Audiences enjoyed both being hoodwinked and watching the contests between mediums and those who tried to expose them.

Zeal for the Civil War

All excitements about local affairs stopped abruptly at the outbreak of the Civil War, as if an earthquake had dislocated everyday life. In spirit, Vermonters were superbly prepared for the war by the revival-born zeal that fueled reforms, especially abolition. The revivals of the late 1850s, except the revival of military training, disappeared. Their spirit merely shifted into the stream of parades, rallies, and victory celebrations that roused emotional support for war goals instead of salvation. These social events left little time and energy for camp meetings, protracted meetings, and prayer meetings. Ministers used to bringing in the sheaves now brought in recruits, welcomed returning heroes, comforted the families of fallen soldiers with private counsel and funeral sermons, and justified the ways of the war to their parishioners.

Yet in spite of the militia revival and the almost universal approval of sacred war aims for freedom and union, the mass of Vermonters were ill prepared for the fight when it came, in willingness to accept military discipline and in ability to fund and forward arms, equipment, and men to war fronts. Not everyone who wanted to restore the Union was willing to make the necessary sacrifices. The nine or ten thousand young men who volunteered during the first year of the war offered their lives for their ideals. Many of the survivors re-enlisted because the job was not finished. But the vast majority, in Vermont as elsewhere, put personal and family goals ahead of abstract war aims.

Vermont localism, when oriented toward the war, expressed itself in the efforts of towns, companies, and churches to supply what by the end of the war state and federal government more efficiently procured. At home, attention focused on the boys in blue and the content of the newspapers reflected this shift of attention with their focus on war stories. Because almost everyone believed that union was a sacred goal worth fighting and if need be dying for, the home folks accepted the loss of help from family and friends away in the service and supported the collection of money and material for them as the least they could do for the cause.

Vermont Chaplains[59]

Although Vermonters thought little about it, they expected chaplains to maintain connections between soldiers and home, as well as between God and the soldiers away from home. Like other nineteenth-century Americans, they did not question the mingling of church and state in chaplaincies for the state prison, the state legislature, Congress, or at frontier army posts. The militia acts of 1779, 1797, and 1837 did not provide for chaplains. These officers represented a vestige of the principle written into the first Vermont constitution, that the state is undergirded with Protestant principles. Citizens are free to behave according to what they think is sacred, but they can be required to practice their religion in a way that upholds the state and accepts its settling of differences when non-violent private settlement fails. In support of this principle, most Vermonters fought to recover a *Christian* Union.

Twenty-eight chaplains, roughly one out of every fifteen Vermont Protestant ministers, served Vermont regiments in the Civil War. The role of the ninety percent who stayed home was to boost morale; so was the chaplains' role with the troops. Chaplains symbolized the hope that religion would remain as central to American character in the restored Union as it appeared to Alexis De Tocqueville a generation before.

Countrywide, they were appointed in various ways.[60] In Vermont they applied to the governor, who appointed them as a small part of his patronage. In these appointments, the decision was the governor's but he listened to a variety of pressures. In the case of Episcopalian John A. Hicks, appointed chaplain of Burlington's Baxter Army Hospital in February 1865, the state senate confirmed the appointment. The Congregationalist *Vermont Chronicle* claimed that chaplains had to be ordained and recommended by five other clergymen. The practice of electing company captains carried over to replacement chaplains, at least in the case of Episcopalian Charles S. Hale, chosen "by formal vote of the line officers" of the Fifth Regiment.[61]

A letter from Charles Wesley Willard, editor of the *Green Mountain Freeman* and successor to Congressman Frederick E. Woodbridge, urged the appointment of Alonzo Webster to the very convenient chaplaincy of Montpelier's Sloan Army Hospital, supported by the signatures of substantial citizens. Webster, prewar editor of the Methodist *Montpelier Christian Messenger*, had a nine-month leave of absence from the chaplaincy of the state prison to serve as chaplain of the Sixteenth Regiment, then served another year as chaplain of the Sixth. He was finding the work in Virginia hard on his health, Willard wrote. Soon after Webster joined the Sixth a correspondent reported his getting a large chapel tent from the U.S. Christian Commission. "Through his energetic efforts" and with help from the men he got the tent "raised upon stockades and furnished with a desk, seats, a stove, &c." It was used for weekly literary society meetings as well as religious services and was the first chapel tent in the brigade since the first year of the war.[62]

Chaplains volunteered for the terms of the regiments they served and received the pay and perquisites of a captain of infantry. By August 1861 Congress provided for and paid for them, generally higher salaries than their churches agreed to pay them. Besides, some church salaries were in arrears, while army pay was prompt. William S. Smart's Benson Congregational Church gave him a leave of absence with pay. St Johnsbury's North Congregational Church gave Ephraim Cummings leave, but whether with pay is buried in the church record.[63]

Vermont chaplains were a varied group, like the other volunteers, only older. The median age of the twelve Congregationalists, about thirty-eight, was probably older than that of other officers, too. They came from all over the state, although half came from the larger villages. Their median length of service was just under a year. Lucius C. Dickinson was the only chaplain of a three-year regiment who served his full time as a chaplain. John Cargill enlisted in the Fifth Regiment as a corporal, was promoted, wounded, and after six months' recuperation returned to complete his three years; then served as chaplain the last nine months of the war. Only Universalist Joseph Sargent of Williston, in the Thirteenth Regiment, died in service, of "camp [typhoid] fever." There were seven Methodists, five Episcopalians, two Baptists, a Unitarian, and a Wesleyan Methodist. I have not found Cargill's affiliation.

None were Catholics. According to Bishop De Goesbriand's estimate, 700 to 1,000 French Canadian and Irish Catholics had by early October, 1861, volunteered for regiments in the first Vermont Brigade of some 5,000 men. A resolution of the joint houses persuaded the governor to appoint Zephyrin Druon, who had been firing up crowds at

Table 1. Vermont Civil War Chaplains

Name and Regiment	Date Comm'd/Date Disch.		Residence
Bayne, Thomas(8)	23 Feb. 65	28 June 65	Irasburg
Bogart, William E.(ll)	18 Aug. 62	*29 Nov. 62	Weybridge
Brastow, Lewis O. (12)	19 Sep. 62	14 Jul. 63	St. Johnsbury
Cargill, John D. (5)	19 Sep. 64	29 Jun. 65	Richmond
Cummings, Ephraim C.(15)	26 Sep. 62	5 Aug. 63	St. Johnsbury
Dayton, Durell W. (2)	18 Aug. 62	*6 Jan. 63	Middlebury
Dickinson, Lucius C. (9)	2 Jul. 62	13 Jun. 65	Cavendish
Frost, Henry M. (7)	25 Jan. 62	*9 Aug. 62	Middlebury
Goodrich, John E. (Cav.)	7 Apr. 64	9 Aug. 65	Burlington
Hale, Charles S. (5)	24 May 62	25 May 63	Brandon
"	8 Aug. 63	15 Sep. 64	"
Haynes, Edwin M. (10)	18 Aug. 62	*2 Oct. 64	Wallingford
Hopkins, William C. (7)	25 Sep. 62	*19 Oct. 65	Northfield
Little, Arthur (11)	20 Mar. 63	24 Jun. 65	Ludlow
Mack, Daniel A. (3)	11 Jan. 62	27 Jul. 64	Royalton
Parmelee, Moses P. (3)	10 Jun. 61	*18 Dec. 61	————
Perry, John B. (10)	23 Mar. 65	7 Jul. 65	Swanton
Plimpton, Salem M. (4)	8 Sep. 61	*1 Sep. 62	Wells River
Randall, Edward H. (13)	5 May 63	#	Burlington
Roberts, John L. (4)	25 Sep. 62	*9 May 63	Chelsea
Sargent, Joseph (13)	9 Oct. 62	+20 Apr. 63	Williston
Simons, Volney M. (5)	24 Aug. 61	*— Mar. 62	Swanton
Smart, William S. (14)	8 Oct. 62	30 Jul. 63	Benson
Smith, Claudius B. (2)	6 Jun. 61	*8 Jul. 62	Brandon
Stone, Edward P. (6)	10 Oct. 61	*23 Aug. 63	Berlin
Stone, Levi H. (1)	26 Apr. 61	15 Aug. 61	Northfield
Webster, Alonzo (16)	16 Oct. 62	10 Aug. 63	Windsor
" (6)	3 Oct. 63	28 Oct. 64	"
Webster, Harvey (6)	13 Nov. 64	26 Jun. 65	Randolph
Williams, Francis C. (8)	20 Dec. 61	22 Jun. 65	Brattleboro
Woodward, John H.(Cav.)	16 Nov. 61	*17 Jul. 63	Westford

Information from the *Revised Roster of Vermont Volunteers*. Number of regiment in parenthesis after name. The First Regiment enlisted for three months; the Twelfth through the Sixteenth, for nine months; the Second through the Eleventh, the Seventeenth, and the First Vermont Cavalry, for three years.
* = Resigned.
+ = Died.
# = Declined commission

recruiting rallies, "to visit and remain with the Vermont Regiments." Druon went to Washington with the Assembly resolution and the governor's letter to the Secretary of War but Cameron vetoed the appointment, either pleading lack of funds or citing rules allowing for regimental chaplains only.[64] Was this Protestant prejudice? Should the pious Protestants have been deprived so that one regiment would have a token Catholic chaplain? The positions of the Vermont Brigade on the Potomac front made it difficult for Catholic soldiers to attend Mass conducted by priests of other state units. At least three Irish regiments had Holy Cross fathers for chaplains: two from New York and one from Massachusetts.[65]

Feisty John Lonergan, ultimately awarded a medal of honor for bravery at Gettysburg, made an issue of the rights of Catholic soldiers. When ordered to turn out his Company A, Thirteenth Regiment, for a Protestant Christmas service, he refused, was disciplined, but exonerated. Coming to Burlington in 1848 with his family of famine refugees from County Tipperary, Ireland, he had joined the Allen Greys of Brandon, the first militia company revived in 1855. He was selling groceries in Winooski when he saw a chance to captain a company in the Second Regiment. The sixty-five men he recruited were too few for a company, the authorities said, and distributed his volunteers among the other companies. He fought to be paid for the work he had done and with the support of his officers eventually won some compensation. He was sergeant of Frontier Cavalry for six months in 1865, an active Fenian, a customs inspector, and when Cleveland Democrats were in power, U. S. consul in Montreal.[66]

How well qualified were the Vermont chaplains? Students of Civil War chaplains throughout both armies have concluded that they were of poor quality, whether from the religious or military point of view. Scraps of evidence about Vermont Civil War chaplains, however, suggest that they varied as much from courage to cowardice, from useless to useful, as other Vermont officers and men; that on the whole, they did their jobs.

They had to earn the respect of Vermont troops, especially in the first two years when they were an afterthought of the authorities, and most volunteers were imbued with the religion of democracy and patriotism. When everything had to be done at once, finding work for chaplains did not get high priority. Those who knew how to find useful things to do made themselves useful. Perhaps many thought of chaplains as in the way, some feeling that they were hiding behind clerical immunity from the dirty work. The Seventeenth Vermont Regiment, enlisted for three years, never had a chaplain. Nearly nine months went by after Chaplain Woodward resigned from the First Vermont Cavalry before another was commissioned, and nearly six months passed before

John B. Perry succeeded Edwin M. Haynes of the Tenth Regiment. When other chaplains resigned there was always some gap in coverage.

In their pastoral function, chaplains had great opportunities from the start, for military life was full of unpleasant surprises for farmer boys. Four months into the war, Chaplain Moses P. Parmelee rounded up signatures for a petition to pardon Private William Scott, sentenced to be executed for sleeping on sentry duty and pardoned in the nick of time. Chaplains seemed free to do whatever soldiers of their unit were ordered to do. Chaplain Woodward of the First Vermont Cavalry led charges, fired at the enemy, and took prisoners. For his martial fervor, his town of Westford honored "the fighting chaplain" with a memorial statue, the only Vermont Civil War monument to a chaplain.[67]

The ups and downs of a chaplain's life are well illustrated in the letters of Edward Payson Stone to "Dear Home" in Berlin.[68] Unlike most other chaplains who were pastors first, Stone taught in Vermont, North Carolina, and near Boston after graduating from Middlebury College in 1853, and was ordained to be a chaplain four days after his commission. His regiment suffered sickness in the winter of 1862 and heavy casualties in McClellan's Peninsular campaign. Writing on July 8, 1862, at Harrison's Landing, where the Vermont Brigade camped for over a month, he reassured his folks that he and his brother had endured "the exposure and hardship better than . . . average. . . . The chaplains of the 4th & 5th are away sick. The chaplain of the 2d was sick when I last saw him and expected to leave soon. Chaplain Mack of the 3d I have not seen for some time. He is away a good deal." "There is hardly any opportunity for meetings of any kind," he concluded. Although he lost his linen coat "when we were shelled out of camp and lost our tents &c," another coat came from home a few weeks later.

Then his tone changed. The chaplains "started a daily prayer meeting in the brick church," he wrote August 8, and rotated Sabbath preaching. He ate well, with the hospital mess, helped build brick ovens, and tied his horse with the others, "and the boys help me take care of him. . . . My bed & writing table is two boards each a foot wide supported on four stakes." He was sorry to leave "the beautiful church" when they broke camp a week later. By November, near Fredericksburg, Virginia, he was gloomy again. "Nearly all our sabbaths are spent" moving, with hardly a chance "to look at my Bible. . . . No chaplain that I have talked with feels. . . that it is of any use for chaplains to be here. They have to hear profanity and obscenity from both officers and men." A month later he complained, "I never saw the men and officers so depressed before except at Harrison Landing. . . I can not see anything human to encourage them." When Col. Elisha Barney, "a praying man," replaced Col. Oscar S. Tuttle in March 1863, Stone's hopes rose again. Soon the Sabbath was filled with meetings morning and afternoon and tent meetings in the evening. Yet he resigned in August, and preached for the United Brethren while waiting for transportation home.

Baptist-Adventist "Father" Isaac Blake, who enlisted as a musician from West Derby, behaved, when not piping his fife, like the minister he had been. Chaplain Francis C. Williams of the Eighth Vermont, serving in Louisiana, was glad of Blake's help visiting the sick and wounded. He allowed Blake to preach to the African Americans when the regiment was near Algiers, across the river from New Orleans. After three months Blake was commissioned chaplain of the third Louisiana Native Guards (colored).[69] Williams shared the chaplain's work from the start. The Eighth Regiment, after a rough winter passage down the Atlantic coast in the ship *Wallace*, had its first divine service the fourth Sunday out of New York. Second Lieutenant Carter H. Mason read the sermon, probably because Chaplain Williams had not found his sea legs.[70] Among other ministers like Blake who served as soldiers, Thomas Kidder (1801-64) enlisted as a private in Company H, 9th Vermont, November 28, 1863, served in the 18th Army Corps as a hospital nurse, and died after almost a year of service.

Chaplains, like other commissioned officers, could resign before the end of their terms; enlisted men could not. Twelve Vermont chaplains, almost half of those appointed, resigned before the end of the terms they had signed up for. This suggests either that their experience did not match their expectations, or their lack of importance to the military. Reasons for resigning varied from individual to individual. Some resignations amounted to medical discharges, as with Simon M. Plimpton.[71]

On the other hand, Moses P. Parmelee resigned to start his life-work as a foreign missionary. Born into a family of Congregational ministers, he worked his way as printer's apprentice and school master through the University of Vermont (A.B. 1855) and Union Theological Seminary. Ordained on graduation, he discovered that the American Board of Commissioners for Foreign Missions, which had accepted him for assignment abroad, had put all departures on hold. So he secured an appointment as chaplain of the three-year Third Vermont Regiment and was commissioned June 10, 1861. A dozen years later, he summarized his war experience: "Immediately after the first Bull Run battle we were ordered to the front, where I remained in service until I learned the American Board was prepared to send me out, when I resigned [December 18, 1861]. . . and began preparation for my life work" in Erzerum, Turkish Armenia. After marrying a West Brattleboro girl, he sailed for Erzerum May 30, 1863.[72]

In 1864, the Christian Commission, the United Service Organization of the Civil War, sent short-term ministers to visit active troops and the sick and wounded in army hospitals around Washington and in the West. They preached and provided tracts, denominational newspapers, testaments, writing paper, and postage, and taught freedmen in Sunday schools.[73] John B. Perry, escaping trouble in his home church,[74] joined the Christian Commission and then filled a vacancy as chaplain of the Tenth Regiment. He went back to Swanton but the old controversy revived, so he left for another church, and eventually, Boston.

According to Wilbur Fisk, the soldiers liked the ministers of the Christian Commission better than regular army chaplains. "The chaplains they say, all they care for is to come out here and see the country, hold office, get a good swad of greenbacks every pay day, perhaps preach. . . if the weather is perfectly right, distribute the mail when it comes, and then when they get tired of this, contrive some way to be out of health, resign, and go home."[75] The *St. Albans Messenger* echoed this attitude, claiming that chaplains earned no respect, did not do their jobs, and spent their time boozing and gambling with the men.[76]

When the war was over, some returned to their parishes, or to other Vermont parishes. Others moved away. C. B. Smith got a government clerkship in Washington. W. C. Hopkins, the Episcopal bishop's son, became rector of Calvary Church, New Orleans, then moved to Missouri. Alonzo Webster went to South Carolina in 1866 and later became presiding elder of the Charleston district. Arthur Little, a New Hampshire native, took a Bedford, New Hampshire church, then moved west and rose to be moderator of the National Congregational Council of 1883. The Rev. John L. Roberts, a Methodist who had served in Marlboro, Putney, and Barre before the war, but never was a Vermont wartime chaplain, won appointment as post chaplain at St. Augustine, Florida.[77]

The ministers' military careers were like the short-term service of pastors from southern New England among the troops in the Champlain theater during the Revolution and like the missions of Connecticut ministers in the 1790s among the new settlements in Vermont.

On the whole, Vermont chaplains were not much different from the rest of the clergy at home, or the rest of the volunteers in the field. If their character and outlook had changed because of their war experience, they were not yet aware of it.

The Home Front

Many of military age had all kinds of reasons for not volunteering for service, or not re-enlisting at the end of their terms of service. The few who could not support the war for religious reasons could remain quiet in their civilian work unless the draft called them in the second half of the war. About a dozen Quakers volunteered for military service and some paid commutation when drafted, as unknown others did. Three Quakers, who refused to bear arms or pay commutation when drafted in mid-July 1863, were discharged November 6, 1863, "by reason of being a Quaker." Cyrus Guernsey Pringle of Charlotte, a convert who married a Quaker minister in 1859, left a diary of his experiences as a conscientious objector until furloughed to hospital work and home.[78]

The unity of opinion about the war suppressed differences of opinion about other matters. Protestants shelved most of their nativism because of the paramount value of every fighting man but some showed their anti-Catholic bias, as in the court-martial of John Lonergan. The first draft of July 1863 caused rioting in New York City and business practically stopped for days in the major Vermont centers. Bishop De Goesbriand, aware that the West Rutland Irish quarriers had organized and armed a "home guard," preached vehemently against draft resistance, racism, and strikes.[79]

In the superabundance of wartime recreation, the puritanically pious detected an insidious note of city corruption. While they blessed patriotic celebrations, target shoots, oyster suppers for soldiers' benefits, and receptions for returning veterans, they felt there was too much betting on horse races, and football in the streets, and entirely too much drinking and illicit sex. They raised no serious objections to the further spread of the baseball fad and tolerated commercial roller-skating and bicycle rinks, magicians, circuses, and exhibitors of war panoramas. The strait-laced objected to raffles, grab bags, and lotteries at local sanitary fairs, which raised money for bandages and other soldier needs. They felt that females should not teach penmanship, read sketches, or declaim in public. In St. Johnsbury, stricter than any other large Vermont village except possibly Windsor, young America patronized a dancing school, which wound up with a ball at the St. Johnsbury House. The North and South Congregational churches got even through the aqueduct company, which closed the hotel the morning after by shutting off its water. The areas where Sabbatarian rules could be enforced, however, were shrinking. Perhaps the advocates of silent Sabbaths and other features of ascetic Protestantism were really objecting to the Roman Catholics, who occupied their leisure and Sundays otherwise.

Some Congregational amd Unitarian ministers spent their leisure and Sundays after service rambling in the woods and fields and wondering how to explain nature and human nature to their people. Pastoral care in that generation apparently did not involve systematic visiting of all the scattered flock in their homes. Visits to those who had to work on the farm from dawn to dark might well have been considered an imposition, not a blessing, short-handed and busy as most of the members were during the war. At most, an eager young pastor might appoint occasional schoolhouse meetings for those who found it hard to get to the village church, in addition to the midweek prayer or Methodist class meetings that were the staple of nineteenth-century Protestant piety, and the preparatory lecture, usually Bible instruction, toward the end of the week. That left a great deal of time to themselves for study. Some pastors, already liberally inclined, took a path which led by the late nineteenth century to "a cluster of liberal ideas" called modernism, discussed in Chapter 6.

On his twenty-third birthday, John Perry had written in his diary, "I trust I may some day be able to reconcile the sciences with each other, and especially with religion." He pursued this goal for a decade in Swanton, with time to hike the hills in search of outcrops and to study the currently debated geological questions. When he died in 1872 he had a faculty appointment at Oberlin College which allowed him to focus directly on the issue.[80]

While Catholics multiplied, two paths seemed to be separating for Protestants facing the postwar world. One led to an accommodation to new conditions and new thought, putting men like Perry to work out a new faith and practice. The other led to an adaptation of the old revival techniques to rural people found in the mill villages, using the same Bible without raising critical questions about its meaning.

Notes to Chapter 5

[1] See graph of Baptist membership, Chapter 3, p. 90.

[2] See John Orvis' grim prophecy quoted in Bassett, *The Growing Edge*, 49, and my essay, "Secular Utopian Socialists."

[3] See Schneider, *Domestication of American Methodism*.

[4] Scott, *Appeal*, and *Grounds for Secession*; Matlack, *Orange Scott*; Sprague, *American Pulpit*, 7:667-671; Wells, *Newbury*, 212, 246. Using almanacs, local histories, and Schedule VI of the manuscript census, I have found Wesleyan Methodists in Chittenden, Ferrisburg, Goshen, Mount Tabor, Shelburne, and Sudbury.

[5] See, for a sample of contemporary Adventist literature, Himes, *Views of the Prophecies*. Many scholars have been intrigued by the Adventists' succeeding after failure, for example, Seventh Day Adventist Nichol, *The Midnight Cry*; Festinger, *When Prophecy Fails*, 12-14, 19-23; Adventist church historian Maxwell, *Tell It To the World*, 26-27, 32-33, 106; Doan, *The Miller Heresy*; Numbers and Butler, *The Disappointed*; Perry, "The Camp Meeting in Millerite Revivalism."

[6] Harriet Hutchinson to Lucius Salisbury, Keytesville, Charlton County, Missouri, December 1, 1844, in Hutchinson, "Letters," 277.

[7] W. H. Eastman, Grantham [New Hampshire], "Jan. 6th, 1843, Bible Time," to C. G. Eastman, Woodstock, in Eastman Papers, Vermont Historical Society, MS41.

[8] I have found evidence, usually not distinguishing between Seventh Day and Christian branches, in the manuscript census (Schedule 6), almanacs, gazetteers, and newspapers, showing Adventist churches in Addison, Bridgewater, Bristol, Burlington, Cabot, Castleton, Enosburg, Hartland, Johnson, Montgomery, Morgan, Mount Holly, New Haven, Poultney, Richford, Rutland, St. Johnsbury, Springfield, Troy, Vernon, Waterbury, Wolcott, and Woodstock. On the Whites' visit to Johnson, see A. C. Bourdeaux in *Vermont Historical Gazetteer*, 2:765.

[9] See Higham, *From Boundlessness to Conslidation*.

[10] Randolph A. Roth, in *The Democratic Dilemma*, 279-290, characterizes religion in the sag after 1843 as sentimental and respectable.

11 Schwartzes, *Flame of Fire*, 127, 140-141. I have used the incomplete and uncertain building dates in the Schwartzes' *A Spreading Flame* to estimate the number of church buildings in 1840. A more refined search would show more.

12 Shedd, "Congregationalism and Symbolism," quotation on p. 11 of reprint. Strout summarized Shedd's ideas in "Faith and History." For the quarrel that led to the 1879 *Protest*, see Chapter 6, p. 210.

13 Roth, *The Democratic Dilemma*, 279, 282, noted for the Connecticut Valley a 26 percent membership drop, 1843-1850, in the "evangelical" denominations, a slower rate of joining "Calvinist" churches, and 61 percent of the disciplinary cases, 1844-1859, for non-attendance at church. One can expect the west side to show about the same figures.

14 Durick summarized the last years of Father O'Callaghan and Bishop De Goesbriand's episcopate in "The Catholic Church in Vermont." Wilson, "Catholicism in Vermont," has reliably collected names, dates, and places for the same period. Lucey, "Diocese of Burlington: 1853," tells a longer story of the early period. The fullest account, by David J. Blow and William Goss, diocesan archivists, awaits publication. My account of the Roman Catholics in this and other periods is based on their work, which they have kindly let me read. A short history of the diocese by Howard Coffin, "profusely illustrated," also drawing heavily on Blow and Goss, is in press. They have used Vatican and episcopal archives that are not easy of access. My earlier use of their research appeared in *The Growing Edge*, 94-97, and I have borrowed heavily from that work in this and some of the next chapter.

15 Quoted in the *Burlington Free Press*, 2 May 1853.

16 Schedules VI, Social Statistics, of the U.S. MS Census for 1850 and 1860 (copies at the Vermont State Library and in the National Archives and Records Administration) show capacity of Protestant houses of worship far beyond the number of adherents. A partial list of December 1858 communions in eleven Roman Catholic churches, however, comes within three hundred of the capacity of those churches in 1860 (typescript copies of Bishop De Goesbriand's diary, 12-13, in the St. Michael's College Library and at UVM.

17 Jeremiah O'Callaghan in Zadock Thompson, *History of Vermont*, 2:202; Burlington. St. Joseph Church. *History*, 7-18.

18 De Goesbriand *Diary*, 4 (March 13, 1854), 19-20 (June 10-14, 1862); see also 12 (February 11, 1858).

[19] Murphy and Potash, "Highgate Affair."

[20] Huden, *State School Administration*, 109-110, 116.

[21] An insightful interpretation of the recurrent invasion of new and unwanted religious groups is R. L. Moore, *Religious Outsiders.* While "mainline" denominations professed an ecumenical goal and prophesied that the invaders would fade, the American reality was pluralism among increasing varieties.

[22] Marsh, *Shadow of Christianity*, 113.

[23] Wright, C. B. *Gleanings from Forefathers*; *Forefathers' Day, 1891*, includes the order of exercises and proceedings reprinted from the *Middlebury Register*, with a summary of the address of the Rev. W. S. Smart of Brandon on "The Puritan Spirit." Violet Chatfield, "Annual Middlebury Event: Forefathers Day Observance Planned," *Burlington Free Press*, 9 December 1965, sec. ii, 9:1-3; Stephen A. Freeman, *Middlebury Congregational Church, 1790-1990*, 107. The church suspended it, 1974-1984, and revived it briefly, 1985-90.

[24] Michaud in Byrne, *Catholic Church in New England*, 2:471.

[25] Fletcher, *Oberlin College*, 61, quotes a letter of May 28, 1825, from John J. Shipherd, Vergennes marble factory supervisor, to his brother Fayette in Cambridge, New York, reporting "about 20. . . French children" in his Sabbath School. Burlington *First Congregational Church Centennial*, 89, mentions a Sunday school for more than eighty French Canadians at Winooski Falls, beginning in May 1830, taught chiefly by college students.

[26] I summarize the political maneuvers of 1854-1856 in *The Growing Edge*, 123-126.

[27] A. M. Hemenway, *Vermont Historical Gazetteer*, 1:503; *Burlington Free Press*, 5 October 1857, reporting his death in a Demerara, Guyana, prison.

[28] See Scrapbook 88 in the Sheldon Museum, Middlebury, containing American Party oaths, notifications, and correspondence. The *Northfield Star of Vermont*, published from late 1854 to May 1856, was the longest-lived of the Know Nothing press. McKeen, *On Romanism*, and Lord, *National Hospitality*, are sample nativist sermons. See *Middlebury Register*, 2:3 (27 August 1856), and John M. Comstock, ed., *Civil Officers*

of Vermont, on Joyce.

29 I describe election day as part of the ritual of Vermont's civil religion in Chapter 2, pp. 41-42.

30 O. Kempton letter dated September 19, 1842, to the editor of the New York *Christian Advocate and Journal*, 17 (5 Oct. 1842): 30.

31 Henry Crocker, *Baptists in Vermont*, 419-426, 458, 460; "The French Baptist Mission," *The Burlington Citizen*, 9 (Dec. 1883): 1, 12, with photograph of the chapel when it had become a school, after 1888.

32 Were the seeds of Hoyt's first conversion sown by Benjamin Hale, Dartmouth professor of chemistry, 1827-1835, an Episcopal deacon who began to conduct private Episcopal services in the spring of 1830, in Hoyt's junior year? See Lord, *Dartmouth College*, 255-258, on Hale.

33 Diary of William Henry Hoyt at UVM; Hoyt, *Hoyt Family*, 64, 92, 64, 92; Memorandum of the distribution of the estate of E. H. Deming, 31 Mar. 1838, in the possession of Robert V. Daniels, Burlington, Vermont; De Goesbriand, "William Henry Hoyt," in *Catholic Memoirs*, 128-143; Clifford, "Abby Hemenway's Road to Rome."

34 See [Hopkins, J. H., Jr.], "Vermont Episcopal Institute, *Life of John Henry Hopkins*, 295-319.

35 F. P. Wells, *History of Newbury*, 208-232, covers the history of the seminary, the Biblical Institute, and the Female Collegiate Institute. Racists did not harm the school when it accepted "a colored girl" (p. 213) in the early 1840s, at the preceptress' insistence.

36 Baptists: The Vermont Literary and Scientific Institution, Brandon (1832), Black River Academy, Ludlow, and the Leland Classical and English School, Townshend (both 1834), and the Derby Literary and Theological Institute (1839). Methodists described below, in Poultney and Newbury (1834), Bakersfield (1846), and Springfield (1847). Universalists: Green Mountain Liberal Institute, South Woodstock (1848), Orleans Liberal Institute, Glover (1852), and Green Mountain Central Institute (1863), which became Goddard Seminary, Barre, soon after it opened in 1870. Free Will Baptists: Green Mountain Seminary, Waterbury Center (1862).

37 This name is the basis of a claim that Ripley Female College was the first "college" in Vermont to admit women. The line between academies and colleges did not become clear until completion of study at an academy became a requirement for college entrance. If the name determines the

claim, the first prize goes to the Newbury Female Collegiate Institute, a
"department" of Newbury Seminary "for the higher education of young
women", chartered in 1849. The Springfield Female Collegiate Institute,
chartered in 1858, was Springfield Wesleyan Seminary's "collegiate
department for ladies. . . added for those who wished to take a higher course
of study than the ordinary seminary course." (Hubbard and Dartt, *History of
Springfield*, 118). Then came Montpelier's "Vermont Conference Seminary
and Female College" in 1865. The Conference bought the Ripley Female
College back in 1873 and restored the old name, Troy Conference Academy,
the next year. D. C. and O. D. Schwartz, *The Story of the Troy Conference*,
215-217, summarize the history of Troy Conference Academy.

38 Stameshkin, *Middlebury College*, 126-189; state geologist Adams,
Second Annual Report, 106-108; Bassett, *The Growing Edge*, 129.

39 Ellis, *Norwich University*, 1:72, 133-137;*Vermont Historical Gazetteer*,
4:657. The *Burlington Free Press* discussed Brattleboro's prospects of
becoming a college town 11 Nov. 1851. Tufts was chartered in 1852 at
Medford, Massachusetts. New England Baptists patronized Brown
University in Providence, Rhode Island, and Colby College, Waterville,
Maine; Free Will Baptists patronized Bates at Lewiston, Maine.

40 The peak period measured by E. C. B[ass]., UVM 1859 (in "Ministers,"
University Cynic), included the classes of 1830 through 1856. The
Methodist author believed that "The intellectual supremacy of a nation. . .
depends upon its pulpit. . . doing something in holding church and state and
school in best relations."

41 See Bassett, "The Classical College."

42 Andrews, "Grammar Schools and Academies," 175-184, discusses the
transition from church-related to public secondary schools, and lists
chronologically by date of charter all the schools chartered from 1780 to
1867, 207-209. Mower, *Morristown*, 43, 86, summarizes People's
Academy history.

43 See Bassett, "Brandon Through a Peep-Hole."

44 See Bassett, "James Buckham."

45 Roth, *The Democratic Dilemma*, 283. MacDonald, *Rebellion in the
Mountains*, details the presence of pastors in her section on "Societies." I
summarized John Gregory's Burlington missions in the *Burlington Free
Press*, 26 Nov., 10, 17 Dec. 1978.

[46] Roth, *The Democratic Dilemma*, 283-284, concludes that Free Will Baptists and Christians were still growing in the Connecticut Valley (nine new churches, 1843-1850).

[47] See discussion of the religious press in Chapter 4, pp. 126-128, and Chapter 6, p. 213; and of the Welsh churches of Rutland County in Chapter 7, pp. 229-230.

[48] Fairbanks, *St. Johnsbury*, 309-310. Graham Newell of St. Johnsbury heard the anti-Methodist motive from a Fairbanks descendant. See transcript of Bassett interview with Newell, 28 January 1998, at UVM.

[49] See Bassett,"College Street Congregational Church," depending on James A. Dailey's and David J. Blow's earlier research. I have told the Methodist story in "Pine Street Methodist Church."

[50] For the details of this story see Bassett, "Pine Street Methodist Church." Quotations are from Castle, *The Methodist Church in Burlington*, 26, and Forest, "Revivals at the Pine Street Methodist Church," *Leterz*, 2 (February 1858), 1.

[51] *Rutland Herald*, 8 Apr. 1858; Fairbanks, *St. Johnsbury*, 317-319.

[52] See Achsah Sprague's diary for December 10, 1855 in Vermont Historical Society *Proceedings*, 9 (September 1941), 156.

[53] Hamilton Child, *Addison County Gazetteer*, 219 (Shoreham); *Rutland Herald*, 14 Apr., 15 Dec.1859 (Brandon); Congregational General Convention *Minutes* (1859), 18, 20 (West Rutland, Norwich).

[54] *Proceedings of the Free Convention*. See Thomas L. Altherr, "'The Fanatics in Grand Conclave': The Rutland, Vermont Free or Reform Convention of 1858," Rutland Historical Society *Quarterly*, 29: 33-48 (1999). See also R. L. Moore, "The Spiritualist Medium."

[55] *Rutland Herald*, 6 Jan. 1859, 1:2.

[56] Carroll, *Spiritualism in Antebellum America*, 6, 8. Carroll pays no attention to Achsah Sprague of Plymouth, a medium who did not publish, except from the podium.

[57] Randall, *Spiritual Manifestations*, identified and described in Kathy Wendling's columns on Woodstock Spiritualism in the *Woodstock*

Standard (November 1991 and January 1992). Ms. Wendling has sent me copies of these columns, excerpts from Charles Cobb's diary, and reference to the notebook of John D. Powers (born 1806) containing messages from spirits. Mary Grace Canfield wrote a 1935 column about Miranda Randall. See Jennison, *Woodstock*, 64-65. In Sherman-Safford Papers, Vermont Historical Society, MS 23: letters of Linus E. Sherman (13 Feb. 1852) and E. H. Sherman (n.d. "the rappers are the chief topic of conversation now"), Fairfield, 13 Feb. and n.d., 1852; and L. Matteson, Shaftsbury, to Brother Alvah T [F] Sherman, 24 Mar. 1852 ("there is very great excitement about here"; Alfred Landon a "pa[r]tial" medium, Aunt Sarah a "half medium"; the elder Smith of South Shaftsbury "is a believer and a medium").

58 Twynham, "Achsah Sprague's Journal," and "Achsah W. Sprague"; R. L. Moore, *In Search of White Crows*, 125.

59 This section on Vermont Civil War chaplains has been accepted for publication in *Vermont History*. See also Marshall, *A War of the People*, e.g., 188-189.

60 Smith, C. E. "Civil War Chaplains," summarizes the findings of Honeywell, *Chaplains of the United States Army*. A one-line record of chaplains' service appears with the commissioned officers of each regiment in the *Revised Roster of Vermont Volunteers*.

61 *Rutland Herald*, 15 February 1865 (Hicks); *Windsor Journal*, 11 June 1864, quoting *Windsor Vermont Chronicle*; G. G. Benedict, *Vermont in the Civil War*, 1:186-187 (Hale).

62 Willard to Woodbridge, July 16, 1864 in the Sheldon Museum, Middlebury; Lieutenant Albert A. Crane of the Sixth to the *Rutland Herald*, 20 January 1864.

63 Benedict, *Vermont in the Civil War*, 2:408, 410 (Smart), 2:411, 413 (Cummings).

64 Vermont House *Journal* (1861), 119; *Vermont Laws* (1861), 76-77; *Rutland Herald*, 28 October 1861. *Burlington Times*, 6 November 1861 ("appointment meets with general acceptance"); Eno, "Quest for a Civil War Chaplain." Vermont Auditor of Accounts *Annual Report* (1862), xi, shows that the state paid for Druon's trip.

65 See Corby, *Memoirs of Chaplain Life*.

66 Coffin, *Stannard's Vermonters*, 9-10, 20-21, 85, 290; *Walton's Vermont*

Register for 1862, 47; *Revised Roster of Vermont Volunteers*, 657.

[67] See Coffin, *Full Duty*, 87-89 (Parmelee), 99, 102, 215 (Woodward); Benedict, *Vermont in the Civil War*, 2:537, 549, 553.

[68] From the Edward P. Stone Papers, Vermont Historical Society, MSS 25 #72, I have quoted from the letters of July 8, 28 or 29, August 8, November 15, December 23, 1862, and March 19, 1863.

[69] G. N. Carpenter, *Eighth Regiment*, 67; portrait opposite 66.

[70] Wickham, *Letters from Press Correspondents*, 2:41.

[71] Alumni record in Amherst College Archives, supplied by Daris D'Arienzo, College Archivist.

[72] Parmelee's "brief autobiography" in the Congregational Library, Boston, dated at Erzeroom, Turkey, March 18, 1875, is among the manuscript responses of several ministers to a suggestion in *The Congregationalist* that they summarize their careers.

[73] The diary, accounts, and report of Rev. P. Stuart Pratt of Dorset, of a forty-day stint, January-February 1865, are among his papers at UVM.

[74] Perry expressed his controversial views in six 1856 sermons delivered during his first year in his first parish, after three years' as interim pastor. Under attack from a few parishioners, he published them as *Discourses Preached in Swanton*, on the experience of heaven and hell on earth.

[75] Fisk, *Civil War Letters*, 213, in a favorable letter about the Christian Commission, dated April 26, 1864. Private Tabor Parcher of Waterbury, however, in a letter of April 3, 1864, to his wife, played down the success of fellow townsman Charles C. Parker of the Commission in stimulating a revival (Tabor Parcher Papers at UVM).

[76]*Windsor Vermont Journal* , ll June 1864, rebutting the charges.

[77] Smith: *Vermont Historical Gazetteer*, 3:501; Hopkins: *Windsor Vermont Chronicle* (13 January 1866); Webster: J. R. Bartlett in *Vermont Historical Gazetteer*, 4:383; Little: Dartmouth College and Andover Theological Seminary general catalogues; Roberts: *Rutland Herald*, 23 March 1865, E. H. Newton in *Vermont Historical Gazetteer*, 5(pt. 2):446, Amos Foster in *Vermont Historical Gazetteer*, 5(pt. 2):238, and J. R. Bartlett, ibid., 4:52.

[78] Pringle, *Diary*.   The others were Peter Dakin of Charlotte, credited to Bridport's quota, and Lindley Murray Macomber of Grand Isle, all in the Fourth Regiment (*Vermont Volunteers*, 119, 131, 133).

[79] James O'Toole, Archivist of the Archdiocese of Boston, provided the Archives of the Diocese of Burlington with a copy of the 19 July 1863 report in the *Boston Pilot* of De Goesbriand's sermon the previous Sunday.

[80] Obituary of John Bulkley Perry (1825-1872) by Clark E. Perrin, University of Vermont trustee, in *Congregational Quarterly* (Apr. 1873), copied in *Vermont Historical Gazetteer,* 4:983-988. State geologist Adams' *Second Annual Report* was available to Perry as an upperclassman at the University of Vermont.

6

Pluralism Settles In, With Infrastructures, 1865-1900

The most important tension for more than a postwar generation was between Catholic and Protestant, but shared war experience had earned mutual respect for comrades in arms. Each group had potential for internal friction: among the Catholics, Irish versus French; among the Protestants, from a variety of centrifugal tendencies, toward modernism, toward holiness, toward the social gospel, toward the formation of new religious societies and centers of religious activity. The memory of shared war effort was sometimes little more than a cosmetic cover over these tensions, but as in earlier divisions, a necessary bond.

In peacetime, too, rubbing shoulders in schools, stores, playgrounds, or anywhere else, confirmed hatred and dislike or removed negative attitudes. Over the long years, on balance, I believe the effects were positive when situations were not aggravated by pain-causing customs. Exclusion of Jews and blacks from restaurants and resorts were such aggravations, until legislation in the late 1950s sharply cut the incidence of discrimination. The sources to test this guess, however, are few and fugitive.

Soon, however, sources of conflict resurfaced, but the conditions of the contest had changed. Catholics in Vermont were on their way to becoming the first denomination by any standard, whether judged by attendance, number of communicants, number of clergy, value of plant, or, eventually, influence on social policy. They therefore need first attention, to understand how they grew under bishops De Goesbriand and Michaud. This growth produced overt Protestant reactions, both in conscious statements against Catholics and in positive movements stimulated by Catholic competition.

But to view a generation of religious history after Johnny came marching home as this rivalry and nothing else would be a distortion.

It would miss the meaning of the pluralism Vermont and the nation had accepted.[1] Deep under consciousness a stream of antagonism still flowed, but on the surface each parish conducted its parochial affairs, beyond the daily work of its parishioners, with short-range attention, raising money, spending it, meeting, gossiping, helping.

While becoming stiffly and outspokenly hostile to distant unreconstructed rebels of the defeated South, Protestant Vermonters seemed to be softening to the children of the thousands of antebellum intruders from Ireland and French Canada, as well as their reinforcements since the war. Although civil on the surface, Protestants and Catholics thought more of their disagreements than of their common Christianity and chose to weave separate webs of institutions, limiting contacts to politics, business, and passing on the street.

Catholic Growth

From being largely landless craftsmen and hand laborers, immigrant Catholics had put down roots, acquired property, developed corner and crossroads stores, and patronized their own professionals. "Mick's" speech had begun to lose its brogue and "Antwine" had shifted his twang to Vermontese. Intermarriages between Irish and French multiplied. The Irish were moving up the social scale more rapidly than the French Canadians, and those whose parents were Irish and Quebecois, like Bishop John Stephen Michaud, often succeeded better than either branch.

The Catholics, first only a few settling in the Champlain Valley, became in the late nineteenth century the most numerous denomination in Vermont, spread over the entire state, although still more thinly in the Connecticut Valley. This growth continued to have its casualties, where the uprooted immigrants, coming from Catholic countries and often lukewarm in the faith, accepted what Protestant churches were available, when Catholic Mass could not be heard. The cool attitudes of Protestants, however, the Catholics' original hostility to Protestants where they had come from, and their hardships, often laid, with some justification, at Protestants' doors, preserved their basic Catholicism until the supply of priests came close to meeting their needs by the end of the century.

Symbolic of this growth, Burlington's $100,000 Cathedral of the Immaculate Conception, designed by Patrick C. Keely of Brooklyn, New York, was consecrated on December 8, 1867. On the same lot, facing Cherry Street, Bishop De Goesbriand lived in a new home from November 1885 until he retired to St. Joseph's orphanage in 1892. Bishop John S. Michaud gave a fourteen-foot, gilded statue of Our Lady of Lourdes, blessed in 1904, as a memorial of his own episcopate, to crown the two-hundred-foot tower of the Cathedral.[2]

Burlington and Winooski had the largest concentration of Catholics, partly because their lake and railroad trade, wood processing, and other industry provided jobs to support over eighteen thousand people. Upwards of five hundred French Canadian Catholics worked in the Burlington Woolen Company's Winooski mill, which had kept busy throughout the war making uniform material. They earned a wide range of wages averaging one dollar for an eleven-and-a-half-hour day (eleven hours after 1875).

When Montreal Oblates came on mission in January 1868, St. Joseph's Church on Fern Hill, Burlington, was so crowded that the already ackowledged need for a parish across the river stirred Bishop De Goesbriand to action. He secured the Rev. Jean Frédéric Audet, a twenty-six-year-old native of St. Césaire, Quebec, who arrived in Burlington March 4. When Audet preached his first sermon on Passion Sunday, March 29, with the bishop singing high Mass, he "saw contentment on all the faces" to have at last "a Canadian parish," with a French Canadian priest. Although Father Quévillon, the first priest at St. Joseph's, came from Quebec, his successors from 1856 to 1868 had been Bretons.[3] Audet moved energetically; after three building seasons the Winooski parish had a convent for the Canadian teaching Sisters of Providence, a new wing on the bilingual parochial school of St. Louis, and a Church of St. Francis Xavier. Simply designed by a Montreal priest and set on the edge of the woods above the village of Winooski, the building represented the cooperative efforts of bishop, *curé*, syndics (building committee), *marguilliers* (prudential committee), local contractors and workmen, and every concerned member of the parish. In his prime, Audet shepherded a median of four hundred families and thirty single communicants, received less than $150 salary (five percent of a median $2,900 in pew rents), plus part of fixed wedding and funeral fees and gifts in kind at "la quête de l'enfant Jesus," the pastor's and *marguilliers'* tour of the parish between Christmas and Epiphany.[4] To this francophone community Fr. Audet was "married" until his death in 1917.

Being a majority in Winooski, the French Canadians did not keep out of politics as most of them did elsewhere, but worked with the Irish minority, first in electing John McGregor to represent Colchester in the legislature in 1867 on the Workingmen's Union ticket, then Democrats Charles Lafountain (1874) and Francis LeClair (1880-82). The Democratic Party chose Lafountain chairman of its state committee for a dozen years and rewarded him with the consulship of Sorel, Quebec, in 1889.[5]

Old St. Joseph's on the hill continued to serve French-speaking

Catholics in Burlington until its pastor, Fr. Jérôme Marie Cloarec, was able by the 1880s to build more centrally downtown, leaving the parish school on the old site. The new St. Joseph's, one of the largest houses of worship in Vermont, seated over twelve hundred.[6] English-speaking Catholics in Winooski went to the Cathedral in Burlington until the bishop established St. Stephen's, Winooski, as a mission in 1871 and as a parish in 1882, with future bishop John Stephen Michaud as first resident pastor. The pastor's father, Stephen Michael Michaud, reached Burlington from Quebec in 1838 and married Irish Catherine Rogan. This background helped the son deal with the tensions between French and Irish.

French Canadians comprised an important part of the wage-earning population in all the other Vermont villages. In the Rutland marble district as in so many other parts of Vermont, the new flavor was French, but the Irish still held most of the jobs, and better jobs than the French. By 1870, two-fifths of West Rutland's common laborers, but only one-sixth of its skilled marble workers, were French. They built the Church of the Sacred Heart of Jesus for the French Canadians, but by 1875, the bishop wrote, there were "but few Canadian families attached to this place."[7] It was tended from Rutland until 1888, when a new wave of immigration from Canada strengthened the francophone presence.

In West Rutland, Rutland, Fair Haven, and St. Albans, the French Catholics felt strong enough to support ethnic parishes with francophone priests. The bishop recruited three Redemptorists in Quebec for an 1869 mission to West Rutland and collected almost four thousand dollars in France and Canada for "l'Oeuvre Canadien" of several more missionaries.

Germans, Spanish, Italians, Greeks, and Syrians (or Lebanese), too few to have churches using their languages, stayed home or attended Catholic services for anglophones. Much of the liturgy was in Latin, the common language of the Roman church, and the rest was in the English they were trying to learn in their everyday life.

In the granite industry of Barre, Hardwick, Woodbury, and Ryegate, expanding from 1880, many immigrants brought anticlerical attitudes toward the Catholic church. The French in Canada looked to their church to protect them against British Americans running their country and Yankee Americans coming to trade and threatening annexation. The Irish looked to their priests to succor them under the oppression of the alien English, and carried much of that loyalty with them across the ocean. But the Italians and fewer Spaniards in the granite quarries had come from Catholic countries where many blamed the church for the sufferings of the poor.

In Catholic Vermont, priests' tenure tended to be short and their charges widely scattered. With their rigorous training, they were the local source of teaching in catechism, theology, and the meaning of the Mass, aided by women religious and laity. Through confession and frequent access to his parishioners, the priest maintained greater contact and yet won more deference from them than did the average Protestant parson.

From the dedication of St. Mary's in 1832, when curious Protestants were impressed with the high quality of the French choir, the Gregorian chanting in the Mass continued a strong tradition. Hymn singing by the congregation, on the other hand, was not the Catholics' forte. Their few surviving hymnbooks with words in Latin, French, and/or English, mainly from late in the century, seem to this singer of Protestant background to lack Lutheran inspiration or Puritan positiveness.

Methodist and Baptist missions in North Barre at the turn of the century made inroads among the Italians there. Some remained alienated from the Catholic church and contributed a radical syndicalism, politics based on labor unions, to the heterogeneity of Barre. From 1900 the Vatican began to discourage the establishment or perpetuation of ethnic parishes in English-speaking countries. It took until World War II before the use of French died out in Vermont churches.[8]

For both the French and the Irish Catholics, churches, schools, convents, and mutual benefit societies mushroomed in the 1870s. Some three dozen buildings were bought or erected by 1880, and St. Peter's on West Street, Rutland, another $100,000 structure designed by Patrick Keely, was blessed in 1873.

Protestants controlling institutional buildings let Catholics use them, and mill owners were cordial to Catholics needing space and financially supportive of Catholic building programs, especially for the French. Seth B. Hunt, Bennington's millionaire shawl manufacturer, donated for the cathedral an expensive transept window made in Nantes, France. Bishop Louis De Goesbriand wrote in his diary for June 18, 1868 at West Castleton, "the Slate Company seem to be anxious to have a Church here, and offered lots for a Church, school house, &c." On August 30, 1868 he noted saying Mass in the former Masonic Hall in Woodstock for French Canadians who had been using "the railroad building." Again, his June 22, 1875 entry mentioned seven Irish landowners and many French Canadians near the Pownal cotton mill: "the Company has offered a lot. . . for a Church." Apparently for the first time on October 6, 1878, he was allowed to preach to the convicts at the Windsor state prison. Redfield Proctor gave the land and a hundred dollars for a church to serve seventy-nine families at Sutherland Falls in 1879, and, later, land for a cemetery. In 1884, William H. Root, Protestant Burlington city clerk, gave all the red sandstone used in St.

Joseph's church.[9]

Catholics created a separate set of parochial schools, taught by almost enough nuns in several orders, living in voluntary poverty. Sisters from Montreal supplied French parish schools, while religious orders in southern New England sent nuns to teach the Irish in Burlington, Rutland, St. Albans, and St. Johnsbury. The first four parochial schools had started between 1854 and 1858. When Bishop Louis De Goesbriand retired in 1892 and John S. Michaud became bishop coadjutor, the diocese had 125 nuns in nine orders and 3,206 pupils in fourteen elementary schools, with the beginnings of diocesan control.[10] Protestants could not see why a duplicate school system was necessary. All they intended was to teach morality in the public schools, based on the ten commandments, which even Moslems accepted.[11]

Beyond the parochial schools, the Sisters of Mercy opened Mount St. Mary's Academy for girls in 1878 and moved it next to their new Burlington convent in 1886. For boys, Father Daniel J. O'Sullivan opened St. Joseph's College in an old Burlington hotel used by the Sisters of Providence as an orphanage until their new building was ready in 1883. "College" meant secondary school, as the French and sometimes the British used the word. Boarders and day students aged twelve and up took a classical or commercial curriculum. In 1890, the bishop transferred O'Sullivan, perhaps judging his failure as an administrator, to St. Mary's parish in St. Albans, where his bilingual abilities would soothe Franco-Irish tensions, and closed St. Joseph's College in June 1891. Because of a shortage of funds and because of the need for clergy in the growing parishes, the bishop stated, "priests could not be spared to teach." On both sides of the cleavage between Protestants and Catholics, women teachers predominated in elementary schools. No one used the old building after the college closed and it was torn down in 1907 to make way for a Catholic hospital, not built until 1924. Bishop Michaud negotiated with the Society of St. Edmund, whose members arrived from anticlerical France in 1892, to use the site, but they chose to open St. Michael's College at Winooski Park, Colchester, in 1904.[12]

From the Catholic strongholds in the Champlain Valley villages came protests against the use of the Protestant Bible in the public schools and demands to equalize for Catholics their financial burdens for schools. A "national convention" of Franco-American provident institutions at St. Albans in 1870 discussed the school question. Antoine Moussette, publisher of *Le Protecteur Canadien* (1868-1871), had revived a Société de St. Jean Baptiste at St. Albans in 1866. He and his editor, the Rev. Zephyrin Druon, back from Brittany after the war as rector of St. Mary's, St. Albans, agitated the issue of the Protestant

Bible in the schools.[13]

Moussette could have trumpeted the unique success of St. Bridget's, West Rutland, in getting tax money for its parochial school. The old schoolhouse and town hall for District 7 was near the corner of Main and Pleasant streets, next to the Congregational church. St. Bridget's was a mile northwest on Pleasant Street, right next to the major quarries and mills, with the Catholic school, built by the town, between the church and the railroad spur that served the quarries. Francis Picart, the first pastor (1857-1859), secured the approval of the notables in school district 7, especially the Congregational minister, Aldace Walker, for a tax-supported Catholic school. Picart's successor, later Vicar General Thomas Lynch, saw the new building opened in 1865, with Catholic teachers and Catholic texts, and serving Catholics all over town. Its four ungraded rooms, crowded with pupils from six to thirteen, totalled 370 in 1867 and 400 in 1877, over an unusually long, forty-week year. A movement to include all children east of the railroad succeeded in the 1896 town meeting, and it "ceased to be a public school for just Catholic students" from all over town. They had taught catechism in the school; after that, in the church.[14]

We might expect that Catholics would have an easier time in the Connecticut Valley where there were fewer for Protestants to worry about. Quite the contrary: as in Burlington during the 1830s, when nativism was most intense and overt, many kinds of prejudicial practice occurred in postwar Brattleboro. When Catholics were ready to build for themselves in 1863, a parishioner fronted the purchase of the church lot on Walnut Street because it was "not prudent to make their intentions too public." Some Protestant businessmen "refused to sell material for its construction." Catholics were unwelcome because their crowd going to Mass "would ruin the market value of all property on the street." But assessments rose on Walnut Street as elsewhere in the growing village. On the Feast of Corpus Christi, June 4, 1874, some schoolchildren attended Mass and were refused admittance when they returned to school. When the court upheld the school board, Fr. Henry Lane promptly started building a church school, opened in 1875 and staffed by Sisters of St. Joseph out of Rutland.[15] The Brattleboro experience suggests that prejudice declined more slowly on the east side of the state where the influx of Catholics came later.

Protestant Answers

For many, not prejudice but recognized difference of beliefs and practices divided Catholics and Protestants.[16] Old-line Protestants saw immigrant Catholics still crowding in and replacing Protestant emigrants in the economy. Even worse in their opinion than the growth of

Roman Catholic numbers were the institutions to sustain these masses and protect them from Protestant influence. A steady home missionary spirit, as already pointed out, and the habit of church support had preserved a defensive Protestantism, no more than holding its own. The long-standing Protestant commitment to win the world for Christ required greater efforts to keep control in one's own city.

Some of the Protestant defense was aggressive, as Civil War prosperity made funds available to build better houses of worship and strengthen evangelism. United Protestant efforts, foreshadowed by the fundraising and material aids for the United States Christian Commission and the United States Sanitary Commission during the Civil War, continued after the war. Trying hard to keep their youth in membership, Protestants invested their war and postwar profits in new or existing denominational academies, run by conference or statewide boards. They invested much energy, more than bricks and mortar, first in the YMCA, then the Vermont Union of Christian Endeavor and the special-interest benevolent associations.[17] Fear of the Roman Catholic church was an underlying motivation then, just as fear of secular materialism and new-age sects fueled the late-twentieth-century ecumenical movement and the rebirth of born-again evangelicalism. Protestants recognized their need to teach young and old better, communicate with members better, and reach the unchurched better.

The first interdenominational effort was a midweek convention in Burlington, September 5-8, 1866, led by Baptist A. B. Earle of Newton, Massachusetts. His purpose was to teach pastors, who came from all over the state, how to conduct revivals. Probably coached not to remind people of the divisions caused by Jedediah Burchard thirty years before, Earle protested that he had no "set of measures," yet his prescription was the same old sequence of prayer, protracted meetings, experience (testimony) meetings, and altar calls.[18]

In Burlington, although Protestant leaders could plainly see that the Catholics had caught up to them, the laity needed arousing to canvass and convert. Edward Hungerford, former University of Vermont science professor whose wife's wealth freed him to lead a crusade, devised a two-pronged project to awaken Protestants to the need for strenuous evangelism. Teams visited from door to door, reporting needs, and took attendance at all area churches on March 3, 1867. Including Burlington's two Catholic and six Protestant churches, Winooski's Methodists and Congregationalists, and those coming from other neighboring towns, they found 52.65 percent of the churchgoers attended Mass at St. Joseph's or the Cathedral, and 53.82 percent (4,270 out of 7,934) of the people in the homes they visited declared themselves Catholic. Having announced the figures, Hungerford trumpeted his call for troops to combat Catholic error with Protestant truth.[19]

In Hungerford's College Street Church two years after his survey, pastor George B. Safford delivered a Fast Day sermon on "The Irrepressible Conflict" between Catholics and Protestants. With the genteel stance of fighting fair, with no persecution using "the weapons of worldly warfare," without violent passion, and giving credit where credit was due, Safford urged his hearers as "catholic christians" to be as faithful to their principles as the Romans were to theirs.[20]

Anti-Catholicism continued strong among active Protestants long past 1900. It was a major plank in the platform of the American Party, which ran John Wolcott Phelps of Brattleboro for president in 1880. Nationwide, he received 707 votes from nativists, prohibitionists, Sabbatarians, and enemies of secret societies.[21]

While overt, public objections to Catholicism all but disappeared, Protestant outreach increased, stimulated by Catholic competition. Local ministers heard a new model of the old gospel in Dwight L. Moody's four-week stand with his musical partner, Ira D. Sankey, in Burlington, October 1877. He was starting a vacation for their voices, as it were, in foliage season, with a five-month, low-key tour of New England cities: after Burlington, Manchester, New Hampshire; Portland, Maine; Providence, Rhode Island; Springfield, Massachusetts; Hartford and New Haven, Connecticut. At the time he felt that the series changed Christian New England's orientation. In the shadow of the violent railroad strikes that summer, Moody inaugurated what the *Burlington Free Press* called "the most remarkable series of meetings ever known in these parts." Moody did not consciously preach an antidote to labor unrest, but his business background and orientation were individualist and capitalist. Businessmen, after four years of depression, were fearful, and supported and contributed to Moody's campaigns as oil for troubled waters.

Moody arrived in Burlington by Central Vermont sleeper Saturday morning, October 6, and checked into "a choice suite of rooms" at the new Van Ness Hotel. Why, asked the *Free Press*, would the great evangelical duo who had packed the largest halls in Philadelphia, New York, and Chicago, come to "our small country city"? State religious leaders, including Congregationalist Franklin Fairbanks of St. Johnsbury, Baptist Jacob J. Estey of Brattleboro, and Methodist Samuel Huntington of Burlington, had signed an appeal to support Moody's evangelistic campaign. The idea, like Earle's a decade before, was to seed the revival by drawing delegates from churches all over the state. Hearing Moody and Sankey, they would "imbibe their spirit" and transmit this inspiration to their churches. The appeal called for special prayers at regular church services, at family altars, and by each private Christian.[22]

Like Billy Graham a century later, Moody attracted millions in the

great cities of the English-speaking world. Without benefit of loud-
speakers he repeatedly preached to congregations of five to ten thousand.
He introduced a new style of eloquence, which people came from across
the lake and from down the valley to hear. A short, stout, powerful man
in early middle age, with full beard and moustache, he used "racy,
idiomatic, direct" words and illustrated from common experience. Gone
were the florid, spread-eagle periods of Daniel Webster's generation and
the thunder of hell-fire revivalists. Setting the tone by the "melting
pathos" of his preaching, in tune with the doctrine of Horace Bushnell,
Connecticut Congregationalist,[23] Moody depended on the quiet prayer
meetings of inquirers. Crowds also came to hear Sankey's glorious
tenor, buy the thirty-cent, paperback hymnals, and join in "What a
Friend We Have in Jesus," "Nearer, My God, to Thee," and "I Need
Thee Every Hour." The massed choirs of four churches, leaders and or-
ganists taking turns, integrated musical praise with preaching and
prayer.

Born in Northfield, Massachusetts, in 1837, with a Connecticut
Valley accent familiar to Vermonters, Moody had left the home farm at
seventeen to work in his uncle's Boston shoe business. In 1856, he
moved to Chicago, where he made more money in a week's selling
shoes, he wrote his brother, than he could make in a month in Boston.
He devoted all his spare time to lay missionary work in Sunday School,
YMCA, and church. In 1861 he abandoned selling shoes for the full-
time sale of the gospel. As agent for the U.S. Christian Commission,
he visited army camps. After the Civil War he perfected his skills as an
evangelist, especially with the YMCA.

The protracted meeting Moody brought to Burlington in 1877 was
housebroken, unlike the version that Jedediah Burchard introduced to
Vermont in 1834-1836. Burchard's mountebank manners in his extended
series of revival sessions had turned off many respectable, orthodox
Protestants. Moody, on the other hand, channeled the emotions that
once erupted into the shouts of exhorters and the screams and yells of
converts into soothing hymns led by Sankey. Early in October a reformed drunkard made the temperance pitch and Moody declared that
what rum does is the work of the devil.

The pastors of Burlington's evangelical churches sat on the platform with Moody at the opening session, and participated throughout
the four weeks. These Congregationalists, Methodists, and Baptists
were loosely connected with the Evangelical Alliance of British and
American churches organized in London in 1846. President Matthew H.
Buckham of the University lent its prestige, or borrowed Moody's. The
visitors did not interfere with the regular Sunday worship but started
that day with a nine o'clock meeting, followed by afternoon and evening
sessions. The weekday program started at noon to catch businessmen

from the stores and snowballed until the management abandoned the city hall, because it was settling and unsafe, and moved to the new Methodist church.

Inquirers and converts asked what to do after the excitement of Moody's meetings. He told them: join a church; take communion; attend church meetings; repeat Bible verses; help others resist temptation; join the YMCA. One immediate result in Burlington was the formation of a Union Committee of Methodists, Baptists and the two Congregational churches in November 1877, consisting of two laymen and the pastor of each church. They held noonday prayer meetings and Sunday evening preaching services, and probably visited households as the 1867 canvass had done.[24] Moody effected no religious revolution, but he reflected if not created an atmosphere in which the YMCA, Christian Endeavor, the Women's Christian Temperance Union, and other benevolent institutions flourished.

Burlington's Evangelical Alliance, an 1890 revival of the Union Committee formed in the wake of Dwight L. Moody's visit in 1877, expressed the continued need for a pan-Protestant front. As before, home visitors supplied Bibles, urged householders to go to church and Sunday school, and found some attending the YMCA who did not go to church. This time the base was broader, including the Episcopalians, and women did the visiting.[25]

Protestant Vitality in the Villages

Main-line Protestants mourned the disappearance of family prayers, the decline in pious Sabbath activities, and the divisive effects of biblical criticism. They knew that country churches were losing their grip, but took comfort that in central places, the churches were confidently on the move. Moody, Safford, and Hungerford, considering themselves spokesmen for evangelical Christianity, were nevertheless Congregationalists primarily concerned with their denomination.

Thinking in terms of Protestant denominations is the way people then and people still think of Protestantism, but this approach does not reveal the common elements of style, structure, and content. Because Congregational churches were in most cases the first in town, they tended to have more prestige than the just as numerous Methodists, and to lead in changes affecting the architecture, music, ministers, schools, media, thought, and polity of the Protestant churches.

The new churches in the industrial villages included space for more uses than an auditorium, while old meetinghouses, located for a different social economy, were left isolated and sometimes abandoned on their hills. Some of the urban ministers, more often seminary-trained than earlier, led the way toward modernism, a movement to reconcile traditional theology with current culture imbued with science. As before the war, they were better paid, longer tenured, and more professional and genteel, an ornament to the upper class. The four Unitarian churches, fed from Harvard, fit the same model. The social and business connections between Unitarians and Congregationalists in the commercial villages of Burlington, Montpelier, Windsor, and Brattleboro insured a cross-fertilization within this elite. The presence of Unitarians and Universalists, and occasional liberals in the pulpits of other denominations, encouraged Congregationalists in those towns to be more liberal than their co-religionists in the country.

Baptists were among the main-line Protestant churches benefiting from urban industrial growth, as they had earlier in the village of Brandon. In Burlington they had needed state support until 1859, but by 1872 they were able to open a mission chapel near the waterfront lumberyards. They moved it by 1877 nearer to where French Canadians lived. Lumber dealers Lawrence Barnes and Mial Davis were principal donors in Burlington; Deacon Jacob Estey and his son-in-law, Levi K. Fuller, contributed liberally from their organ company profits to the Brattleboro Baptists, as did Alanson Allen, in slate, for the churches in Hydeville and Fair Haven.

People moving into the growing industrial centers either swelled the ranks of existing groups, joined missions of denominations not hitherto present, as in the case of the Episcopalians in Lyndonville and the Universalists in Rutland, or were satisfied with the rites of the many fraternal orders and other associations, flourishing again after the Masons had been silenced half a century before.[26]

Newcomers increased the pool of financial supporters which kept five major denominations viable in twenty-eight large towns. Roman Catholics, Congregationalists, and Methodists had clergy in all of them. Baptists (including Free Baptists with whom they merged early in the next century) had ministers or missionaries in all but Swanton and Barton, and Episcopalians in all but Derby and Waterbury. By contrast, Universalists held on in only twelve, and ten other groups (including "Union" churches in Cambridgeport and Derby Line) had three or less.[27]

Pluralism at its widest developed in St. Johnsbury and Burlington. In St. Johnsbury the regular Baptists, ignoring the presence of the Free Will Baptist church, organized in 1874 and built a large hall in the factory section. A Second Advent church followed the next year. The Reformed Presbyterians organized in 1879, ordained their minister in 1880, built on Eastern Avenue in 1883, and discontinued services in 1895. With the addition of the Salvation Army, a second Catholic church (St. Aloysius, anglophone), and Christian Science, St. Johnsbury village offered a dozen church choices.[28]

In Burlington the story is similar, the main flow going to the Big Five, but with four newcomers butting in. The Spiritualists bought Queen City Park in 1880; the Salvation Army showed up in 1885; a Seventh Day Adventist church organized in 1886, with a building by 1894; and Free Methodists organized in 1893 but were still renting a hall in 1900. Perhaps other church missions sowed, but on stony ground.[29]

All these denominations in the same towns shared many common practices: the church-going habit, seminary training for clergy, common styles of architecture in the same periods, and similar hymns and anthems enhancing worship.

Architecture and Music

Building and renovation of every denomination's houses of worship, born of war prosperity from 1863, was a response to needs long delayed, the existence of available funds, village pride, and denominational competition.[30] Church members wanted the places where they worshiped to be as fine as they could afford. They either needed more space for increased membership, achieved or expected, or different arrangements for added functions.

The Congregationalists usually led in making architectural changes. The Methodists, like the Episcopalians following a somewhat different drummer, came into the centers late, and tended to harmonize with existing non-Episcopalian structures. After the Civil War, the characteristic Methodist building had a side spire and an assymetrical entrance on the broad gable end as in Ludlow (1875), Randolph (1888), or Middlebury (1893). The Methodists added the most buildings in this period, although the Catholics probably spent more money on larger buildings. Methodists in many places were still sharing space with other denominations or subsisting in public space or as house churches. They acquired fifty-nine houses of worship in this period, and another sixteen received major renovations, with the peak construction of sixteen buildings during the depression of 1874-78. The Methodists were doing their bit for work relief, as they did again with ten more projects during the hard times of the mid-1890s.[31]

Changes in what happened in church caused changes in church architecture. The sanctuary of Henry Searles' 1842 Congregational church in Burlington was only a few feet above ground level, with no usable basement. Both the Pine Street Methodist (1856) and the College Street Congregational (1863-1865) buildings in Burlington had lecture halls, the latter with a raised platform, below the sanctuary. These enabled the congregation to start worship in the new space as soon as the first floor was enclosed. Also, the basement could be divided into rooms convenient for Sunday school classes and prayer meetings. Smaller spaces amd low ceilings were easier to heat. Elsewhere, wooden buildings were jacked up and cellars dug to provide usable basements.

Competition to have the most elegant, most modern, tallest church building in town was most intense in Burlington. The Baptists dedicated their proud spire in mid-December 1864; the College Street Congregationalists ten weeks later, the Cathedral of the Immaculate Conception in December 1867, and the reunited Methodists in 1870. The Pine Street Methodists felt strongly against paying for pews, so in the new building they compromised by having the even-numbered pews rent free. This system continued until 1943.[32] St. Joseph's had won the seating capacity contest in 1887. The Cathedral became the tallest when Bishop Michaud gave a statue of Mary, whose halo reached 200 feet.

Burlington's First Congregational Church, also competitive, in 1871 replaced its "vestry" with a large "lecture room" or parish hall now called the chapel, parallel to and north of the original building, with basement, first, and second floors. Pastor Edward H. Griffin recalled that the small wooden building at the east edge of the lot, used for social meetings, with women on one side and men on the other, was "ill heated, ill ventilated, cold in winter and hot in summer." They added a new parsonage, since 1983 the Ronald McDonald House, in 1874-1877.[33] The 1816 Unitarian church at the head of Church Street, Burlington, also spent competitive money on improvements: a new organ in 1862, a new clock and an extension on the north or pulpit end for parlors in 1867, more renovation in 1893, and a new parsonage on Williams Street near Pearl.[34]

What happened to church building in Burlington and a few other bellwether towns among the Congregationalists was imitated far and wide in smaller towns and other denominations, including the Catholics. The St. Mary's of 1842 could not be identified as Catholic except for the cross on the cupola. And St. Joseph's (1850) did not even have a cross. You can tell a late-Victorian church building by its borrowing some "Gothic" and sometimes Romanesque features: arched or pointed openings or circular rose windows and, when congregations could afford it, extra ornament.

Inside, gaslight or kerosene had supplanted candles and whale oil; with some exceptions, electric lighting awaited the twentieth century.[35] Architects softened the light with stained glass, golden and brown tints. From then until a recent shift, churches remembered major donors and deacons with wall plaques in the sanctuary. The church was no more dominated by its substantial members than in the early days, but it now felt it should honor in ornament the elders who shared their wealth and wisdom.

Church suppers, first supplied like a potluck, became more efficiently produced with the addition of a range burning wood, coal, or kerosene. When a village provided the services, water became available for cooking and dishwashing. Churches installed water closets with the advent of village sewer systems, beginning in Burlington by the end of 1867.

The hymns heard in Congregational churches in the 1860s most often came from "Watts and Select," a hymnbook with psalms versified by Isaac Watts in eighteenth-century England. It was easier for choirs than for congregational singing. For the congregation the editions had words only and many of the tunes assigned to the words were, according to John Goodrich, "unsingable." Young Eldridge Mix, coming to Burlington's First Congregational Church in 1862 from New York City, supported a movement to transfer from the choir to the congregation the hymns before and after the sermon, from new hymnbooks. The trend, however, was not universal. Strong characters who insisted on keeping the old books might block the purchase of something easier for the ordinary voice to sing. Some village churches preferred to hire "four voices on a shelf," as Henry Ward Beecher called the paid quartet, to show how superior their choir was and to inspire the congregation.[36]

Congregational singing was one place, whether Protestants were aware of it or not, where they all sang a range of poems, from Anglican John Henry Newman's "Lead, Kindly Light" (1833) to Quaker John Greenleaf Whittier's "Dear Lord and Father of Mankind" (1872). The music spoke an ecumenical language.

The purchase of a pipe organ was probably the most important milestone in the history of late-Victorian church music in Vermont.[37] Buying an organ might come with the surge of spending for a new building or later when the church could raise more money, or perhaps when it changed choir directors or bought new hymnbooks.

Churchgoers tend to want old favorite hymns but a revolution every generation could be effected with the popularity of a new young minister or after enough deaths. Few treasured hymnbooks as historical sources and no one has analyzed the fugitive remnants. But as Vermont churches took their styles from the cities, it is a safe guess that in most cases, nationwide popularity meant Vermont popularity.

English composers Joseph Barnby (1838-1896) and John Bacchus Dykes (1823-1876) wrote hymn tunes that lasted in successive editions for a century. Dykes set John Henry Newman's "Lead, Kindly Light" to music in 1865. Barnby gave us a tune for Sabine Baring-Gould's "Now the Day Is Over" in 1868. In the city revivals conducted by Dwight L. Moody, Ira D. Sankey popularized the *Gospel Hymns* he published in 1874 with Philip Paul Bliss, composer of "Hold the Fort for I Am Coming" and "Pull for the Shore." George Coles Stebbins (1846-

1945), who joined Moody's traveling team in 1876 and succeeded
Sankey as soloist in 1884, wrote hundreds of hymns, including "Have
Thine Own Way, Lord" (1907). Perhaps no hymn captures the femi-
nine, personal nature of the evangelical conversion experience of this
period so well as Will L. Thompson's words and music for "Softly and
Tenderly Jesus Is Calling" (1880). "We Three Kings of Orient," created
by John Henry Hopkins, Jr. in 1857, had worked its way into long-
term Protestant popularity before the century was out.

As in every age, writers of sacred poems and providers of hymn
tunes and offertories borrowed from contemporary composers. Across
the denominational board, after the "wedding of the century" in 1858 between Queen Victoria's eldest daughter and the eldest son of the German
emperor, many weddings started with the bridal chorus from Wagner's
Lohengrin and ended with Mendelssohn's "Wedding March" from his *A
Midsummer Night's Dream.*

Ministers and Bishops

The sacred music of Congregational worship was secondary to
preaching, and the sermon counted more than pastoral care. In fact, the
clergy held the keys to the Kingdom, whether in the pulpit, in guiding
the superintendent of the Sunday school and the leader of the prayer
meeting, in teaching in the church-related academy, in sustaining the
denominational press.

Most parish and town histories stick to the non-judgmental record
book and make clear that the minister's first duty was preaching. In
Burlington's First Congregational Church, a contemporary's review of
the features of each pastorate discloses how carefully they had to tread in
suggesting innovations and in satisfying deacons and donors.[38]

The sermons of Spencer Marsh (1856-1860) were "carefully elaborated" and spiced with literary allusions. He was asked to leave and
eventually found his vocation as a librarian. Under young Eldridge Mix
(1862-1867) the church moved the second Sunday service from two o'-
clock to the evening, after the ladies voted that they did not fear being
out at night. By the mid-1880s most other churches had abandoned the
Sunday afternoon service and members used the free time to call on
their friends and neighbors, while the well-to-do took their infirm elders
for carriage rides and the young went for a ramble in the country. Pious
Protestant families still banned "secular" amusements on Sunday.

The next two pastors of Burlington's First Congregational Church,
Edward Herrick Griffin (1868-1872) and Lewis Ormond Brastow (1873-
1885), left for professors' chairs. Griffin, an ambitious young product
of Williams College and Princeton and Union seminaries, spoke clearly
to the unlearned but the straitlaced among the congregation called him

to account. When he joined a club that read Shakespeare's plays, "two saintly women" warned him against the evils of theater, so he withdrew from the club and soon left for a career at Williams. Griffin's contemporary in Montpelier, William H. Lord, pastor of Bethany Church, Congregational, called to serve on a church council in a case of a Connecticut River church, found that the substance of the charge against its pastor, according to his son's recollection, was his playing blind man's buff.[39] Members of other evangelical churches had the same ascetic attitudes.

Pastor Brastow, chaplain of the Twelfth Vermont Regiment, with twelve years' experience in St. Johnsbury when he came to Burlington, addressed his sermons "to alert and active minds." That is, it was hard for some to keep up with his developing themes. He resigned to teach at Yale Divinity School. Edward Hawes (1885-1899), out of Bowdoin College and Bangor Seminary, had the church's longest tenure in the century, his climax career, because he "preached the old gospel in the old ways."

Congregational ministers, by and large local products, usually left city churches for larger parishes in larger cities. St. Albans is an example of a major congregation that lost its longer-term pastors (four in twenty-eight years from 1873) to Springfield and New Bedford, Massachusetts; Newark, New Jersey; and Auburn, Maine. As earlier, churches just getting a toehold in a town or with congregations unwilling or unable to pay as much, settled for less training and experience, and shorter tenure. As before, a small fraction, perhaps a tenth of the newly chosen Congregational ministers in this period, were born in Canada, Scotland, or England and stayed briefly in poorer parishes.[40]

Methodist clergy, as they settled into their parsonages with less concern that the bishop would move them soon, became more refined, respectable, and sentimental. They were refined because they had studied more than the Bible-taught itinerants of the converting generation had studied. They were respectable because they behaved with one eye on the patterns shaped by the village elite, though usually not accepted in top social circles. In the early days their own society had sufficed. They were sentimental in their emphases on love and benevolence. Preaching, prayer, and praise continued to be the staples of worship, with only minor variations in style and content. Methodist tradition for two generations continued to be served by fervent prayer meetings supplementing weekly worship. Their people were earnest, comfortable, and "puritan" in their habits of piety.

As in other denominations, the roles of Methodist women were expanding. The Methodist Vermont Conference, meeting in Barre April 12, 1896, adopted by a 50 to 7 vote the "Baltimore amendment" which, if accepted by all conferences, would have admitted women to their

General Conference. Although the Methodists had allowed such women as Phoebe Palmer to be evangelists in the 1850s and used others as "supply preachers" toward the end of the century, they did not choose their first Vermont deaconess until 1900, and did not "fully ordain" a woman until 1963.[41]

Methodists expected their ministers to set a good example in maintaining their defenses against the world's evils by their "puritanical" code. A Troy Conference resolution of 1867 listed "Games of chance, or of skill, as cards, billiards, chequers, backgammon. . . and dancing, horse-racing" or attending "theatres, operas, circuses or minstrels" as "wholly incompatible" with Christian practice. This list was virtually the same as in the unenforced Vermont legal codes of 1880 and 1906. In 1870, soon after Andrew I. Goodhue, who became President Calvin Coolidge's father-in-law, joined his wife's Methodist church in Burlington, he burned his packs of cards.[42] A proposal at the annual Methodist Troy conference of 1892 to change the 1867 statement was somehow slipped through the opposition and sent on to the General Conference. The aroused conservatives disavowed the proposal in 1893 and in the new *Discipline* of 1896 continued the 1867 list of prohibitions of "Imprudent and Unchristian Conduct," with expulsion from Methodist membership on third offense. This remained in force until 1944, when the prohibition was limited to "Taking such diversions as cannot be used in the name of the Lord Jesus," omitting the list of specifics.[43] This attitude toward vain amusements was more or less common to all Christians, with less emphasis among the Universalists and Unitarians at one end of the denominational spectrum, and among the Episcopalians and Roman Catholics at the other.

This oversimplified portrait applies to the regular Baptist elders, except that their congregations chose them, and many of them still worked to supplement their salaries. The Free Will Baptists differed less from the regulars than they had before the war. They sent their first woman delegate to their Vermont Yearly Meeting Conference in 1877.[44] They had, since the tours of Clarissa Danforth, shown a willingness to use the talents of women as exhorters and revivalists. But with a shrinking membership, one suspects that opportunities for women were limited. The men swept into the ministry by the revivalism ending in the early 1840s still needed places to preach as aging veterans a generation later.

The Universalists, faced with the same shortage of ministers, found it more economical to hire woman pastors, unless they could get a couple for the price of one. They claim Olympia Brown, who became the Universalist minister at Marshfield and East Montpelier in 1863, as "the first woman to gain full ministerial status in any denomination in this country." Two other Universalist women appear in the haystack of male ministers. Ruth A. Damon, trained at the seminary of St. Lawrence University, preached in Cavendish and Springfield, 1867-1869, and after her marriage to James B. Taber, was active in Bethel, Gaysville, and Williamsville. Annette Shaw preached in Barton and Charleston in the late 1870s.[45]

Episcopal bishop William Henry Augustus Bissell (1868-93), a gentle, pious, ordinary man with no enemies, had been twenty years rector of Trinity Church, Geneva, New York, when chosen Hopkins' successor. He was not elected for his rhetoric or his writings. He published nothing but his mandatory addresses to the annual diocesan conventions. He was a native Vermonter brought up a Congregationalist in Randolph and converted soon after graduating from the University of Vermont. The convention hoped he would understand and nourish his people and he jusified their hopes, as far "as health would allow."

The diocese continued to grew under Bishop Bissell for the same reasons it had grown under Bishop Hopkins, "owing to . . . the increase of parishes, to the breaking down of prejudices against the church and to a more general advancement in wealth and liberality," rector Alonzo Flanders of St. Albans concluded in his memorial sermon. In other words, changes in Vermont society enabled its stately ritual and creed not argued about to appeal broadly, from the lower middle class to such wealthy patrons as LeGrand B. Cannon. The diocese added seven priests to care for an increase of over a thousand communicants in Bissell's first fourteen yers. From 1884, however, he "showed signs of failing health," spending the cold months in warmer climes, and his management weakened. His successor inherited only twenty-two priests, four less than when Bissell came, and the two Rock Point schools whose administration Bissell had turned over to others, in financial trouble.[46]

The choice of pastors and leaders of state organizations was still a matter of the private networks of religious leaders, as perhaps it always is in part. For example, Bishop Bissell died in May 1893 and in June the diocesan convention elected a man who declined. Right after, the Rutland wife of the diocesan treasurer and the wife of the rector of St. Michael's Episcopal Church in Brattleboro were visiting their brother, who recommended his friend Arthur C. A. Hall. The sisters wired their husbands, who consulted the diocesan leadership, called a special convention, and elected Hall before the end of August.[47]

Vermont Episcopalians probably chose better than they knew in electing Arthur Crawshay Alliston Hall (1847-1930) their third bishop in 1893. They may have heard of Hall as a powerful preacher with missionary zeal, with an attraction for the Anglo-Catholic movement, and a supporter of the liberal Bishop Phillips Brooks of Massachusetts. A country squire's son, Oxford-trained, Hall entered the Church of England as a monk of the order of St. John the Evangelist, known as the

Cowley Fathers. He served eighteen years as a missionary in Boston, with a summer among lumbermen, gold miners, and railroad workers in British Columbia. Combining the military discipline of his soldier father and his own stubborn frankness in urging his independent views, he accepted his removal as provincial superior in the United States and returned to England in 1891, to the deep regret of his wide circle of associates. From that distance, he came to the bishop's house at Rock Point, Burlington, to be for a generation assiduous in pastoral care, voluminous in publishing his opinions on many aspects of doctrine and practice, an example of piety, active in his national church, a man who got things done. But the diocese felt most of the power of his personality after 1900, when he had won its settled approval.

Modernists

Professionals were having difficulty fitting the articles of their faith, "which was once for all delivered to the saints" (Jude, 3), to conditions vastly different from those years of primitive Christianity. The case of Senator Edmunds demonstrates the restlessness of some Congregational churches under the weight of their tradition, and exemplifies the basic differences between their Puritan heritage and the Protestant Episcopal Diocese of Vermont.

George F. Edmunds, Burlington's state senator, former speaker of the House, and leading lawyer, married a charter member of the College Street Congregational Church. Apparently not a church member, but of Quaker background, he was willing to join her church in 1862 if the articles on Providence and predestination were not included as essential tests.

The church, many of whose members were University of Vermont officers and faculty with views like his, regretfully responded that it could not act independently of the Chittenden County Conference. Perhaps this answer concealed objections to change from a few weighty, old-guard, orthodox members. When two ministers belonging to the church signed the *Protest* of 1879, they did not defer to the County Conference. The church, after prolonged discussion, adopted a resolution worded by Matthew H. Buckham, Congregational minister's son and next president of the university. This recognized that human understanding of doctrine is inevitably clouded and expressed variously. Therefore candidates need assent to the articles of faith in substance and not in explicit detail. This did not satisfy Edmunds. In 1870, during his first term as U.S. senator, he and his wife joined a Washington D.C. Episcopal church.[48] In 1872 the Edmundses' former church adopted a new form of covenant not mentioning Providence or predestination, but asserting that it neither modified nor abandoned the old articles.

One of the most obvious conflicts among the clergy, causing questions for most of two centuries, was between the findings of scientists and the theories they built on them, and the Bible stories. After the Civil War, John William Draper and Andrew Dickson White called this the warfare of science with religion (or theology).[49] How could a person who had been taught the age of rocks reconcile geology and Genesis? How could a college graduate, taught Darwinian or even Lamarckian biology, accept any literal explanation of the creation story?

The roots of modernism reach back to the eighteenth-century appreciation of nature and reason. Ever since Schleiermacher, who published in the first third of the nineteenth century, one set of theologians had felt the necessity of considering culture and religion as both expressing human glimpses of God. Modernism, a name ascribed to the movement by the early twentieth century, derived from three basic assumptions at odds with traditional Christianity. First, it assumed that religion is entangled with culture, that in each age the good news must be declared to people in their languages and adapted to their current conditions. The modernists' opponents charged that this gave ultimate authority to human science and culture rather than to God. Working on this premise and adapting religion to science, the theologian could not interpret the Bible literally. The second modernist assumption was the belief in divine immanence in nature, persons, and societies, rather than divine transcendence, invading the world with judgment beyond the limits of human comprehension. Third, if God is somehow in human culture and revealed through it, that culture must be moving toward but perhaps never achieving the Kingdom of God, "on earth as it is in heaven."[50]

This was a formulation that followed half a century and more of groping by Unitarians from William Ellery Channing to Octavius B. Frothingham, with notable contributions by Congregationalist Horace Bushnell of Hartford and Presbyterian David Swing of Chicago, among many others. The theologies of the travelers on the road from old-time orthodoxy had varied emphases.

Shailer Mathews, for example, announced his version of modernism in *The Faith of Modernism* (1924): "What then is Modernism?...It is the use of the methods of modern science to find, state and use the permanent and central values of inherited orthodoxy in meeting the needs of a modern world."[51] He attempted to escape what he considered the authoritarianism of the churches that focused on dogma. He favored examining the Christian inheritance and discarding elements that did not meet the needs of ever new situations.

Modernists with these assumptions were preoccupied with the issues of the relations between the theories of science, the scholarly exegesis of the Bible, and the fundamentals of the New England theology. For thirty years before the war, the debate over whether the Bible sanctioned slavery had depended for both sides on assembling proof texts. Could some Northerners have been weaned from literalism partly because their opponents collected an abundance of pro-slavery quotations?

Protestants especially, with their emphasis on the authority of the Bible, faced with archeological, geological, and other scientific findings over the previous century, had problems with the literal interpretation of Scripture. Vermonters had this dilemma at least since Charles B. Adams' reports as state geologist in the 1840s, if not before. His second (1846) report spent several paragraphs proving that he was a Christian scientist who believed in the Bible and accepted evidence of long geological history.[52] Adams essentially put Christianity and geology in two compartments and believed both. No evidence has surfaced that the English controversy over Darwin's publication of *The Origin of Species* on the eve of the war attracted any immediate attention in Vermont until after the war.

John Perry had wrestled with this problem since his college days. After the war he returned to Swanton as a minister, both a geologist and a Christian. The prewar criticism that he was theologically unsound led to another church council of neighboring ministers. This council concluded in 1865, without judging the issue, that the prolonged fight had spread bad feeling across northwestern Vermont so that reconciliation seemed impossible. Perry accepted dismissal, spent a year in Wilmington, Vermont, married a second time in 1867, and supplied pulpits near Boston. His career took an unexpected turn when his paper presented to the Boston Society of Natural History won Louis Agassiz's approval and appointment as curator of paleontology at Harvard in 1868. Teaching natural science for a term at the University of Vermont, he concluded with a lecture on the "Relation of Geology to Scripture," using hard-rock evidence to reject the literal view of the creation stories. By 1870 he proposed that seminaries should create departments of science and religion, an idea which Oberlin College acted on by appointing him to such a post.[53]

George Frederick Wright, Perry's successor in a similar Oberlin chair, also incubated his modernism in northwestern Vermont. Born in Whitehall, New York, and trained at Oberlin College, Wright stirred Bakersfield to life in the decade after his discharge for physical disability from the Sixth Ohio Regiment in 1862. "At the outset, I began to devote my forenoons sacredly to study," he recalled. He was "probably the only minister on either side of the Atlantic who, while fulfilling his clerical duties, read the Bible through in the original languages, translated Kant's *Critique of Pure Reason*, studied the philosophical works of [John Stuart] Mill, [William] Hamilton, and Noah Porter, and read appreciatively the *Origin of Species* and [Charles] Lyell's *Antiquity of Man*." He also "found time. . . to become an authority on the glacial geology of his region," and in communication with Asa Gray, developed a version of Christian Darwinism.[54] He proceeded to a pastorate at Andover, Massachusetts, next door to the seminary that would mediate new thought through its graduates. From there he went to Oberlin and eventually occupied a chair on the harmony of science and religion.[55]

Ministers like John Perry and George Wright, and John H. Worcester, who moved toward modernism in the forty years after he retired from preaching in 1854, tried to reconcile traditional theology with the conclusions of modern science. Their development resulted from corresponding with others of the same interest and reading the Bible, classics, and contemporary thinkers with a fresh eye. This struggle moved the leaders away from the views of church members who had little time for adult self-education. To be sure, many towns had their ladies' fortnightlies, which could meet at teatime, and village men's clubs after supper, also concerned with world affairs and opinion. Each town had from occasional to frequent lecturer-entertainers who put a thick coating of respectable beliefs over anything new they might insert. But the village elite learned at a snail's pace without consciously compromising their traditional views, while the other church members accepted the articles of their faith, not having pondered them much since joining, if then. Some of the clergy, with so much college and seminary training and so much free time, still claiming to be evangelical, were moving down the road toward modernism. They either prudently kept their new insights to themselves or mediated them most circumspectly in their sermons, finding a safety valve in confidants at home or away.

John Dewey, who graduated from the University of Vermont in 1879, attended the lectures and demonstrations of George Henry Perkins (Yale Ph.D. 1869) in geology and zoology. He recalled that Perkins "ordered his presentation of material on the theory of evolution. . . . the emphasis on evolution caused little, if any, visible resentment."[56] Perkins published descriptive articles in all branches of natural history throughout his long life, but did not show his Christian Darwinism until 1895, when his public lecture, "The Relation of Theories of Evolution to Religious Belief," appeared in the local paper. In this talk he reconciled his faith in progress with faith in evolutionary science, a popular view judging by the large and sympathetic crowd that heard him.[57] His offices as president of the Vermont Christian Endeavor Union in 1886 and vice president of the Burlington YMCA in 1889 indicate his active piety.[58] Across the state, the Rev. Edward T. Fairbanks was casually saying, without arousing antagonism, that the divine way takes eons.[59]

Exposure to evolutionary ideas did not faze the Burlington and other urbane elites. The farm community, however, with only superficial exposure to the new ideas, looked on UVM with ambivalent suspicion and pride. They favored science to improve breeds and yields and wanted to see results in a demonstration farm run by an agricultural college. They justifiably feared that UVM, whose classical college shaped its curriculum to prepare professionals, would not offer what dirt farmers wanted, vocational training or the practical experiments in the field. Some of this fear, felt by orthodox literalists, spilled over into suspicion of the Burlington faculty and some UVM alumni as unsound on Scripture.

In the late 1870s a disagreement among Congregational ministers surfaced which bore obliquely on the modernism issue. In 1878, a state Congregational convention resolution took to heart William G. T. Shedd's 1858 advice to pull the denomination together by requiring its pastors to accept "the historic belief of these Churches." The chairman of the resolution committee, writing to his opponents and representing the evangelical majority, felt "Vermont was a good place to begin" to shore up the walls against modernism. The next year's convention adopted the resolution by a large majority and defeated an amendment supporting appeal from "all human creeds to the word of God" and to church councils. This evoked *A Protest Addressed to the Congregational Churches and Ministers of Vermont*, signed by ten Congregational ministers, all but one from the large villages of the Champlain Valley.[60]

This is a time of active theological discussion, the protesters wrote. The Perry case of a passionate geologist and pastor dismissed because too many parishioners found fault with his theology, was warm in their memories. They were in basic agreement with the traditional orthodoxy, but objected to binding "a living church, nourished and growing by the living word, to any creed" written by "uninspired men," or "to join a varying orthodoxy to an unvarying formula." "New problems are arising," they continued, "and old problems are presenting themselves in new lights . . . some scriptural interpretations need re-examination, and some doctrines long established are challenged from unexpected quarters."[61] One modernist, George Angier Gordon, would have supported these protesters. We should prize our ideas of the gospel, he wrote, "but we must never make the mistake of supposing that our ideas are the gospel."[62]

No one mentioned Darwin's name nor the debate over the creation, but the spirit of evolutionary science was in the protesters. Andover Theological Seminary, where many Vermont Congregationalists trained, had debated the theological ramifications of accepting the new science and concluded in 1878 to accept the endowment of a chair of "Relations of Christianity and Science."

In Burlington, an exodus from the original First Baptist Church appears to have been a group of modernists uncomfortable with its conservatism. The Berean Baptist Church organized June 9, 1884, as its colony, with Professor Ezra P. Gould from Newton Theological Seminary its first pastor. By 1886 it had a building a block north of the First Congregational Church and less than five blocks from its parent church. One of Gould's star scholars, Frederick Eli Dewhurst, succeeded him because he was too modernist for his church near Boston. Congregationalist President Matthew H. Buckham made Dewhurst adjunct lecturer in political economy at the University of Vermont, 1889-1892. Still hounded by traditionalists, Dewhurst left his denomination in 1892 for the pulpit of the Plymouth Congregational Church, Indianapolis, and finished his career at the liberal University Congregational Church, Chicago. The Bereans next chose James Ten Broek, also with a modernist pedigree (Middlebury 1884, Rochester Seminary 1887, Yale Ph.D. 1891, fresh from a year at the University of Berlin). When Ten Broek accepted an appointment as professor of philosophy at McMaster University in Toronto in 1895, they gave up and sold their building to the WCTU the next year.[63] Membership rolls of Burlington's College Street Congregational Church show an accession of about a dozen from the Berean Baptist Church.

The two Baptist churches in Burlington had been a third pair of Protestant churches of the same denomination in the central village of a town. The discontinuance of the Berean Baptists left only two such pairs, discussed in chapter 5: the Congregational churches in St. Johnsbury and Burlington.

The fight in the Congregational state conventions of 1878-1879 was not only about theology but also about power. It proved that the dismissal of John Perry from Swanton had not contained, but spread the controversy. In the long run, however, the gods of the valley villages carried the body of the main-line churches with them. The spirit of the Bible, and not a creedal formula, was basic to them.[64]

Home Missions, Schools, and Press

Although no case occurred in which the state convention vetoed a decision of a church council, the state denominational organizations, in place for half a century and more, quietly expanded their spheres of influence and power. State-supported denominational evangelists like one Potter who raised the membership in Rupert in 1873, reached into the hills.[65] Through the Vermont Domestic Missionary Society, home missionaries supplemented or took the place of pastors whom the smaller, weaker hill churches could not quite afford.

In 1886, Henry Fairbanks took a census of forty-four towns in five counties and reported that half the population never attended worship.

After 1888, when the women's Home Missionary Union decided to manage its own funds, they diverted some money from national to local needs. This paid for pairs of female evangelists trained at the Moody schools in Northfield, Massachusetts, and Chicago, and working in rural parishes. Florence Yarrow, one of the first, reported that the people of Plymouth welcomed their work but that a Spiritualist convention had pre-empted the hall. From 1891 to World War I, sixty-four women followed Yarrow.[66]

At the level of religious education, churches indoctrinated adults in catechism, confirmation, and Sunday or study groups. Sunday schools thrived for the pre-adolescent, using denominational materials nationally produced or by the American Sunday School Union. Each denomination except Congregational and Catholic had settled, by the end of the century, on one church-related academy, always in financial difficulty.

While the Methodists' Troy Conference Academy, deeply in debt, had been sold in 1863 to become the proprietary "Ripley Female College," after a decade the conference negotiated for its return debt-free. It continued to serve western Vermont Methodists, once again for both sexes. For the Vermont Conference Methodists established a strong new seminary on the Sloan military hospital site in Montpelier. A study of membership changes among academy students would indicate the vitality of the school as a church mission. Records of conversion to Catholicism by girls such as Fanny Allen who attended convent schools suggest the value of such a study. At any rate, the presence of a church-related school certainly strengthened the church in its town.[67]

The Baptists raised $70,000 in hard times to endow Vermont Academy at Saxtons River, near Bellows Falls, which opened in 1876, with Jacob Estey, Levi K. Fuller (Brattleboro organs), Lawrence Barnes, Mial Davis (Burlington lumber), and Alanson Allen (Fair Haven slate) among the incorporators. It built beyond its means and set tuition too low to cover operating expenses, so that the state convention had to come to its rescue in 1900. It lent the school $25,000 and guaranteed a subsidy of $1,000 a year for ten years.[68]

Free Will Baptists raised nearly $27,000 to build Green Mountain Seminary at Waterbury Center and opened it in 1869. In spite of the effort to increase enrollment by adding a commercial department in 1881, it closed in 1906.[69]

The Universalists closed their Orleans Liberal Institute at Glover in 1872, while their Green Mountain Perkins Institute in South Woodstock lasted until 1898. Goddard Seminary in Barre, although it survived to be transformed into Plainfield's Goddard College, traveled "the same rocky road."[70]

After Bishop Hopkins' death in 1868, his Vermont Episcopal Institute became essentially a military academy, with Bishop Hopkins

Hall, a girls' finishing school, added in 1887. Financial difficulties forced the closing of both Rock Point schools in 1899.[71]

In the three Vermont colleges at Middlebury, Northfield, and Burlington, religion was still important, but less important than it had been. The University of Vermont had lay presidents from 1866 although Matthew H. Buckham at the helm behaved like a minister. Middlebury College's presidents were Congregational ministers until Ezra Brainerd was elected in 1885. Brainerd graduated from Andover Theological Seminary but like Buckham became a professor and was never ordained. At Norwich University a series of Episcopal priests held the presidency until 1876, but the diocese never became a solid sponsor. The century turned with another Episcopal clergyman in charge, Alan D. Brown.

Protestants depended on state and national publications to keep them informed. While official state publications maintained membership in organizations of doctors, druggists, dairymen, Grangers, antiquarians, and many more, the state denominational press all but vanished. The cost of publication and the competition of local newspapers fighting national competition with emphasis on local news, forced the religious press to centralize nationally.

The Congregationalists came to a crisis in 1866, when Lyman J. McIndoe added their *Vermont Chronicle* to his string of Connecticut Valley weeklies and reduced it to a virtual department of a weekly with general coverage. The clergy complained, but McIndoe retorted that he met his obligations by printing their news and opinion. He implied that a purely religious state organ could not survive.[72] On the modest scale of a printed newsletter it could, and did. When the *Vermont Chronicle* died in 1898, the monthly *Vermont Missionary*, started in 1889, expanded its coverage to become a general Congregational mouthpiece, called *Congregational Vermont* from 1935.

Methodists could not continue a state denominational organ against their own national competition. Elisha J. Scott, founder of the Methodist *Christian Messenger*, died in 1866 and the paper limped along into the 1880s with much turnover. Long-term editor Eli Ballou died in 1870 and his executors promptly sold his *Universalist Watchman*'s subscription list to the Boston *Universalist*.

Toward the end of the century, the Episcopalians started an official missionary newsletter. Bishop Hall, even before his consecration, assigned diocesan missionary and Congregational convert William J. Harris to edit the quarterly *Mountain Echo*, beginning in January 1894. The *Mountain Echo* continues into its second century as a monthly, distributed with the denomination's national monthly newspaper, *Episcopal Life*.

Denominational Numbers

Those splinter groups whose strength was in the hills suffered with the decline of the hill country. Those who stayed home and learned how to maintain their acres and keep their rural ways were more often Congregationalist, Methodist, or Baptist. Some denominational fragments, listed at the end of chapter 3 (Quakers, two other kinds of Methodists), hung on in a few places without enough life to change and grow. Or if they changed, as some Quakers did in the 1880s, adopting old-time revivalist religion, they also ran in the race for converts. The Mormons wisely called their converts to come together, and therefore left no trace in the state until they sent new teams of missionaries in the twentieth century. The Wesleyan Methodists, founded on the dated antislavery issue, continued on inertia, as did the Protestant Methodists, less worried about the power of bishops than earlier. Adventists continued their expectancy, but divided on whether to worship on Saturday or Sunday. The Advent Christians conformed to the Christian world about them and worshiped on Sunday. The more numerous Seventh Day Adventists followed a sensible literalism that at the creation God rested after six days of work. Without being feminist, the Advent Christians let Mrs. L. C. McKinstry preach in the house of worship she built in Richford in 1899 as a memorial to her minister husband.[73]

The Free Will Baptists, born in an atmosphere of protest against strict Calvinism, had reached a peak of 85 ministers and 4,409 members in 1844, about the same time as the regular Baptists. Their corps was down to 46 ministers and only 2,673 members in 1889, with a continued slide in the next twenty years. Because the regular Baptists had become more liberal on the issues that had originally divided them, a merger was not far off.[74]

Universalists entering these commercial-industrial villages joined a liberal church nearest to what they had left, usually the Unitarian. In Windsor, Montpelier, and probably Burlington, the 1961 merger of the two denominations had already occurred locally. The new Montpelier Church of the Messiah (1864), succeeding where an earlier liberal church failed, had a majority of Universalists with a sprinkling of Unitarians and Spiritualists. During the sixteen-year life of the Liberal Christian Society of Castleton, 1867-1883, both Universalists and Unitarians joined.

On the other hand, new Universalist life strengthened the Brattleboro and Barre churches, established before the war, planted a strong new church in Rutland in 1885, and created new outposts with their own trademark in the northern villages (Derby and Swanton briefly; Newport, St. Albans, and St. Johnsbury into the twentieth century).

The Universalists in Brattleboro became the largest of some thirty of its active churches in the 1870s and merged with the Unitarians in 1921.[75]

Whether in town or country, church going continued among an influential fraction of the people. They kept Sunday laws on the books if not fully enforced. They were losing ground, although fighting rear-guard actions against trains operating on Sunday, carrying milk to the cheese factory on Sunday, and partial observance. Herman C. Riggs' Thanksgiving sermon in 1869 decried the growing popularity of the "continental Sabbath," going to church Sunday morning and then spending the rest of the day in correspondence, visits, parties, reading secular publications, and other "self-gratification." Yet when labor unions and others supported limiting activity, it was for the sake of rest (in harmony with Genesis 2:2), not devotional observance. Stores, post offices, and places of amusement were still closed on Sunday in the interests of church people, contrary to the interests of Seventh Day Adventists, Jews, and many of the unchurched. Neither the Rutland and Burlington *Sunday Sentinel* (1879-1880), nor the Rutland *News* (1891-1893?), daily and Sunday, survived long defying the sabbatarians, but several weeklies published on Saturday for Sunday reading.[76]

Henry Fairbanks of St. Johnsbury wrote perhaps the clearest expression of the belief that Puritan independency is the necessary foundation of democracy in America and shield against Catholic hierarchy and autocracy. He read his paper, "The Influence of Congregationalism Upon Vermont," before the annual Congregational state convention at Bennington, June 12, 1895. The Congregational way, he declared, was primitive Christianity revived, after centuries of departure from the congregational principles of St. Stephen and the Jerusalem elders. Although he was speaking to Congregationalists and claiming that they had the right way, all the brethren who had separated from them, from Unitarian to Adventist, could claim as much. Fairbanks, like Rowland Robinson, lamented the replacement of departing Yankees by invading immigrants, but also regretted the native stock's "drifting away from all religious influences." He concluded his jeremiad, "The guiding moral power seems to have lost its hold, the rudder chains are broken."[77]

In statistical language, this discouragement translated into a period nearly level in membership reports of around 23,500 Congregationalists from 1877 to 1885. Then the totals rose gradually to 26,552 in 1901 and continued slowly upward for another half century. Fairbanks knew, however, that the figures concealed an increasing proportion of non-residents, and a large number of churches (140 in 1873) without settled pastors, certainly a sign of ill health.[78]

No one has compiled for the Methodists, although enviously known as the Methodist "Statistical" church, a summary of the numbers available in their press for the Vermont churches in the Troy Conference and for the Vermont Conference.

The Baptists, the next largest group of Protestants, had rallied after the war on evangelists barnstorming the major villages within reach of the rails. These visitors were responsible for the peak of 9,870 Baptist members in 1880, more than a thousand below the peak of 1840. Although thereafter the Baptists lost ground until 1906, their losses would have been greater without the evangelists' help. Their chief jolter, A. B. Earle, came to Vermont five times from 1867 to 1883, mainly to towns on the Rutland line of the railroad, and other Baptist evangelists followed him. More than other Protestant churches, they appealed to the unchurched working class in the industrial villages.[79]

The Episcopalians shared with the Congregationalists and the Baptists in gains up to 1880. Without the benefit of immigration like the Catholics or revivalism like the Baptists, the diocese grew from 2,381 to 3,488 communicants by 1882. Bissell added seven priests to the twenty-six he inherited from Hopkins as pastors for forty-eight active parishes using $476,000 worth of church buildings and rectories. St. Paul's Burlington had doubled and Christ Church Montpelier had tripled its adherents in thirty years.[80] As the bishop's health began to fail, however, things slipped.

Bishop Louis De Goesbriand minded his own business while protesting the unfairness of Protestant arrangements. Catholics were double-taxed for schools. They had no chaplains in the Vermont regiments. While Republican business managers, recognizing their value as labor and voters, let them use public property and contributed to their building funds, Catholic laity felt intangible social pressures.

Over forty years, De Goesbriand found space for worship, priests to conduct it, and nuns to teach in Catholic schools. In 1854 he invited the Sisters of Providence to run the first orphanage in Vermont. Approaching 1900, his coadjutor from 1892 started to modernize the diocese. John Stephen Michaud, born of French and Irish parents, the first native priest ordained in the diocese, in 1873, was preparing his people for the twentieth century. Vermont's largest denomination soon had its own Fanny Allen Hospital (1894), its incorporation (1896), and its own St. Michael's College (1904).

A symbol of newly acquired Catholic self-esteem was the establishment in 1893 of the shrine of Ste. Anne on Isle La Motte.[81] "We are not Jean come lately," it quietly proclaimed. "We are not only the biggest; we were here first." New England Yankees had their Plymouth Rock and Vermonters their Bennington Battle Monument, dedicated with great fanfare in 1891. Catholics now had their shrine at the site of the 1666 French fort and chapel, the first European outpost in Vermont. In 1903 Bishop Michaud added the great tower to his cathedral, crowned with a gilded statue of Our Lady of Lourdes, to make its two hundred feet the tallest building in Vermont.

In another part of the pasture, Protestants bestirred themselves in the face of the Catholic challenge. The Methodists, while not growing by conversions the way they had early in the century, escaped schism with their holiness wing, especially through their institutionalized camp meetings. Twenty-eight ministers shared the trials of the Civil War with Vermont regiments. Where out-migration and indifference racked the rural churches, domestic missionaries, many of them women, strove to fill the gaps. In the villages, new spires arose and new flocks gathered, testing the tolerance of main-line churches. Spiritualism, Christian Science, and the Salvation Army, all bent on healing the body and the soul, crept in to gather the crumbs under the main-line table. While immigration still favored the Catholics, Welsh and Swedish industrial workers formed new Protestant congregations worshiping in their own languages. Jews arriving from eastern Europe imposed a new test of tolerance, forming an enclave in Burlington, both as defense against prejudice and as balm for the uprooted.

Competition continued among religious societies, more diverse than ever, but competition was more severe between the churches and a multitude of "secular" associations, each of them a church outside the church. First there were organizations to meet particular, recognized needs: intemperance (the WCTU and others), homes for orphans, homes for youths escaping the churches (the YMCA/YWCA, Christian Endeavor), hospitals for the sick, as homelike as possible, homes for the aged, fraternal orders to pay death benefits and satisfy with mysterious rituals. Most potent of all these one-purpose institutions was the Grange, from 1871 expressing the pain of farmers as they realized their decreasing roles in the enlarging nation and the urbanizing country.

The failure of feeble union efforts in Burlington in 1877 and 1890 and the persistent reluctance to share worship between poor congregations all signified that denominational distinctives were still worth working to preserve. If a little time was left over for an ecumenical gesture, good. Central to each group's survival was their own church. Unfortunately for clarity and power in their programs, they were agreed only that they should help people, but had less agreement than ever before on what people needed help and what kind of help they needed. Most of them had accommodated too much to their pluralistic society.

Notes to Chapter 6

[1] Circumstances had forced the country into the pluralism that some students of Christian history are saying was present in Christianity since its beginning. See Riley, *One Jesus, Many Christs*.

[2] C. E. Allen, *About Burlington*, 27-28.

[3] Audet, *Congrégation Canadienne de Winooski*, 41. See also Blow, "French Canadian Culture in Winooski."

[4] See Blow, "Financial History of St. Francis Xavier Parish, 1873-1900," Table I in his "French-Canadian Culture in Winooski," 66.

[5] Ibid., 72-73.

[6] For details and illustrations of the new St. Joseph's see Burlington. St. Joseph Church. *History*, 46-55. The crest of the cock above St. Joseph's vane was six inches lower than Mary's halo on the 1904 cathedral.

[7] In *Vermont Historical Gazetteer*, 3:1050. Bassett, "Urban Penetration of Rural Vermont," 586-588, analyzes the ethnic composition of West Rutland quarry labor.

[8] Senécal, "Franco-Americans in Vermont," 5.

[9] Burlington. St. Joseph Church. *History*, 48.

[10] Blow, "Parochial Schools of Burlington," 150, 157.

[11] See Seaver, *Moral Teaching*, 6-8.

[12] Geno, "St. Michael's College"; Duquette, *Sisters of Mercy*, 176; Blow, "St. Joseph's College"; and "Parochial Schools of Burlington," 149. Blow's Table 1, 157, includes nine orders of nuns in eleven villages, with dates of arrival (and departure in four cases).

[13] *Le Protecteur* also emphasized issues of naturalization, repatriation, and Canadian annexation, but otherwise avoided politics. Frédéric Houde succeeded Druon as editor in 1871, changing the paper's name to *L'Avenir National*, and moved it to Troy, New York, the next year. Daggett, "Vermont's French Newspapers," supplies details of other attempts in Burlington and Vergennes.

14 Hannon, *West Rutland*, 106-117; Beers, *Atlas of Rutland Co.*, 27 (West Rutland and Center Rutland).

15 Patrick Cunningham, "Irish Catholics in Brattleboro," the rector's 1898 answers to the diocesan questionnaire; Blow, "Brattleboro School Affair"; Shaw, "'Yankee Priest' in Brattleboro."   Fr. Shaw spent eight weeks at the Wesselhoeft Water Cure, hearing confessions, celebrating Mass, preaching, baptizing, and marrying in the area. He read Mass daily in his hotel room but kept the shutters closed so that no one could see his candlelight.

16 Anderson, *We Americans*, 3-96, weaves the nineteenth-century history of Burlington into the description of its situation in the early depression of the 1930s.

17 For a discussion of these associations, see Chapter 7.

18 Earle, "Vermont Meeting," in *Bringing In Sheaves*, 167-174.

19 Edward Hungerford, *Report*, based on "Religious Canvass of Burlington," printed tables filled in with numbers, and "Remarks," from canvassers' notebooks, at UVM. Hungerford (1829-1911) served churches in Meriden, Conn. (1871-1877) and Adams, Mass. (1884-1887), and intermittently supplied the Congregational mission in Winooski. In retirement he wrote for the periodical press and published liturgical works. See Bassett, "The College Street Congregational Church," 110-112.

20 Printed in *Burlington Free Press*, April 10, 1869, in full.

21 See Messner, "Phelps and Conservative Reform." How many of the 109 "scattering" Vermont votes in 1880 were for Phelps? Crockett, *Vermont*, 4:120, does not say.

22 Moody sent two assistants to spread the word in Rutland. This discussion of Moody's visit revises the treatment in Tom Bassett, "Moody," in *Burlington Free Press*, February 4, 11, 18, 1979, based on sympathetic daily coverage in the 1877 *Free Press*.

23 See Edwards, *Horace Bushnell*.

24 The "Records of the Union Committee," 1877-1878, 1890, are in the archives of the College Street Church, Burlington, because its member, H. O. Wheeler, was secretary of the committee. See above on Edward Hungerford's canvass.

25 The "Records of Union Committee" in the College Street Church archives show the monthly, mainly statistical, reports of the visitors in 1890.

26 I discuss these associations in Chapter 7.

27 *Walton's Register for 1895*, supplemented with information from denominational sources, showed Catholics, Congregationalists, and Methodists with clergy in all twenty-eight towns over 2,500 in 1900, including Vergennes and Windsor. I discuss the comparative failure of the Universalists and the other small denominations to invade the central places in Chapter 5, pp. 160-161.

28 Fairbanks, *St. Johnsbury*, 305-315.

29 Allen, *About Burlington*, 32. The Salvation Army appeared in Brattleboro the same year.

30 The following sketch is built from fragments in church anniversary histories that mention when buildings were erected but are too focused on ministers to tell many details.

31 Schwartz, *Spreading Flame*, contains a page for each Vermont church, including a photograph of each building and dates of construction or dedication.

32 Greene, "Methodism in Burlingon."

33 Edward H. Griffin's reminiscence in *Burlington First Congregational Church*, 77-78; see also Blow. *Historic Guide to Burlington*, 1:149-151.

34 Allen, *About Burlington Vermont*, 20, and author's consultation with Unitarian Universalist church archivist Elizabeth Dow.

35 In Burlington, where electric power was available in the late 1880s, the Unitarians installed electric lighting in 1893 and its superiority, cleanliness, and apparent cheapness induced other churches to follow suit as soon as power became available. Elizabeth Dow, Unitarian Universalist Archivist, has checked the record for me. The Wells River Congregational Church had electric lights in 1894 (Wells, *Newbury*, 188).

36 Goodrich, "Historical Discourse" (1905), 35.

37 For details on Vermont organs, see Owen, *Organ in New England*.

[38] Goodrich, "Historical Discourse," *Burlington First Congregational Church*, 34-41.

[39] Montpelier. Bethany Congregational Church *Hundredth Anniversary* , 24.

[40] Among the 282 clergymen whose names begin with A or B in Comstock, *Vermont Congregational Churches*, 159-169, comprising about one sixth of his whole list, besides the British from abroad, two Swedish-speaking pastors successively served marble workers in Proctor and Rutland Town, 1890-1902, and one bilingual Belanger from Quebec City and Oberlin Seminary served a decade in Wallingford and Wells River from 1899.

[41] C. D. and O. D. Schwartz, *Flame of Fire*, 326-333, 344. On Vermont Methodists' favoring women in General Conference, see *Burlington Free Press*, 14 Apr. 1896, 2:4. Passage failed by eighteen votes of the three-quarters majority needed (*Free Press*, 25 June 1896, 4:2). The General Conference approved full ordination of women in 1956, admitted Doris Hartman on trial in 1959, and ordained her in 1963.

[42] Coolidge, *Autobiography*, 11..

[43] C. D. and O. D. Schwartz, *Flame of Fire*, 256-258.

[44] Henderson and Phillips, *Vermont Yearly Meeting of Free Will Baptists*, 37.

[45] MacDonald, *Rebellion in the Mountains*, 134, 177, 78; *Woodstock Spirit of the Age*, 19 Sept. 1867, 3:1. Cazden, *Antoinette Brown Blackwell*, 74-82, demonstrates Brown's primacy in the pulpit by ten years. She became pastor of the South Butler, New York, Congregational church in the spring of 1853 and was ordained September 15, 1853.

[46] Bailey, *Episcopal Church in Vermont*, 16; Vermont (Diocese, Episcopal), *In Memoriam: Wm. H. A. Bissell*, 4-5, 8, 14-15; Carleton, *Genealogical and Family History*, 2:174-175; George L. Richardson, *Arthur C. A. Hall*, 158, 161.

[47] Richardson, *Arthur C. A. Hall*, 1-133, tells of Hall's life before coming to Vermont; 134-158, of his life as bishop in the 1890s.

[48] I tell Edmunds' story in "College Street Congregational Church," 108-109.

49 Draper, *Conflict Between Religion and Science*, and White, *Warfare of Science with Theology,* accepted modern theories in the physical and biological sciences.

50 See Hutchison, *Modernist Impulse*, especially 1-9 and 48-144.

51 Mathews, "Faith of a Modernist," 2:238-245, quotation on 240.

52 See Bassett, *Vermont Geological Surveys*, 5.

53 For Perry's difficulties before the war, see Chapter 5, pp. 173, 184n.74.

54 Wright, *Story of My Life*, 115-117, 128; Moore, *Post-Darwinian Controversies*, 280-298, quotation on 281, evidence of the earliest attention to Darwin in Vermont.

55 See McGiffert, "Christian Darwinism," 65-76.

56 Dewey, "Biography of John Dewey," 10.

57 See Bassett, *Vermont Geological Surveys*, 19-24; Dann, "George Henry Perkins," especially 138-148; see also 118.

58 Vermont Christian Endeavor Union, *Journal of Annnual Meetings*, 6; Burlington City Directory for 1889-90, 40.

59 Fairbanks, *Wrought Brim*, 5.

60 *Protest*, [1], [2] (quotations from resolution, and defeated amendment, and resolutions committee chairman), signed by George B. Safford, Lewis O. Brastow, and John E. Goodrich of Burlington, George E. Hall of Vergennes, Sedgewick P. Wilder of Brandon, Charles Van Norden of St. Albans, Charles F. Watson of Sheldon, Samuel I. Briant of Hartford Village, Professor Edwin H. Higley of Middlebury College, and an unidentified layman. Seventeen more voted against the resolution but did not sign the protest. On Shedd, see chapter 5, p. 147.

61 *Protest*, [6], [8].

62 Hutchison, *Modernist Impulse*, 138.

63 Letter from Kenneth R. Morgan, Director, Canadian Baptist Archives,

McMaster Divinity College, Hamilton, Ontario, received November 5, 1998, with an appreciation of James Ten Broek in *The Canadian Baptist* (November 11, 1937). On Dewhurst, see his *Memorial,* and Allen, *About Burlington,* 22.

[64] John E. Goodrich, one of the protesters, summarized the change in theological climate in Burlington. First Congregational Church. *Hundredth Anniversary,* 39-40, 42-44.

[65] In Pratt, "State of religion in Bennington County," 2, the Dorset pastor points to small Congregational gains in Rupert, Peru, North Bennington, and Manchester.

[66] Washington, "Women's Fellowship," 182-184. See also Yarrow's letters, "The Work in Tyson," and the summary in Merrill, *Historical Address.*

[67] I discuss whether Ripley Female College was an academy or a college in chapter 5, n31. Troy Conference Academy in Poultney and Montpelier Seminary became junior colleges in the 1930s, and forty years later dissolved their formal connection with Methodism because in fact the church connection had become tenuous, and for the sake of state aid.

[68] Henry Crocker, *Baptists in Vermont,* 545-550, 503-504.

[69] *Waterbury, 1915-1991,* 12; photograph of new building, faculty and students, 13.

[70] MacDonald, *Rebellion in the Mountains,* 45-48; Mary Canfield, *Valley of the Kedron,* 172-190.

[71] Bailey, *Episcopal Church in Vermont During the Last Fifty Years*; Ross, "Vermont Episcopal Institute and Bishop Hopkins Hall," photograph of Hopkins Hall, 117, description, 119-120; Richardson, *Arthur C. A. Hall,* 138.

[72] Gilman, *Bibliography of Vermont,* 214; among the many articles in the 1866 *Vermont Chronicle,* those of June 2 (4:1-3), July 7 (2:2), September 22 (2:2-3), and October 6 (2:2-3), carry the gist of the arguments.

[73] Mary-John Atwood on McKinstry in *Rural Vermonter,* 1 (Fall 1962): 16.

[74] Henderson and Phillips, *The Vermont Yearly Meeting of Free Will*

Baptists, 12, 41; Crocker, *Baptists in Vermont*, 618.

75 See MacDonald, *Rebellion in the Mountains*, under "Societies" for the towns named. Cabot, *Annals of Brattleboro*, 385-388, 891, recounts the Universalists' antebellum history.

76 *Windsor Vermont Chronicle*, 17 March 1866, 1:6; Riggs, *Supremacy of Man*, 23; printed petition against Sunday trains (Sheldon Museum, Middlebury, manuscript S44 (1892), 85).

77 Henry Fairbanks, "Influence of Congregationalism," offprint at UVM from an unidentified newspaper, n.p., n.d. [1895] (*St. Johnsbury Caledonian? Windsor Vermont Chronicle? Bennington Banner?*) Also read to the Passumpsic Congregational Club at Newport. For Robinson's comment see Bassett, *The Growing Edge*, 175.

78 These conclusions are based on figures in the synopses of each year's annual convention reports in Nutting, *Becoming The United Church of Christ*, 188-262, and the compressed graph, 20.

79 Crocker, *Baptists in Vermont*, 169-170, 402, 482; see graph of membership, fig. 1 in chapter 3. Baptists in Maine, with double the membership, showed the same, but less severe trends. See table in Burrage, *Baptists in Maine*, 480-481. The Baptists' next Vermont peak was not until after World War II.

80 Bailey, *Episcopal Fiftieth Anniversary*, passim.

81 Joseph Marie Kerlidou, *St. Anne of Isle La Mott in Lake Champlain: Its History, Rules of the Confraternity, Prayers, Novena* (Burlington: Free Press, 1895).

7

New Groups and Associations, 1865-1900

In every society, the parts grow or decline at different rates and in different directions, depending on a particular congeries of conditions. After the Civil War, Americans and Vermonters kept getting more diverse, both within the Catholic fold, and among the Protestant denominations, both statewide and in any particular location. Without considering themselves intolerant, every group sold its wares in the open market, assuming that its message was necessary for everyone's salvation. Style, however, dictated that some classes would be turned off, either by the noise or the sedation, by the rigidities or the flabbiness, by spareness or fulsomeness. In reaction to increasing diversity, Protestants formed associations to pool their benevolences, always aiming to reproduce the favored qualities of home and family in the larger society.

In the denominational pie, more than half the late-Victorian Vermonters probably had no ties, or very tenuous ties, to any organized faith. No new denomination challenged the Big Five (Catholic, Congregational, Methodist, Baptist, Episcopalian) after the Civil War the way the Methodists did in the generation after 1800. They had come from nothing to reach the front in less than forty years. Little invaders, however, nibbled at the edges. The holiness variety appealed to the poor and the poorly educated. All kinds of ethnic outsiders, mystics, and others trying to reconcile science and religion attracted small congregations.

Into a society racked by two depressions and blessed with only minimal and spotty growth, small groups from abroad took advantage of the formal welcome American institutions promised the immigrant. Welcomed for their special skills, as cheap labor, or as buyers of farms the natives no longer wanted to farm, they were expected to shift for themselves as Vermonters had always done, with no more than normal neighborliness for the stresses of getting settled. If they were Catholics using languages neither English nor French, they were perforce second-class communicants in English language parishes. Welsh, Swedish, and Yiddish speakers went off by themselves, as did in the next century many of the Slavs and Greeks of Orthodox orientation, and the non-Catholic refugees from Europe's and Asia's wars. These few new sects did not threaten, but seemed merely bizarre, extreme, and expected to fade away, as established insiders usually view most new minorities.

Stronger challenges erupted from within, because of the shocks experienced as corporate industry broke antebellum patterns. In terms of vested interests, private benevolent associations, founded by the churches to be their activist arms, proved greater threats to existing denominations than new sects or immigrants. Some organizations, like the Grange and the Women's Christian Temperance Union, absorbed the attentions and energies of their advocates until they became, in effect, substitute churches. The old issue, fought first among the Baptists, whether the church is a missionary society or whether there needs to be a separate institution for each missionary field, arose again, with most of the votes for separate associations.

After brief sketches of additions to the denominational constellation, the main burden of this chapter will be to trace how Protestants established private charitable institutions to deal with the needs of the young, the sick, the aged, women, and the poor. The Catholics, using orders of religious, had already begun such institutions of their own in the 1850s.

Spiritualists

The Spiritualists surfaced in Vermont early in the 1850s as a religious phenomenon, not an organized faith. The movement had proven to be more than a transient craze, but rather part of the mid-century "harmonial religion" assuming that right relations with the cosmos would produce spiritual composure, physical health, and even economic comfort. Obvserving what they interpreted as an American society emptying itself of religious significance while science and popular pragmatism took over, spiritualists tried to re-spiritualize society and populated the cosmos with spirits, if not spirit. Their individualism was obvious, but like so many Americans, they sought order. Vermont spiritualists, too, wanted freedom *and* unity.

Spiritualists were looking for a solid basis for their faith that could meet the tests that growing faith in science required. Hence their efforts to prove the presence of communicating spirits. Quakers and others emphasizing the action of the Holy Spirit in the world felt that proof lay in behavioral changes ("You shall know them by their fruits" Matt. 7:16).

Although their spokespersons differed widely, Spiritualists' ideology included all the parts of a full-fledged religion. Their "spiritualist republicanism" had a cosmology, a creed, a clergy in their mediums, rituals in their circles or séances producing similar benefits to members that Methodist classes produced, and similar results in social behavior.[1] No wide, coordinating organization formed until the National Association of Spiritualists in 1893, but annual conventions of Vermont Spiritualists had begun as soon as the war was over.[2]

In Vermont they continued their devout, sometimes charlatan séances after Achsah Sprague's death during the Civil War. Angelina Miller left a rare Vermont source of what the spirits of her relatives and friends told her during the 1860s in Williston. The first entries in her journal record "progressive" messages from spirits opposing "church[,] Bible and creed worshipers." While valuing the Bible, the departed spirit urged the "great work of reform," seeking "the sunlight of nature's truth." Yet soon after the war, according to Angelina, the spirit of Nathan B. Haswell was telling "Mrs. B," "You are the one to establish the church of the new dispensation" in Burlington.[3]

Sprinkled thinly over the whole state were believers in the possibility of communication with the spirit world. Stowe Spiritualists organized in 1868, with articles of association "allowing perfect freedom of thought and expression to all . . . according to the dictates of their conscience." Mina M. Hinds, who lived on a farm in Eden, recorded frequent contact with spirit friends. "A Miss Davis came in a medium controlled by her brother," she wrote, "to talk sing examining my health test my disposition and surroundings my past and present and to work over me and to make a prayer." Thomas P. James, tramp printer and Brattleboro medium, published Charles Dickens' novel, *The Mystery of Edwin Drood*, unfinished at his death in 1870, with the last 284 pages completed, according to James, by the dictation of Dickens' spirit.[4]

While most outsiders treated the Spiritualists as queer curiosities, Sarah Giddings, a servant girl and Enosburg woolen mill worker, felt damaged by her excursion into the cult. She told how she had visions in her "struggle for perfection," and "had gone astray into the paths of Spiritualism."[5]

In July, 1874, the Spiritualist *Banner of Light* published an account of the "solidification of phantom forms" at William and Horatio Eddy's in Chittenden, Vermont. The Eddy family (no close relative of Christian Science founder Mary Baker Eddy's third husband) ran what amounted to a tourist business as the curious from far and wide came to see William's performances. Madame Helena P. Blavatsky spent twelve weeks that fall at the Eddys, then returned to New York and published her belief in their authenticity, and founded the Theosophical Society the next year.[6]

Vermont Spiritualists bought Queen City Park, along a cove south of Burlington, from the Central Vermont Railroad in 1880, and formed a joint stock association to operate the park as a sort of camp meeting center. They ran no-liquor, no-gambling grounds; forenoons free to "all who wish to express their ideas on any progressive subject"; speakers and séances in the evenings. The Burlington Traction Company extended its trolley line to Queen City Park in 1893. Universalists for many years held "grove meetings" here.[7]

"Sleeping Lucy" Ainsworth Cooke (1819-1895) was no less religious in her trance cures and herbal drug business than Achsah Sprague and subsequent mediums, who depended on other spirits. The miracle of healing wins converts, from Jesus to Catholic missions among the Indians in Canada and Latin America. "Sleeping Lucy," born in Calais, Vermont, began to heal by mesmeric clairvoyance on her marriage to Charles R. Cook, a Vermonter transplanted to Moriah, New York. They lived in Reading, Vermont, until her husband's death in 1855, and she practiced for sixteen years (1860-1876) in Montpelier. Her brother Luther, an herb doctor, was her business manager. Her advertisements breathe no word of religion, but the success that enabled her to make a living as a healer was part of the background of mesmerism and spiritualism out of which Mary Baker Eddy developed Christian Science a generation later.[8]

Related to Spiritualism in a mutual concern for psychic healing, Christian Science was the last new nineteenth-century sect in Vermont. Healing was an aspect of New Testament religion which most Protestants had long ignored. Soon after Mary Baker Eddy's third husband died June 3, 1882, she took a summer vacation in Barton, Vermont. Her lecture in its Methodist house of worship "made a big stir," she wrote a friend. In the next dozen years, Christian Science publications out of Boston carried advertising cards of Vermont practitioners and teachers trained by Mrs. Eddy and her pupils, and testimonials of cures. Practitioners were those who had successfully completed "primary class" instruction from a teacher of Christian Science. Teachers were those who had healed successfully for three years and had completed the Christian Science Metaphysical College course in Boston. Before the first Vermont church organized in Barre in October 1894, small groups were meeting to read the King James version of the Bible and the latest edition of Eddy's text, *Science and Health with Key to the Scriptures.*

After the First Church of Christ, Scientist, completed its headquarters building in Boston in 1897, the church regularized the amorphous growth in the hinterland. In 1898 the *Christian Science Journal* listed eighteen Vermont practitioners in eleven towns. In these larger places, groups were performing some of the functions of a "branch": renting rooms for services on Sundays and Wednesday evening testimony meetings, maintaining reading rooms, putting copies of *Science and Health* in public libraries, and electing readers of the Bible and Mrs. Eddy's commentaries. In Burlington, Christian Scientists began services in the summer of 1896 and rented rooms in the new Masonic Temple, dedicated in June 1898. In St. Johnsbury they chartered the church in January 1898 and first met in Odd Fellows Hall.

Statistical analysis has not yet revealed what kind of convert Christian Science attracted. They were probably educated above average, more wealthy and prosperous than average. Unmoved by main-line and revivalist traditions, they were looking for something "spiritual" in the face of modern urban tensions. They testified that Mrs. Eddy's Science had improved their health. In polity, the Church of Christ, Scientist, was autocratic under Mary Baker Eddy; in theology it was progressive in recognizing the divine as including the essence of both male and female; in science it was prophetic, repeating at each Sunday service, out of *Science and Health*, "Spirit is immortal truth; matter is mortal error." In an age discovering new ways of looking at the sciences related to health, Christian Scientists were the strongest group in a wide band of seekers after assurance, prosperity, and health in an uncertain world of change.[9]

Ethnic Groups

Ethnic religious societies, formed to allow immigrants to worship in a language they could understand, were commonest among the French Canadians of the mill towns. Non-Catholics also formed congregations in the slate district of western Rutland County, the Rutland marble district, in Swedeville near Brattleboro's Estey Organ Company factory, and in Burlington's Old North End.

Welsh

Welsh with experience in the slate quarries of Caernarvonshire and Denbighshire, North Wales, and Northampton County, Pennsylvania, came to the sides of the Mettawee, Poultney, and Castleton river valleys in eastern Washington County, New York, and western Rutland County, Vermont, beginning about 1850. Railroads had reached the region and could cheaply carry heavy stone from the slate belt to urban markets. The Welsh in Wales suffered high taxes, high tithes, high rents, and many intangible indignities from English-speaking, Anglican landlords, bosses, and courts. It was hard to find a landowner who would sell them a freehold for a home or a chapel. The Welsh slate industry was depressed at the time the emigration began. In America, they hoped to find better working, living, and worshiping conditions.

They united with other Welsh speakers of various views, and divided when one group felt strong enough to support a preacher and perhaps build a chapel. In at least two cases, when a union church decided to split, it auctioned the house of worship, the winner taking the building and the loser able to build elsewhere with the money the winner paid. They supported their preachers by attendance but expected them, as the Baptists had expected their preachers, to earn all or most of their own living. Welsh ministers worked slate, planted gardens, and tended a few animals. The state boundary was of little importance in sharing services and helping one another build chapels.

The most numerous Calvinistic Methodists became Presbyterians by joining in a "cymanfa" (Welsh-language assembly or synod) from 1866 to 1936, when the remnant after much anguish joined the anglophone Troy Presbytery. The Welsh Wesleyans developed an Arminian interpretation of Wesley's doctrines and had no connection with the later antislavery Wesleyan Methodism of Orange Scott and his associates. Welsh Congregationalists and Baptists also harvested some of the disenchanted Anglicans.

Not reinforced by sufficient Welsh immigration, Welshness thinned out. Chapel, however, was a consolation as labor problems arose in the 1880s, even with their own Welsh who had risen to own quarries. Tension from the beginning had marred relations with Irish Catholic laborers and with a second generation straying from Welsh ways. Contact with English speakers, especially Yankee farmers and merchants who controlled their larger society, made the young reluctant to marginalize themselves by cleaving to Welsh culture. Only nostalgia could restore it.[10]

Swedish

The marble managers and the Esteys consciously favored and recruited Protestant Scandinavian workmen. Swedes were numerous enough to form Lutheran churches in both Brattleboro and the Rutland marble district. St. Paul's Evangelical Lutheran church connected with the Augustana Synod organized in Proctor in February, 1890, and the members built a house of worship dedicated that November. The Congregationalists started a mission to Proctor and West Rutland Swedes in 1881 and organized an evangelical church in 1888. Other Scandinavians who worked with the Swedes probably preferred to worship where Swedish was spoken. When the need for the Swedish language was no longer felt, the church died by attrition.[11]

Jews

Jews came to Vermont, unlike other European immigrants, as petty merchants or peddlers, not as industrial labor. As isolated individuals, they had to organize or perish. Jews would try not to settle where they could not find enough other Jews for worship together. If they chose to reside on the outer edge of their five-state peddling circuit out of New York or Boston, they had to face the handicaps suffered by unwelcome strangers.

Historians have found traces of a Jewish presence in eighteenth-century Vermont, but the individuals wandered in and out, married out of faith, and disappeared into the population, as many Catholics and Quakers did in the early nineteenth century. Bernard Jacob Heineberg (1809-1878) is a notable example of an individual lost in a sea of otherness, but able to find a new life in a new environment, as did the Hudson Valley Dutch farmers of Bennington County and the first French Canadians.[12]

Perhaps Heineberg's parents or grandparents had converted from Judaism. He first graduated from the University of Bonn, then earned an M.D. from Göttingen in 1834. He came to Burlington hoping for a post at the University of Vermont medical school, but it closed soon after he arrived. After a successful life as physician, local official, and real estate investor, he earned a glowing obituary at his death on July 3, 1878. It concluded that although "tinged with German skepticism" about some evangelical tenets, "he was a Christian man."

In the 1850s an occasional German, Jewish or not, joined the ranks of the Yankee peddlers,[13] and acquired with the competition the ill repute in which settled people held those "tramps." Peddlers had to pay for an annual state license, scaled according to whether they were on foot ($15), with a draft animal ($30), or sold articles of precious metal and patent medicines ($60). They had to be United States citizens and residents of Vermont for the previous year.[14] Enforcement was probably occasional or rare, because farmer's wives were glad to have a store brought to their doors. A recent arrival from the neighborhood of Kaunas, Lithuania, where many Burlington Jews originated, could not qualify for a license without living in Vermont for a year, and could not live in Vermont a year without peddling. Jews on the road tended to rendezvous to restock or celebrate Holy Days in Poultney, Enosburg Falls, and Plattsburgh rather than Burlington. Could it be that because Burlington was the headquarters of Morillo Noyes, who employed nearly two dozen Yankee peddlers, Jewish peddlers had trouble breaking into the territory? Was it mere coincidence that Noyes went bankrupt about 1880, just as the number of East European Jewish peddlers increased enough to form a congregation in Burlington?

After the Civil War, more than half a million Jews fled the pogroms of Eastern Europe, attracted by the promise of America. A small fraction filled their packs in the city or other depots, sold or swapped the contents in upstate New York and northern New England, and disposed of the junk taken in trade where they could. Jewish peddlers arriving in Burlington during the 1870s were able to form a *minyan* (ten males over thirteen) for worship by 1880. Five years later they organized a synagogue, which they named Ohavi Zedek (Hebrew for "Lovers of Justice"), with a house of worship at the northwest corner of Hyde and Archibald streets. They filed articles of association with the city clerk in 1887.[15]

The synagogue had been organized as an offshoot of the more important *chevra kadisha* or burial society, formed in 1884, with a *degel* or roster of watchers who sat with the sick and with the dead before burial. The *chevra* was central to the life of the community. All adult male Jews gathered once a week or oftener and discussed problems of brothers in distress: individual grievances, which people needed help getting settled, who could provide an interest-free loan.[16]

All told, some six hundred Jewish immigrants came to Burlington between 1880 and 1920. The number of residents at any time grew from 160 in 1890 to a plateau of more than a thousand from 1910 on. The leading families were pious, orthodox, Yiddish-speaking, coming from the environs of Kaunas, Lithuania. They came having to rent, and those who married sought to own their homes, as they had not been allowed to own property in the Old Country. They had little difficulty borrowing from non-Jews. They found living in Burlington good. They had a high birthrate: Until the early 1920s the majority were under sixteen. They served as a religious magnet for isolated Jews over a wide area.

The unique characteristic of this Jewish enclave was its persistence, resisting the pressures of its non-Jewish surroundings for a generation or more. It recreated many features of a Lithuanian *shtetl*, a rural village with room for pasturing a cow, a horse, and poultry, with access to the Winooski River for ritual bathing, near Hyman Wasserman's orchard. Some became even more rigorously orthodox and observant than they had been in Europe. Informants recalled that relatives came not particularly pious and felt pressures to conform. As the community grew, it grew more densely Jewish, rather than spreading out into the city.

Yet in some respects there was a symbiotic relationship with non-Jews. Father Cloarec at St. Joseph's rectory studied the Pentateuch with some of the elders. Older Gentile children would light the fires in Jewish households on Sabbath morning, lead the horses to the trough and bring the *cholent*, a casserole of lentils and beans from the bakers, as no observant Jew should do these chores on the Sabbath.

Their upward mobility was steady and comparatively rapid. They quickly learned French and traded with the Canadians who shared the North End. They were super-patriots in the Spanish American War, and their patriotic attitude continued in the next two wars. They tended to take an interest in local politics as Republicans. The young helped in the home and the shops and went to Hebrew school after public school each day. While they learned Hebrew for worship, they spoke Yiddish among themselves and used English in dealing with the non-Jewish world. It was an intensely patriarchal society, although women had great influence in the home and shared the work of burial preparation. In the synagogue, women sat in the balcony, which ran halfway toward the front on each side. Readers of the scrolls used the lectern (*amud*) in the middle of the assembly room so that the women above could hear better. Only the women on the inner edge of a balcony bench could watch the rites or look for prospective beaux and husbands. The government of the community was in male hands, perhaps even more than elsewhere in American society.

In 1889, the relatives and other connections of Morris Levin formed the Chai Adam (meaning "the life of man") synagogue. It lasted half a century. Buried in schisms are personal antagonisms, with parties changing attitudes toward different issues at different rates. Morris Levin was not allowed to use the lectern because he kept his store open on the Sabbath, but Elias Spear, who had married out of faith, was. Very soon the community tolerated Sabbath breaking, perhaps because, during the depression after 1893, every nickel gained from Saturday trade with non-Jews helped keep Jews from failing. Non-Jewish Sabbath observance had declined earlier. But the congregation still frowned on mixed marriages.[17]

Christians soon noticed the Jews' presence. Rev. Norman Seaver, Rutland Congregationalist, thought he was being fair in praising their care of their own poor, their rarely going to jail, their not divorcing, and their trustworthiness as bankers. Despite "their almost necessary vices and immoralities," he concluded, God intended to bless their descendants.[18]

The Salvation Army

Where Spiritualists and Christian Scientists drew adherents from the middle of the class structure, and the Welsh and Scandinavian Protestants gathered wage earners, the Salvation Army aimed at the bums on the bottom. Catherine and William Booth, English Methodist holiness evangelists in East End London, established an independent Christian Mission in the 1860s, called the Salvation Army from 1878.

It sent a team of one male commissioner and seven women to the United States in 1880, and by 1885 had spread into northern New England, including Brattleboro, Burlington, and St. Johnsbury.

Booth concluded that trying to feed the soul without feeding the body did more harm than good. The Army was a social service agency but first and last an evangelical movement. What distinguished the army was its military government, an elected monarchy giving women and men equal status and responsibility. Like the Gandhi family in India, the Booth family held the leadership for a long generation after the founders died in 1890. All members of the Army were Christian soldiers tied to the general by chain of command. It spread because it reached people that the older churches failed to reach.

It was Protestant, with Bible authority the first article of its faith. The other ten articles expressed orthodox, trinitarian, holiness Protestantism. Quoting Jesus' words, "Why do you call me good? Only God is good" (Matt. 19:17), Salvationists distinguished between the absolute perfection of God and the possibility that the converted can repeatedly and continually do the will of God. No officer in the organization could be efficient without this blessing. Although the Salvation Army fed articles to the *Burlington Free Press* summarizing its history and principles,[19] thus indicating its presence, it otherwise escaped early public notice. Other groups beneath notice may have come but did not have the durability of the Army organization. In 1917 the judge advocate of the U.S. Army recognized the Salvation Army, for the purpose of appointing chaplains, to be a denomination.[20]

Camp Meetings: Holiness Strongholds

The major Methodist problem was to keep their holiness wing within the fold. From a holiness perspective, it was to keep Methodists faithful to Wesley's original perfectionism. A group in northwestern Vermont formed a Methodist Holiness Association in the early 1890s, apparently wanting the Troy Conference to pay more attention to sanctification.[21] Camp meetings, feeding the lambs as Francis Asbury fed them a century before, and increasingly sponsored by holiness Methodists, seemed to show that the old-time religion was still ascendant.

Annual camp meetings climaxed the year for the devout. Once started from necessity, because they had no house of worship, the camp meeting had been a major source of conversions. Adopted by Adventists and whatever group had no access to indoor space, it became a fixed feature of Methodist worship. No longer borrowing a field, Methodists owned their acres. No longer in temporary tents, church people regularly built themselves wooden cottages. They scheduled their gatherings for late August or early September, to avoid the worst heat and mosquitoes. Because all kinds of Methodists supported the camp meeting in 1865, it was a source of solidarity.

In west-side Vermont the Troy Conference had annual week-long sessions at Spring Grove, New Haven, as early as 1857. The New Haven Camp-Meeting Association, chartered in 1868, acquired a lot on the west side of the Rutland Railroad, a mile and a half from Belden's Falls and a third of a mile from present U. S. Route 7. Called Spring Grove because of its two essentials for a viable camp site, shady pines and a plentiful cold spring, it also had easy access to rail and highway. Those who could come only for an evening or Sunday had only a few miles to go from Middlebury, New Haven, and Vergennes villages. The site had wooden shelters, built over the years by regular attenders and used until about 1916. Riverside, beside the Missisquoi in Sheldon, served the St. Albans District from 1882.[22]

The St. Johnsbury District of the Methodists' Vermont Conference held its first camp meeting in the "Railroad Grove" of the Passumpsic Railroad (later the Boston and Maine) in Lyndonville, September 9-15, 1867, and its last in 1915. Billed as the largest meeting of any kind ever held in northern Vermont, it attracted by rail and wagon seven (some estimated ten) thousand from Newbury to Troy and Eden to Granby, with one group coming from New Hampshire. The local paper

A camp meeting in Lyndonville, 1867 (from Shores, Lyndon: Gem in the Green; *used by permission of the Lyndonville Historical Society).*

listed two dozen tents for churches in twenty-eight towns and reported fifty conversions. The next year the railroad built a boardinghouse, and, later, frames for plank seats and tents, and refreshment shacks. Fences, to check the rowdies and provide hitching for the horses, bordered the three land sides of the twenty-acre tract. Morning, afternoon, and evening, the people under the shade of a canvas stretched over half the seats, or some of the time shaded by trees, heard from returned missionaries, WCTU exhorters, bishops, and Bible scholars. The legend on the arch over the speakers' platform read, "Holiness unto the Lord." In 1905 they advertised a new feature, several periods set aside for croquet, tennis, baseball, and golf.[23] Rest and recreation had always been a by-product but ground laid out for particular games required ownership of the site—ownership in this case by the railroad interested in thousands of half-fares—or a camp meeting association to attract and handle the crowds. Worcester, Barre, and Northfield had their own sites for different periods after Lyndonville's.

The camp meeting at Claremont, New Hampshire, drew from both sides of the Connecticut River. One vivid reminiscence emphasizes an eight-year-old girl's excitement, anticipating the sights and scents of the buggy ride to Claremont, the extra-large Sunday crowd in its Sunday best, listening to the presiding elder in his Prince Albert, black broadcloth trousers, boiled white shirt, and white tie, and the happy weariness, clutter, and confusion, packing up to go home.[24]

Gradually, the support given camp meetings by the National Camp Meeting Association for the Promotion of Holiness, began to create a new schism by the end of the century. The examples of Silver Lake, Leicester, and Ithiel Falls, Johnson, illustrate this trend.

The irresistible enthusiasm of Frank Chandler created a camp meeting site at virtually inaccessible Silver Lake, a mile above Lake Dunmore in Leicester. Chandler got religion, established a Methodist mission in Montreal, and answered a cry for help that led to inheriting 2,500 acres in Leicester. Between 1879 and about 1902, he ran Silver Lake as a summer resort as well as a camp meeting site, on the "unbusinesslike" basis of making everything free and depending on freewill offerings. Missionaries came for preparation to serve abroad; impecunious ministers came for refreshment. Chandler kept expanding his building as conference center and hotel whenever he had the money, until the porch on its lake side was two hundred feet long. Characteristic of revivalist evangelicals after the Civil War, those who came to Silver Lake downplayed their denomination and preached "only Christ, and him crucified" (1 Corinthians, 2:2). Methodist support is clear: Silver Lake opened in 1879 with Mrs. Hammond, a Methodist evangelist, sponsored by attenders at the earlier Spring Grove camp meeting that year. These were clearly holiness Methodists: The only contemporary account of Silver Lake was published by the Holiness Book Concern of the Rev. E. Davies of Reading, Massachusetts.[25]

Toward the end of the camp meeting half century, the Ithiel Falls Camp Meeting Ground at Johnson, also a Methodist project, was built the way barns used to be raised and the way Jehovah's Witnesses still construct their houses of worship. Everyone from Adventists to Catholics brought their tools, lumber, and food, clearing and leveling the ground and building the structures. They made "Vermont mahogany" bedsteads out of rough timber, fitted with straw ticking on springs. For one bee ninety men came from considerable distances, divided into three teams; forty came to another until the cottages were built. The ground was dedicated in August 1899, late in the second season of work, with William McDonald of Boston, president of the National Camp Meeting Association, and B. S. Taylor of Mooers, New York, "the Cyclone Evangelist," principal orators. Out of experience at Ithiel Falls, more than from anywhere else, came the converts who founded the Church of the Nazarene in Vermont.[26] Although camp meetings died out among Vermont Methodists by World War I, latter-day Evangelicals have continued the style.

Charitable Associations

What the existing denominations did to strengthen their position in the Vermont market for souls occurred not only in an atmosphere of competition between them, but in an environment where, instead of the church and its individual members doing charity, private associations cared for those in every kind of need. Social ills were beyond what individuals could manage. Few had hitherto thought the towns should do more than appoint an overseer of the poor to dole out relief to individuals who had no church connections, and maintain a poor farm as a catch-all for every kind of welfare. The law limited the state to paying for patients in a private insane asylum, funding prisons for convicts, or sending the worthy deaf or blind to out-of-state institutions.

Towns and the state had provided "secular" welfare. By the end of the century there were competing organizations to supply needs beyond what state and local government felt obliged to provide for, although both levels were providing much more welfare. The many new private associations had to compete for members. The Young Men's Christian Association, for example, although mainly patronized by church youths, served as a church for some who were unaffiliated. The revived fraternal orders such as the Masons and the Odd Fellows, basically mutual benefit insurance societies, flourished as support systems for people in trouble, when unemployment, disability, or death hit their families. Lodges met to be sociable. They were pan-Protestant groups aiming to maintain Protestant values in local communities. The Benevolent and Protective Order of Elks declared this purpose in establishing two lodges before 1900. With so much competition between Elks, Red Men, Eagles, Moose, etc., barriers tended to lower in order to win initiation fees and dues to pay for the costumes, the equipment, and the hall. The Vatican told Catholics not to join the Masons or any other secret order, but Catholics had no Vermont alternatives until the 1890s: the Catholic Order of Foresters (1892) and the Knights of Columbus (1894). The latter rose on the swell of interest in the Columbian Exposition.[27]

Associations declared off limits by one church or another, or that required no religious tests, such as the few feeble craft unions, provided focus for some laboring men's lives. Competition, however, from ethnic, benefit, fraternal, political, and religious associations fragmented their attention. Many immigrants had been class conscious abroad but lost the sense of solidarity with others in Vermont shops and quarries. Justice for labor was one sacred goal; the sanctity of life lost in disasters also won non-sectarian relief. After the Chicago fire of 1871, eighty-three citizens of many faiths pledged $546 in Burlington for aid to the sufferers.[28]

The Patrons of Husbandry, usually called the Grange, was the most important "church outside the church" in this period. Grangers organized in Vermont in 1871, to maintain and increase support in the legislature for solutions to the new problems facing farmers. They saw their old familiar staples of wood, grain, meat, and wool bring lower prices in world competition. In the evolving dairy industry, they were bewildered by the invasion of new cattle diseases, impoverished by the destruction of their infected herds, or fearing such a blow. Like the Masons, the Grange had a Christian ritual. Its creed in essence declared that farming is the foundation of democracy, close to nature and close to God. Its masters were ministers of this gospel, comforting troubled Vermont farmers.

An early peak of over eleven thousand members in 1875 could not be sustained when the Grange's venture into cooperative buying during the depression failed from bad management and price competition. At nadir with scarcely a thousand members in 1885, the organization reversed the trend with a new, militant leader focusing on agricultural colleges and state agricultural policies. After its heyday before World War I with twenty thousand members, the Grange survived as primarily a social and recreational organization. Passing through a town like Ferrisburg one could not tell its Grange hall from the church building it had once been.[29]

During this third of a century, individuals, especially women, invested much energy and some money in pan-Protestant enterprises for the orphaned, the young, the aged, the sick, and the delinquent, and through these agencies, indirectly for the poor. They joined volunteers in various churches because they did not feel their own church was strong enough to do good by itself where the needs were so great. They did not invite the Catholics, whom they considered competitors. Catholic orphanages and hospitals integrated the mundane care of children and the sick with religious observances that could not be reconciled with Protestant rites. They cared for women by admitting them to nunneries if they had authentic vocations.

Associations for the Young

In good times, people gave some of their surplus for building and outreach, and whatever the economic weather, they worried about how to help society's victims. The ladies' first postwar project was launching Burlington's Home for Destitute Children late in 1865, intended to "be associated . . . with Religion." Within their first year they acquired Burlington's Civil War hospital, vacated by veterans. Although men from several local Protestant churches dominated the ceremonies consecrating their new home, women controlled the governing board and a matron managed the children, as a home needed a mother most. Here, "our Saviour's principles were daily inculcated."[30]

The Home taught its girls sewing amd knitting, both to keep them out of mischief and as a skill for self-help. An outgrowth of the Burlington Relief Association, founded at the beginning of the Civil War to help soldiers' families, it aspired to be more than a holding tank for orphans like many earlier orphan asylums, here and abroad. No doubt St. Joseph's orphanage in Burlington (1854), and the Warner Home for Little Wanderers in St. Albans (1882), aspired to discipline and educate as well as keep, but their means were limited. The wives of Burlington Protestant business and political leaders, with a few well-to-do single women, were responding to conditions of poverty revealed in health officer Samuel W. Thayer's report of 1866, and they reached all over the state, as St. Joseph's did, for funds and wards.

Near the turn of the century, out-of-state donors planted another kind of orphanage. As Vermont was becoming a resort for well-to-do tourists and refugees from the cities, the state also became an attractive site for charitable establishments. The New England Kurn Hattin Homes were located in Westminster West (boys) and Saxtons River (girls) in 1894 because their Boston founders wanted a Christian atmosphere and a rural environment where the boys' work on the farm could help support the institution. The Rev. Charles A. Dickinson of Boston's Berkeley Temple had known Francis Clark in Portland, Maine, when he founded Christian Endeavor. They fished together on the Allagash River in Maine and inspected Mrs. Dickinson's Westminster home farm as a site for their charity. Clark said the view across the Connecticut reminded him of "the Horns [Kurn] of Hattin," where Jesus supposedly said the beatitudes. Vermonters were on its board, but the main funding came from Boston—from Francis G. Pratt, publisher of *The Youth's Companion*, until he died intestate.[31]

After orphaned children, the young were the next group to receive special attention, as they had for a century as objects for conversion in revivals. YMCAs, budded in 1855-59 in St. Johnsbury, Rutland, and Springfield, blossomed in the late 1860s. Several town locals sent delegates to the 1867 international conference in Montreal and the Portland conference of 1869.

The Burlington YMCA, founded in May 1866, opened a reading room and parlor in the spring of 1870, turned over its library to the new Fletcher Free Library in 1874, but continued in rented quarters of increasing size where Protestants met across denominational lines. They held regular meetings in their rooms, at first meeting at six, the hour before the evening church services, then moved to the mid-afternoon space when some churches left it vacant. The St. Johnsbury YMCA, backed by the Fairbanks family, reorganized in 1867 with a reading room and lecture series. It sponsored a successful revival in 1875.

The YWCA often joined the YMCA in visiting jails and holding prayer meetings in the parks, but the young women went farther in benevolent work. Hungerford's house-to-house canvass of March 1867 revealed slum poverty, and children who could not go to Sunday school for lack of clothing. To address this need, and following the lead of the Home for Destitute Children, the Burlington YWCA started an industrial school for girls in February 1868. The ladies collected forty girls between six and fifteen, cut the cloth or supplied the yarn, and hired a superintendent to teach sewing and knitting. With tickets issued "for regular attendance and good behavior" the girls outfitted themselves with the clothes they had made.[32] The new Vermont Reform School, for juvenile offenders, also enveloped with Protestant piety, followed the same philosophy, but did not take girls, reportedly for lack of adequately segregated space, until the late 1870s.[33]

In the early 1880s, the YWCA's industrial school became the ward of the Howard Relief Society, which was the Ladies Aid Society of the late 1860s, enriched with new endowment in 1882. The YWCA had disappeared from listings in sources now available, perhaps because the young women helped out in other organizations, and later became active in Christian Endeavor.

With the YW in eclipse, the YMCA prospered in villages such as St. Johnsbury, Bellows Falls, and Brattleboro, along the Connecticut; Barre; and on the west side, Burlington, Middlebury, and Rutland. Now primarily missions to young men rather than through them to the needy, they branched out to the University of Vermont and to schools like Vermont Academy. In 1879, St. Johnsbury's North Congregational Church, to clear the ground for a new house of worship, moved its old building across Main Street, where the YMCA used it until 1885. A general secretary from 1882 led his committees, Bible study, and many other religious meetings. Three years later, on condition the YMCA always hire a director, Henry Fairbanks provided the western part of his new brick block on Eastern Avenue with a parlor, reading room, music hall, gymnasium, and boys' room. After a dip in interest and probably funds during the depression of the 1890s, a renovation after a 1907 fund drive added eighteen dormitory rooms, a bowling alley, and a billiard room, the complex now occupying the whole building.[34]

Village rivalry pushed the Burlington YMCA to hire a general secretary as soon as St. Johnsbury did, in 1882. That year it moved to the southwest corner of Church and College Streets, a central business location where it hoped to have a building of its own. The YMCA bought the lot in 1886 and when the building burned the next year, it started to raise money for a five-story block. The Y used rentals from the street-level stores to finish paying for the $105,000 cost of the property, and to maintain services after it opened in 1889. The new building's parlor and reading room were open from 8:30 a.m. to 10 p.m. on weekdays, more hours than the city library, and for four hours on Sunday afternoon, with a gospel service. The only new features of the Burlington building were a kitchen on the main (second) floor, so that the lecture room could be used for banquets, and a game room. As Burlington was twice as populous as St. Johnsbury, it had more office space for a staff, which grew to four, a larger and better equipped gymnasium, and more seats for public events. It boasted the largest membership (770 in 1904) of any YMCA in a city under 25,000. Byron N. "Dad" Clark founded the YMCA Camp Abnaki in North Hero in 1902 and became state secretary for twenty years from 1909.[35]

The Catholic Young Men's Union, organized in 1882 for "practical catholic" married men between eighteen and forty, was only an approximation of the Protestant YMCA. Except for a spiritual adviser appointed by the bishop, who said mass monthly for deceased members, they behaved like any other fraternal order.[36]

On the surface it looks as if the YMCA aimed initially at young men who were loosely if at all connected with churches. Without changing the old-time emphasis on the need for conversion, the Y tried to lure the young clerk or mechanic with an appeal to self-improvement, health, and recreation, where he might be exposed to Christian literature and Christian activities. Burlington City Clerk Charles E. Allen concluded his description of the local Y, "Its activity in training and helping young men in moral and physical culture. . . has contributed largely to the development of a spirit of Christian endeavor and unity."[37]

If the children of pious, church-going families had thronged to the Y, the Young People's Society of Christian Endeavor would not have bloomed so vigorously in the years after 1882. Francis E. Clark, founder of Christian Endeavor, on graduating from Andover Theological Seminary in 1876, tackled a three-year-old mission parish in Portland, Maine. He saw an opportunity in the young people's "unusual interest" developing in the fall of 1880, which led to several commitments to Christ during the church's annual January week of prayer. Previous methods had not prevented "the dreadful leak between the Sunday School and the church," the evaporation of young members as they grew up and lost interest. He and his wife invited the converts and some older youth to the parsonage to consider the meaning of their commitment, and eventually persuaded fifty-seven of them to sign a constitution. The signers pledged to attend regular prayer meetings and monthly "experience" (soon called "consecration") meetings.

Next to Sunday worship, Protestant prayer meetings throughout the nineteenth century kept faithful the core of the committed but had not attracted many youth except during periods of revival. What distinguished Clark's group was the combination of discipline with a measure of freedom from domination by elders and a balance between piety and service. The YMCA separated the boys from the girls; C.E. did not. The proceedings of the annual state YMCA conventions in the 1880s printed a constitution "recommended for adoption," whose preamble has the same purpose as Christian Endeavor's, "to promote the interests of evangelical religion in this town and vicinity, especially among young men," and under membership it adds in brackets, "No limitation of age or sex." Previously, the pastor, a deacon, or other senior, or perhaps an older youth marked for the ministry, had led the youth groups and the young were expected to follow. In contrast, the *Young People's* Society of Christian Endeavor aimed to be of young people and by young people, instead of just for them. The new organization expected full participation by youths practicing churchmanship by running their own meetings. Their committees (lookout, prayer-meeting, social, missionary, Sunday school, and flower) had even more liberty to practice being Christians without elders supervising their every move. The lookout committee recruited members and monitored their performance. Each member agreed to pray and read the Bible daily, and at monthly roll call "take some part, aside from singing." All these young Christians were equal, older or younger, male or female, articulate or bumbling, in the commitment to participate in Christian Endeavor. Rather than being preached at, they would be inspired to lead a Christian life.[38]

The Vermont Christian Endeavor Union's third annual meeting in 1888, six years after the first Vermont local organized, affirmed the following prayer-meeting pledge:

> Trusting in the Lord Jesus Christ for strength, we promise Him that we will strive to do whatever He would have us do; that we will pray to Him and read the Bible every day, and that so far as we know how, throughout our life we will endeavor to lead a Christian life. As active members, we promise to be present at, and to participate in every prayer meeting unless prevented by some reason which we can conscientiously give as an excuse to our Master. If obliged to be absent from the monthly Consecration meeting, we will if possible send an excuse for absence to the society.[39]

Christian Endeavor, with its concept of harnessing youth for prayer and praise, piety and service, took off like a rocket. Its advantages in the competition for the attention of youth and the approval of their elders were many. It supported, it did not compete with the church. Members promised to *follow* Christ rather than to believe in Christ in some prescribed way. Elders were not breathing down their necks, although they were in a watchtower only a little removed. It sought to develop well-rounded Christians, where the competition emphasized one aspect like prayer or temperance. Since Christian Endeavor balanced service and prayer and did not spell out a creed, both evangelicals and modernists could join in the same organization.

Forty delegates of local societies came to Burlington in 1886, with Francis Clark present to be helpful. A year later 1,733 active members belonged to nearly seventy Vermont locals, nine of which were "union" or interdenominational. Only eighteen to twenty-two locals sent delegates to state Y conventions in 1880 and 1883-84. In 1888, in a full-scale debate on the union issue, proponents argued that it taught tolerance and was good for small places; opponents argued that it was better to keep their youth, even though few, in their own churches. The later development of denominational youth groups shows what those against union locals feared. Francis Clark may have heard echoes of an injudicious remark at the close of the St. Albans convention of 1887 that Christian Endeavor was "the church of the next generation," for he spoke diplomatically that union societies were "not in harmony with the original idea of the society," which was to nourish each church the way Sunday schools do, and *not* like the YMCA. He would not, however, abolish or discourage union societies.

By 1890, the Vermont total had swelled to over five thousand actives with 1,254 copies of the *Golden Rule*, official Christian Endeavor organ, circulating in the state. While Congregationalists flocked to Christian Endeavor most readily, in slates of officers and on conference programs, Methodists and Baptists balanced the ticket. A sprinkling of single and married women spoke their pieces along with young pastors.

The movement peaked in the early 1890s. The 1888 debate over union societies foreshadowed fears among the Methodists and Baptists that their youth would escape to another fold. Epworth Leagues for young people, started in 1889 and approved by the Methodist General Conference in 1892, had 255 chapters in the Troy Conference by 1896, with 15,890 members. The Methodist Vermont Conference welcomed the Epworth League with equal enthusiasm.[40]

The Baptists felt the same uneasiness with Christian Endeavor. The Vermont Baptist State Convention of 1891, believing that the interests of Baptist youth "will be best secured by alliance with our denominational organization," urged forming *Baptist* young people's unions. That summer "a large number of delegates" from the new Baptist unions met in Burlington and a strong minority opposed the movement as "antagonistic to the Christian Endeavor Societies." A majority voted to continue and the 1892 Baptist State Convention endorsed the state young people's organization. Its statistical peak in 1896 was 1,739 members in 54 societies that received literature.

In 1910 Christian Endeavor and the Baptist Union arranged a sort of merger, disbanding the Baptist local and state organizations, and "united in one organization all Baptist Young People's Societies of every name [i.e., some were called Christian Endeavor societies] for the single purpose of denominational unity." Thereafter all Baptist Young People's would be called Christian Endeavor societies and the Baptist contributions would go to the young people's societies of the Vermont Baptist State Convention, its treasurer forwarding half to the Vermont Christian Endeavor Union.[41]

By the late 1890s, junior societies for little children and intermediate societies for pre-adolescents had split off. Rutland Methodists organized the first junior society in the winter of 1888-89. On top of these, Mothers' Christian Endeavor societies helped children keep their pledges. Union societies were still popular in the sparsely populated northeastern hills. Emphasis on pleasure and recreation increased, as with the Y and camp meetings, in the years just before World War I. A Cavendish broadside advertised a midsummer lawn party and concert by the Ludlow band with this jingle: "Ice cream will be served / On this glorious night; / Watermelon and cake / Will fill in just right . . ./ So hitch up your horse / Or put gas in the tank / And get up some muscle / To turn that old crank."[42]

Care of the Sick and Aged

While children and youth received the most attention as the sphere where help would do the most good in the long run, some benevolent Protestants founded Burlington's Home for Aged Women in 1868. This inaugurated a new stage in Vermont's institutional care for the elderly outside of the family, church, poorhouses, and the Brattleboro Retreat. Other homes for the aged followed: the Vermont Soldiers' Home on the north edge of Bennington (1885), the Gill Odd Fellows Home of Vermont in Ludlow (dedicated 1896), and the Brattleboro Home for the Aged and Disabled (dedicated 1897).[43]

The ideal of the old people's "home" was betrayed at the outset by the collective scale of the institution. Their managers tried to restore the comforts of home, but they were essentially a step toward hospitals. They combined nursing care with warehousing of the senile. Medicine was rapidly changing, with the acceptance of the germ theory in the 1880s. Vermont physicians reflected this revolution by promoting the establishment of the State Board of Health in 1886.

After Mary Fletcher endowed her Burlington hospital (organized in 1876, opened in 1879), a decade went by without hospitals in other towns. Then in the followng quarter century, beginning with Chauncey Warner's 1888 gift to St. Albans, seven more centers acquired one, while Burlington and St. Johnsbury had two, one with Protestant and one with Catholic management. Bishop John Michaud invited the Religious Hospitallers of St. Joseph from Montreal to staff the Hotel Dieu of St. Joseph Fanny Allen Hospital, opening in 1894 in the renovatedd Dunbar's tavern. The next year the Rev. J. A. Boissoneault opened the St. Johnsbury Hospital, staffed by Sisters of Providence, also from Montreal. The St. Johnsbury Protestants countered in 1899 with the Brightlook Hospital. A few were built as hospitals, but the common pattern was to start with the remodeled private mansions of the donor-philanthropists.[44]

Before the development of psychiatry, the private Vermont Asylum for the Insane in Brattleboro was the sole Vermont mental hospital until the Waterbury State Asylum for the Insane opened in 1891. After the Civil War many individual physicians ran rest cures, retreats, and sanitariums, similar to the water cures of antebellum days, without hydropathic theory behind them.[45]

Several of the largest villages mirrored the Burlington profile of benevolence, each with a slightly different complex. Brattleboro's Y went into decline after 1907. Some of its citizens established the first Vermont Society for the Prevention of Cruelty to Animals, January 9, 1877, probably related to the Vermont Humane Society, organized in the next decade. In St. Johnsbury the prime movers operated out of the Woman's Club.[46]

Associations For and By Women

The cult of domesticity, assuming that "woman's place is in the home," allowed respectable women various ways to take their first steps into public space. Some managed ladies' bazaars at the town hall. Mrs. G. G. Benedict played the piano at Dwight L. Moody's prayer meetings. Some worked through the YWCA or the Vermont branch of the WCTU, or served on boards of charitable institutions.

Hardly any women felt free to urge their husbands to bolt the Republican Party for any reform. Prohibitionists, Greenbackers, nativists, and Populists persuaded few Vermont church people and fewer ministers to join them. Females, once drawn into running their own benevolent institutions after the Civil War, continued to expand their charitable activities and influence in the 1880s. Sharing the leadership of Christian Endeavor, they ran the WCTU, and figured prominently in all village charities. In Burlington they ran the Howard Relief, the Burlington Cancer Relief Association (1886), later merged with the Howard Relief, the Adams Mission, and the Home for Friendless Women (unwed mothers, 1890), later called the Elizabeth Lund Home. The Mary Fletcher Hospital (1879), founded by the daughter of its namesake, conformed in policy to her wishes, although run by a board dominated by male physicians. These charities had a large component of Burlington women's participation, and other urban centers reflected the same impetus.[47]

The Vermont Women's Christian Temperance Union participated in a national temperance movement whose origins reached back to the early republic. Its postwar phase was colored by the lax enforcement of the state prohibition law of 1852, the intemperance of war veterans, and the anxieties caused by the wandering unemployed. But it operated on the premise still deemed valid by professionals, that alcoholism, next to smoking tobacco the commonest form of drug abuse, leads to a multitude of social ills. Protestants perceived these as mainly Catholic French Canadian and Irish, in threatening numbers during the depressions of 1873-1878 and 1893-1898.

Women who knew the reputation of Diocletian Lewis as a temperance orator, found him with several hours to wait for a train in St. Albans, in March 1874. He persuaded an audience of quickly gathered women to organize a new temperance association, to lobby the local government, to persuade property owners not to lease to saloons, and to win teetotal pledges from liquor dealers and the poor. On one spring day, fifty members marched singing through the streets and won pledges from inn and saloonkeepers. Mrs. E. G. Greene, later president of the state WCTU, recalled the mysterious thrill she and other quiet home-makers felt, keeping step to a battle hymn against rum. That particular religious crusade, spreading to half a dozen towns, lasted less than two months.[48]

When the national WCTU was organized in November 1874, Vermont delegates were there, and came back to organize a state branch in the dead of the following winter. Membership increased from 466 in 1878 to 2,375 ten years later. They lobbied into law an act allowing women to vote in school meetings—if they paid their property taxes. Since men owned most of the property, few women voted in school meetings. When Frances Willard, the national president, tried to link temperance with woman suffrage and with the Prohibition Party, Anna C. Park of Bennington, who opposed both woman suffrage and the WCTU's endorsement of the Prohibition Party, led a substantial group to withdraw from the organization, which lost much of its vitality. A loyal remnant was able to buy the Berean Baptist church building in Burlington for a "temple." This name suggests that for some women the WCTU was their real church home, as Masonry was "a church out-side the church."[49] They continued their routines, alongside the Good Templars and the Sons of Temperance, through much of the twentieth century. The Anti-Saloon League joined them as the new century dawned. Beside these Protestant groups, the Roman Catholic Total Ab-stinence Society and other Catholic organizations to fight alcoholism, marched in temperance ranks under different banners. Perhaps the com-petition between all the do-good organizations as much as the aversion to women in politics doomed the WCTU. Women with neither servants nor kitchen gadgets and all the work to do at home had limited spare time.

The Howard Relief Society in the 1880s broadened its charities to include an employment office and other work relief. The ladies used the Howard as an instrument of social control, investigating each need and barring aid to the intemperate, the truant, and other undeserving poor. In one related outreach, women's organizations from each Burlington Protestant church took monthly turns for twenty years, 1885-1905, running and paying the expenses of the Adams Mission. Located in the Follett House on lower College Street, it aimed to educate and entertain young children from its working-class neighborhood.

The wisdom of the *Brattleboro Household* (1868-1890) was to hold together in the cult of domesticity a broad readership of all kinds of middle-class women. Its creed assumed that the American housewife, chief supporter of the churches, reigned in the home, "be it ever so humble," as its masthead announced. Devoted to the queen of this heaven, the Brattleboro journal won national leadership among modern home magazines. Organized by rooms in the home, from veranda to kitchen, it had no room for the family altar and printed scarce a word about religion, because the whole house was an altar to the goddess of domesticity. It was easy for the *Household* to merge in 1890 with a Boston monthly which merged with the Rev. W. H. H. "Adirondack" Murray's *The Golden Rule*, and was sold by 1898 to the national Christian Endeavor organization that had patronized it for nearly a decade.

The non-denominational but basically Protestant women's social and charitable organizations had wonderfully expanded by the end of the century. For many of the more social, an umbrella institution organized in 1896: the Vermont Federation of Women's Clubs. After over thirty years of interdenominational experience, Protestants published the *Burlington Friend and Helper* in 1900, edited by Walter H. Crockett, giving news of local private charities.[50]

The Brattleboro reaches of the Connecticut Valley captivated another pair of tourists like the Dickinsons who founded the Kurn Hattin Homes. Boston millionaire Thomas Thompson and his wife Elizabeth visited in the 1860s. When he died in March 1869, his will punished Boston for its high property taxes and established a trust whose income amounted to some $30,000 a year, available on the death of his widow, to "poor seamstresses, needle-women and shop girls" in Brattleboro and Newburgh, New York. Elizabeth Thompson did not die until 1899, however, so the effects of this gift occurred entirely in the twentieth century.[51]

The Communitarian Fringe

In the heyday of community socialism, from 1820 to 1855, people with a vision of Pentecostal sharing, deeply wounded by American society, found some farm-owning believer in having all things in common (Acts 2:44, 4:32). They lived on his land briefly, that is, while they were solvent. Those who "knew how to meet a payroll," such as John Humphrey Noyes, Brigham Young, and a few others, kept their communities afloat. The rest found close, "family" living without some recognized religious glue beyond their capabilities and soon dissolved their communities.[52] The impulse to commit community has continued to hover on the outskirts of American society. Before the counter-culture communes of the years of the Vietnam War, two partial manifestations occurred in Vermont.

Orren Shipman had a 210-acre farm in Colchester between the Winooski Intervale and Malletts Bay. On that good soil in the twentieth century, truck gardens have prospered. In 1874, impressed with the ideas of John Wilcox of Wisconsin, Shipman persuaded Wilcox to put his ideas to a practical test. They incorporated the Dawn Valcour Agricultural and Horticultural Association, whose purpose was to support "celebates[sic], Free Lovers, and Believers in the sacredness of marriage." All twenty-two members shared Shipman's property on the anarchist principle of "absolute social freedom" and "complete universal free love." They used Shipman's two hundred acres on Valcour Island in Lake Champlain as a base, but much of the productive acreage was near Shipman Hill. Congregating at the end of August, they had failed by the next spring, from bad timing, personality clashes, bad management, and unqualified labor.[53]

A communitarian, prohibitionist general without an army was N. D. Bartlett, sometime constable of Searsburg, Vermont, who long advertised, apparently without takers, a cross between a tourist home and a home for wayward everybody. He published his Christian socialist ideas, in the tradition of John Humphrey Noyes and Orson S. Murray, from 1883 to 1926, whenever he had the money to print them. His proposed Home Institute was Bible-based, "practical Christianity practically applied to the church," for both sexes, guaranteed to reform the criminal, cure the physically and mentally ill, comfort the orphan, mend broken families, and raise "fallen" girls in the "bracing balsam-laden air" of Searsburg. It would be self-supporting because of the work of the residents. As in all the other "homes" of the period, the idealized family atmosphere was presumed to nourish its members into health and happiness. His wisdom was in seeing that social ills are interlocked.[54]

Very likely the cooperative spirit promoted in Christian Endeavor and the initiatives of Edward Hungerford and revivalists like Dwight L. Moody overcame the fears of denominations weaker in a particular village that their rivals would draw off their youth in the name of unity. Many church people felt that the social evils of the time were drinking, "immorality," as they referred to sexual deviations from their moral code, and gambling on horse races. A redeeming feature of this narrow view was the assumption that those evils were so enormous that only a concerted attack could defeat them.

The cooperative spirit, however, brought churches together for limited objectives. The isolated example of the Proctor Union Church Society, organized in 1889, although it appeared to be prophetic of the twentieth-century movement toward church union, could have happened only in the 1880s and in Proctor, a town with one economic interest, the Vermont Marble Company, formed in 1880 to combine two thirds of the county's marble interests. The new society followed a succession of schools and a chapel where existing denominations shared space, as in the early days, but it operated on different principles.

Redfield Proctor, in helping form a church in his new town, incorporated in 1886 from pieces of Pittsford, Rutland, and West Rutland, had no entrenched sectarian or municipal traditions to combat. He wisely saw that all Protestants had a great deal in common, and that it was advantageous for his firm, when it had a concern involving religion, to deal with one main Protestant church rather than many. Instead of arguing over doctrine, members of about a dozen denominations accepted a statement of faith consisting of Bible quotations. Members declared that they were in "substantial" agreement with those texts and, like the members of Christian Endeavor, they were "willing to live a Christian life." This was a unique exception to the pattern of many denominations competing in growing industrial villages.

After the chapel burned in 1889, the Union Church Society rebuilt in elegant blue marble, with oak pews, a pipe organ, and soon, electric lights. Although congregational in polity, they agreed to transfer members to churches of their choice, to send representatives to the several church councils, to exchange ministers, and to divide mission offerings proportionally between the Baptists, Congregationalists, and Methodists, the bulk of the membership. The town historian detected "the pervasive influence" of Redfield Proctor.[55]

Turn-of-the-Century Religious Landscape

Looking out from the end of the century, what was Vermont's religious landscape? Physically speaking, where were church buildings in the village and country panoramaa? How axial, how focused, were places of worship as symbols of religion's importance? Aesthetically speaking, how well did worship in song and story, prayer and praise, satisfy the communicants and express a common Christian liturgy? Morally speaking, did religious norms, repeated by preachers and aimed at by members, still call people to follow the gleam? How had the character of the clergyman changed? Constitutionally speaking, how much freedom had been won by the so-called separation of church and state of 1807—freedom from other people's religion as well as for one's own? In terms of church polity, how had the balance shifted between local laity and their pastors, and the layers of executives above them? What kind of equilibrium can we see between basic Christianity and denominational distinctives?

Village skylines were still centered on steeples and other church towers, and the cupolas and domes of academies and colleges. Only a few smokestacks for steam-powered factories and a score of four-story village and lake resort hotels were beginning to intrude.[56] In the country, the early-twentieth-century landscape came to be dominated by the churchlike cowbarn with its gambrel roof and silo steeple, reminiscent of the first barn-meetinghouses. Silos were the new feature of the late

1880s and 1890s. Burlington's first two Congregational churches were axial, the liberal (Unitarian, 1816) at the head of Church, the main business street, and the other (1842) at the head of Cherry Street that crossed Church. Lavius Fillmore's Old Bennington (1805) and Middlebury (1809) buildings were more subtly focused, unquestionably the crowns of their respective villages. Later comers, still centrally located, clustered alongside in practically all the urban centers, the way shops vending the same wares cluster. Site was also determined by limited availability in the built-up center, and for the convenience of members. The Cathedral of the Immaculate Conception did assert symbolically, with its tallest tower in Vermont, that its Roman Catholics were Number One. In other villages Catholics chose the most prestigious site available: in Montpelier the old courthouse next to the capitol; in Bennington, St. Francis de Sales was the landmark on the eastern edge of Old Bennington hill. The earlier, plain church buildings housed worship only while the new ones housed many activities. Now oftener in more expensive stone or brick, their style was highly decorated and eclectic "Victorian Gothic."

In Protestant Vermont, the minister's original contract spelled out what he and the church expected him to do; his honeymoon period was his best chance to increase the membership, reshape the liturgy, and update the Sunday schools. The clergy taught Bible and theology and modelled for morals. The sources of local sermon style for the late-Victorian era are not yet analyzed. The content did not change: explaining beliefs and relating the Bible to contemporary thought; inveighing against perceived evils—wine, women, and dancing—or against Catholics or Protestants (most often indirectly), varying with the preacher. Shrillness and the volume of noise depended on the denomination and the requirements of the hall.

Who the Vermont Protestant minister was did not change much from antebellum days. If he was a village Congregational, Episcopal, Presbyterian, and Unitarian minister, he had college and seminary degrees. He had better pay than if he had been in a rural church, and longer tenure, especially if he had the cachet of Yale or Dartmouth. Among the Universalists, Free Will Baptists, and Adventists, a few women had invaded the realm of male preachers, mainly because the low salaries could not attract male preachers. The main change in the character of the Catholic priest was the gradual disappearance of the European-born and European-trained, as more anglophone and francophone natives prepared for the priesthood in American seminaries.

The crystal of liturgy continued unfractured in its various denominational styles. When a church replaced its hymnals the congregation found a few unfamiliar poems and tunes. The files of the Estey Organ Company showed an expanding Vermont church market for its pipe organs and some indication of the competition to sell church organs.

Protestant ministers and deacons and their wives took oversight of "morals," defined in their minds as personal departures from respectable norms, beyond the medieval seven deadly sins. Besides condemning breaches of contract and other crimes mainly against property, they agreed with Anthony Comstock, Secretary of the Society for the Suppression of Vice, 1873-1915, in identifying vice as sexual. And they extended the sexual to innocent party games. With a celibate priesthood, the Irish Catholics were likely to be just as "Victorian" as their prudish Protestant neighbors, but perhaps the French somewhat less so. In games and recreation, the Protestants made it clear that Catholics were much too unbuttoned.

Hal Goldman's forthcoming study of the trial records of four Vermont county courts from 1780 to 1920 has led to some remarkable but very tentative conclusions about how Vermont courts dealt with illicit sexual activity. Early Vermonters, if they disciplined sexual behavior at all, seem to have left it to community pressures or to the churches. Laws against incest, lewdness, brothel keeping, and obscenity, remained in being but only sporadically enforced. Vermont early legislated against obscenity but had not prohibited fornication since the eighteenth century. Local ordinances, not state law, dealt with prostitution. In family matters, state law had penalized abortion since 1846 and now allowed more grounds for divorce. More Vermonters divorced than before, either because of the legal changes, or the law changed because more pressed for divorce. The law raising the age of consent for girls from eleven to fourteen (1886) then to sixteen (1897) led to "a flood of statutory rape cases" with many older men convicted of having sex with young girls. "Prosecutions for adultery. . . increased dramatically" after about 1880, with nearly two dozen cases in 1901 alone. Jury trials open to the public, with gossip distributing through the town the explicit evidence that juries and courtroom audiences heard, publicized the danger to the home beyond anything the newspapers felt free to print.[57] Anthony Comstock's organization and the host of uplift organizations like the WCTU found reason for concern. If the home glorified in the *Brattleboro Household* was being corrupted, as evidence introduced in the courts seemed to suggest, benevolent associations needed to get busy.

The Protestant minister's responsibilities were stretched not only by the increased concern over morals, but also by the need to care for several weak congregations in neighboring small towns. Here was another reversion to the early days when Methodists made circuit riding an advantage. Many Catholic priests had always had to serve communicants beyond their parishes. These hard times for hill churches would lead in the new century to federation and other forms of Protestant cooperation.

The body of the Protestant churches was content with the end of the multiple establishment in 1807, and Catholic protests went unheeded. The change allowed churches to compete for members and denied town tax support for any. Vermonters felt that a firm boundary prevented the state from interfering on behalf of favorites. In this generation, few complained of the remaining religious benefits from state connections.

State-paid chaplains, none Catholic, usually chosen in rotation among available Protestant divines, still blessed state institutions and celebrations. When the Assembly incorporated the University of Vermont and State Agricultural College in 1865, Section 2 specified that "all future elections or appointments. . . shall be made with special reference to prevent any religious denominational preponderance in said Board."[58] Schoolteachers could read the Bible and hold religious exercises in school, and Roman Catholics protested in vain that their children were thus subjected to Protestant preferences. Aside from these repeated Catholic complaints, however, citizens' practice nullified old blue laws and let the sleeping dog of church-state relations lie.

In church polity, what had been the stark necessity of local control in the beginning had over the years continued as a shibboleth. Indeed, in the twentieth century local control has continued as a myth while town meetings have lost the management of schools, roads, welfare, and much more to state and federal power and local churches likewise to larger bodies. The more complex society of 1900 allowed input at every level, so that it had become impossible to assert in any meaningful sense that congregations enjoyed full local autonomy. While church bylaws paid allegiance to various congregational, federal, and episcopal models, the reality was more complicated. The trend of power, however, was definitely upward and outward.

At the other extreme one could not safely say, as Protestants persisted in saying, that Catholics suffered under autocracy. The bishops of Rome and the bishops of Burlington, like the Episcopal bishops of Vermont, the Methodist bishops of the Troy and Vermont conferences, the general of the Salvation Army, and Christian Science led by Mary Baker Eddy, were very limited monarchies. For example, the seven religious orders of Catholic women, invited by the bishop to staff schools, orphanages, and the Fanny Allen Hospital, were responsible to their mother houses, most of them outside Vermont. The bishop could only order them to leave. The Society of St. Edmund had similar independence, supplying some parishes at the bishop's invitation, and teaching.

The Persistence of Civil Religion

My attention has been on the variations among Christians and Jews. What about the majority, unwashed in the blood of the Lamb? Their civil religion was firm, but its content and forms had shifted. Their religion baptized with the fire-water of patriotism, with fresh memories of the crusade in their country's defense. Although the ante-bellum bellowers had yelled to the world that republican democracy worked, doubters abroad had croaked that Americans would never be able to deal with sectional schism without turning to tyranny. Vermonters were sure that the paradox of Freedom and Unity had worked. From the point of view of the defeated South, their liberty was lost in the war while their investment in the Union was diminished by the tyranny of alien Black Reconstruction. Victorious Vermonters shared Lincoln's conviction that the federal Constitution was just and worked and that the Civil War proved it.

In the hubris of victory, the Vermont press reflected assurance that the South needed investment of Yankee capital and Yankee ways. There was a new market to win, for traders' profits, and a population to teach. Vermonters would enjoy the sunny South, and attract more Southern tourists to its hills and waters. While the focus was on their own share in the fruits of victory, many presumed that the exchange would help the South too.

In the last two decades of the century, something like the Southern victory over radical reconstruction occurred in Vermont. From disappointment in the apparent failure of their mission to make over the South in their own image, and from alarm at the multitude of problems at home, Vermonters turned their attention inward or elsewhere. They followed the local band in torchlight processions chanting "Blaine, Blaine, from the State of Maine," or stood before the local telegraph office as the announcer called, "Another county heard from." More Americans, including the same class of Vermonters, went abroad, either to wear status symbols of having been to Europe, or for professional training, or to probe markets for new manufactures. Whether Congregationalists or Episcopalians, they came back proud that they were Americans, like Mark Twain's *Connecticut Yankee in King Arthur's Court* (1889). They also came back changed.

Probably no earlier period had placed the flag so consistently in the van for holiday parades and celebrations. The market ballooned for flags in schools and other public buildings. After brief persecution of those "snakes in the grass," Copperhead Democrats, the weak opposition party acquired loyalty status. As the splinter parties (Greenbacker, Populist, Prohibition, Socialist, etc.) claimed, but without persuading many, the major national parties were but two sides of the same coin.

Members of the unaffiliated majority practiced much Christian behavior, and when asked, "substantially" agreed with much Christian belief. Their camouflage was adequate to avoid criticism, because on the whole they accepted the way things were.

After all the postbellum bad times, the century ended for Vermonters with a bang in 1898. Within a week after Dewey's May Day victory in Manila Bay, the news set off a series of celebrations keeping patriotic fervor at fever pitch for a year and a half. The climax came in October 1899, when unprecedented throngs hailed the naval hero's return, through the glory of autumn foliage, to his native Montpelier. Schools and shops closed, and politicians harangued the thousands gathered at numerous depots en route. Dewey, inexperienced in his role as public figure, his arm swollen from endless handshaking in Washington and New York, bowed from the rear platform of Seward Webb's private car.

Other causes for celebration maintained the excitement, as of the old-time protracted meetings. In May 1898, crowds cheered a thousand in the Vermont Regiment along its route from Fort Ethan Allen in Colchester to New London, Connecticut, destined for three disease-ridden months in Chickamauga, Georgia. Captain Charles E. Clark took the battleship *Oregon* from San Francisco through the Straits of Magellan to Key West in sixty-six days, in time to take part in the battle of Santiago Harbor, Cuba. Here was more cause for legislative resolutions in his honor, commissions for his official portrait along with Dewey's, and eventually a hero's welcome to his Montpelier home.

Then, on the last day of 1898, Congress assembled to pay its final respects to Senator Justin S. Morrill, who had died three days before. Morrill had served in their halls since elected to the House in 1854. Funereal honors continued in Vermont for weeks, putting the century into its grave with Justin Morrill.

Vermonters found the Victorian legacy perplexing. On the surface the glorious little Spanish war was bully, to use the popular Theodore Roosevelt's favorite word. It was right to "take up the white man's burden" in Cuba, Puerto Rico, Hawaii, and the Philippines and teach those gooks in the tropical isles something about civilization. And at home, life seemed simple to President McKinley, William Jennings Bryan, and Governor Grout. A popular song asserted their simple truth: "There are two sides to every question: right and wrong."

On the other hand, faint voices questioned this imperialist trend. The State Democratic Convention in May 1898, whose slate won less than twenty-eight percent of the votes in the September election, included an anti-annexationist plank in its platform. In 1900, the Democrats supported William Jennings Bryan's anti-imperialist campaign. Senator Justin S. Morrill had opposed the annexation of Hawaii, and generally opposed including Latin (Catholic) countries in the Union. Morrill, however, did not object to protecting American business or medical missionaries abroad. Sarah Cleghorn recorded in her autobiography that the accounts of U.S. cruelties to Filipinos sickened her. But nobody in Manchester except her father agreed with her. She was "perplexed. . . by our keeping the captured islands."[59] Finley Peter Dunne, Chicago columnist who created bartender Mr. Dooley, claimed the annexation of the "Ph'lippeens" was not his concern. He would leave the issue up to his cousin Admiral Dooley. "He started without askin' our lave, an' I don't see what we've got to do with th' way he finishes."[60]

Notes to Chapter 7

1 Carroll, *Spiritualism in Antebellum America*, finds a unity in Spiritualists' Swedenborgian and liberal Protestant origins, and in their working out through diverse individual voices a complete set of religious characteristics. He builds on the work of a considerable body of scholars, notably Moore, *In Search of White Crows*, and Braude, *Radical Spirits*.

2 See newspaper notices and commentary in *Rutland Herald*, 8, 29 August 1865 (meeting in Ludlow); 6 June 1866; 26 August, 5, 8, 9 September 1868 (Danby); *Woodstock Spirit of the Age*, 6 September 1866 (Montpelier); 24 August 1867 (Montpelier); 2 September (West Randolph) and 9 December 1869 (St. Albans); *Burlington Free Press*, 6 January 1880 (Waterbury). The *Age* (28 November 1867) noted the single issue of Nathaniel Randall's *The Age of Reason*, Montpelier. Twentieth-century notices of Spiritualist annual meetings, e.g. *Burlington Free Press*, October 4, 1966, seem to have settled on 1869 as the founding date of their annual gatherings.

3 My transcript of the privately owned notebook of Angelina Miller (1804-1878) is at UVM.

4 *Vermont Historical Gazetteer*, 2:716-717 (Stowe Spiritualists); entry for April 19, 1870 in Mina Hinds' diary, Schlesinger Library (A/H 662), Radcliffe College. See Cabot, *Brattleboro*, 855-856 on James' *Mystery of Edwin Drood*.

5 Giddings, *In the Enemies Land*, 5-27, quotations, 6, 19.

6 Blavatsky's original story of her visit to the Eddys appeared in the New York *Spiritual Scientist* (3 Dec. 1874). Olcott, a believer, described the Eddys' operation in *Inside the Occult*, especially 1-11, 62-71.

7 See also *Burlington Free Press*, 1, 3 August 1891, detailing the month's program of their August summer conference, and *Queen City Park Spiritualist Camp Meeting*, [4].

8 Newkirk, *Sleeping Lucy*, has her portrait on the cover, with wrapper facsimile of her medical advertisement, after 1886 because issued from North Cambridge, Massachusetts, where she lived, 1887-1895.

9 Parsons, *Christian Science In Vermont*, 3-4, 14-16, 18-19, and passim. Parsons has combed Christian Science publications and recorded many scraps of information about active Vermont promoters of the faith. A notable example of those who left the state for the church's activities

elsewhere is James Franklin Gilman, who illustrated some of Mrs. Eddy's books. See Dawson, *James Franklin Gilman*; also church listings in city and village directories for the 1890s; and the even-handed treatment of Eddy's life by Sydney E. Ahlstrom in *Notable American Women*, 1:551-561.

[10] Gwilym Roberts, *New Lives in the Valley*, 37-79 (Welsh background), 52 (distribution of dissenters); and "The Creation of Welsh Institutions in the Slate Valley," 81-109. Welsh Methodists seceded from the Church of England in 1811. By 1851, sixteen Anglican parishes in Anglesey and Caernarvonshire were only 8.8% Anglican, with the following distribution of dissenters: 8,442 Calvinistic Methodists
                        3,000 Independents (Congregationalists)
                        1,058 Wesleyan Methodists
                        642 Baptists
J. G. Williams, *Welsh Churches Beyond Britain*, 255-260, traces the vicissitudes since 1851 of the three main varieties of Welsh Protestants, with photographs of two Poultney and two Granville chapels.

[11] See Gale, *Proctor*, 202, 205-206; "Svenskarna i [Swedes in] Proctor, Vermont," 1, 3. The Swedish article tells how Redfield Proctor helped the immigrant Swedes. "New Swedish Church," 4, sketches the first ten years of the "Swedish Evangelical Mission of the Congregational Church." The Brattleboro Swedes who worked for the Estey Organ Company had both Lutheran and Evangelical Reform churches by 1894 (Mary R. Cabot, *Annals of Brattleboro*, 892; *Walton's Register...for 1895*, 61).

[12] According to Kaufman, *College of Medicine*, 38-39, Heineberg had Jewish relatives in the United States. The entry for "Dr. Heineberg" in Edward Hungerford's "Religious Canvass" of 1867, 29, indicates that the household of five at the American House had no church members and one churchgoer (probably his second wife), but has no "Remarks" as in the case of the clothing merchant, Morris Berwin: "Jews--attend no Church" (32). See Heineberg's obituary in the *Burlington Free Press*, 4 July 1878, 3:2, and Samuelson, *Jewish Community of Burlington*, 41-42.

[13] For example, Manivon [Emmanuel ben?] Abraham, 24, peddler, living with Jacob Abraham, 26, tinman, $1,000 real property, both born in Germany, recorded in the 1850 manuscript census September 2 at household 1242, family 1291 in Barnet; Kolp, 38, peddler born in Bavaria, with wife, 34, and two children, the one-year-old born in Vermont, ibid. 42:51, in Burlington.

[14]*Vermont Laws* (1847), 24, substantially the same in *Revised Laws (R.L.) 1880*.

15 Samuelson, *Burlington Jewish Community*, 9-66. Bercuvitz, "Neighborhood and Community," supplements Samuelson with quantitative analysis and more interviews of immigrant members of the community.

16 Samuelson, *Burlington Jewish Community*, 64; see also 74-99.

17 Ibid., 99-108.

18 Norman Seaver, *Moral Teaching*, 3-5.

19 *Burlington Free Press*, 14 January 1885, 4:2; 9 April, 6:2; 1 October, 4:3; 5 October, 1886, 7:3; 23 June 1891, 2:2. See also Cabot, *Annals of Brattleboro*, 2:292 (Salvation Army incorporated Nov. 1885); Fairbanks, *St. Johnsbury*, 314-315 (street work begun in the summer of 1885, continued to 1913).

20 For background, see *Handbook of Salvation Army Doctrine*; Robert Sandall, *History of Salvation Army*; and McKinley, *Marching to Glory*. Walker, "Catherine Booth," in *Women Preachers and Prophets*, 288-302, traces the origins of women's equality in the Army.

21 Listed in *Walton's Vermont Register* for the 1890s only.

22 [Cate], "Spring Grove Revisited"; Beers, *Atlas of Addison Co.*, 20, called it "Meth. Camp Ground"; 9 (Ferrisburgh), labeled Long Point "Camp Grove." For the institution of the camp meeting in the Troy Conference, see C. D. and O. D. Schwartz, *Flame of Fire*, 234-243, and O. D. Schwartz, "Missisquoi Campground."

23 Shores, *Lyndon*, 178-185 with illus.; *Horace Ward Bailey*, 156-157. Harriet F. Fisher of Lyndonville has shared her columns in the local press and other extensive material on Railroad Grove.

24 Bleakney, "Old-Time Camp Meeting," a reminiscence of August 1889.

25 Davies, *Silver Lake Camp Meeting*; Estabrook, "Silver Lake Camp Meetings."

26 I. T. Johnson, *Story of My Life,* 143-147; Bassett, "Church of the Nazarene."

27 See Stone, "Fraternal Organizations," in *Vermont of Today*, 2:635-664.

28 Pledge list of Burlington Citizens Committee at UVM.

29 Rozwenc, *Agricultural Policies*, 19-21; Stone, *Vermont of Today*, 2:647-651. By 1928 there were at least forty Grange halls in towns like Ferrisburg, whose hall had once housed Congregationalists.

30 See the first annual report in the *Vermont Chronicle* (10 November 1866), 4:1-2, also published separately. True, "Middle-Class Women and Civic Improvement," traces how Burlington Protestant women organized to combat poverty in the quarter century after the Civil War, thereby influencing official policies toward the poor.

31 Hurd, *Kurn Hattin*, 77-93.

32 *Burlington Free Press*, 18 October 1867, 4:1, 15 February 1868, 4:2.

33 *Vermont Laws* (1865), sec. 5, p. 5, provided that "whenever any male or female under... eighteen" was found delinquent, the court could commit to the Vermont Reform School. The *Burlington Free Press*, 15 June 1866, reported the religious ceremonies at its opening and the views of John Sullivan Adams, orator of the day, on juvenile delinquency.

34 Fairbanks, *St. Johnsbury*, 316-320.

35 Allen, *About Burlington*, 79-81, view of building looking southwest, 80; Auld, *Picturesque Burlington*, 73-75. Clark: Stone, *Vermont of Today*, 862.

36 Catholic Young Men's Union. Burlington, Vermont. *Constitution and By-laws*.

37 Allen, *About Burlington*, 81.

38 Nordbeck, "Legacy of Francis Clark," 3-13.

39 Vermont Christian Endeavor Union, *Journal of Annual Meetings, 1886-1888*, 16.

40 Schwartz and Schwartz, *Flame of Fire*, 293-295, using Hutchinson, *Epworth League* and Vermont Conference *Minutes*.

41 Crocker, *Baptists in Vermont*, 575-577.

[42] Barre, Vermont. Congregational Church. *Centennial*, 43-48; Marvin, "Y.P.S.C.E."; *Our Church Work* (Barton, January 1898), 2-3, (July 1898), 2-3; *Band Concert July 21, 1911*, broadside at UVM.

[43] True, "Middle-Class Women"; *Walton's Register* (1886), 217 (Soldiers' Home); Stone, *Vermont of Today*, 653 (Gill Odd Fellows Home); Cabot, *Annals of Brattleboro*, 873.

[44] Orton, *Mary Fletcher*; *Look Around Colchester*, 14; Healy, *Fanny Allen Hospital*; A. F. Stone, *The Vermont of Today*, 1:319-320, with photograph of St. Johnsbury Hospital opposite 320; Fairbanks, *St. Johnsbury*, 328-330; *Walton's Register for 1895*, 74.

   The other prewar hospitals: Rutland and Proctor (1896), Brattleboro (funded by the Thompson Trust, 1904), Barre (1907), Bellows Falls (1910), Springfield (1914). Bennington followed after the war. See Crockett, *Vermont*, 5:634-638.

[45] See Swift and Beach, *Brattleboro Retreat*, 66, and passim.

[46] Fairbanks, *St. Johnsbury*, 494-495; Cabot, *Annals of Brattleboro*, 868-875 (SPCA, 869, YMCA, 874-875). *Walton's Vermont Register for 1885* (209) and *for 1895* (305) list a Vermont Humane Society.

[47] The dates of founding are from Burlington city directories. In addition to references already cited, see S. W. Smith, "Burlington Cancer Relief Association."

[48] Clifford, "Women's War Against Rum." Photograph of the Temple, 1896-1928, 145.

[49] See Coates, *Masonry, a Church Outside the Church.*

[50] True, "Middle-Class Women," 112, focuses on the women who ran the Home for Destitute Children and the Ladies Aid Society, continued after 1882 as the Howard Relief Society. See also his "Howard Relief to Howard Mental Health," 8-13, 21-23.

[51] Blackwell, *Poor Women, Charity, and Medicine*, 5, 27.

[52] See Persons, "Christian Communitarianism in America," 1:125-151, and Bassett, "Secular Utopian Socialists," 1:153-211, and the pre-Marxian sections of some topical chapters in Egbert and Persons, *Socialism and American Life.*

[53] See David J. Blow's summary in *Look Around Colchester*, 8, and articles in the press, e.g. *Burlington Free Press*, 1 and 11 September 1874. No records of the community have been found.

[54] [Bartlett], *Home Institute*, 1-4; *The Christian Citizen*, (March 1913, February, April 1926); Prohibition Song Leaflet No. 2 (May 1909), "originally prepared in 1898," scattered copies in Vermont Historical Society; *Walton's Vermont Register* (1896), 196.

[55] G. W. C. Hill, "Union Church, Proctor"; Gale, *Proctor*, 189-203.

[56] Wriston, *Vermont Inns*, 342, shows the Montvert (1871) in Middletown Springs with five stories. Burlington's Van Ness House (1870), 160, Newport's Memphremagog House (ca. 1870), front cover and 378-377, and Brattleboro's Brooks House (1872), 140, had five stories in parts. The Randall in Morrisville, 362, had the standard three stories with three more levels of an octagonal "steeple," apparently with windows on all sides.

[57] Hal Goldman, Ph.D. diss. in progress, University of Massachusetts.

[58] *Vermont Laws* (1865), 98.

[59] Cleghorn, *Threescore*, 113.

[60] Finley Peter Dunne, "On Admiral Dewey's Activity," *Mr. Dooley in Peace and in War* (Boston: Small, Maynard, 1898), 39-42.

8

Conclusion

The assumption behind this story has been that *all* Vermonters have *always* been religious; they all have had "spirituality." The human and the holy are intertwined. This makes the history of one topic in one place, with the end open to recent times, extraordinarily difficult, and a summary even more so. Topical history is not a series of compartments, but the whole history of humanity from a series of perspectives. Beyond that, the whole history relates human nature to the rest of nature, also imbued with the sacred. The difference between this view and pantheism is the difference between the creator and creation. The Holy Spirit, or the spirit of holiness, is in but not of the world. The difference between this view and the secular is the assumption of permeating holiness. With this reminder of the promise of the preface, this conclusion recapitulates the religious aspects of life in Vermont.

The only way to suggest how the Western Abenaki, as predators with supplementary horticulture, lived in balance with their environment is to sketch their total culture, because a religious spirit infused the whole. In dangerous waters and dangerous woods, the Indians felt protected by shamans because these "ministers" best understood, interpreted, and made use of the spirits of each part of nature. So European clergy understood the Bible and the Christian tradition, and "justified the ways of God to man," as Milton wrote. At the time of first contact with Europeans, white and Indian mostly failed to understand each other's religion because they were on different planes. The Abenaki understood the danger of being squeezed to death between imperial France and imperial Britain, so they chose the side that seemed least likely to hurt them, if they could not keep out of the way.

A majority of Vermonters were unaffiliated with any church until some time in the twentieth century, when church membership crept over fifty percent. The "civil religion" of this majority derived from the generic Puritan Christianity they had absorbed in their previous homes.

When settlers, in those awesome, dark forests, had no minister, they worshiped by gathering to read a sermon or scripture, with hymns and prayers. They also worshiped by helping other settlers. In the frequent hardships of first settlement they shared grain brought on the back for miles on crooked paths. They joined in the hunt for the bears, wolves and catamounts that killed their stock and ate their stores.

They expressed revolutionary religious principles also in their original constitution of 1777. These principles of the Republic of Vermont fit those of the revolutionary thirteen states except that Vermonters carried freedom farther. Their constitution extended suffrage to most adult males and abolished adult slavery.

Church members or not, they expressed the creed of their constitution in their moderating motto, "Freedom and Unity": not unlimited freedom nor forced unity. Vermonters celebrated the principles of their Republic on the Fourth of July, the country's birthday. Vermont had only bit parts in the drama of the American Revolution, but as often happens, some of those minor actors made major differences. Benedict Arnold threatened Quebec and with Ethan Allen captured the key fort of Ticonderoga in 1775. Arnold checked the British at Valcour Island in 1776, delaying their invasion a year. Vermont rangers and militia under Seth Warner, John Stark, and Samuel Herrick resisted at Hubbardton and Bennington in 1777, and blocked the paths through the wilderness between Ticonderoga and the Hudson. These events, sapping the strength of Burgoyne's advance, were the stuff of the Vermont story. They provided the scriptures of Vermont's civil religion, rehearsed every Independence Day. Vermont's Exodus was winning freedom from British Egypt. Its conquest of Canaan was the winning of the New Hampshire Grants.

Beyond the climax celebration on the Fourth, the state had its own calendar of inherited Puritan feasts and fasts, all with Vermont overtones: Thanksgiving, New Year's Day, Fast Day, June training, academic exhibitions or commencements, Bennington Battle Day (celebrated mainly in Bennington), and Election Day.

By the 1830s, Vermonters had a symbolic state house, and soon after, a hero in Ethan Allen. The only other change in Vermont's calendar of civil religion was the fading of Fast Day and June training, the failure of Arbor Day, the mid-nineteenth-century village version of modern Green-up Day, and the emergence of Memorial Day. The War of 1812 was a mere coda to the symphony of the Revolution, and the northern border skirmishes and the Mexican War evoked only partisan loyalties.

The impulse to decorate the graves of Union soldiers, however, struck the right chord for Vermonters. Freedom and Unity had a special meaning after their war that preserved the Union and freed the slaves. The meaning was enhanced by love for the martyred president who led the Union forces to victory. Abraham Lincoln, although only a forty percent choice of the country in 1860, was the choice of seventy-six percent of Vermont voters in both his elections. His image increasingly fused with Memorial Day. Vermonters, whether in school or at home, were more sympathetic toward the gaunt democrat who rose from a log cabin to the White House than toward George Washington, the Southern patrician slaveholder.

Patriotic societies organized toward the end of the nineteenth century to promote observance of patriotic holidays. The young soldiers of the 1860s, middle-aged and eager for office in the 1880s, made the Reunion of Vermont Officers and the Grand Army of the Republic strong political forces in the dominant Republican Party. The Women's Auxiliary of the G.A.R. and the Daughters of the American Revolution (1894) campaigned for flags in the schools and ritual pledges of allegiance, while the Women's Christian Temperance Union campaigned for pledges against liquor. For such pure causes, women were taking their first organized steps out of the home and into politics.

The minority that belonged to some church or other started from scratch. In a wilderness without churches, every sort had to send salesmen to win adherents. The Episcopalians and Quakers, present before the Revolution and both of dubious patriotism because of their reluctance to fight the British, depended on rare visits from traveling ministers. The Congregationalists, Baptists, and Universalists persuaded by debates and revivalism. Since meetinghouses were scarce, revivals were most often at camp meetings, held outdoors. When a town decided to afford a meetinghouse it was often a "union" meetinghouse, with denominations negotiating shares in its use.

In most towns the Congregationalists organized first and tried by fair means or foul to keep others out, but others kept coming in. A pattern repeated itself throughout the century: The insiders called the invaders the lunatic fringe, infiltrating with their devilish ways but without staying power. Neither Methodist circuit riders nor the first Roman Catholic priest could amount to much, the insiders told themselves. But a "ranting Arminian" in 1789, and "Crazy Dow" ten years later, were merely the first to raise up a horde of Methodists. Jeremiah O'Callaghan, "the reverend paddy," "a shatter-brained disorganizer," could not last, the insiders said. But he covered the state until reinforced with other priests and increasing thousands of Irish and French Canadian immigrants. From the Baptists to the absurd Adventists and the outlandish Jews, the newcomers came to stay, making the constellation of faiths ever more varied. While most of the new groups filled little niches, the Baptists, Methodists, and Catholics rose as a spring tide contending with the Congregationalists for leadership among the churches.

The eighteenth-century Baptists were chief victims of harassment, having an ox or cow taken for taxes to support the "majority" minister. Once penalized, they learned that to be exempt from church taxes they had to get a certificate from a neighboring minister of their own denomination. They led the assault on the "multiple establishment," a system that purported to let each church support its own but worked to the advantage of the Congregationalists.

The final separation of church and state in 1807 owed much to the Baptist alliance with the rising Methodists and Universalists in the Jeffersonian Republican party. These were the strongest of several groups rejecting the contemporary version of orthodox Calvinism. Actually, the Methodists were not all as "Arminian" as their opponents accused them of being. What they rejected was more a style and a polity than a theology. "Crazy Dow" was an early and extreme example of Methodist circuit riders: young, able to withstand abuse, equipped with Bible, maybe a hymn book, and a book of discipline, but without much training, who endured hardship for Christ. Dow and other itinerants were neither capable of nor interested in arguing the fine points of pre-destination and Providence. Methodist circuit riders, in Vermont from 1789, arranged "classes" where probationers learned by hearing and giving testimony, and warmed themselves in the enthusiasm of a neighborhood group of converts.

In southern New England, Congregationalists, and Presbyterians in their pockets of Scottish settlement, had been wounded by traveling ministers in eighteenth-century revivals. They would not lower their high standards of ministerial training. With few exceptions, they would not compromise their system of one minister, one congregation. They believed in the freshening of revival under the guidance of pastors. Not until the 1830s did one wing espouse the "new measures" of protracted meetings, altar calls, and mourners' benches, which Charles G. Finney had used successfully in upstate New York. Finneyite Jedediah Burchard toured both sides of Vermont, 1834-1836, but met with organized opposition who claimed his conversions were shallow and temporary. Some of them were, but partly because of the cold reception of lower-class converts by respectable members.

By 1840 the Methodists, as strong and numerous as the Congregationalists, began to give up their itinerancy and become solid, respectable, "domesticated" main-liners. A final fervor of millennialism, aroused by William Miller and also dependent on revivals, excited Protestants in the early 1840s. When Miller's predictions of the end of the world failed, a remnant survived as Adventists. One wing of Methodism, emphasizing the Wesleys' original holiness theology, gathered strength, especially through institutionalized camp meetings, but unlike the handful of antislavery Methodists, did not leave main-line Methodism until the twentieth century.

Meanwhile, immigrant Catholics began to pose a graver threat to all Protestants. Before there were enough Catholics in Vermont to shake a stick at, they represented the stereotyped, evil world force Protestants opposed everywhere. As nearby French Canadians and far-off alien Irish began seeping into the Champlain Valley, hostility toward them rose to its worst level. Low-paid muscle laborers, always needed, kept escaping to better opportunities elsewhere. Vermont, like the rest of the country, consisted of immigrants who had always needed a welcome as much as the latest arrivals.

Yet the heirs of the pioneer immigrants did not like the Catholic immigrant. They used, abused, ridiculed, and discriminated against their missionary priest, Jeremiah O'Callaghan, and his poor statewide flock. Some Protestants, to be sure, when they saw an advantage or just because it was fair, allowed Catholics to use public space for worship or conributed to their building funds. College students gave them Bibles and taught their chilren. The well-to-do expected their Catholic servants as well as slumdwellers to learn the better, Protestant way. But the Catholics merely multiplied. Numerous enough to have their own diocese of Burlington and bishop from 1853, they built a separate system of schools, convents, and orphanages, all the while pressing for equal rights. After the Civil War, in one category after another, the numbers showed that the Catholics had forged ahead.

Protestant reactions to this obvious new threat were various. Some repeated the old revivalist efforts, which worked for the Baptists and checked the decline of the Methodists. Congregationalists liked the simple, businesslike style of revivalist Dwight L. Moody. Protestants also formed interdenominational associations both to deal with specific social needs and through those missions to win members.

Beyond worrying over Catholic gains, Protestant leadership was divided between modernism and traditionalism. The Fairbanks dynasty of St. Johnsbury invested liberally in rural missions, to shore up churches weakened by emigration and indifference. They wanted Congregationalism to consolidate its forces and lead the defense of Protestantism. Many recent seminary graduates, facing an urban industrial society their grandfathers had not known, sloughed off many of the doctrines that had almost gone without saying in antebellum ordination examinations. These young ministers came to be called modernist, a name attached by the early twentieth century to a movement that was still amorphous in previous decades. Modernism assumed that in each age, the gospel must be interpreted in the language of contemporary culture and that God is immanent in that culture, which is progressing toward the kingdom of God on earth. Many felt that the emphasis on immanence tended toward humanism and lacked the mystery and awe associated with a transcendent deity. The idea of progress was the most widely accepted modernist principle, but there was less agreement on the goals of progress.

Some put their energies into Protestant union and organized the Federal Council of Churches. Others felt that the purification of politics, business, and culture depended on raising women to equality with men. The modernist tendency to promote the social gospel, that institutions need to be saved as well as individuals, further distanced them from the fundamentalists, especially since some social gospellers were Christian socialists. In a period of Balkan, Asian, and African wars, many Christians hoped for peace through a world court or world government. Fears evoked by the flood of East European immigration before World War I encouraged the eugenics movement for the improvement of humanity, with its racist and antisemitic overtones. These were only the more popular of the astonishing variety of twentieth-century religious movements, from healing to hallucination and from liturgical reform to lay empowerment.

All this concern with the world instead of the hereafter was alarming "secularization" to the fundamentalists of the new century. To the unaffiliated, the secular had been gaining ground for a long time. Only the modernists refused to see the trend as detracting from religion. To them it was just the opposite: The spirit of religion was penetrating the whole culture.

What was happening in other aspects of American culture was also happening to Vermont religion. Those of all faiths or none talked local control but accepted and used power beyond the town and parish. The exasperation of evangelicals with modernists for being "soft on science" would lead to ruptures soon. Both sides had prescriptions for what they understood to be the ills of society. Some had a vague sense that they ought to do something for the working poor, and those with handicaps. Many in the middle thought in terms of Christian Endeavor, the YMCA, and the elimination of the saloon and the Sunday edition. Few church people had plans to overhaul the whole society. Dominant Protestantism had not won the world for Christ in the past century, but felt undefeated and willing to keep striving onward and upward.

Other conclusions about the legacy of the nineteenth century all emphasize the fundamental pluralism of American and therefore Vermont society. Though without racial diversity, Vermont had increasing ethnic diversity, contributing to the ever-widening religious diversity. For the first time, in the 1880s, religious pluralism had reached beyond Christianity with the arrival of organized Jewry. Before another century closed, however, all the world religions were represented by the latest immigrants and converts to their faiths. Pluralism meant competition for members and continued change in the balance of religious forces.

Bibliography

Aiken, Wellington E. "Benson (1783-1933) in Epitome." *Vermont Quarterly*, 19 (July 1951): 147-158.

Allen, C. E. *About Burlington, Vermont.* Burlington: Hobart J. Shanley, 1905.

Allen, Ethan. *A Narrative of Col. Ethan Allen's Captivity.* Burlington: H. Johnson, 1838.

————. *Reason the Only Oracle of Man.* Bennington: Anthony Haswell. 1784.

Allen, Ira (1751-1814). *The Natural and Political History of the State of Vermont.* London: J. W. Myers, 1798.

Allen, Ira. *Thoughts on the Practice of Hiring Preaching.* Weathersfield: Isaac Eddy for the author, 1816.

Altherr, Thomas L. "'The Fanatics in Grand Conclave': The Rutland, Vermont, Free or Reform Convention of 1858," Rutland Historical Society *Quarterly*, 29: 33-48 (1999).

Anderson, Elin L. *We Americans: A Study of Cleavage in an American City.* Cambridge: Harvard University Press, 1937.

Andrews, Edward D. "The County Grammar Schools and Academies of Vermont." Vermont Historical Society *Proceedings* 4 (September 1936): 117-211.

Andrews, Mary Raymond Shipman. *The Perfect Tribute.* New York: Scribner, 1906.

Asbury, Francis. *Journal and Letters.* 3 vols. London: Epworth Press, and Nashville: Abingdon Press, 1958.

Atwood, Mary-John. "Women Ministers of Vermont." *Rural Vermonter* 1 (Fall 1962):16-20.

Audet, Jean-Frédéric. *Histoire de la Congrégation Canadienne de Winooski, au Vermont.* Montreal: Imprimerie de l'Institution des Sourds-Muets, 1906.

Auld, Joseph. *Picturesque Burlington: A Handbook of Burlington, Vermont, and Lake Champlain.* Burlington: Free Press, 1893.

Avery, David. *The Papers of David Avery 1746-1818.* ed. J. M. Mulder. Princeton: Princeton Theological Seminary, 1979.

Avery, David. *Narrative of the Rise and Progress of the Difficulties Which Have Issued in the Separation Between the Minister and People of Bennington, 1783; With a Valedictory Address.* Bennington: Haswell and Russell, 1783.

Bail, Hamilton Vaughn. "Zadock Wright, That 'Devilish' Tory of Hartland." *Vermont History* 36 (Autumn 1968): 186-203.

Bailey, Albert H. *A Sermon Sketching the History of the Protestant Episcopal Church in Vermont.* Montpelier: Argus and Patriot Job Printing, 1882.

Bailey, Elijah. *Thoughts on the Nature and Principles of Government Both Civil and Ecclesiastical.* Bennington, 1828.

Bailey, Horace Ward. *Vermonter: A Memorial by his Friends* ed. Frank L. Fish. Rutland: Tuttle, 1914.

Bailyn, Bernard. *Voyagers to the West.* New York: Knopf, 1986.

Baker, Charles Baker. *Second Annual Report on the Geology of the State of Vermont.* Burlington: Free Press, 1846.

Ballou, Adin. *An Elaborate History and Genealogy of the Ballous.* Providence: E. L. Freeman and Son, 1888.

Bandel, Betty. *Sing the Lord's Song in a Strange Land: The Life of Justin Morgan.* Rutherford, N.J.: Fairleigh Dickinson University Press, 1981.

Barclay, Robert. *Barclay's Apology in Modern English.* ed. Dean Freiday. Manasquam, N.J.: Dean Freiday (Sowers Printing), 1967.

[Barnes, Melvin]. *A Circular, or Short Biography of Col. Ebenezer Allen, Known as Captain or Major, in the New Hamnpshire Grants, and Its Rangers, A. D., 1777, and After* [Grand Isle, Dec. 1851]; reprint, Plattsburgh, N.Y.: J. W. Tuttle, 1852.

Barnouw, Eric. "The Benson Exodus of 1833: Mormon Converts and the Westward Movement." *Vermont History* 54 (Summer 1986): 133-148.

Barre, Vermont. Congregational Church. *The Centennial. . .1899.* Barre: E. W. Cummings, 1899.

Barron, Harold Seth. *Those Who Stayed Behind: Rural Society in Nineteenth-Century New England.* New York: Cambridge University Press, 1984.

[Bartlett, N. D.]. *The Home Institute: A Prospective Home for the Unfortunate of All Classes.* Wilmington, Vt.?, 1899.

B[ass], E. C. "Ministers: A Little Study of the General Catalogue of University of Vermont," *University Cynic*, 23 (May 27, 1905): 26-27

Bassett, T. D. S. "Father of a College President: James Buckham (1795-1886)," Chittenden County Historical Society *Bulletin*, 24 (Summer 1989): 4.

————. "Irish Migration to Vermont Before the Famine," Chittenden County Historical Society *Bulletin* No. 4 (March 17, 1966): 1-4.

Bassett, T. D. Seymour. "Brandon Through a Peep-Hole: William M. Field's Record of Preachers, Texts and Attendance at the Brandon Congregational Church, 1855-1856" (TS filed with Field's *Record* at UVM.

————. "Cabin Religion in Vermont, 1724-1791," *Vermont History* 62 (Spring 1994): 69-87.

————. "The Church of the Nazarene in Burlington, 1928-1969." Chittenden County Historical Society *Bulletin* 32 (Winter 1998): 25-30.

————. "The Classical College," in R. V. Daniels, ed., *The University of Vermont*, 81-85.

————. "The College Street Congregational Church, Burlington, and Its First Pastor, 1860-82." *Vermont History* 57 (Spring 1989):103-120.

————. "500 Miles of Trouble and Excitement: Vermont Railroads, 1848-1861." *Vermont History* 49 (Summer 1981): 133-154.

————. *The Growing Edge: Vermont Villages, 1840-1880*. Montpelier: Vermont Historical Society, 1992.

————. *A History of the Vermont Geological Surveys and State Geologists*. Burlington: Vermont Geological Survey, 1976.

————. "'The Mightiest Revival That Burlington Ever Saw' and Its Consequences: The Pine Street Methodist Church, 1855-1866." Chittenden County Historical Society *Bulletin*, 30 (Spring 1996): 7-12.

————."Origins of UVM, 1791-1833: Overview," in Daniels, *University of Vermont*, 9-17.

————. "The Rise of Cornelius P. Van Ness, 1782-1826," Vermont Historical Society *Proceedings*, 10 (March 1942): 3-20.

————. "The Secular Utopian Socialists," in *Socialism and American Life*. ed. Donald Drew Egbert and Stow Persons. 2 vols. Princeton, N. J.: Princeton University Press, 1952, 1:153-211.

————. "Urban Penetration of Rural Vermont, 1840-80." 2 vols. Ph.D. diss. Harvard University, 1952.

————. "Vermont's Nineteenth Century Civil Religion." *Vermont History* 67 (Winter/Spring 1999), 27-53.

————. "Vermont's Second State House: A Temple of Republican Democracy." *Vermont History* 64 (Spring 1996): 99-107.

Bassett, T. D. Seymour, ed. "A Letter by William Lloyd Garrison, Written from Bennington, Vermont, on March 30, 1829," *Vermont History* 37 (Autumn 1969): 256-264.

————. *Outsiders Inside Vermont: Three Centuries of Visitors' Viewpoints on the Green Mountain State*, 1963. 2nd ed. Canaan, N.H.: Phoenix Publishing, 1976.

Bassett Thomas. "Migration of Friends to the Upper Hudson and Champlain Valleys," in Hugh Barbour and others, *Quaker Crosscurrents: Three Hundred Years of Friends in the New York Yearly Meetings* (Syracuse, N.Y.: Syracuse University Press, 1995), 30-36, 38-40.

Bassett, Tom. "History of Religion in Burlington," in *Burlington Free Press*, October 9, 1977 - July 8, 1979. Ira Allen: October 23, 30, 1977; Ethan Allen: November 6, 13, 1977; Dwight L. Moody: February 4, 11, 18, 1979.

Baxter, Norman Allen. *History of the Freewill Baptists: A Study in New England Separatism*. Rochester, N.Y.: American Baptist Historical Society, 1957.

Beach, Mona. See Swift.

Belknap, Jeremy. *History of New Hampshire*. 2 vols. Dover: John Farmer, 1812.

Beers, Frederick W. *Atlas of Addison Co. Vermont, from Actual Surveys*. New York: F. W. Beers, 1871.

————. *Atlas of Rutland Co. Vermont, from Actual Surveys*. New York: F. W. Beers, A. D. Ellis & C. G. Soule, 1869.

Bellesiles, Michael. *Revolutionary Outlaws: Ethan Allen and the Struggle for Independence on the Early American Frontier* Charlottesville: Virginia University Press, 1992.

Benedict, George Grenville. *Vermont in the Civil War: A History of the Part Taken by Vermont Soldiers and Sailors in the War for the Union, 1861-5*. 2 vols. Burlington: Free Press, 1886-1888.

Benedict, David. *A General History of the Baptist Denomination in America and Other Parts of the World*. New York: Lewis Colby, 1848.

Bercuvitz, Richard Alan. "Neighborhood and Community: A Social History of the Jewish Community of Burlington, Vermont (1880-1940)." Master's thesis, University of Vermont, 1994.

Biddle, Arthur W., and Paul A. Eschholz, eds., *The Literature of Vernont: A Sampler*. Hanover: University Press of New England, 1973.

Big Event Band Concert and Lawn Party at the Village Park, Cavendish, Given by the Christian Endeavor Society. . . Friday evening, July 21, 1911, broadside at UVM.

Bigelow, Edwin L., and Nancy H. Otis. *Manchester, Vermont, 1761-1961: A Pleasant Land Among the Mountains*. Manchester: The Town, 1961.

Black, Jeannette D., and William G. Roelker, ed. *A Rhode Island Chaplain in the Revolution*. Fort Washington, N. Y.: Kennikat Press, 1949.

Blackwell, Marilyn S., and James M. Holway, "Reflections on Jacksonian Democracy and Militia Reform: The Waitsfield Militia Petition of 1836," *Vermont History* 55 (Winter 1987): 5-15

———. *Entitled to Relief: Poor Women, Charity, and Medicine, 1900-1920*. Ann Arbor, MI: UMI Dissertation Services, 1996.

Bleakney, Julia Chappel. "Vermont's Old-Time Camp Meeting." *Vermonter* 43 (February 1938): 34-35.

Blood, Caleb. *A Sermon Preached Before the Honorable Legislature of the State of Vermont, Convened at Rutland, October 11th, 1792. Being the Day of General Election*. Windsor: Alden Spooner, [1792].

Blow, David J. "The Brattleboro School Affair: An Episode in Vermont Catholic History," *Vermont Catholic Tribune*, 23 (February 16, 1979), 1, 3.

———. "The Catholic Parochial Schools of Burlington, 1853-1918," *Vermont History* 54 (Summer 1986): 149-163.

———. "The Establishment and Erosion of French Canadian Culture in Winooski, Vermont, 1867-1900." *Vermont History* 43 (Winter 1975): 59-74.

———. *Historic Guide to Burlington Neighborhoods*. ed Lilian Baker Carlisle. 2 vols. Burlington: Chittenden County Historical Society, 1991-1997.

———. "St. Joseph's College, 1884-91." Chittenden County Historical Society *Bulletin*, 2 (June 12, 1967): 1-7.

Bogart, Walter Thompson. *The Vermont Lease Lands*. Montpelier: Vermont Historical Society, 1950.

Bradley, A. Day. See Hughes, C. W. "Quaker Meetings."

Bratt, James D. "The Reorientation of American Protestantism, 1835-1845." *Church History* 67 (March 1998): 52-82.

Brooke, John L. *The Refiner's Fire: The Making of Mormon Cosmology, 1644-1844.* New York: Cambridge University Press, 1994.

Brown, Clark. *The Moral and Benevolent Design of Christianity and Freemasonry.* Danville: Ebenezer Eaton, 1808.

———. *The Utility of Moral and Religious Societies and of the Masonick in Particular.* Keene, N.H.: John Prentiss, 1814.

Brush, George Robert. *St. James' Episcopal Church, Arlington, Vermont.* Arlington: G. R. Brush, 1941.

Burlington, Vt. Cathedral Church of St. Paul. Document Committee. *A Goodly Heritage: The Episcopal Church in Vermont.* ed. Kenneth S. Rothwell. Burlington: The Committee (George Little, Pr.), 1973.

Burlington, Vt. First Congregtional Church. *The Hundredth Anniversary of the Founding of the First Church, Burlington, Vt.,* Burlington: The Church, 1905.

Burlington, Vt. St. Joseph Church. ed. Robert J. Keenan and Francis R. Privé. *History of Saint Joseph Parish, Burlington, Vermont, 1830-1987.* Burlington: The Parish, 1988.

Burrage, Henry S. *History of the Baptists in Maine.* Portland: Marks Printing, 1904.

Burton, Asa. *The Life of Asa Burton, Written by Himself.* ed. Charles Latham, Jr. Thetford, Vt.: First Congregational Church, 1973.

Butler, Jonathan M. See Numbers, Donald L.

Buzzell, John. *The Life of Elder Benjamin Randal.* Limerick, Maine: Hobb, Woodman, 1827.

Cabot, Mary R. *Annals of Brattleboro, 1681-1895.* 2 vols. Brattleboro: E. L. Hildreth, 1921.

Canfield, Mary Grace. *Lafayette in Vermont.* Rochester, N.Y.: Canfield and Tack, 1934.

———. *The Valley of the Kedron: The Story of the South Parish, Woodstock, Vermont.* South Woodstock: Kedron Associates, 1940.

Carleton, Hiram. ed. *Genealogical and Family History of the State of Vermont.* 2 vols. New York and Chicago: Lewis Publishing, 1903.

Carlisle, Lilian Baker. See Blow, *Historic Guide,* and *Look Around Colchester.*

Carpenter, George N. *History of the Eighth Regiment, Vermont Volunteers, 1861-1865.* Boston: Deland and Barta, 1866.

Carpenter, Jonathan. *Jonathan Carpenter's Journal: Being the Diary of a Revolutionary War Soldier and Pioneer Settler of Vermont,* ed. Miriam and Wes Herwig. Randolph Center:Greenhill Books, 1994.

Carroll, Bret E. *Spiritualism in Antebellum America*. Bloomington: Indiana University Press, 1997.

Castle, Cassius A. *A History of the Methodist Episcopal Church in Burlington, Vermont*. Burlington: Free Press Association, 1903.

[Cate, Weston A.]. "Spring Grove Revisited." *Vermont History News*, 28 (May-June 1977): 44-46.

Catholic Young Men's Union. Burlingon, Vermont. *Constitution and By-Laws*. Burlington: Free Press Association, 1896.

Cazden, Elizabeth. *Antoinette Brown Blackwell: A Biography*. Old Westbury, N.Y.: Feminist Press, 1983.

Chase, Frederick. *A History of Dartmouth College and the Town of Hanover, New Hampshire*, ed. John K. Lord. vol. 1. Cambridge: John Wilson and Son, 1891.

Child, Hamilton, comp., *Gazetteer and Business Directory of Windsor County, Vt., for 1883-84*. Syracuse: Journal Office, 1884.

Civil War Soldier Correspondents, see Wickham.

Cleghorn, Sarah N. *Threescore: The Autobiography of Sarah N. Cleghorn*. New York: Harrison Smith and Robert Haas, 1936.

Clifford, Deborah P. "Abby Hemenway's Road to Rome." *Vermont History*, 63 (Fall 1995): 197-213.

———. "The Women's War Against Rum." *Vermont History* 52 (Summer 1984): 141-160.

Coates, Walter J. *Masonry: A Church Outside the Church*. North Montpelier: Driftwind Press, 1934.

Cockerham, B. F. "Levi Allen (1746-1801): Opportunism and the Problem of Allegiance." M.A. thesis, University of Vermont, August 1965.

Coffin, Howard. *Full Duty: Vermonters in the Civil War*. Woodstock: Countryman Press, 1993.

———. *Nine Months to Gettysburg: Stannard's Vermonters and the Repulse of Pickett's Charge*. Woodstock: The Countryman Press, 1997.

Colby, John. *The Life, Experience and Travels of John Colby [1787-1817], Preacher of the Gospel*. 1815; Dover, N. H.: Free-Will Baptist Printing, 1854.

Collamer, Jacob. *Oration Delivered at Fairfax, Vt., On the Anniversary of American Independence, July 4th, 1811*. Burlington: Samuel Mills, 1811.

[Collamer]. *Addresses on the Presentation of the Statue of Jacob Collamer, of Vermont, by Hon. James M. Tyler, of Vermont, Hon. Geo. B. Loring, of Massachusetts, Hon. Alexander H. Stephens, of Georgia, delivered in the House of Representatives, Tuesday,*

February 15, 1881. Washington [Government Printing Office], 1881.

Committee for a New England Bibliography. 8 vols. *Bibliographies of New England History.* Boston and Hanover: The Committee, 1976-1990.

Comstock, John M. *The Congregational Churches of Vermont and Their Ministry, 1762-1942.* 1914; St. Johnsbury: The Cowles Press, 1942.

Comstock, John M. ed. *Principal Civil Officers of Vermont.* See Vermont. Secretary of State.

Conforti, Joseph A. *Samuel Hopkins and the New Divinity Movement: Calvinism, the Congregational Ministry, and Reform in New England Between the Great Awakenings.* Grand Rapids: William B. Eerdmans, 1981.

Coolidge, Guy Omeron. "The French Occupation of the Champlain Valley from 1609 to 1759," Vermont Historical Society *Proceedings* n.s. 6 (September 1938): 143-313, with *Biographical Index,* Montpelier: Vermont Historical Society, 1938; 40p.

Coolidge, Grace Goodhue. *Grace Coolidge: An Autobiography.* Worland, Wyo.: High Plains Publishing, 1992.

Corby, William. C.S.C. *Memoirs of Chaplain Life.* ed. Lawrence S. Kohl. 1893; New York: Fordham University Press, 1992.

Cox, Francis A. *Baptists in America: A Narrative of the Deputation from the Baptist Union in England to the United states and Canada.* London: T. Ward, 1836.

Crespel, Emmanuel. *Travels in North America.* London: printed by and for S. Low, 1797.

Crockett, Larrimore Clyde. *Safe Thus Far: A History of the Guilford Congregational Church, a.k.a. The Guilford Community Church, United Church of Christ in Guilford, Vermont, 1767-1997. With Appendices.* Dummerston: Black Mountain Press, 1999.

Crockett, Walter H. *Vermont: The Green Mountain State.* 5 vols. New York: Century History, 1921-1923.

Crocker, Henry. *History of the Baptists in Vermont.* Bellows Falls: P.H. Bobie Press, 1913.

Cross, Whitney R. *The Burned-Over District: The Social and Intellectual History of Enthusiastic Religion in Western New York, 1800-1850.* 1950; New York: Harper & Row, 1965.

Cunningham, Patrick. "Irish Catholics in a Yankee Town: A Report About Brattleboro, 1847-1898," *Vermont History* 44 (Fall 1976): 189-197.

Curti, Merle E. *The Growth of American Thought*, 3rd ed. New York: Columbia University Press, 1946.

Daggett, Malcolm D. "Vermont's French Newspapers." *Vermont History* 27 (January 1959): 69-75.

Dana, Henry S. *History of Woodstock, Vermont.* Boston: Houghton Mifflin, 1889.

Daniels, Robert V. ed. See University of Vermont.

Dann, Kevin T. "The Natural Sciences and George Henry Perkins," in Daniels, *The University of Vermont*, 138-159.

Davies, E. *History of Silver Lake Camp Meeting, near Brandon, Vermont.* Reading, Mass.: Holiness Book Concern, [1887?].

Davis, Almond H. *The Female Preacher, or, Memoir of Salome Lincoln, Afterwards the Wife of Elder Junia S. Mowry.* Providence, R.I.: J. S. Mowry, 1843.

Dawson, Adele Godchaux. *James Franklin Gilman, Nineteenth Century Painter.* Canaan, N.H.: Phoenix Publishing, 1975.

Day, Jeremiah. "A Missionary Tour to Vermont, 1788." Vermont Historical Society *Proceedings*, n.s. 1: (Dec. 1930): 169-176.

De Puy, Henry W. *Ethan Allen and the Green Mountain Boys of '76.* Buffalo: Phinney, 1853.

Desmond, Harry W. "A Forgotten Colonial Church." *Architectural Record*, 14 (August 1903), 94-106.

Dewey, John. "Biography of John Dewey. . . by [his] . . .daughters. . . from material which he furnished," in *The Philosophy of John Dewey.* ed. P. A. Schilpp. 2nd ed. New York: Tudor Publishing, 1951.

Dewhurst, Frederick E. *A Memorial: Frederic E. Dewhurst, Pastor of the University Congregational Church of Chicago, Illinois.* Chicago: Priv.Pr., 1907.

Demos, John. *The Undredeemed Captive: A Family Story From Early America.* New York: A. A. Knopf, 1994.

Dexter, Franklin B. *Biographical Sketches of the Graduates of Yale College: With Annals of the College History.* 6 vols. New York: Holt, 1885-1912.

Dickens, Charles, and Thomas P. James. *The Mystery of Edwin Drood, Complete.* 1870; Brattleboro: T. P. James, 1873; 284 out of its 488 pages, according to James, delivered by the spirit of Dickens through James.

Doan, Ruth Alden. *The Miller Heresy: Millenialism and American Culture.* Philadelphia: Temple University Press, 1987.

Dollier de Casson, François. *Histoire de Montréal.* ed. Ralph Flenley. London: Dent-Dutton, 1928.

Dow, Lorenzo. *History of Cosmopolite; or, The Four Volumes of Lorenzo Dow's Journal Concentrated in One, Containing his Experience and Travels, from Childhood to Near his Fiftieth Year. . . . Also his Polemical Writings. . . to Which is Added the `Journey of Life' of Peggy Dow*, 5th ed. Wheeling, Va.: Joshua Martin, 1848.

Draper, John William. *History of the Conflict Between Religion and Science.* New York: Appleton, 1875.

Drysdale, Alexander B. *Bennington's Book: Being the Complete Chronicle of a New England Village.* [Troy, N.Y.: Troy Times Art Pr.], 1927.

Duffy, John J., ed. *Coleridge's American Disciples: The Selected Correspondence of James Marsh.* Amherst: University of Massachusetts Press, 1973.

Duffy, John J., and H. Nicholas Muller III, "An Aesculapius of the Soul," in *An Anxious Democracy: Aspects of the 1830s.* Westport, Conn.: Greenwood Press, 1982, 17-42.

Duquette, Marion. *The Sisters of Mercy of Vermont, 1872-1991.* [Burlington: Sisters of Mercy], 1991.

Durick, Jeremiah K. "The Catholic Church in Vermont: A Centenary History," in *One Hundred Years of Achievement by the Catholic Church in the Diocese of Burlington, Vermont.* Burlington: The Diocese, 1953, 25-29.

Dwight, Timothy. *Travels in New England and New York.* 1821-1822. ed. Barbara Miller Solomon and Patricia M. King. 4 vols. Cambridge, Mass.: Harvard University Press, 1969.

Earle, A. B. *Bringing In Sheaves.* 1868; Boston: James H. Earle, 1884.

Eastman, C. G. *Sermons, Addresses & Exhortations by Rev. Jedediah Burchard: With an Appendix, Containing Some Account of Proceedings During Protracted Meetings, Held Under His Direction, in Burlington, Williston, and Hinesburgh, Vt., December, 1835 and January, 1836.* Burlington: Chauncey Goodrich, 1836.

Edwards, Robert L. *Of Singular Genius, Of Singular Grace: A Biography of Horace Bushnell.* Cleveland: Pilgrim Press, 1992.

Ellis, William Arba. *Norwich University, 1819-1911: Her History, Her Graduates, Her Roll of Honor.* 3 vols. Montpelier: Capital City Press, 1911.

Emerson, Eleanor Read. *The Religious Experiences of Eleanor Read Emerson, Formerly Preceptress of a School in Bennington.* Bennington: Anthony Haswell, 1809.

Eno, Paul F. "Quest for a Civil War Chaplain." *Vermont Catholic Tribune,* (14 August 1974).

Eschholz, Paul A. See Biddle.

Estabrook, Seeley. "The Story of the Silver Lake Camp Meetings." *Middlebury Valley Voice*, (July 9, 1975), 3, 28; (July 16, 1975), 17, 27.

Ethan Allen Engine Company. *Exercises Attending the Twenty-Fifth Anniversary of Ethan Allen Engine Company Number 4, Burlington, Vermont. April 14th, 1882. Including Historical Address by Hon. George H. Bigelow*. Burlington: Free Press Association, 1882.

Fairbanks, Edward T. *The Town of St. Johnsbury Vt: A Review of One Hundred Twenty-five Years to the Anniversary Pageant, 1912*. St. Johnsbury: Cowles Press, 1914.

————. *The Wrought Brim: Twelve Discourses Given in the South Church, St. Johnsbury, Vermont*. St. Johnsbury: W. W. Hubbard, Caledonian Press, 1902.

Fairbanks, Henry. "The Influence of Congregationalism." Offprint from newspaper, n.p., n.d. [1895]. At University of Vermont.

Festinger, Leon. *When Prophecy Fails*. New York: Harper and Row, 1964.

Finke, Roger, and Rodney Stark. *The Churching of America, 1776-1990: Winners and Losers in Our Religious Economy*. New Brunswick: Rutgers University Press, 1992.

Fisher, Dorothy Canfield. *The Vermont Tradition: a Biography of an Outlook on Life*. Boston: Little, Brown, 1953.

Fisk, Wilbur. *Hard Marching Every Day: The Civil War Letters of Private Wilbur Fisk, 1861-1865*. 1983; Lawrence, Kan.: University Press of Kansas, 1992.

Fletcher, Robert S. *The History of Oberlin College*. Oberlin: Oberlin College, 1943.

Forefathers' Day, 271st Anniversary: Proceedings at Middlebury, Vermont, Monday Evening, December 21, 1891. Middlebury: Middlebury Historical Society, 1891.

Forest, Jon R. "An Exposition of Revivals az[sic] Exemplified at the Pine Street Methodist Episcopal Church, Burlington, Vermont, February 1858." In *Leterz, Moral Political and Theological*, 2 (February 1858), 1.

Free Baptist Cyclopaedia. ed. Gideon A. Burgess and J. T. Ward. Chicago: Free Baptist Cyclopaedia, 1889.

Freewill Baptist Connection. *Minutes of the General Conference of the Freewill Baptist Connection*. Dover: Freewill Baptist Printing, 1859.

Freeman, Stephen A. *The Congregational Church of Middlebury, Vermont, 1790-1990: A Bicentennial History.* Middlebury: The Church, 1990.

Fraetax, Josiah A. See Melville, J. [pseud.]

Fulop, Timothy E. "Gospel Liberty, Freewill Baptists and the Christian Connection: Charisma and Routinization in Early National New England." Paper presented at the American Society of Church History meeting, April 12, 1996.

Gale, David C. *Proctor: The Story of a Marble Town.* Brattleboro: Vermont Printing, 1922.

Gay, Bunker. "A Particular Account of the Captivity of Mrs. Jemima Howe, by the Rev. Bunker Gay, of Hinsdale, in a Letter to the Author," in Jeremy Belknap. *History of New Hampshire.* 3 vols. Dover: John Farmer, 1812, 3:177-190.

Geno, Thomas H. "From Le Mont-Saint-Michel to Saint Michael's College: Early Edmundite Years in Vermont, 1892-1904." Paper presented to the Center for Research on Vermont, Burlington, February 1992.

Giddings, Sarah Powell. *In the Enemies Land: A Personal Experience.* Chicago: Regan Printing, 1899.

Gilbert, Alfred Holley. *Parsons Stuart Pratt, D.D. Life and Ministry, Dorset, Vermont, 1822-1906.* Dorset: Dorset Historical Society, 1975.

Gillies, Paul S. See Sanford, D. Gregory

Gilman, Marcus Davis. *The Bibliography of Vermont, or, A List of Books and Pamphlets Relating in Any Way to the State. With Biographical and Other Notes.* ed. George Grenville Benedict. Burlington: Free Press, 1897.

Gilmore, William J. *Reading Becomes a Necessity of Life: Material and Cultural Life in Rural New England, 1780-1835.* Knoxville: University of Tennessee Press, 1989.

Goen, C. C. "The Evangelical Bond," in *Broken Churches, Broken Nation: Denominational Schisms and the Coming of the Civil War.* Macon, Ga.: Mercer University Press, 1985.

Goesbriand, Louis de. "Reverend William Henry Hoyt." *Catholic Memoirs of Vermont and New Hampshire.* Burlington: The Author, 1886.

Goldman, Hal. Ph.D. diss. in progress, University of Massachusetts.

Goodrich, John E. "Immigration to Vermont: Was Immigration to Vermont Stimulated—and To What Extent—in the Years 1760-90 by Persecution on the Part of the 'Standing Order' in Massachusetts and Connecticut." *Vermont Review* 1 (January-February 1907): 23-28, 70-74.

Goss, C. C. *Statistical History of the First Century of American Methodism*. New York: Carlton and Porter, 1866.

Graffagnino, J. Kevin. "The Vermont `Story': Continuity and Change in Vermont Historiography," *Vermont History* 46 (Spring 1978): 77-99.

Greene, Florence. "Methodism in Burlington." Chittenden County Historical Society *Bulletin*, 15 (April 1980): 6-8.

Gribbin, William. "Vermont's Universalist Controversy of 1824." *Vermont History* 41 (Spring 1973): 82-94.

Griswold, Rufus W. "Ethan Allen. Written on Visiting His Tomb, Near Burlington, Vt." *New-Yorker* 9 (July 18, 1840), 275.

Guilford. *Official History of Guilford, Vermont, 1678-1961. With Genealogies and Biographical Sketches*. Guilford: The Town and Broad Brook Grange No. 151, 1961.

Guyette, Elise. "Black Lives and White Racism in Vermont, 1760-1870." Master's thesis, University of Vermont, 1992.

Hamm, Thomas D. *God's Government Begun: The Society for Universal Inquiry and Reform, 1842-1846*. Bloomington, Indiana: Indiana University Press, 1995.

Handbook of Salvation Army Doctrine. New York: Salvation Army, 1923.

Hannon, Patrick T. *Historical Sketches on West Rutland, Vermont, Celebrating Its Centennial, 1886-1986*. ed. Victor A. and Ethel P. Sevigny. Rutland: Academy Books, 1986.

[Hastings, Susannah Willard Johnson]. *A Narrtive of the Captivity of Mrs. Johnson...1796*. 3rd ed. Windsor, Vt.: Thomas Pomeroy, 1814.

Haviland, William A., and Marjory W. Power. *The Original Vermonters: Native Inhabitants, Past and Present*. 2nd ed. Hanover, N. H.: University Press of New England, 1994.

Hayes, Lyman Simpson, and William Danvorth Hayes. *The Old Rockingham Meeting House, Erected 1787 and the First Church in Rockingham, Vermont, 1773-1840*. Bellows Falls: P. H. Gobie, pr.,1915.

Hayward, John. *A Gazetteer of Vermont: Containing Descriptions of All the Counties, Towns, and Districts in the State, and of its Principal Mountains, Rivers, Waterfalls, Harbors, Islands, and Curious Places. To Which are Added, Statistical Accounts of Its Agriculture, Commerce and Manufactures; With a Great Variety of Other Useful Information*. Boston: Tappan, Whittemore, and Mason, 1849.

Headley, Joel Tyler. *The Chaplains and Clergy of the Revolution*. New York: Charles Scribner, 1864.

Healy, Michael J. *Walking in the Spirit: Fanny Allen Hospital, 1894 to 1994*. Colchester: The Hospital, 1993.

Hemenway, Abby Maria, ed. *Poets and Poetry of Vermont*. Rutland: Charles A. Tuttle, 1858.

Hemenway, Abby Maria, ed. See *Vermont Historical Gazetteer*.

Henderson, Moses C., and J. Phillips. *An Historical Sketch of the Vermont Yearly Meeting of Free Will Baptists from 1808 to 1889*. St. Johnsbury: Republican Press, 1890.

Higham, John. *From Boundlessness to Consolidation: The Transformation of American Culture, 1848-1860*. Ann Arbor: William L. Clements Library, 1969.

Hill, George W. C. "The Union Church, Proctor, Vermont." *Vermonter* 8 (February 1903): 231-232.

Hill, Ralph Nading. *Yankee Kingdom*. New York: Harper, 1960.

Himes, Joshua V. *Views of the Prophecies and Prophetic Chronology, Selected From the Manuscripts of William Miller, With a Memoir of His Life*. Boston: J. V. Himes, 1841.

Hoag, Joseph. *Journal of the Life of Joseph Hoag*. 1861; repr. London: A. W. Bennett, 1862.

Hollister, Hiel. *Pawlet For One Hundred Years*. Albany: Joel Munsell, 1867.

Honeywell, Roy J. *Chaplains of the United States Army*. Washington: Government Printing Office, 1958.

Hopkins. John Henry. *Essay on Gothic Architecture, with Various Plans and Drawings for Churches: Designed Chiefly for the Use of the Clergy*. Burlington: Smith & Harrington, 1836.

————. *Twelve Canzonets: Sacred Songs; Words and Music; for the Use of Christian Families*. Burlington: Chauncey Goodrich, 1840.

[Hopkins, John H., Jr.]. "The Vermont Episcopal Institute," in *The Life of the Right Reverend John Henry Hopkins, First Bishop of Vermont, and Seventh Presiding Bishop*. By one of his sons. New York: F. J. Huntington, 1873, 295-319.

Horace Ward Bailey. See Bailey, Horace Ward.

Hoskins, Nathan. *A History of the State of Vermont*. Vergennes: J. Shedd, 1831.

How, Nehemiah. *A Narrative of the Captivity of Nehemiah How*. Boston: Printed and Sold opposite to the Prison in Queen Street, 1748.

Hoyt, David W. *Hoyt Family: A Genealogical History of John Hoyt of Salisbury and David Hoyt of Deerfield (Massachusetts,) and Their Descendants.* Boston: C. Benjamin Richardson, 1857.

Hubbard, Charles H., and Justus Dartt. *History of the Town of Springfield, Vermont . . . 1752-1895.* Boston: G. M. Walker, 1895.

Hubbell, Seth. *A Narrative of the Sufferings of Seth Hubbell & Family, in his Beginning a Settlement in the Town of Wolcott, in the State of Vermont.* Danville: E. & W. Eaton, 1829.

Huden, John C. *Development of State School Administration in Vermont.* Montpelier: Vermont Historical Society, 1943.

Hughes, Charles W., and A. Day Bradley, "The Early Quaker Meetings of Vermont." *Vermont History* 29 (July 1961): 153-167.

Hughes, Charles W., and Carleton Sprague Smith. *American Hymns, Old and New: Notes on the Hymns and Biographies of the Authors and Composers.* 2 vols. New York: Columbia University Press, 1980.

Hungerford, Edward. *A Report on the Moral and Religious Condition of the Community, Being an Address Before a Union of Evangelical Churches, in the City of Burlington, Vt., Delivered in the White St. Cong. Church, March 10, 1867.* Burlington: Free Press Steam Print., 1867.

Huntington, Lee Pennock. *Brothers in Arms.* Taftsville, Vt.: The Countryman Press, 1976.

Hurd, John Laurence. *Kurn Hattin: The Story of Home.* Westminster, Vt.: Kurn Hattin Home, 1989.

Hutchinson, Harriet. "The Girl He Left Behind: The Letters of Harriet Hutchinson Salisbury." ed. Allen F. Davis. *Vermont History* 33 (January 1965): 274-282.

Hutchinson, Paul. *The Story of the Epworth League.* New York: Methodist Book Concern, 1927.

Hutchison, William R. *The Modernist Impulse in American Protestantism.* Cambridge and London: Harvard University Press, 1976.

Jacob, Stephen. *A Poetical Essay, Delivered at Bennington on the Anniversary of the 16th of August, 1777. . . 1778.* Hartford: Watson & Goodwin, 1779, reprinted in Vermont Historical Society *Collections*, 1:263-270.

James, Thomas P. See Dickens.

Jennings, Isaac. *Memorials of a Century: Embracing a Record of Individuals and Events, Chiefly in the Early History of Bennington, Vt., and its First Church.* Boston: Gould and Lincoln, 1869.

————. *The One Hundred Year Old Meetinghouse of the Church of Christ in Bennington, Vermont; Being a Record of the Centennial of the Same Held in the Meetinghouse, August the 19th and 20th, 1906.* Cambridge, Massachusetts: Riverside Press, 1907.

Jennison, Peter S. *The History of Woodstock, Vermont, 1890-1993.* Woodstock: The Countryman Press, 1985.

Johnson, Ithiel T. *Story of My Life.* Burlington: Free Press Printing, 1912.

Johnson, Otto T. tr. See Svenskarna...

Johnson, Susannah Willard. *A Narrative of the Captivity of Mrs. .Johnson.* 3rd ed. Windsor: Thomas M. Pomroy, 1814.

Jones, Abner. *Autobiography.* Exeter, N.H.: Norris & Sawyer for the author, 1807.

Jones, Abner Dumont. *Memoir of Elder Abner Jones.* Boston: W. Crosby, 1842.

Jones, Matt Bushnell. *History of the Town of Waitsfield, Vermont, 1782-1908.* Boston: George E. Littlefield, 1909.

Kaufman, Martin. *The University of Vermont College of Medicine.* Hanover: University Press of New England, 1979.

Kelley, Brooks Mather. *Yale: A History.* New Haven: Yale University Press, 1974.

Kellogg, John. *A Narrative of the Facts Connected With . . . the Author's Withdrawal from the Congregational Church in Benson, Vt., April, 1838.* Castleton: L. R. H. Robinson, 1841.

Krueger, John W. "Troop Life at the Champlain Valley Forts During the American Revolution." Fort Ticonderoga Museum *Bulletin* 14 (September 1982): 165-177.

Lawrence, Robert F. *The New Hampshire Churches: Comprising Histories of the Congregational and Presbyterian Churches in the State, with Notices of Other Denominations. . .* [Claremont]: Published for the Author, 1856.

Lewis, John W. *The Life, Labors, and Travels of Elder Charles Bowles of the Free Will Baptist Denomination.* Watertown, N.Y.: Inglass & Stowell, 1852.

Look Around Colchester and Milton, Vermont. ed. Lilian Baker Carlisle. Burlington: Chittenden County Historical Society, 1975.

Lord, John King. *A History of Dartmouth College, 1815-1909.* Concord, N.H.: Rumford Press, 1913.

Lord, William H. *A Tract for the Times: National Hospitality.* Montpelier: E. P. Walton, 1855.

Lossing, Benson J. *The Pictorial Field-Book of the Revolution.* New York: Harper, 1851.

Lovejoy, Evelyn Mary Wood. *History of Royalton, Vermont*. Royalton: The Town and the Republican Woman's Club, 1911.

Lucey, William Leo. "The Diocese of Burlington, Vermont: 1853," *Records of the American Catholic Historical Society of Philadelphia*, 44 (Sept. 1953): 123-149; "The Position of Catholics in Vermont: 1853," (Dec. 1953): 213-235.

Ludlum, David M. *Social Ferment in Vermont, 1791-1850*. New York: Columbia University Press, 1939.

Lund, John M. "Vermont Nativism: William Paul Dillingham and U.S. Immigration Legislation." *Vermont History* 63(Winter 1995): 16-29.

MacDonald, Edith Fox. *Rebellion in the Mountains: The Story of Universalism and Unitarianism in Vermont*. Concord, N.H.: Unitarian Universalist Association, New Hampshire-Vermont District, 1976.

Manchester, Vt. Zion Episcopal Church. *Jubilate: A History of the Zion Episcopal Church, 1782-1982*. North Adams, Excelsior Printing, 1982.

Map of the State of Vermont As It Was About A. D. 1791, A. Montpelier: Vermont Department of Highways, 1941.

[Margaret of Scotland] (Sister). *Light in the Tower: William Henry Hoyt (1813-1883); Episcopal Minister, Lawyer, Editor, Organist, Catholic Priest*. By a Sister of Charity of Providence. Montreal, 1950.

Marini, Stephen A. *Radical Sects of Revolutionary New England*. Cambridge: Harvard University Press, 1982.

Marsh, Leonard. *The Shadow of Christianity, or, The Genesis of the Christian State: A Treatise for the Times*. New York: Hurd and Houghton, 1865.

Marshall, Jeffrey D. *A War of the People: Vermont Civil War Letters*. Hanover: University Press of New England, 1999.

Marvin, Cynthia L. "Y.P.S.C.E." *Vermonter* 1 (Apr. 1896): 176-177.

Mathews, Shailer. "The Faith of a Modernist," in *American Christianity: An Interpretation with Historical Documents*. ed. H. Shelton Smith, Robert T. Handy, and Lefferts A. Loetscher. 2 vols. New York: Scribner's, 1963.

Matlack, Lucius S. *The Life of Rev. Orange Scott*. New York: C. Prindle and L. S. Matlack, 1847.

Maxwell, C. Mervyn. *Tell It To the World*. Boise, Idaho: Pacific Press, 1977.

McCorison, Marcus A. *Vermont Imprints, 1778-1820.* Worcester: American Antiquarian Society, 1963. The compiler refers to "Additions and Corrections" of 1968, 1973, 1985, and 1992 in the introduction to what he hopes is a final list, in *Vermont History*, 67 (Winter/Spring 1999): 54-66.

McGiffert, Michael. "Christian Darwinism: The Partnership of Asa Gray and George Frederick Wright, 1874-1881." Ph.D. diss. Yale University, 1958.

McKeen, Silas. *A History of Bradford, Vermont.* Montpelier: J. D. Clark, 1875.

————. *Sermon on Romanism.* Bradford?, 1854.

McKinley, Edward H. *Marching to Glory: The History of the Salvation Army in the United States of America, 1880-1980.* New York: Harper and Row, 1980.

McWilliams, John. "The Faces of Ethan Allen, 1760-1860." *New England Quarterly* 49 (June 1976): 257-282.

Melville, J. [pseud. for Josiah A. Fraetax]. *Ethan Allen: or, The King's Men, an Historical Novel.* New York: W. H. Graham, 1846.

Memorial of Rev. Simeon Parmelee, D. D. Boston: Beacon Press, 1882.

Merrill, Charles Henry. *An Historical Address in Commemoration of the One Hundredth Anniversary of the Vermont Do mestic Missionary Society, Before the Meeting Held in Lyndonville, May 22, 1918.* [St. Johnsbury: Cowles Press, 1918].

Messner, William F. "General John Wolcott Phelps and Conservative Reform in Nineteenth Century America." *Vermont History* 53 (January 1985), 17-35.

Michaud, John S. "Diocese of Burlington," in William Byrne et al. *History of the Catholic Church in the New England States.* 2 vols. Boston: Hurd and Everts, 1899.

Mitchell, William. "An Enquiry into the Utility of Modern Evangelists, and Their Measures." *Literary and Theological Review*, 2 (Sept 1835): 494-507.

Montpelier. Bethany Congregational Church. *The Hundredth Anniversary of the Founding of Bethany Congregational Church, Montpelier, Vermont, July 19 and 20, 1908.* Montpelier: Argus and Patriot, 1908.

Moore, James R. *The Post-Darwinian Controversies: A Study of the Protestant Struggle to Come to Terms With Darwin in Great Britain and America, 1870-1900.* Cambridge, England: Cambridge University Press, 1979.

Moore, Hugh. *Memoir of Col. Ethan Allen.* Plattsburgh, N.Y.: O. R. Cook, 1834.

Moore, R. Laurence. *In Search of White Crows: Spiritualism, Parapsychology, and American Culture.* New York: Oxford University Press, 1977.

————. *Religious Outsiders and the Making of Americans.* New York: Oxford University Press, 1986.

————. "The Spiritualist Medium: A Study of Female Professionalism in Victorian America." *American Quarterly,* 27 (May 1975): 212.

Morrill, Milo True. "The Christians." *Vermonter* 8 (Feb. 1903), 228-231.

Morrill, Justin S., and George F. Edmunds. *Report of Justin S. Morrill and George F. Edmunds, Commissioners for Vermont, on the National Statuary Hall, in the Capitol, at Washington.* Montpelier: Walton's Steam Printing, 1866.

Morton, Daniel O. *A Narrative of a Revival of Religion in Springfield, Vermont.* Springfield: The Author, 1834.

Mower, Anna L. *History of Morristown, Vermont, in Morristown Two Times.* Morrisville: Morristown Historical Society, 1982.

Mudge, James. *History of the New England Conference of the Methodist Episcopal Church, 1796-1910.* Boston: The Conference, 1910.

Muller, H. Nicholas, III. See Duffy.

Murphy, Ronald C., and Paul Jeffrey Potash. "The Highgate Affair: Episode in Establishing the Authority of the Roman Catholic Diocese of Burlington." *Vermont History* 52 (Winter 1984): 33-43.

Murray, Donald M., and Robert M. Rodney, "Sylvia Drake, 1784-1868: The Self-Portrait of a Seamstress." *Vermont History* 34 (April 1966): 123-135.

Nash, Hope. *Royalton, Vermont.* Royalton: The Town, South Royalton Woman's Club, Royalton Historical Society, 1975.

New Hampshire Yearly Meeting of Free Baptists. *Centennial Souvenir. . . 1792-1892.* ed. Frederick L. Wiley. Laconia, New Hampshire: Yearly Meeting Board of Directors, 1892.

"New Swedish Church." *Vermont Missionary,* 2 (November 1890), 4.

Newell, Fanny. *Memoirs of Fanny Newell Written by Herself.* Springfield, Massachusetts, 1833.

Newfane, Vt. *Centennial Proceedings and Other Historical Facts and Incidents Relating to Newfane, the County Seat of Windham County, Vermont, 1773-1874.* Brattleboro: DeWitt Leonard, 1877.

Newkirk, McDonald. *Sleeping Lucy.* Chicago: The Author, 1973.

Newton, Earle. *The Vermont Story: A History of the People of the Green Mountain State, 1749-1949*. Montpelier: Vermont Historical Society, 1949.

Nichol, Francis D. *The Midnight Cry: A Defense of the Character and Conduct of William Miller and the Millerites, Who Mistakenly Believed That the Second Coming of Christ Would Take Place in the Year 1844*. Tacoma Park, Washington, D.C.: Review and Herald Publishing, 1944.

Nordbeck, Elizabeth C. "The Legacy of Francis E. Clark." Congregational Library *Bulletin* 47 (Fall 1995-Spring/Summer 1996): 3-13. Presented at Bangor Theological Seminary March 2, 1996 and first published in its *Horizon*, v.2, Spring 1996.

Norwich, Vt. *"Know Your Town": The 1940 Survev of Norwich, Vermont*. Norwich: Norwich Woman's Club, 1942.

Notable American Women, 1607-1950: A Biographical Dictionary. ed. Edward T. James, Janet Wilson James and Paul S. Boyer. 3 vols. Cambridge: Belknap Press of Harvard University Press, 1971.

Noyes, George Wallingford. ed. *John Humphrey Noyes: The Putney Community*. Oneida, N.Y., 1931.

———. *The Religious Experience of John Humphrey Noyes*

Noyes, John Humphrey. *The Religious Experience of John Humphrey Noyes, Founder of the Oneida Community*. ed. George Wallingford Noyes. New York: Macmillan, 1923.

———. *The Way of Holiness*. Putney, Vermont: The Author, 1838.

Numbers, Donald L., and Jonathan M. Butler. *The Disappointed: Millerism and Millenarianism in the Nineteenth Century*. Bloomington: Indiana University Press, 1987.

Nuttall, Geoffrey Fillingham. *The Holy Spirit in Puritan Faith and Experience*. Oxford: Blackwell, 1946.

Nutting, John. *Becoming the United Church of Christ in Vermont, 1795-1995*. Burlington: John Nutting, Christopher Scott, and Nancy Des Coteaux for the Vermont Conference of the United Church of Christ, 1996.

Nye, Mary G. *Vermont's State House*. Montpelier: Vermont Publicity Service, 1936.

O'Callaghan, Jeremiah. *Usury; or, Lending Money at Interest; also, The Exaction and Payment of Certain Church-Fees, Such as Pew-Rents, Burial-Fees, and the Like, Together with Forestalling Traffic, All Proved to be Repugnant to the Divine and Ecclesiastical Law, and Destructive of Civil Society. To Which is Prefixed a Narrative of the Controversy Between the Author and Bishop Coppinger, and of the Sufferings of the Former in Consequence of* *his Adherence to the Truth. With a Dedication to the `Society of Friends.'* 1824; 3rd ed. London: William Cobbett, 1828.

————. *Usury, or Lending at Interest.* New York, 1824.

Olcott, Henry Steel. *Inside the Occult: The True Story of Madame H. P. Blavatsky.* 1st ed. entitled *Old Diary Leaves,* 1875. Philadelphia: Running Press, 1975.

Orton, Vrest. *Mary Fletcher Comes Back.* Burlington: Mary Fletcher Hospital, 1941.

Owen, Barbara. *The Organ in New England . . . Use and Manufacture to the End of the Nineteenth Century.* Raleigh, N.C.: Sunbury Press, 1979.

Parkman, Francis. *The Journal of Francis Parkman.* ed. Mason Wade. 2 vols. New York: Harper, 1947.

Parsons, Cynthia. *"I Never Found a Kindlier People": The Early History of Christian Science in Vermont.* Chester: Vermont Schoolhouse Press, 1996.

Peak, John. *Memoir of Elder Peak, Written by Himself.* Boston: Printed by John Howe, 1832.

Peladeau, Marius B., ed. See Tyler

Perkins, Nathan. *A Narrative of a Tour Through the State of Vermont from April 27 to June 12.* ed. Charles V. S. Borst. 1920; Rutland: Tuttle, 1964.

Perry, John Bulkley. *Discourses Preached in Swanton.* Burlington: Free Press, 1861. At head of title: "Life and Death, or the Recompense of the Righteous and the Wicked on earth."

Perry, Milton L. "The Role of the Camp Meeting in Millerite Revivalism, 1842-1844." Ph.D. diss., Baylor University, 1994.

Persons, Stow. "Christian Communitarianism in America," in *Socialism and American Life.* ed. Donald D. Egbert and Stow Persons. 2 vols. Princeton: Princeton University Press, 1952.

Pettibone, John S. "Early History of Manchester." Vermont Historical Society *Proceedings,* n.s. 1 (Dec. 1930): 147-166.

Pièces Justificatives. Burlington: H. B. Stacy, 1843.

Potash, P. Jeffrey. "Jedediah Burchard and the Revival of 1835," in *Vermont's Burned-over District: Patterns of Community Development and Religious Activity, 1761-1850.* Brooklyn, N.Y: Carlson Publishing, 1991, 171-182.

————. See Murphy.

Power, Marjory W. See Haviland.

Pratt, Parsons Stuart. "State of Religion in Bennington County." *Manchester Journal,* July 16, 1874.

Pringle, Cyrus Guernsey. *The Record of a Quaker Conscience: Cyrus Pringle's Diary.* Intro. by Rufus M. Jones. New York: Macmillan, 1918, repr. as Pendle Hill Pamphlet No. 122, Wallingford, Pa.: Pendle Hill Publications, 1962.

Proceedings of the Free Convention Held at Rutland, Vt., July 25th, 26th, and 27th, 1858. Boston: J. B. Yerrinton, 1858.

A Protest Addressed to the Congregational Churches and Ministers of Vermont. n.p., n.d., unpaged reprint from a Vermont newspaper, perhaps the *Vermont Chronicle.*

Queen City Park Spiritualist Camp Meeting, Queen City Park Hotel, S. Burlington, Vt. Twenty-fourth Annual Assembly, From July 31 to September 4, 1904. Burlington, 1904.

Rambo, Lewis Ray. *Understanding Religious Conversion.* New Haven: Yale University Press, 1993.

Randall, Miranda. *Mystery: Spiritual Manifestations.* Woodstock: Nahum Haskell, 1852.

Raney, William F. "Recruiting and Crimping in Canada, 1861-1865." *Mississippi Valley Historical Review,* 10 (June 1923): 21-33.

Reed, Andrew, and James Matheson. *A Narrative of the Visit to the American Churches by the Deputation from the Congregational Union of England and Wales.* 2 vols. London, 1835.

Reformed Methodist Church. *"History of the Reformed Methodist Church,"* in Israel D. Rupp, ed., *History of All the Religious Denominations in the United States.* Philadelphia: Charles De Silber, 1871, 399-403.

The Reformer's Discipline. Bennington: Printed for the [Reformed Methodist] Society, 1816.

Richardson, George L. *Arthur C. A. Hall, Third Bishop of Vermont.* Boston: Houghton, Mifflin, 1932.

Riggs, Herman C. *The Supremacy of Man: A Thanksgiving Day Sermon Delivered Thursday, Nov. 18, 1869.* St. Albans: E. B. & W. H. Whiting, 1870.

Riley, Gregory. *One Jesus, Many Christs: The Truth About Christian Origins.* San Francisco: Harper, 1997.

Robbins, Ammi R. *Journal of the Rev. Ammi R. Robbins.* New Haven, Conn.: B. L. Hamlen, 1850.

Robbins, Daniel. *The Vermont State House: A History & Guide.* Montpelier: Vermont State House Preservation Committee, 1980.

Roberts, Gwilym. *New Lives in the Valley: Slate Quarries and Quarry Villages in North Wales, New York, and Vermont, 1850-1920.* Somersworth, NH: New Hampshire Printers, 1998.

Rockingham, Vt. First Congregational Church. *Records from Its Orga-nization, October 27, 1773, to September 25, 1839.* Copied by Thomas Bellows Peck, with an Historical Introduction. Boston: David Clapp & Son, 1902. Reprinted from *New England Histori-cal and Genealogical Register*(April 1900 - October 1902).

Rodney, Robert M. See Murray.

Roelker, William G. See Black.

Ross, Henry H. "The Vermont Episcopal Institute and Bishop Hopkins Hall," *Vermonter* (Feb. 2, 1897): 116-120.

Roth, Randolph A. *The Democratic Dilemma: Religion, Reform, and the Social Order in the Connecticut River Valley of Vermont, 1791-1850.* Cambridge: Cambridge University Press, 1987.

————. "Spousal Murder in Northern New England, 1776-1865," in Christine Daniels and Michael V. Kennedy, eds., *Over the Thresh-old: Intimate Violence in Early America, 1640-1865* (New York: Routledge, 1999), 65-93.

Rowley, Thomas. See Biddle and Eschholz.

Rozwenc, Edwin C. *Agricultural Policies in Vermont, 1860-1945.* Montpelier: Vermont Historical Society, 1981.

Rupp, Israel D., ed. "History of the Reformed Methodist Church," in his *History of All the Religious Denominations in the United States.* Philadelphia: Charles De Silber, 1871.

Sabin, Elijah R. *A Discourse on Gospel Discipline in Three Parts.* Windsor: Alden Spooner, 1805.

Sabin, James, ed. See Waterbury.

Safford, George B. "The Irrepressible Conflict," in *Burlington Free Press*, April 10, 1869.

Saillant, John. "A Doctrinal Controversy Between the Hopkintonian and the Universalist: Religion, Race, and Ideology in Post-rev-olu-tionary Vermont." *Vermont History* 61 (Fall 1993): 197-216.

Samuelson, Myron. *The Story of the Jewish Community of Burlington, Vermont.* Burlington: Myron Samuelson, 1976.

Sandall, Robert. *The History of the Salvation Army.* London: Thomas Nelson, 1955.

Sanford, D. Gregory, and Paul S. Gillies, eds. *Records of the Council of Censors of the State of Vermont.* Montpelier, Vt.: Secretary of State, 1991.

Schilpp, see Dewey, John.

Schneider, A. Gregory. *The Way of the Cross Leads Home: The Do-mestication of American Methodism.* Bloomington: Indiana Uni-versity Press, 1993.

Schwartz, Charles Downer, and Ouida Davis Schwarz. *A Flame of Fire: The Story of the Troy Annual Conference.* Rutland: Academy Books, 1982.

————. *A Spreading Flame: The Stories of the Churches of Troy Annual Conference.* Rutland: Troy Conference (Academy Books), 1986.

Schwartz, Ouida Davis. "The History of Missisquoi Campground," duplicated typescript with illus., n.p.: Commission on Archives and History, Troy Annual Conference, June 1990.

Scott, Orange. *An Appeal to the Methodist Episcopal Church* Boston: D. H. Ela, 1838; 156p.

————. *The Grounds of Secession from the M. E. Church: or, Book for the Times Being an Examination of Her Connection with Slavery and Also of Her Form of Government.* rev. ed. New York: C. Prindle, 1848; 229p.

————. *New and Improved Camp-Meeting Hymn Book.* Brookfield, Massachusetts: E. & G. Merriam, 1831.

Seaver, Norman. *Moral Teaching the Duty of the State: A Sermon Delivered in the Congregational Church, Rutland, Vt., August 2nd, 1885.* Rutland: Tuttle, 1885.

Senécal, André Joseph. "The Franco-Americans in Vermont: A Chronology." Prepared for the American Canadian Genealogical Society Fall Conference, Burlington, 1986.

Shaw, Joseph C. "The 'Yankee Priest' Says Mass in Brattleboro: Joseph Coolidge Shaw Describes His Visit in 1848." *Vermont History,* 44 (Fall 1976): 198-202.

Shedd, William Greenough Thayer. "Congregationalism and Symbolism." *Bibliotheca Sacra* (July 1858), reprinted, Andover: Warren F. Draper, 1859.

Shores, Venila Lovina. *Lyndon: Gem in the Green.* ed. Ruth Hopkins McCarty. Lyndonville: Town of Lyndon, 1986.

Shuttlesworth, Samuel. *A Discourse Delivered in Presence of Excellency, Thomas Chittenden, Esq. Governor, His Honor Olcott, Esq. Lieutenant Governor, the Honorable Council, and of Representatives of the State of Vermont: at Windsor, October 1791.* Windsor: Printed by James Reed Hutchins for . . . the Assembly, 1791.

Skinner, Gladys. *Heritage of the Old South Church, Windsor, Vermont.* 1963; [Windsor]: Old South Church, 1976.

Sloane, David C. *The Last Great Necessity: Cemeteries in American History.* Baltimore: Johns Hopkins University Press, 1991.

Smith, Charles Edward. "The Work of the Civil War Chaplains." Master's thesis, University of Arizona, 1965.

Smith, Donald A. "Green Mountain Insurgency: Transformation of New York's Forty-Year Land War." *Vermont History* 64 (Fall 1996): 197-235.

————. "Legacy of Dissent: Religion and Politics in Revolutionary Vermont, 1749-1784." Ph.D. diss. Clark University, 1980; copy in Vermont Historical Society Library.

Smith, Elias. *The Life, Conversion, Preaching, Travels, and Sufferings of Elias Smith, Written by Himself.* Portsmouth, N. H.: Beck & Foster, 1816.

Smith, John Talbot. *A History of the Diocese of Ogdensburg.* New York: John Lovell, 1885.

Smith, Sybil Watts. "One Hundred Years of Caring: The Burlington Cancer Relief Association, 1886-1986." Chittenden County Historical Society *Bulletin*, 22 (Winter 1987): 1-4.

Spargo, John. *Anthony Haswell, Printer-Patriot-Ballader: A Biographical Study with a Selection of His Ballads and an Annotated Bibliographical List of His Imprints.* Rutland: Tuttle, 1925.

Sparks, Jared. *The Life of Col. Ethan Allen.* Boston: Hilliard and Gray, 1834.

Spicer, Tobias. *Autobiography Containing Incidents and Observations; and Some Account of the Visit to England.* 3rd ed. New York: Carlton and Porter, 1860.

Sprague, Achsah. See Twynham.

Sprague, William Buell. *Annals of the American Pulpit; or, Commemorative Notices of Distinguished American Clergymen of Various Denominations, From the Early Settlement of the Country to the Close of the Year 1855.* 9 vols. New York: Robert Carter, 1857-1869.

Stameshkin, David. "Troubled Times, 1835-1880," in *The Town's College: Middlebury College, 1800-1915.* Middlebury: Middlebury College Press, 1985, 126-189.

Stanton, Phoebe B. *The Gothic Revival and American Church Architecture.* Baltimore: Johns Hopkins University Press, 1968.

Stark, Rodney. See Finke, Roger.

Steele, Zadock. *The Indian Captive: or, A Narrative of the Captivity and Sufferings of Zadock Steele. . . . To Which Is Prefixed an Account of the Burning of Royalton.* 1818; Springfield, Massachusetts: H. R. Huntting, 1908.

Stewart, Isaac Dalton. *The History of the Free Will Baptists for Half a Century.* Dover, New Hampshire: Freewill Baptist Printing, 1862.

Stiles, Ezra. *The Literary Diary of Ezra Stiles*, ed. Franklin B. Dexter. 2 vols. New York: C. Scribner's Sons, 1901.

Stilwell, Lewis D. "Migration from Vermont, 1776-1860." Vermont Historical Society *Proceedings*, n.s. 5 (June 1937), 63-245.

Stone, Arthur F. *Vermont of Today: With Its Historic Background, Attractions and People*. 4 vols. New York: Lewis Publishing, 1929.

Stratton, Allen L. *History of the South Hero Island: Being the Towns of South Hero & Grand Isle, Vermont*. North Hero: A. L. Stratton, 1980.

Streeter, Russell. *A Mirror of Calvinistic, Fanatical Revivals, or Jedediah Burchard & Co. During a Protracted Meeting of Twenty-six Days, in Woodstock, To Which is Added the "Preamble and Resolutions" of the Town, Declaring Said Burchard a Nuisance to Society*. Woodstock: The Author, 1835.

Strout, Cushing. "Faith and History: The Mind of William T. Shedd." *Journal of the History of Ideas*, 15 (January 1954): 153-162.

"Svenskarna i Proctor." *Allsvensk Samling* (May 17, 1932). trans. by Otto T. Johnson, at University of Vermont.

Sweet, Douglas Hardy. *Church and Community: Town Life and Ministerial Ideals in Revolutionary New Hampshire*. Ph.D. diss. Columbia University, 1978.

Swift, Esther Munroe, and Mona Beach. *Brattleboro Retreat: 150 Years of Caring, 1834-1984*. Brattleboro: The Retreat, 1984.

————. *Vermont Place Names: Footprints of History*. Brattleboro: Stephen Green Press, 1977.

Thompson, Charles Miner. *Independent Vermont*. Boston: Houghton Mifflin, 1942.

Thompson, Daniel Pierce. *The Green Mountain Boys: A Historical Tale of the Early Settlement of Vermont*. 2 vols. Montpelier: E. P. Walton, 1839.

————. *History of the Town of Montpelier*. Montpelier: E. P. Walton, 1860.

Thompson, Zadock. *History of the State of Vermont*. Burlington: Edward Smith, 1833.

————. *History of Vermont, Natural, Civil, and Statistical*. 3 pts. in 1 vol. Burlington: Chauncey Goodrich, 1842.

Tichenor, Isaac. *Proclamation, for a Day of Humiliation, Fasting and Prayer . . . Given Under My Hand at Bennington, This 18th Day of March, Anno Domini 1805*. n.p., n.d. [Bennington? Haswell & Smead?, 1805]. Copy in Boston Public Library.

Torrey, Henry A. P. "In Memoriam—Abraham Lincoln," undated MS in University of Vermont Archives.

Torrey, Mary C. "A Brief History of the Sunday School," in Burlington. First Congregational Church. *Hundredth Anniversary.* Burlington: The Church, 1905.

Towle, Nancy. *Vicissitudes Illustrated in the Experience of Nancy Towle in Europe and America.* 2nd ed. Portsmouth, N.H.: John Caldwell for the author, 1833.

Truair, John. *The Alarm Trumpet: A Discourse, Delivered at Berkshire, (Vt.) Sept. 9, 1813, the Day of the National Fast, Appointed by the President, on Account of the War.* Montpelier: Walton & Goss, 1813.

———. *The Doctrine of Christian Holiness.* Northampton, 1833.

True, Marshall. "From Howard Relief to Howard Mental Health: The Changing Role of the Howard in Burlington, Vermont," in *Social Service in Vermont: The Community and the State.* Occasional Paper No. 5. Burlington: University of Vermont, Center for Research on Vermont, 1981.

———. "Middle-Class Women and Civic Improvement in Burlington, 1865-1890." *Vermont History,* 56 (Spring 1988): 112-127.

———. "Slavery in Burlington? An Historical Note." *Vermont History,* 50 (Fall 1982): 227-232

Twynham, Leonard, pseud., "Selections from Achsa W. Sprague's Diary and Journal." Vermont Historical Society *Proceedings* 9 (Sept. 1941):131-184; "Achsah W. Sprague (1827-1862)." ibid., 271-279.

Tyler, Royall. *The Prose of Royall Tyler,* ed. Marius B. Peladeau. Montpelier: Vermont Historical Society and Rutland: Charles E. Tuttle, 1972.

———. *The Verse of Royall Tyler.* ed. Marius B. Peladeau. Charlottesville: University Press of Virginia, 1968.

The University of Vermont: The First Two Hundred Years. ed. Robert V. Daniels. Burlington: The University, 1991.

Vermont. Adjutant and Inspector General's Office. *Revised Roster of Vermont Volunteers and Lists of Vermonters Who Served In the War of the Rebellion, 1861-66.* Montpelier: Adjutant-General's Office, 1892.

Vermont Almanac. . . for. . . 1844. Woodstock: Haskell & Palmer, 1843. Other almanacs with various imprints and compilers.

Vermont (Diocese, Episcopal). *The Documentary History of the Protestant Episcopal Church in the Diocese of Vermont, Including the Conventions From the Year 1792 to 1832, Inclusive.* [ed. Albert H. Bailey, C. R. Batchelder and George B. Mansur]. New York: Potts & Amery for The Diocese[Claremont, N.H., Manufacturing], 1870.

————. *In Memoriam: The Rt. Rev. Wm. H. A. Bissell, D.D. Entered into Rest May 14th, 1893*. [Burlington: The Diocese, 1893].

Vermont Christian Endeavor Union. *Journal of Annual Meetings: Burlington, Dec. 14 and 15, 1886; St. Albans, Nov. 1 and 2, 1887; Montpelier, Dec. 5 and 6, 1888*. St. Albans: Messenger and Advertiser Print, 1889.

Vermont Historical Gazetteer: A Local History of all the Towns in the State, Civil, Educational, Biographical, Religious and Military. Abby Maria Hemenway, ed. 5 vols. Burlington &c.: A. M. Hemenway, 1867-1892. *Index to the Contents of the Vermont Historical Gazetteer* Rutland: Tuttle, 1923.

Vermont Historical Society, *Collections*. 2 vols. Montpelier: J. & J. M. Poland, 1870-1871.

Vermont Laws. For each session, cited with date.

Vermont Laws to 1824. Windsor: Simeon Ide for the State, 1825.

Vermont. *Records of the Council of Safety and Governor and Council of the State of Vermont, to Which Are Prefixed the Records of the General Conventions from July 1775 to December 1777*. ed. E. P. Walton. 8 vols. Montpelier: J. & J. M. Poland, 1873-1880.

Vermont. *Revised Laws of Vermont, 1880*. Rutland: Tuttle, 1881. Cited as R. L.

Vermont. *The Revised Statutes of the State of Vermont, Passed November 19, 1839, To Which Are Added Several Public Acts Now in Force*. Burlington: Chauncey Goodrich for the Legislature, 1840. Cited as R.S.

Vermont. Secretary of State. *A List of the Principal Civil Officers of Vermont from 1777 to 1918*. ed. John M. Comstock. St. Albans: Messenger, 1918.

————. *State Papers of Vermont*. Various eds. 17 vols. Montpelier: Secretary of State, 1918-1978.

Vermont State Papers. William Slade, comp. Middlebury: J. W. Copeland, 1823.

Vermont. University. *General Catalogue of the University of Vermont and State Agricultural College, Burlington, Vermont, 1791-1900*. Burlington: Free Press, 1901.

Vicars, William. *A Companion to the Altar: Shewing the Nature and Necessity of a Sacramental Preparation in Order to Our Worthy [sic] Receiving the Holy Communion. . . .* Burlington: Samuel Mills, 1810.

Wagner, Carol Christine. "A Ministry Suppressed: John Truair's Vermont Ministry in the 1830s." Chittenden County Historical Society *Bulletin* 26 (Winter 1991): 1-7.

Walker, Pamela J. "A Chaste and Fervid Eloquence: Catherine Booth and the Ministry of Women in the Salvation Army," in *Women Preachers and Prophets Through Two Millennia of Christianity.* ed. Beverly Mayne Kienzle and Pamela J. Walker. Berkeley, California: University of California Press, 1998.

Walter, Dorothy C. "Perfectionists in the Westminster Church." Vermont Historical Society *Proceedings*, n.s. 8(June 1940): 190-193.

Walzer, Michael. *On Toleration.* New Haven: Yale University Press, 1997.

Ward, Donal. "Religious Enthusiasm in Vermont, 1761-1847." Ph.D. diss., University of Notre Dame, 1980. Copy at University of Vermont.

Washington, Ida H. "A History of the Women's Fellowship, Vermont Conference, U.C.C., and the Organizations Out of Which It Grew, 1870-1995," in John Nutting, *Becoming the United Church of Christ*, 102-104, also published separately by the Fellowship.

Waterbury. *History of Waterbury, Vermont, 1915-1991*, James Sabin, editor-in-chief. Waterbury: Waterbury Historical Society, 1991.

Wells, Elsie. *History of Bakersfield: The Way It Was, the Way It Is.* Canaan, N.H.: Phoenix Publishing, 1976.

Wells, Frederic P. *History of Barnet, Vermont.* Burlington: Free Press Printing, 1923.

————. *History of Newbury, Vermont, from the Discovery of the Coös Country to the Present Time. With Genealogical Records of Many Famlies.* St. Johnsbury: Caledonian, 1902.

White, Andrew D. *History of the Warfare of Science with Theology in Christendom.* 2 vols. New York: Appleton, 1896.

Wickham, Donald H. ed. *Letters to Vermont from Her Civil War Soldier Correspondents to the Home Press.* 2 vols. Bennington, Vt.: Images from the Past, 1998.

Williams, Alvin Dighton. *The Rhode Island Freewill Baptist Pulpit.* Boston: Gould and Lincoln, 1852.

Williams, Edward H., III. "History of the Christian Church, Woodstock, Vermont." 1950, TS in Norman Williams Public Library, Woodstock.

Williams, Jay G., III. *Songs of Praise: Welsh-Rooted Churches Beyond Britain.* Clinton, N.Y.: Gwen Prewi Santes Press, 1996.

Williams, John C. *The History and Map of Danby, Vermont.* Rutland: McLean & Robbins, 1869.

Williams, Samuel. *The Love of Country. . . .* Salem, New-England: printed by Samuel and Ebenezer Hall, 1775.

————. *The Love of Country: . . . a Discourse Delivered October 21, 1792, at Rutland*. Rutland: A. Haswell, 1792.

————. *The Natural and Civil History of Vermont*. Walpole, N. H.: Isaiah Thomas and David Carlisle, Jr., 1794. 2nd ed. 2 vols. Burlington: Samuel Mills, 1809.

————. *Philosophical Lectures on the Constitution, Duty, and Religion of Man*. ed. Merle Curti and William Tillman. Philadelphia: American Philosophical Society, 1970, in its *Transactions*, n.s. 60 (pt. 3).

Wilson, Frederick R. "A History of Catholicism in Vermont." *Vermont Quarterly*, 21 (July 1953): 212-216,

Woolman, John. *The Journal and Major Essays of John Woolman*. ed. Phillips P. Moulton. New York: Oxford University Press, 1971.

Worcester, Leonard. *An Oration, Pronounced at Peacham, in Commemoration of the Death of the Late Gen. George Washington, February 22d, 1800*. Peacham: Farley & Goss, 1800.

Wright, Charles B. *Gleanings from Forefathers: A Memorial Souvenir*. Middlebury: Middlebury Historical Society (printed by D. B. Updike, Merrymount Press, Boston), 1926.

Wright, Chester. *The Devil in the Nineteenth Century: Two Discourses Delivered at Hardwick, Vermont, May 6, 1838*. Montpelier: E. P. Walton & Son, 1838.

Wright, George Frederick. *The Story of My Life*. Oberlin: Bibliotheca Sacra, 1916.

Wriston, John C. Jr. *Vermont Inns & Taverns, Pre-Revolution to 1925: An Illustrated and Annotated Checklist*. Rutland: Academy Books, 1991.

Yarrow, Florence. "The Work in Tyson," in the *Vermont Missionary*, 3 (Aug. 1892): 189.

Young, Daniel. *Autobiography of Daniel Young*. ed. W. P. Strickland. New York, 1860.

Zielinski, Stanley A. *The Story of the Farnham Meeting, a Quaker Meeting in Allen's Corner, East Farnham Township, Brome County, Province of Quebec, Canada, 1820-1902*. Fulford, P.Q.: The Author, 1961.

Index

Page numbers in italics refer to illustrations or tables. Unless otherwise indicated, all towns named are in Vermont.